W9-BYS-338

Politics in Russia

Seventh Edition

THOMAS F. Remington

Emory University

Longman
Boston   Columbus   Indianapolis   New York   San Francisco   Upper Saddle River
Amsterdam   Cape Town   Dubai   London   Madrid   Milan   Munich   Paris   Montreal   Toronto
Delhi   Mexico City   Sao Paulo   Sydney   Hong Kong   Seoul   Singapore   Taipei   Tokyo

Senior Acquisitions Editor: Vikram Mukhija
Editorial Assistant: Beverly Fong
Senior Marketing Manager: Lindsey Prudhomme
Production Manager: Fran Russello
Project Coordination and Composition: Abinaya Rajendran / Integra
Cover Design Manager: Jayne Conte
Cover Designer: Suzanne Behnke
Cover Illustration/Photo: © Dmitry Astakhov/Pool/epa/Corbis
Printer and Binder: Courier Companies, Inc.

Copyright © 2012, 2010, 2008 by Pearson Education, Inc. All rights reserved. No part of this publication may be reproduced, stored in a retrieval system, or transmitted, in any form or by any means, electronic, mechanical, photocopying, recording, or otherwise, without the prior written permission of the publisher. Printed in the United States. To obtain permission to use material from this work, please submit a written request to Pearson Education, Inc., Permissions Department, 1900 E. Lake Ave., Glenview, IL 60025 or fax to (847) 486-3938 or e-mail glenview.permissions@pearsoned.com. For information regarding permissions, call (847) 486-2635.

Library of Congress Cataloging-in-Publication Data

Remington, Thomas F.
    Politics in Russia / Thomas F. Remington — 7th ed.
        p. cm.
    Includes bibliographical references and index.
    ISBN-13: 978-0-205-00579-6 (alk. paper)
    ISBN-10: 0-205-00579-9 (alk. paper)
    1. Russia (Federation)—Politics and government—1991   2. Constitutional history—Russia (Federation) 3. Soviet Union—Politics and government. I. Title.
JN6695.R46 2012
320.947—dc22
                                                                2010041647

2 3 4 5 6 7 8 9 10   V092   14 13

Longman
is an imprint of

www.pearsonhighered.com

ISBN-13: 978-0-205-00579-6
ISBN-10: 0-205-00579-9

ACC LIBRARY SERVICES AUSTIN, TX

BRIEF CONTENTS

CONTENTS

PREFACE

The image on the cover shows Russian president Dmitrii Medvedev at his inauguration in May 2008. Former president Vladimir Putin looks on as Medvedev steps up to the podium to take the oath of office. Upon assuming power, Medvedev immediately appointed Putin his prime minister, ensuring continuity in policy and personnel in leadership. But over time, Medvedev has shifted the themes and priorities in foreign and domestic policy. The photo illustrates the uncertainties that accompany any change of leadership in a centralized system such as that of Russia. This new edition of *Politics in Russia* assesses the evolving relationship between the two top leaders as they cope with the policy challenges—both short-term and long-term—facing the country.

NEW TO THIS EDITION

Russia's political life remains subject to rapid change. This edition of *Politics in Russia* covers events through the summer of 2010. It has been substantially revised to take account of the many developments that have occurred in Russian political life since the sixth edition was published, among them the effects of the global economic crisis on Russia, President Medvedev's drive for modernization and innovation, and the evolving "tandem" leadership of Putin and Medvedev. Among the elements new to this edition are the following:

- A discussion of the unusual "tandem" leadership of Putin and Medvedev. As president, Medvedev has staked out some important policy objectives that point Russia in the direction toward political liberalization and democratization, but so far he has not reversed any of the moves Putin made to close the political system and centralize power. If their close working relationship were to give way to overt rivalry, the consequences could be to destabilize the regime.
- A discussion of Medvedev's call for modernizing Russia's economy. He has painted a dramatic picture of the dire consequences of Russia's overdependence on revenues from the exports of oil and gas and other natural commodities, and clearly recognizes that without upgrading its capacity for technological innovation, Russia will slip fatally and permanently behind in the global competition for wealth and power. But his call for modernization and innovation runs counter to the need to use rents from energy exports to maintain the regime's power base and cope with the consequences of the economic recession that began in 2008.
- An overview of the impact of the global economic crisis on Russia. Fiscally dependent on revenues from the export of oil and gas, the budget suffered devastating deficits as world energy prices plummeted. The value of the shares sold on the Russian stock market fell by three-quarters in

less than a year's time. And the crisis escalated throughout the economy as businesses closed down production and laid off hundreds of thousands of workers. The crisis exposed the vulnerability of the economy to external economic shocks and the urgency of deep reforms.

- A new close-up on the problems of company towns ("mono-cities," as they are called in Russia) is included using the illustration of the car maker AvtoVAZ, located in the city of Togliatti, where one in seven adults works for the troubled company. There are hundreds more such cities in Russia, a legacy of the Soviet system that poses a continuing challenge to the present-day authorities.
- An update of Russia's dire demographic situation, which includes low birthrates, high mortality, and a declining population. In recent years, the situation has eased somewhat, but the public health and demographic situation remains serious, and the country is increasingly dependent on immigrant labor for its workforce.
- Finally, a discussion of the way modern online communications are changing patterns of state–society relations. Episodes of the mobilization of automobile drivers against the abuses by the authorities in cities around the country (including the "blue buckets" movement in Moscow) is discussed as one example of the way new technologies enable grassroots protest movements to form.

FEATURES

In order to understand recent developments, we have to understand the longer-term dynamics shaping Russian politics. The book takes the view that in the post-communist era, Russia is engaged in rebuilding the power of the state at home and abroad. An authoritarian ruler such as Putin focuses on increasing state power by reducing the power of other sources of independent initiative in society, such as opposition parties, the mass media, independent civil society groups, the judiciary, and the regional government. But in the longer run, the state can be made stronger only if the economy and civil society become stronger. These require observance of the rule of law and checks on the ability of corrupt and power-hungry state officials to prey on the private sector. Throughout the book, we see examples of the tension between these two strategies for state building—the one that seeks to centralize power at the expense of society, and the other that encourages the development of a strong economy capable of sustained growth and a mutually supportive relationship between state and society.

Chapter 1 offers an overview of the policy agenda faced by the current Russian leadership under President Dmitrii Medvedev and Prime Minister Vladimir Putin. It discusses the transition from the presidency of Vladimir Putin to that of Dmitrii Medvedev and the anomalous power-sharing arrangement between Medvedev as president and Putin as prime minister. The book argues that although Putin and Medvedev have made the strengthening of state power their top priority, there is a fundamental incompatibility between their call for diversifying the economy so as to rid it of its dependence on energy exports and the actual reliance on oil, gas, and other natural resources to expand the state's power at home and abroad.

The book also relates the post-Soviet political system to the legacy of the communist era and the postcommunist period. Much of Putin's strategy was a reaction to the loss of cohesion in the state that occurred in the 1990s. In order to centralize power, Putin reverted to some of the authoritarian methods of rule used by the Soviet regime. Because we can understand Russia's postcommunist era only in relation to the Soviet regime that was in power from 1917 to 1991, Chapter 2 covers the Soviet system, in particular the period of Gorbachev's reforms, which ended in the disintegration of the Soviet state, while Chapter 3 traces the establishment of Russia's present-day political arrangements out of the turmoil of the late 1980s and early 1990s.

Chapter 4 looks at the ways the state and the society interact by showing how people take part in political processes, by voting, joining parties and civic groups, or assuming positions of leadership and responsibility. It traces the paths by which people enter the political elite and the ways in which the power of money is intertwined with political power.

Chapter 5 deals with the cultural dimension of Russian politics. It addresses the seeming puzzle that although Russians value democratic freedoms and consider themselves much freer today than they were in the Soviet era, they also value the stability and order that Putin represents. It looks at the long-term changes that have occurred in Russian society, as well as the influences of education and the mass media that are shaping the attitudes and values people bring to the political world. It also analyzes the way religion is tied to national identity, both for the dominant ethnic Russian majority and for the many ethnic minorities making up one-fifth of the population. It looks at the form of ethnic federalism Russia uses to give political representation to ethnic minorities and shows how these political institutions shape the exercise of power.

Chapter 6 looks at interest groups and political parties. It shows that, in contrast to the old Soviet era, there are hundreds of thousands of organized interest groups, many quite influential. Some are active in the political arena, others concern themselves with occupational or social issues. The chapter discusses the mixed strategy the state pursues in dealing with interest groups—seeking to coopt some into friendly relations with the authorities, while excluding or repressing others. It takes the view that there is a dialogue between the state and the civil society, but one hampered by the political and organizational handicaps that civil society labors under in a country as physically vast and politically centralized as Russia.

The second part of the chapter analyzes the role that political parties play in contemporary Russia. It explains how, after a decade in which a system of viable, competitive political parties failed to take shape, the authorities were able to create a single dominant political party—United Russia—that unites political elites at all levels and allows the authorities to dominate elections and legislative debates throughout the country. The formation of United Russia and its establishment as a unifying political force throughout the country comes at the expense of the opportunity for citizens to express their political voice and choice through democratic party competition and to hold officials accountable for their performance.

In Chapter 7, we analyze the relationship between the economy and politics. The chapter discusses the painful transition from the communist economic system—the severe depression of the immediate post-Soviet period. This was followed by a decade of recovery and relative prosperity, thanks to high and rising international prices for oil and gas. It shows that Russia's economy remained susceptible to economic shocks, as the global economic crisis of 2008–2009 demonstrated. The chapter analyzes the reasons the economy is so vulnerable to economic shocks and the ways in which it has responded to the current crisis.

We examine Russia's legal system in Chapter 8. Although the old Soviet institutions of justice have been reformed, the leaders' unwillingness to relinquish political control over the procuracy, the police, and the courts, let alone the security services, has meant that the judiciary is independent of political influence only in cases where the state's interests are not directly implicated. Moreover, the chapter shows that movement toward the rule of law is hampered by the worsening problem of corruption, the legacy of unaccountable bureaucratic power, and the authorities' use of the legal system for political ends.

In Chapter 9, we survey Russia's relations with the outside world, particularly its neighbors in the territory of the former Soviet Union. It argues that Russia's leaders want to dominate the former Soviet region to increase their security and the security of their oil and gas pipelines, but they also want to deepen Russia's integration into the international economy. These conflicting goals have created a series of dilemmas for Russian policy.

Students who would like to read more about particular topics are directed to consult the endnotes, which contain references to some of the English-language and Russian primary and secondary sources that discuss the topics covered in the book. The book also incorporates a series of "close-ups," which are capsule summaries containing biographies of some of the individuals who feature in the book (such as Putin, Medvedev, and Yeltsin), accounts of important episodes of recent times (such as the arrest of oil oligarch Mikhail Khodorkovsky and the breakup of his company, Yukos), or important concepts for undertstanding Russian politics (such as the ideas of socialism, communism, Marxism, and Leninism).

I hope that students and instructors, while reading through the text, will use the book to form their own judgments about where Russia is going and why. Postcommunist Russia presents any number of paradoxes and problems that are important for understanding how political regimes change. Russia remains a powerful, fascinating, and often puzzling country. While this book does not pretend to offer a definitive interpretation of its politics, it may help its readers understand what the crucial issues are on which its future may depend.

SUPPLEMENTS

Longman is pleased to offer several resources to qualified adopters of *Politics in Russia* and their students that will make teaching and learning from this book even more effective and enjoyable.

Passport for Comparative Politics With Passport, choose the resources you want from MyPoliSciKit and put links to them into your course management system. If there is assessment associated with those resources, it also can be uploaded, allowing the results to feed directly into your course management system's gradebook. With over 150 MyPoliSciKit assets like video case studies, mapping exercises, comparative exercises, simulations, podcasts, *Financial Times* newsfeeds, current events quizzes, politics blog, and much more, Passport is available for any Pearson introductory or upper-level political science book. Use ISBN 0-205-07411-1 to order Passport with this book. To learn more, please contact your Pearson representative.

MySearchLab
Need help with a paper? MySearchLab saves time and improves results by offering start-to-finish guidance on the research/writing process and full-text access to academic journals and periodicals. Use ISBN 0-205-07399-9 to order MySearchLab with this book. To learn more, please visit www.my searchlab.com or contact your Pearson representative.

The Economist
Every week, *The Economist* analyzes the important happenings around the globe. From business to politics, to the arts and science, its coverage connects seemingly unrelated events in unexpected ways. Use ISBN 0-205-00259-5 to order a 15-week subscription with this book for a small additional charge. To learn more, please contact your Pearson representative.

The Financial Times
Featuring international news and analysis from journalists in more than 50 countries, the *Financial Times* provides insights into and perspectives on political and economic developments around the world. Use ISBN 0-205-07394-8 to order a 15-week subscription with this book for a small additional charge. To learn more, please contact your Pearson representative.

ACKNOWLEDGMENTS

I remain deeply indebted to friends and colleagues in Russia for generously sharing with me their knowledge and understanding of developments in their country. I would also like to express my appreciation to colleagues in this · country whose studies of Russian politics have advanced our knowledge of present-day Russia and enriched the field of political science. Finally, I would like to thank those reviewers who provided feedback on the sixth edition to help give shape to this seventh edition: Donald Peinkos of the University of Wisconsin–Milwaukee, Fabian Katalin of Lafayette University, and Mohsin Hashim of Mulhenberg State University.

Like the previous editions, the seventh edition of this book is dedicated to my son, Alexander Frederick Remington.

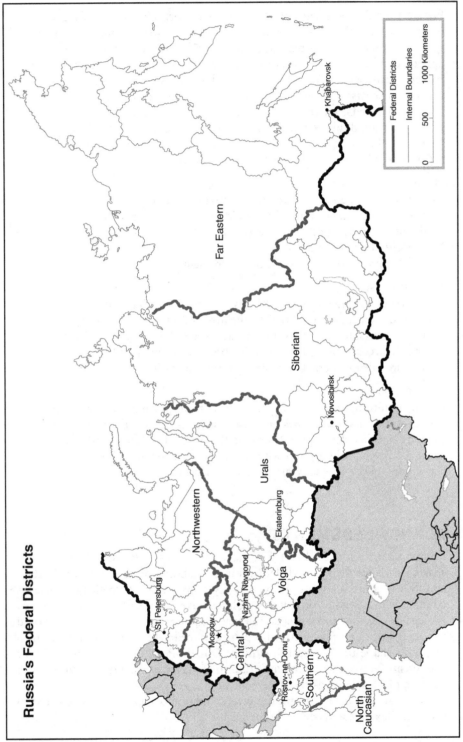

Russia's Federal Districts

Far Eastern

Siberian

Novosibirsk

Urals

Ekaterinburg

Northwestern

St. Petersburg

Nizhnii Novgorod

Volga

Moscow

Central

Rostov-na-Donu

Southern

North Caucasian

Khabarovsk

Federal Districts
Internal Boundaries

0   500   1000 Kilometers

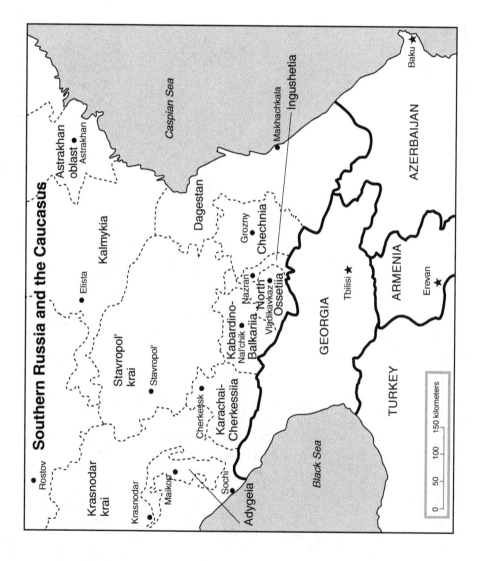

Southern Russia and the Caucasus

Rostov

Krasnodar krai

Krasnodar

Maikop

Sochi

Adygeia

Cherkessk

Karachai-Cherkessiia

Stavropol' krai

Stavropol'

Elista

Kalmykia

Nal'chik

Kabardino-Balkariia

Nazran'

Vladikavkaz

North Ossetiia

Astrakhan oblast

Astrakhan

Caspian Sea

Dagestan

Grozny

Chechnia

Makhachkala

Ingushetia

Baku

AZERBAIJAN

ARMENIA

Erevan

Tbilisi

GEORGIA

TURKEY

Black Sea

0   50   100   150 kilometers

xiii

Location of the Regions of Western Russia

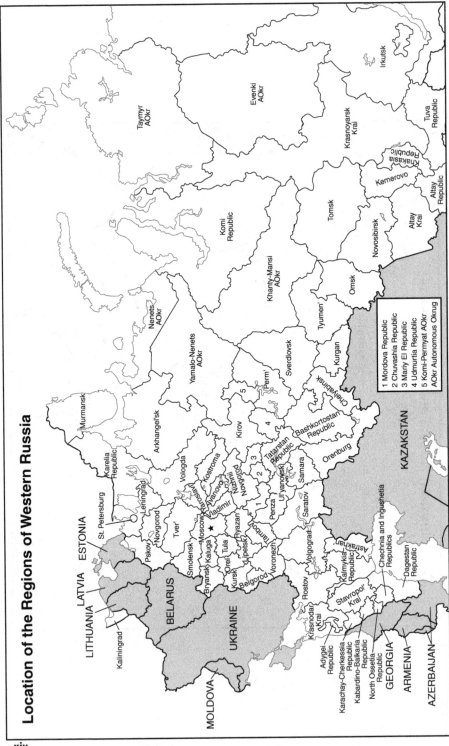

1 Mordova Republic
2 Chuvashia Republic
3 Mariy El Republic
4 Udmurtia Republic
5 Komi-Permyat AOkr
AOkr Autonomous Okrug

Source: Center for International Research, U.S. Bureau of the Census

State and Regime in Russia

THE DUAL EXECUTIVE

On May 7, 2008, **Dmitrii Anatol'evich Medvedev** took the oath of office as president of the Russian Federation. The solemnity of the occasion, which was attended by his predecessor, Vladimir Putin, the Russian Orthodox Patriarch of Russia, Alexii II, and other dignitaries, signaled that the leadership was united around the choice of the new president. Elsewhere in the countries of the former Soviet Union, the succession from one president to another has sometimes triggered a struggle for power among contending political forces, leading to popular uprisings with unpredictable outcomes.[1] The Russian authorities were determined not to allow a similar rupture in the transfer of power from one president to the next.

The succession was smooth but it was hardly democratic. Formally, the presidential election itself took place on March 2, but every aspect of the election process was closely controlled so that no impediment to Medvedev's victory could arise. Once Putin had decided that Medvedev would succeed him—a choice he announced the previous December—the Kremlin took no chances on the outcome. The state-controlled mass media, regional governors, big business, and the election commission all fell into line. The manipulated election process demonstrated to the world and to any would-be opponents that the entire Russian political elite was united in supporting Medvedev.

Adding to the display of unity and continuity was the fact that Vladimir Putin himself stayed on in power as prime minister. Medvedev's first act as newly inaugurated president was to name Putin as prime minister. This neat exchange of offices—Putin made Medvedev his successor, Medvedev kept Putin in power—solved several problems at once. Putin's exceptional popularity among the public, and the authorities' fear of a destabilizing split among the ruling elite, made it desirable to find a post-presidency role for Putin that would ensure continuity and legitimate the new president. At the same time, the authorities deemed it important to observe the niceties of constitutional

1

law, which requires that a president serve no more than two consecutive terms. Putin's move therefore allowed him to comply with the constitution while holding on to the main levers of power.

The new "tandem" leadership arrangement created some uncertainty in elite circles about who was really in charge. With time, Medvedev has expanded the sphere of his influence by announcing major new policy initiatives and replacing senior government officials, but he has not altered any of the basic policies or institutional arrangements established when Putin was president. Most Russians believe that Medvedev is basically continuing Putin's policies.[2] However, as the next presidential election—scheduled for 2012—draws closer, it is possible that competition between Medvedev and Putin will grow, particularly if Medvedev chooses to run again for president. (See Close-Up 1.1: The Putin–Medvedev Tandem.)

CLOSE-UP 1.1

The Putin–Medvedev Tandem

The team leadership of Vladimir Putin as prime minister and Dmitrii Medvedev as president—known as the "tandem"—invites constant speculation inside and outside Russia about the nature of the relationship of the two men. Is Putin still running Russia, with Medvedev a mere decorative appendage? Do the two share power, with Medvedev exercising policy-making power in some issue areas? Is Medvedev personally ambitious enough to want to move Putin out of the way now that he is president? Observers watch keenly for any indication of policy differences between them that might lead to an all-out power struggle. Such a contest could have destabilizing consequences for the country as the political elites divide into opposing factions. Power struggles of this kind invite popular protests and a breakdown in public order, as has happened in other postcommunist states.* So far, however, little tension between them has been evident.

Although the tandem arrangement itself is anomalous, it is based on the well-established pattern of a patron–client relationship. Since Medvedev first started working for Putin in 1990, Putin has kept him close. As Putin moved up in the hierarchy, he brought Medvedev with him. Medvedev has served Putin faithfully, advancing his policy goals and gaining experience but never breaking away to establish an independent political career. Putin has held a number of top executive posts (e.g., running the Federal Security Service, the presidential administration, and the government, before becoming president in his own right). In contrast, Medvedev's career has largely been in staff jobs, providing legal support or heading advisory commissions. Even when he served as first deputy prime minister, he did not have responsibility for setting overall government policy.

---

*Henry E. Hale, "Regime Cycles: Democracy, Autocracy and Revolution in Post-Soviet Eurasia," *World Politics* 58 (2005): 133–165.

It is likely, therefore, that even as president, he continues to defer to Putin. In such a patron–client relationship, the patron is superior in power and gives his client opportunities for power and career advancement in return for personal loyalty. This has clearly been the case with Putin and Medvedev and probably continues even while Medvedev holds the most powerful position in the state.

Putin is Medvedev's senior by 13 years, Putin having been born in 1952, Medvedev in 1965. Their association began in 1990, when Putin became head of the external affairs department of the mayor's office of the city of St. Petersburg and made Medvedev his legal advisor. Putin had returned to St. Petersburg after serving for 15 years in the KGB (the Soviet Committee on State Security), five of which he served in East Germany. Medvedev had just completed a graduate degree in law at St. Petersburg State University. In 1996 Putin moved to Moscow to take a job in Yeltsin's presidential administration. Here his career took off. In July 1998, Yeltsin named Putin head of the Federal Security Bureau (FSB), and in March 1999, secretary of the Security Council as well. In August 1999, President Yeltsin appointed him prime minister. Thanks in part to his decisive handling of the federal military operation in Chechnia, Putin's popularity ratings rose quickly. On December 31, 1999, Yeltsin resigned, automatically making Putin acting president. Putin went on to run for the presidency and, on March 26, 2000, he won with an outright majority of the votes in the first round. He was reelected president in March 2004 by a wide margin.

In 1999 Putin brought Medvedev to Moscow. Medvedev ran Putin's successful presidential election campaign, and after Putin was inaugurated as president, Putin made him deputy chief of staff in the presidential administration. He also named him deputy chairman of the board of the giant state gas company, Gazprom, where he presumably served as Putin's eyes and ears. Putin named Medvedev to several high-profile advisory commissions, including one on reforming Gazprom and another on civil service reform. In 2002 Putin made Medvedev chairman of the board of Gazprom and in 2003 he made him head of the presidential administration.

In 2005, probably with a view to grooming him as a successor, Putin named Medvedev first deputy prime minister. This position gave Medvedev visibility and allowed him to widen his support in the federal government and the regions (aided by the fact that Putin put him in charge of the "national projects," a set of popular spending programs in education, public health, agriculture, and housing). Consistent with his career pattern of serving in support positions rather than chief executive posts, Medvedev did not have overall responsibility for setting government fiscal policy or basic policy priorities. In addition to overseeing the "national projects," he also supervised social, demographic, migration, and youth policy. None of these was an area from which he could cultivate an independent political base.

Medvedev is identified with a faction in the Putin entourage associated with the ideas of market reform and the rule of law. Putin balanced this faction

(continued)

against another that was based in the security agencies. It included several people Putin had served with during his days in the KGB. This latter faction—generally called the "siloviki" because the security agencies are nicknamed the "silovye struktury" or force structures—has a generally conservative, nationalist, statist tendency. Throughout his tenure as president, Putin took pains to surround himself both with representatives of the "liberal" faction, such as Medvedev, and with "siloviki." For example, at the same time he named Medvedev first deputy prime minister, he also named defense minister Sergei Ivanov to be deputy prime minister and secretary of the Security Council. Observers agreed that Putin was effectively giving the two a chance to compete to prove themselves as potential successors to Putin. Then in late 2007, Putin declared that Medvedev was his choice for president but that he intended to stay on in some position of responsibility. Observers expected that Medvedev would name him prime minister, as indeed Medvedev did immediately upon being inaugurated as president. All the resources of the Kremlin and the United Russia party were deployed to ensure Medvedev's election.

Putin and Medvedev project quite different public personas, although these do not necessarily translate into different policies. Putin cultivates an image of a tough, decisive, down-to-earth leader. Generally unemotional and mild-mannered, he occasionally allows himself to indulge in sarcastic or profane language to make a point. At other times, he projects an affable, relaxed demeanor. He is often shown in active, outdoor settings. Putin is self-possessed and guarded in dealing with others. Although he appears uncomfortable with the give and take of public politics, he is adept at handling live call-in programs where ordinary citizens can pose their questions and complaints. He is skillful at explaining complex issues in clear and plain language. Foreign business and political leaders who have met with him come away impressed at his master of policy detail.

Medvedev, in contrast, projects a cultivated, scholarly demeanor. His public statements are much more unequivocal than Putin about the need for Russia to embrace liberal democratic and market-oriented values, to respect the rule of law, and to reform its economic and political institutions. He has been more willing than Putin was to make concessions to the United States and other Western countries on issues such as arms control, membership in the World Trade Organization, and international sanctions against Iran. Probably on these issues he has not crossed Putin but has won Putin's consent to move Russia slightly more in a pro-Western direction. Putin has supported him in his drive for economic and political modernization, but since this strategy has not—so far—upset any major existing interests, it probably costs Putin nothing to let Medvedev stake out his own policy agenda at the level of rhetoric. If any of Medvedev's announced initiatives, such as the call for a serious anticorruption campaign or for dismantling the large state corporations that Putin helped to create, were to be given more than lip service, it would probably lead to a rift between the two. A still more irreparable breach in the tandem arrangement would certainly arise if Medvedev and Putin ran against each other for president in 2012.

So far, though, the two have maintained a remarkably harmonious relationship as president and prime minister based on their 20 years of association and the clear rules defining such patron–client relations. As President Medvedev noted in an interview with a French newspaper, he and Putin have an effective "working alliance." What's more, he added, they recently discovered that they have the same blood type, "in the medical sense."*

_____

*Polit.ru, February 25, 2010.

The peculiarity of the situation arises from the gap between the formal constitutional rules and the informal understandings that guide the exercise of power. Formally, Russia's constitution provides both for a directly elected president and a prime minister who is chosen by the president but must enjoy the confidence of parliament. France under the constitution of the Fifth Republic has demonstrated that a president of one party can coexist reasonably well with a prime minister of an opposing party so long as they agree on how to divide responsibilities and do not fight too openly. But Russia has never had successful experience with the sharing of power between two leaders. As Boris Yeltsin once put it, "in Russia, only one person can be number one." For most of the period since Russia's present-day constitution has been in force, the president has been the clearly dominant political figure, while the prime minister has mainly been responsible for managing the economy and carrying out the president's commands. However, Putin accumulated a great deal of power during his tenure as president, using such classic power-consolidation tactics as rewarding supporters with lucrative posts in ministries and state corporations, eliminating opposition centers of power, and launching new policy initiatives. He maintained impressively high public support, in large part thanks to the economy's robust performance until 2008. He retained his power and popularity when he moved to head the government and continued to dominate the decision-making process in most spheres of policy regardless of the formal lines of authority. Still, as president, Dmitrii Medvedev has considerable institutional prerogatives and has sought to use them to consolidate his own base of power. As a result, under the "tandem" arrangement of Medvedev and Putin, it is often unclear which of them has the predominant power to set policy in any given issue area. So far, the arrangement has worked harmoniously, but the breakout of an open rivalry between the two would split the political elite and destabilize the regime.

Today's Russia is the successor to the Soviet state, formally called the Union of Soviet Socialist Republics (USSR) or the Soviet Union. The Soviet state was a nominally federal union of 15 national republics ruled by a centralized Communist Party. But in 1991, it fell apart into its constituent national republics, and Russia, the largest of the 15 republics, emerged as a newly independent country and heir to the Soviet Union under international law (for instance, Russia inherited the Soviet Union's seat in the Security Council of the United Nations). The transition was painful in many ways. Bloody ethnic conflicts erupted in several regions on Russia's periphery. Within Russia, people's high expectations for a smooth transition to Western-style living standards, featuring democracy and capitalism, were dashed. The country's role on the world stage was greatly reduced, and Russia was unable to prevent neighboring countries that it had once controlled from joining Western defense and economic alliances.

The weakening of Russia's state in the 1990s resulted from the fact that the institutions of the old regime broke down much more quickly than new institutions could be established. This pattern of radical regime breakdown accompanied by a loss of state power, is a recurrent one in Russia's thousand-year history. The previous time the old regime fell apart was the Russian Revolution of 1917 and the Civil War that followed it. But the revolutionary changes of regime that took place in the late 1980s and 1990s in Russia occurred in an era of mass communications, universal literacy, high educational attainments, and widespread faith in democratic values. Many of the initial changes in political institutions in the 1980s and 1990s, therefore, were aimed at replacing the authoritarian, overbureaucratized, and stagnant communist regime with one that was democratic and dynamic. But President Boris Yeltsin made a number of political compromises along the way, trading off large swaths of state authority to business tycoons and regional governors in order to hold on to power.

In 2000, Vladimir Putin succeeded Boris Yeltsin as president in another smooth but carefully stage-managed succession. His agenda was clear: to rebuild the power of the state. That meant, as he understood it, making the bureaucracy accountable to the top political leadership; reining in the regional governors and big business; making parliament and the courts reliable, compliant instruments of policy making; reinforcing the power of the police, security forces, and military to enforce the leaders' will; putting the economy on a growth path; and building back Russia's power and prestige abroad.

To a large extent, Putin accomplished these goals. During the eight years of Putin's presidency (2000–2008), Russia's economy recovered and its internal political order regained predictability and coherence. Russians derived understandable satisfaction from the fact that there was steady economic growth, the country's role as a major oil and gas exporter gave it significant international leverage, poverty and unemployment fell, and real incomes grew sharply. At the same time, Putin centralized power internally. Independent centers of power, such as courts, parliament, the media, and civil society, were tamed. Nevertheless, popular confidence in Putin built quickly and remained high throughout his presidency. Putin's continued role as prime minister only reinforced the sense of stability and security. The economic crisis beginning in late 2008 shook but did not shatter public confidence in Putin's leadership. Putin was at the height of his power and popularity when he turned over the presidency to Medvedev.

Still, as the severe economic crisis of 2008–2009 demonstrated, the state's power rests on a weak foundation. This is not only because most of the tentative democratic gains of the 1990s have been reversed. It is also because the economic and social base of state power is not secure. Putin and Medvedev have pursued policies following a traditional Russian political pattern in which Russia's rulers seek to build the power of the state by diminishing the realm of free association outside the state, meaning that most of the initiative to respond to opportunities and challenges comes from the state rather than from society. As in the Soviet and tsarist eras, bureaucratic overcentralization, the obsessive control of public information, the suppression of potential opposition, and pervasive clientelism and corruption leave the state poorly equipped to respond to crises. Moreover, contemporary Russia's heavy dependence on oil and gas revenues for its budget makes it vulnerable to the so-called "resource curse," the pattern found in countries where, as a result of windfall revenues from state-owned natural resources, the leaders avoid investing in the skills and knowledge of the population. As a result, the societies wind up with lower levels of development than in resource-poor countries. Such states typically exhibit high levels of corruption, low accountability, and low investment in human capital—and suffer a devastating fiscal crisis when world energy prices fall. Finally, Russia continues to experience a severe demographic crisis. In view of these deeper structural dilemmas, the longer-term sustainability of Russia's political and economic recovery, therefore, will require far-reaching institutional reform.

CURRENT POLICY CHALLENGES

Dmitrii Medvedev took over as president at a moment of national optimism about the future. Russia's role as a leading world exporter of fuels and metals meant that as world prices on oil, gas, metals, and other export commodities rose, many parts of the country enjoyed a period of prosperity. Annual growth rates of gross national product were in the range of 7–8 percent from 1999 through summer 2008. Under Putin, the government carried out major programs to rebuild schools, hospitals, housing, and agricultural infrastructure. Real incomes tripled between 2000 and 2008, while poverty and unemployment plummeted. Public opinion surveys suggest that the population was pleased with the current trends: Before the 2008 economic crisis, some 60 percent of the population believed the country was headed in the right direction. Compare that with the nadir of the troubles of the 1990s, in early 1999, when only 6 percent thought the country was going the right way. Medvedev's performance as president was approved by 73 percent of the country.[3]

A question debated actively at home in Russia and abroad is how much credit Vladimir Putin and his authoritarian style of rule deserve for Russia's turnaround—was he a successful leader, or was he merely lucky? Many who think he was an effective leader operate on the assumption that after a turbulent political transition, a spell of authoritarian rule is often the only way that a country can make a decisive turn toward economic growth and prosperity, with democracy only possible once the institutions of market capitalism are firmly installed (many point to China as a case in point). Some also say that, whatever the experience of other countries, Russia can only be governed autocratically.

The "luck" theory holds that Putin's actions as leader had relatively little to do with Russia's success. Skeptics argue that any country where oil and gas make up over 60 percent of exports would have realized a huge windfall from the sharp increase in world oil prices. (From 1999 to 2008, the average price of a barrel of crude oil on world markets rose tenfold—from $10 to $100.) Moreover, some argue that the market reforms of the 1990s opened up opportunities for capitalism to take hold. Therefore, they say, Russia in the 2000s was merely reaping the benefits of the tough reforms of the 1990s.[4]

But whichever perspective is right, the fact remains that Russia still faces fundamental tests of the resilience and capacity of the state. In fact, shortly after Medvedev took over as president, he and Prime Minister Putin faced two crises. First was a brief war with Russia's southern neighbor Georgia in August. (Chapter 9 discusses the war and its aftermath in more detail.) Second, starting in late summer 2008, Russia's economy was hit hard by the world financial and economic crisis. The effects were rapid and devastating: the sharp drop in world oil prices meant that Russia's budget, which had run a surplus for almost a decade, suddenly fell into deficit; the value of the stock market fell almost 80 percent in six months; economic output contracted sharply, shrinking by almost 8 percent in 2009—more than in any other major economy. The government was able to pump hundreds of billions of rubles into failing banks, industrial enterprises, unemployment benefits, and pensions. As a result, many Russians were shielded from poverty and the country was spared the massive financial instability that broke out in other heavily indebted states that lacked Russia's deep reserves. But the shaky foundations of the boom of the 2000s were laid bare.

Both Putin and Medvedev have repeatedly warned that it is dangerous for Russia to be economically dependent on its raw materials exports for economic growth. Instead, they have declared, in the future the country must grow through continuous technological innovation and productivity growth. "The main problem of the Russian economy today is its extreme inefficiency," Putin declared shortly before stepping down as president. "Labor productivity in Russia remains unacceptably low. We have the same expenditures of labor as in the most developed countries but in Russia they bring several times less return. And that is doubly dangerous in conditions of growing global competition and rising costs for skilled labor and energy."[5] Likewise, in a widely discussed article published in September 2009, President Medvedev denounced Russia's current economic structure as "primitive" for its dependence on natural resource production, its "chronic corruption, the outdated habit of relying on the state to solve our problems, on foreign countries, on some sort of 'all-powerful doctrine,' on anything and everything except on ourselves." He noted that "the energy efficiency and labor productivity of most our enterprises are shamefully low" and added that the real tragedy was that most owners, managers, and state officials do not appear to be particularly worried about the situation.[6]

But while Russian leaders have admitted the gravity of the problems the country faces, they have been unable to break through the obstacles standing in the way of solving them. Three in particular have proven to be stumbling blocks: the resistance by state officials to any reforms that weaken their power; the vast physical size of the country that impedes efforts to forge coalitions in society around broad common interests in support of significant reform; and the legacy of the Soviet development model that concentrated resources in giant state-owned enterprises—often located in remote, harsh regions—that are nearly impossible to convert into competitive capitalist firms viable in a global marketplace. Taken together, these factors stack the deck against modernizing and democratizing reforms.

THE PUTIN FACTOR

Putin's successes as president probably owed something *both* to luck *and* to strategy. Certainly Russia was ready for new leadership at the time Putin took office as president. His succession in fact was quite dramatic. Putin's predecessor, Boris Yeltsin, had served as president of Russia since 1991. On December 31, 1999, Yeltsin appeared on national television to announce that he was resigning as president as of midnight. Although his term was not due to expire until June 2000, he had decided to resign early so as to allow his chosen successor, Vladimir Putin, to take over at the beginning of the new millennium. Putin was Yeltsin's prime minister and enjoyed Yeltsin's confidence, although he was not well known at home or abroad. As acting president, Putin had a substantial advantage in the impending presidential elections, which under the constitution had to be held within three months of the president's departure. Putin's first move was to issue a decree guaranteeing Yeltsin and his family lifetime immunity from criminal prosecution. Although the manner in which the succession occurred was not illegal, it appeared to reflect an unseemly bargain: Yeltsin gave the presidency to Putin in return for security for himself.

Putin went on to win election as president in his own right in March 2000 and to exercise the powers of the presidential office forcefully. Enjoying a strong base of popular confidence, Putin undertook a steady effort to recentralize state power. He attacked the power of the so-called **oligarchs**—the small group of extremely wealthy figures who held controlling shares of Russia's major natural resource, manufacturing, financial, and media companies and exercised disproportionate influence over government—through prosecutions of two particularly prominent ones. He systematically weakened the independence of the chief executives of the country's regions—the **governors**—by establishing new federal districts overseen by presidentially appointed representatives, securing the power to dismiss governors for violations of the law, and removing them as ex officio members of the upper chamber of parliament. Putin placed people whom he had worked with closely in the past into positions of responsibility in the government and the presidential administration.

Putin enjoyed exceptionally high levels of public approval as president and continued to do so since becoming prime minister. Moreover, much of his popularity has rubbed off onto Dmitrii Medvedev (see Figure 1.1). This has given him considerable latitude in choosing policies to achieve his goals. He sought to restore Russia to its place as a major world power, a status it lost with the collapse of the Soviet Union. In the economy, he worked to achieve high, sustainable growth under a model in which there is substantial private, including foreign, ownership and investment coupled with state ownership and control of sectors deemed to be strategically important to the state, notably oil and gas. In politics, he preserved the framework of democratic institutions, while steadily eliminating competition from the political arena. Elections are held, but their outcomes are predetermined; civil society is allowed to exist within certain restricted limits; individual rights are honored to the extent they do not conflict with the prerogatives of the state. Putin sought to integrate Russia into the international economic system but at the same time to defend an expansive conception of state sovereignty. A strong state, for Putin, meant an unbroken chain of executive authority stretching from the president down to the head of each region and district, with accountability running upwards to the center rather than downwards to the citizenry. Putin accepted that Russia forms part of Europe and European civilization, but regarded the value of democracy as secondary to that of state sovereignty. His premise seems to be that the capacity and sovereignty of the state require the centralization of authority in the executive.

Putin has not accomplished all his goals. For example, he proposed several ambitious reforms of the civil service, the military, and the economy that were blocked in implementation by powerful entrenched interests. Putin has relied on the country's "force structures" (the interior ministry with its police and security troops, the regular armed forces, the law enforcement system, and the secret services) to remove or intimidate his rivals and to enforce discipline in the bureaucracy. This weakens more purely political mechanisms of consensus building and makes it harder for the center to monitor bureaucratic performance. Actual improvements in the quality of governance under Putin have been modest, and all the evidence suggests that the scale of corruption has risen substantially under Putin (fueled, certainly, by the enormous flood of petro-revenues entering the country). Putin has been much more successful in undercutting democratic checks and balances on central power than in making the new authoritarian system work effectively.

Russia's transformation over the past two decades gives us a unique opportunity to analyze the factors that influence political change. How do long-term, slow-acting social changes combine with short-term conjunctures of circumstance to produce new patterns of political life? As we shall see, the Soviet regime pursued a program of social modernization that had cumulative effects over the decades of Soviet rule, creating pressures for adaptation that the regime could not accommodate. Changes such as urbanization, mass

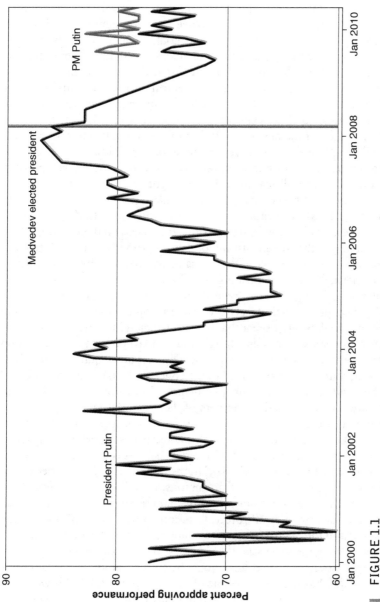

FIGURE 1.1
Putin and Medvedev Approval Ratings, 2000–2009

Both presidents have enjoyed very high approval ratings. As president, Medvedev's ratings are slightly lower than are Putin's ratings as prime minister.

Source: Levada Center, various dates.

11

education, and industrialization resulted in a more demanding and articulate society in the Soviet Union. When the reformist Gorbachev leadership in the late 1980s opened up greater freedom of speech and association, Soviet citizens responded with explosive energy to voice demands and to organize for collective action.[7] Politics became freer, more open, and more contested. Leaders such as Gorbachev and Yeltsin strove to create new political institutions that would enable them to realize their goals. Not surprisingly, though, in view of the huge uncertainty and rapid change surrounding them in the late 1980s and early 1990s, they often miscalculated the consequences of their actions. For instance, it is now clear that the central party leadership in the late 1980s seriously underestimated the strength of ethnic-national attachments in the union republics, so that when they granted greater political liberty to Soviet citizens, much of the new ferment that followed swelled into nationalist movements demanding independence for the union republics.

Another critical issue in understanding regime change is the relationship between economic and political liberalization. The monopoly on productive property—that is, wealth such as factories, banks and land which produces wealth—held by the state meant that the state's rulers could dispose of the country's resources as they saw fit with no effective check on their power. Marx and Lenin had taught that the institution of private property is inimical to communism because it is associated with a class of independent property owners who will defend their rights against a government that tries to confiscate their wealth. The reformers fighting for freedom and democracy in Russia therefore regarded the demand to institute private property rights, the rule of law, and a market economy as being inseparable from the demand for democratic rights in the political sphere. Communists fought intensely to prevent the restoration of private property and a market economy. They argued—quite accurately—that privatizing state assets would lead to the concentration of huge wealth and power in the hands of a small number of owners. They downplayed the point that privatization would also deprive them of their lock on political power.

The communist regime's monopoly on power and property also meant that there were few autonomous social groups that could lend support to newly rising political movements. One of the most distinctive features of communist systems is their effort to transform all social associations into instruments furthering the reach of the state into people's lives. Trade unions, youth leagues, hobby groups, professional associations, communications media, religious bodies, educational institutions, and the arts were all forced to become instruments of mass mobilization on behalf of the regime. Among the impediments to the establishment of a fully democratic regime in Russia, the weakness of civil society—the sphere of organized social associations that link people by their common interests outside family and friends—has proven to be one of the most powerful.[8] This weakness has continued to hold back Russia's postcommunist political development.

The study of Russia's transformation is not only of academic interest. Policy makers throughout the world have drawn lessons from it for their own development strategies. For some observers, Russia's poor performance in the 1990s is often regarded as a devastating indictment of the strategies pursued by the IMF and Western governments in their aid and advice to transitional economies; instead of preaching open markets and fiscal austerity, critics argue, the world should have been promoting efforts to increase the state's ability to steer the economy.[9] Russia and China are often contrasted as opposing models of reform. Some critics argue that Gorbachev erred in democratizing the political system before opening up the economy, on the grounds that loosening political controls invited a surge of nationalism, corruption, civil war, and administrative decomposition that ultimately brought about the collapse of the state—all without improving the economy.[10] Others argue that under Yeltsin the Russian leadership abandoned its controls over the economy before new market-oriented institutions were in place. The result was a catastrophic decline in production, the loss of much of the country's economic capacity, the flourishing of barter, corruption, and underground economic activity, and the takeover of most of Russia's most profitable resources by a few unscrupulous tycoons. In contrast, say the critics, China has preserved its communist political controls but encouraged entrepreneurship, foreign investment, and profit making in agriculture, with the result that it has enjoyed a long period of extremely high economic growth without experiencing the loss of political order.[11]

As we shall see in Chapter 7, whatever the flaws of the economic reform program, certainly its implementation of the program was fatally compromised from the start by political factors.[12] Other postcommunist states pursued similar programs of radical reform with far better results. Some reasons for Russia's problems lie in the starting conditions under which Russia launched its reforms and the particular path it took to postcommunism. We should be wary of assuming that Russian leaders had the same options that Chinese leaders had.

Russia's political evolution also affects international security. Legally, Russia is the successor of the Soviet Union in international law, and, as a practical matter, it has inherited an enormous military arsenal and vital geo-political location. Russia's military might has declined considerably since the 1980s, but, with around 5,200 nuclear weapons still in its active inventory (and another 8,800 or so in reserve or scheduled for dismantlement), it remains one of the two world nuclear superpowers.[13] Of even greater concern for international security than its active nuclear stockpiles, however, is the legacy of its history as a producer of nuclear, chemical, and biological weapons. Many of its factories and laboratories still have the capability of supplying nuclear fuel and other raw materials that could be used to produce weapons of mass destruction. Loose control over nuclear, biological, and chemical materials in the former Soviet Union, in fact, is considered to be the weakest link in international efforts to prevent the proliferation of weapons of mass destruction.[14] The Soviet Union built up a large pool of scientific and technical experts in the production of biological, chemical, and nuclear weapons, and there is widespread concern about their willingness to sell their services to radical states or to terrorist groups.

The stockpiles of weapons of mass destruction and their associated labs, factories, raw materials, and technical expertise that exist in the United States and Russia are the legacy of decades of competition between the two super-powers during the Cold War. From the late 1940s until the late 1980s, the United States and other Western democracies fought with the Soviet Union for influence over Europe, Asia, the Middle East, and other regions of the world. The United States committed itself by treaty to defending the security of Europe and other regions, with the threat of nuclear war backing up its commitment. The Soviet Union, in turn, countered by building up its arsenal of nuclear, biological, and chemical weapons to levels that would allow it to deter any military threat to its national interests.[15] In the end, of course, the huge military power at the disposal of the regime proved incapable of preventing its collapse. Indeed, the regime's insatiable appetite for military spending was one reason its economy lagged far behind the West in most other areas.

The origins of the Cold War conflict between the superpowers lie in the revolutionary aims of the communist movement in the first half of the century, when Russia sponsored an international communist movement aimed at overthrowing international capitalism and "bourgeois" (liberal democratic) governments around the world. From the time that the communists took power in Russia in 1917, their regime adopted a posture of fundamental hostility to the West. For most of the period of communist rule (1917–1991), Soviet rulers alternated between an aggressive, expansionist policy toward the Western world and an accommodative and pragmatic one. They pursued "peaceful coexistence" but competed for influence by supporting radical socialist movements and fought the spread of the basic democratic and capitalist values of the West. Observers noted that in its external relations, the Soviet Union proceeded along two tracks simultaneously.[16] On one track, the regime sought stable economic and diplomatic relations with the powerful countries of the capitalist world. On the other, it constructed a network of political and military alliances with socialist and revolutionary regimes and groups with the goal of increasing its global influence at the expense of that of the West. In turn, the United States also forged a system of alliances and treaty relationships around the world to try to contain the expansion of Soviet influence, provided economic assistance to developing countries, and exerted its power to prevent communism from spreading. The antagonism between the democratic and market-oriented states of the West and the socialist bloc led by the Soviet Union created a bipolar structure of power in world politics which lasted from shortly after World War II until the momentous reforms of Mikhail Gorbachev.[17]

The strategic rivalry between the two superpowers, the United States and the Soviet Union, shaped both political and military relations. Both countries devoted enormous efforts to preparing for possible war. Each side came to accept that a general nuclear war between them would be so devastating to each side, no matter which began it, that it could never be fought; but each accepted that the terrible threat of such a war served to deter the other from taking excessive or provocative risks. Both, moreover, continually upgraded their nuclear arsenals during this period, emphasizing qualities such as destructive power, accuracy, invulnerability, and mobility.

Russia and the United States agree on the desirability of deep reductions in their nuclear arsenals and have negotiated a series of agreements to that end. In 1991, Presidents Bush (the elder) and Yeltsin signed a treaty on strategic arms reductions (START), reducing the number of nuclear weapons to 6,000 warheads on each side. A subsequent treaty, called START-II, committed them to further reductions, but after President Bush (younger) abrogated the Anti-Ballistic Missile (ABM) Treaty in 2002, Russia declared that it would no longer abide by START-II. In May 2002, Presidents Bush (younger) and Putin signed a treaty (known as the Strategic Offensive Reductions Treaty, or SORT) committing each side to removing around two-thirds of their remaining nuclear weapons from deployment over the next 10 years, leaving between 1,700 and 2,200 for each country.[18] Presidents Obama and Medvedev signed a new START treaty in April 2010 that set further limits on each side's nuclear arsenal. The treaty set the maximum number of warheads on each side to 1,550 and specified additional limits on the number of deployed and nondeployed missiles and bombers that each side could keep.[19]

During the Cold War, the United States and the Soviet Union waged a great ideological contest between capitalist democracy and Marxist-Leninist socialism. Each country treated its own political and economic system as a model, and both used their ideologies to defend and expand their power internationally. Soviet doctrine claimed that the socialist system was intrinsically superior to capitalism both because it did away with the exploitation of labor by capitalists and because it concentrated control over productive resources in the hands of leaders who could build up the country's productive potential. The doctrine held that unlike capitalism, socialism had a clear goal and would one day bring society to the "communist" stage of development, where all property and power would be held in common and all people would be equal. In earlier periods, many Soviet citizens as well as sympathetic foreign observers believed that the Soviet system did indeed offer an alternative model of economic development and social justice to that represented by capitalism. Over time, however, the socialist model showed that it was unable to generate self-sustaining economic growth, technological progress, or political liberty. The Soviet populace lost faith that the bright future of communism would ever arrive. When the communist system collapsed, it collapsed quickly, indicating how little popular support communist rule in fact possessed.

Nevertheless, although the deep ideological confrontation between the Soviet bloc and the American bloc has vanished, there remains a distinct possibility of a new cold war if Russia seeks to "balance" against the West rather than to integrate itself into the fabric of political and economic institutions of the West.[20] Emergence of a democratic, open political system in Russia would make it more likely that Russia and the West would be able to cooperate in countering the global proliferation of weapons of mass destruction and terrorism rather than engaging in an arms race or political competition. An economically healthy and democratic Russia would be a stabilizing factor in the multiple regions on which Russia borders: Eastern Europe, the Middle East, and Northeast and Northwest Asia.

FOUR DOMAINS OF CHANGE

Let us look more closely at the changes that have occurred in the last two decades in four basic domains of state and regime: state structure, political regime, economic system, and national identity.

State Structure: From Soviet Union to Russian Federation

As of January 1, 1992, the Union of Soviet Socialist Republics (USSR, also often called Soviet Union) ceased to exist. The Soviet Union's red flag with its hammer and sickle no longer flew over Moscow's Kremlin, which has been the seat of Russian state power for 400 years. In its place was Russia's white-blue-red tricolor flag. Soviet communism had come to an end, and a newly sovereign Russia took control of that portion of the USSR's territory—comprising three-quarters of the physical area and half the population—which had formed the Russian Soviet Federative Socialist Republic (RSFSR). Today, the RSFSR is called "the Russian Federation" or simply Russia.

The relationship between the Soviet Union and postcommunist Russia can be confusing, both for outside observers and for the people who suddenly found themselves citizens of a new state. Many people thought of "Russia" and the "Soviet Union" as interchangeable names for the same country. This was an understandable mental shortcut given Russia's dominance of the union politically and culturally. Formally, however, Russia was only one of fifteen nominally equal federal republics making up the union. Each republic had an ethnic-national identity, but the union itself had no ethnic or national affiliation—only an ideological one.

The union collapsed when the governments of Russia and other member republics refused to accept the authority of the central government any longer. Mikhail Gorbachev, the reform-minded leader of the Soviet Union, struggled to find some new framework to preserve the unity of the union, but he was outmaneuvered by Boris Yeltsin, head of the Russian Republic, and frustrated by the powerful aspirations for self-rule on the part of peoples in many of the republics. On June 12, 1990, the Russian Congress of People's Deputies—the newly elected legislative assembly of the RSFSR—approved a statement claiming Russian sovereignty within the USSR, according to which Russia would only observe those USSR laws that it consented to obey. A year later, on June 12, 1991, Boris Yeltsin was elected president of Russia in the first direct popular presidential elections that Russia had ever had. Probably few Russians foresaw that the union itself would eventually collapse as an outgrowth of these developments. Other events were equally momentous. The Communist Party ceased to rule the country. The familiar contours of the state-owned, state-planned economy were giving way to contradictory tendencies: Production in the state enterprises fell, while energetic if frequently corrupt private entrepreneurship spread. Inequality and poverty increased sharply. Everyone agreed that the old Soviet system was breaking down, while a new system had not fully formed.

The final breakup came in 1991. In August 1991, a group of leaders of the main bureaucratic structures of the union government (army, KGB, state economic ministries, and so on) arrested Gorbachev and made a desperate attempt to restore the old Soviet order. Their coup attempt failed, however, on the third day, when key elements of the army and security police refused to follow their orders. Thereafter, through the fall of 1991, the breakdown of Soviet state authority accelerated. One by one the union republics issued declarations of independence. The power structures of the union soon were unable to exercise authority. The Finance Ministry could not collect taxes; the military could not conscript soldiers. Trade ties were breaking down across regions and republics. As revenues fell, the Central Bank pumped more and more money into circulation that was not backed up by real values. The economy was sinking into chaos. Union bureaucracies operating on Russian territory were taken over by the Russian government; those in other republics were similarly nationalized by their governments.

In October 1991, Yeltsin announced that Russia would proceed with radical market-oriented reform designed to move the economy from communism to a market system irreversibly. On December 1, 1991, a referendum was held in the Ukrainian Republic on national independence. When the proposal to declare Ukrainian independence passed with 90 percent of the vote, politicians throughout the Soviet Union recognized that the breakup of the union was inevitable, and they looked for ways to preserve at least some of the formal ties among the republics. The leaders of the three Slavic core states—Russia, Ukraine, and Belorussia (now called Belarus)—met near Minsk, capital of Belorussia, on December 8, and on their own authority declared the USSR dissolved. In its place, they agreed to form a new entity to coordinate their economic and strategic relations, called the "Commonwealth of Independent States" (CIS). Thirteen days later, the CIS was expanded to include all the former republics except for Georgia and the three Baltic states of Lithuania, Latvia, and Estonia. In 1993, Georgia also joined, although it left again in 2008. As we will see in Chapter 9, however, the CIS has never evolved into an effective mechanism for coordinating political and economic decisions in its member states and has largely been replaced by more specific functional groupings of subsets of its members.

The breakup of the Soviet state enjoyed widespread initial support in Russia and more still in most of the other former Soviet republics. Very soon, however, opinion polls in Russia were registering a wave of public regret at the loss of the Soviet state. Already by late 1993, a large majority of Russian citizens condemned the breakup of the Soviet Union as harmful.[21] By 2001, some three quarters of the population regretted its demise.[22] But gradually opinion shifted. In June 2008, 18 years after Russia declared its independence, the number of people who thought that independence was for the good had risen from 27 percent in 1998 to 61 percent, and the number of those who thought it was for the worse had fallen from 57 percent to only 17 percent. Evidently, the improvement in economic conditions and the succession of generations had brought about a major shift toward acceptance of the breakup of the Soviet Union.[23]

Regime Change

Concurrent with the breakup of the USSR into its component republics, Russia undertook the revolutionary task of remaking its political institutions. The first steps in democratizing the communist system were taken by Mikhail Gorbachev, who came to power as General Secretary of the Communist Party of the Soviet Union (CPSU) in 1985. Although Gorbachev did not intend for his reform policies to bring about the dissolution of the Soviet Union, he did push for a far-reaching and radical set of changes in the economic and political institutions of the regime. These changes, in turn, stimulated demands for still more autonomy by regional leaders and led to the mobilization of protest against the existing regime by large segments of the population in many republics. In Russia, Boris Yeltsin and other political leaders successfully challenged Gorbachev and the union government for power by championing the cause of liberal democracy, the market economy, and national sovereignty for Russia. After the breakup of the Soviet Union, President Yeltsin and his government continued to press for market-oriented economic reform. In doing so, Yeltsin sometimes resorted to undemocratic methods, most spectacularly in 1993, when he dissolved parliament.

Under Putin and Medvedev, there has been a significant decline in political freedom. Independent media outlets have been taken over by owners friendly to the state, political parties are tightly controlled, and NGOs are closely supervised. Yet, even though the scope of free political activity today is narrower than it was in the 1990s, Russia remains freer than it was in the Soviet era before Gorbachev.

Individual Rights   The barriers to individual political liberties that the communist regime imposed are largely removed: the intrusive Communist Party mechanisms for indoctrinating the population and for enforcing ideological discipline in public discourse are gone and with them, the network of political informers who reported to the secret police on "anti-Soviet" speech. Citizens may now organize new political parties and associations, albeit under increasingly burdensome registration requirements. And citizens are free to practice their religion.[24] Citizens' ability to defend their rights against encroachment by central or local authorities is tenuous, however. The courts are usually reluctant to uphold citizens' rights in disputes with powerful central and regional authorities. Political parties and associations that directly challenge the regime are suppressed: they are refused permission to hold rallies, their leaders are arrested on trumped-up charges, or their registration papers are rejected.

Still, there is a significant difference between the current regime and the communist regime in the degree of freedom for civic organizations. In the Soviet era, public organizations were monitored and controlled by the Communist Party and had to serve the goals set by the regime. In the Stalin era (1928–1953), the major public organizations, such as trade unions and youth leagues, were considered to be "transmission belts" linking society to the political authorities. "Transmission belt" organizations provided regime-sponsored outlets for organized collective action and ensured that all organized activity would serve the interests of the regime. In the Gorbachev period, a huge number of new, autonomous social organizations sprang up as a result of the regime's political reforms. Some had avowedly political purposes, while others pursued cultural or avocational interests.[25] After the end of the communist regime, many of these vanished. With time, however, a more stable set of interest groups began to develop. Among these are organizations defending the interests of regions, collective and state farms, state industrial firms, entrepreneurs, private farmers, bankers, and industrial workers. Chapter 6 will discuss the activity of these associational groups in more detail, but here it is worth noting simply that whereas in the old Soviet regime, associational groups were considered to be anti-Soviet if they were not directly controlled and guided by the Communist Party, now, associational groups are tolerated so long as they do not directly challenge the authorities.[26]

A third difference between the present regime and the communist regime is that elections have become regular and more competitive. Between the first contested elections of USSR deputies in 1989 and the presidential election of March 2008, Russian voters went to the polls 14 times in nationwide elections:

March 1989: election of USSR deputies
March 1990: election of RSFSR and local deputies
March 1991: referenda on preserving union and creating Russian presidency
June 1991: election of RSFSR president
April 1993: referendum on approval of Yeltsin and government
December 1993: election of deputies to new parliament and referendum on draft constitution
December 1995: election of deputies to parliament
June 1996: election of president
December 1999: election of deputies to parliament
March 2000: election of president
December 2003: election of deputies to parliament
March 2004: election of president
December 2007: election of deputies to parliament
March 2008: election of president

In addition to these nationwide elections, there have also been numerous regional and local elections of executive and legislative officials. However, especially since Putin took office, elections have increasingly become subject to manipulation by state officials through unequal access to media publicity, rigged court decisions about the eligibility of candidates, fraudulent vote counting, and other abuses.[27] In the 2007–2008 parliamentary and presidential elections, the outcome was predetermined from the start. Yet, despite the substantial manipulation of the process, voters and leaders take elections seriously as a means of conferring legitimacy on political leaders. Russia has become an example of "electoral authoritarianism," where an authoritarian regime holds elections that have the appearance of competition while ensuring that there is no real challenge to the ruling authorities.[28] National elections now bear little resemblance to the elections of the 1990s, when the authorities faced serious challenges to their rule and opposition parties won majorities in the national and regional legislatures.

Authoritarian Trends Since Putin entered office, the authoritarian elements of the political system have grown stronger, while the democratic elements have weakened. One factor facilitating this trend is the heavy concentration of power in the presidency. Ironically, this was the legacy of the democratic movement of 1989–1991, which strived to create a powerful state presidency invested with sufficient power to overcome resistance to reform. The new constitution ratified in the nationwide referendum in December 1993 embodied President Yeltsin's conception of the presidency. Under it, the president has wide powers to form and direct the government, to appoint executives throughout the country, to issue decrees with the force of law, and to command the armed forces. The president directly oversees foreign policy and national security. Presidents Yeltsin, Putin, and Medvedev have interpreted presidential power broadly. Citing the constitutional provision that the president is the supreme commander-in-chief of the armed forces, they have claimed the right to order the armed forces into action to preserve order without parliamentary authorization.

In December 1994 and again in September 1999, President Yeltsin ordered the army and security troops to defeat the armed forces fighting for the independence of the separatist Chechen Republic, an ethnic enclave within the Russian Federation. In neither case did the president seek parliamentary approval for the action. The military campaign by the federal forces in 1994–1996 and again in 1999–2000 resulted in massive destruction of Grozny, the capital city, and of many other cities and towns in the republic. Tens of thousands of people have been killed, hundreds of thousands of people have fled the republic, and hundreds of thousands more were left homeless by the fighting. A group of legislators challenged President Yeltsin's use of his decree power to wage war in Chechnia by appealing to the Constitutional Court, but the Court found that Yeltsin had acted constitutionally in dealing with a threat to national security. President Yeltsin sometimes used the powers of the presidency to take unconstitutional action. In September 1993, Yeltsin issued a decree summarily dissolving parliament and ordering the holding of elections for a new parliament to be held in December of that year. When a group of hard-line parliamentarians resisted and barricaded themselves in the parliament building, Yeltsin ordered the army to shell the building. Under Yeltsin, television broadcasters also came under pressure to support the Kremlin's candidates in elections. For example, state media coverage of the 1999 parliamentary elections was severely biased in favor of the pro-Kremlin parties.[29] Putin went much further to limit media freedom, taking over and reorganizing independent television channels.[30]

The concentration of political power in the president and the executive agencies he oversees is reinforced by the weakness of checks on its use. The institutions that could monitor and expose malfeasance by the president and government, such as parliament, the mass media, and interest groups, are hampered by the cloak of secrecy that surrounds the executive and by the fact that the executive controls many of the material and informational resources that they depend on for their activity. For instance, the government can deny licenses to opposition-minded broadcast companies and newspapers. The presidential administration controls a wide array of material resources and administrative levers with which to check the independence of both the legislative and judicial branches.

Thus, without explicitly violating any constitutional limits on his power, and without abolishing elections or other democratic institutions, Putin effectively negated the constitutional limits on his power built into the constitution. Using the president's extensive powers over the executive branch, he neutralized and marginalized all independent sources of political authority, meantime observing formal constitutional procedures. For example, he enacted his policy program by passing legislation through parliament rather than by relying on his decree power. But having used his control over electoral processes to secure overwhelming majority support in both chambers, parliamentary approval of his proposed agenda is assured. This pattern has continued under President Medvedev.

Putin and Yeltsin differed substantially in the degree to which they respected democratic principles. Yeltsin used his presidential powers erratically and impulsively, but respected certain limits on his power: he did not suppress media criticism, and he tolerated political opposition.[31] Faced with an opposition-led parliament, Yeltsin was willing to compromise with his opponents to enact legislation. However, Yeltsin grew dependent on a coterie of powerful financial-media-industrial tycoons for support and let them acquire substantial influence. Likewise, Yeltsin allowed regional bosses to flout federal authority with impunity because he found it much less costly to accommodate them than to fight them. In contrast, Putin focused on regaining much of the central power lost in the 1990s. In doing so, he reduced some of the political freedoms that Russians gained with the collapse of communism. Simplifying only a little, we could say that Putin strengthened the state by concentrating state power in the executive (reinforcing what the Russians call "the vertical of power"—akin to the "chain of command" in a military organization), and placing the entire executive branch under his direct control. He accomplished this by reducing the autonomy of other centers of political power in the country, among them the parliament, parties, regional governments, the mass media, and civil society.

The loss of state capacity under Yeltsin illustrates one danger of an overcentralized political system: when the president does not effectively command the powers of the office, power drifts to other institutions. The presidency in the 2000s illustrates the opposite danger. When Putin took over, he was faced with the task of reversing the breakdown of political control and responsibility that had accelerated under Yeltsin. Although Putin and Medvedev have repeatedly called for a system based on respect for the rule of law, they have also relied on authoritarian methods to rule. Putin himself captured the contradictory quality of this vision in his 2004 message to parliament, when he said that creating "a free society of free people is the very most important of our tasks" but at the same time warned that any attempts to effect a significant change in his policy "could lead to irreversible consequences. And they must be absolutely excluded."[32]

Economic Transformation

In addition to the momentous changes in state structure and political regime, a third and equally dramatic change has been the transformation from the state-owned, centrally administered economy to one approximating a market system. In a market economy, the right of private ownership of productive resources enjoys legal guarantees, decisions on production and consumption are made by producers and consumers, and coordination of the myriad activities of individuals and organizations is accomplished primarily through their interaction in a competitive environment. Russia remains far from having reached this point—in fact, no economy in the real world completely matches this description. But in Russia, although the state still owns and controls large parts of the economy, a capitalist, market-based system has largely replaced the old planned economy. Russia's 1992 economic reform—a stabilization program that tightened the money supply, cut state spending sharply, and raised taxes—was called "shock therapy." Russia's version of shock therapy was crude and harsh, but in fact it was never fully implemented and it was often quietly sabotaged in practice. It may have been the only means available to policy makers for making rapid and irreversible changes in the behavior of economic actors, but it had many unwanted side effects.[33] Chapter 7 will describe the program and its results in more detail.

Painful as they were, the economic reforms of the early 1990s did effect some significant changes in the economy's structure. One was to create a rudimentary system of market institutions, such as banks, stock exchanges, and property rights. Another was to end most shortages of goods and services in major cities. The public's demand for basic consumer needs could be satisfied, and both domestic and imported food and other goods became widely available throughout the country.

Economic stabilization was only one prong of economic reform in Russia. The other was a shift to private ownership of productive resources through the privatization of state enterprises and the creation of independent businesses.[34] By 1999, the private sector had grown to the point where it exceeded the state sector in share of employed workers.[35] The results of these policies have been mixed. Market forces now play a far greater role than in the past. But control over real economic assets of factories and farms often remains in the hands of the same managers and officials who held them in the past. Many of those who held power under the old system wound up in positions of wealth and power in the new system. Nevertheless, privatization generally improved the economic performance of privatized firms, although only modestly in most industries.

The Question of Identity: Imperial Russia—USSR—Russian Federation

The breakdown and reconstruction of Russia's state structure, political institutions, and economic system created enormous uncertainty for Russians. No less unsettling was the dislocation of national identity. Although today's Russian Federation is the direct successor of a thousand-year-old tradition of statehood, the political forms and boundaries of the state as it exists today differ from any that Russia has known. From the late fifteenth century until the early twentieth century, Russia's state was constituted as an imperial monarchy ruling a contiguous expanse of territories and peoples. As a result, Russia's political evolution differed from the typical path taken by Western countries.[36] In Western Europe, nations formed as social communities in territories defined through wars and treaties among state rulers. In Russia, by contrast, the state created a territorial empire spanning a huge landmass and populated by a diverse array of European and Asian peoples, who differed profoundly among themselves in religion, way of life, and relationship to Russian authority. Russian national consciousness was not based on ethnicity, therefore, so much as it was on identification with a powerful imperial state. Russia's history lacks a model of a nation-state to serve as a precedent for the postcommunist period.

In the Soviet era, Russia was the core republic of a communist-ruled union of national republics, and Russians were often treated as the "elder brother" of the other peoples of the multinational country. Russia lent its language and much of its political culture to the Soviet Union but in the process it gave up its own character as a distinct nation-state. In effect, the Soviet Union was a new kind of empire, one whose culture was partly Russian, but which claimed to be a higher type of political organization. Over time, many Russians came to feel that Russia itself as a national entity was being shortchanged by the terms of its membership in the union.

Following the demise of the Soviet Union, Russians were once again called upon to form attachments to a redefined state, now called the Russian Federation. As had been the case for much of Russian history, postcommunist Russia's leaders have generally chosen not to base the identity of the newly independent state on an *ethnic* principle. No doubt this was partly out of the practical consideration that some 20 percent of the population was not ethnically Russian, but it also reflected the historical tradition of defining Russia as a multiethnic state rather than as a nation-state in which some ethnic minorities have coexisted with Russians for hundreds of years. Generally, Russia's leaders have characterized the state as a multinational federation in which the largest ethnic communities have their own territorial units. To build loyalty to the new Russia, the leaders have emphasized Russian and Soviet historical achievements in war, industry, science, technology, and the arts, but they have also sharply distinguished the new post-Soviet Russia from both its communist-era and tsarist predecessors. They aim at creating a set of concentric identities for citizens, including the sense of belonging to a particular ethnic community (Russian, Tatar, etc.) within the multiethnic Russian state.[37]

In retrospect, the breakup of the Soviet Union into its constituent republics may appear to have been the logical culmination of the Soviet state's development, but until 1991, most observers considered breakup to be highly unlikely— and some still think it could have been avoided. The reason is that the communist rulers were committed to a long-term goal of eradicating differences among peoples based on ethnic or linguistic characteristics, and instead building a new Soviet national identity based on the Soviet socialist way of life. As a practical matter, though, they recognized that harmony in the Soviet state required preserving some cultural rights for territorially based national groups. Therefore, they provided territorial political institutions for larger nationalities through which the traditional languages and cultures could be maintained.

In nearly every case, the national minorities in the Soviet Union were the same groups occupying the same lands that the tsarist Russian empire had conquered in previous centuries. But denying that the multinational, communist state was in any way a Russian empire, the communist regime imposed a common socialist model of economic ownership and administration on the entire territory of the state. Although Soviet ideology held that in the long run, national differences would be subsumed in a common Soviet national identity, during the late 1980s, leaders in the 15 republics pursued demands for greater autonomy for their republics and in many republics, mass movements for national independence grew powerful. This was even true in Russia: the structures of the union itself were so firmly associated in many people's minds with a rigid, exploitative political arrangement that both nationalist conservatives and democratic reformers in Russia agreed that progress for Russia was only possible if Russia escaped the USSR's political straitjacket.

Many Russians believe that the Russian state requires a great national mission as a foundation for its values, goals, and legitimacy. They cite the fact that the tsarist political order had regarded itself as the preserver of the true Christian faith and that the Soviet regime considered itself to be the base of a worldwide revolutionary struggle for socialism. In 1996, shortly after his reelection as president, President Yeltsin called for the formulation of a "new national idea." He observed that previous eras of Russian history had been characterized by overarching political ideologies, such as monarchy, totalitarianism, or perestroika. The new Russian state demanded a new national idea, he declared. However, the team he charged with discovering such a unifying ideology in a year's time reported a year later that they had been unsuccessful in devising one. Perhaps, as one of Yeltsin's advisors commented at the time, it was impossible to frame a single doctrine that could encompass the full range of contradictory realities of the new political situation. Rather, perhaps the never-ending *search* for a national idea was itself the Russian idea.

CHOICES AND CHANGES IN RUSSIAN POLITICS

There have been huge changes—breakup of the Soviet Union, dismantling of the communist political system, a shift toward market capitalism, and the change in the very national identity of the state. How have they affected Russian citizens? How much have they changed the distribution of *real* power in the country?

The upheavals of the last decade are equivalent to a revolutionary break with the past, comparable to the formation of the Soviet regime in 1917.[38] Certainly, older patterns of political life are reappearing, such as the hyper-centralization of power, the dual executive of autocrat and government, the impotence of legal institutions and pervasiveness of corruption, the proliferation of centralized state agencies together with the inability to accomplish stated policy purposes, the power and autonomy of the security police, and the pervasive state control over the economy. Looking at these phenomena, we might jump to the conclusion that following a decade of disorder in the 1990s, eternal Russian patterns of political life have returned.[39] Many Russians today say that the apparent democratic revolution in Russia was a fraud and illusion that simply allowed a new group of greedy, power-hungry elites to win a share of control of the country's property and power. Some observers say that one form of authoritarianism and imperialism has simply been replaced by another.

However, it would be as wrong to exaggerate the degree of continuity with the past as it would to overlook the important changes in the political system that have occurred. The dismantling of the old Communist Party mechanisms for exercising its monopolistic power, especially the all-pervasive control over ideology, means that political processes are more open. The pluralistic diversity of political interests has now moved from the arena of behind-the-scenes bureaucratic politics to a more open competition of interest groups and parties for influence over policy. Individual rights are better protected than in the past. Contact between Russia and the outside world has expanded enormously. There is a flourishing private economic sector. Overall, these changes in national identity, political institutions, and economic system amount to a vast transformation. When we consider the level of violence required to carry out the communist revolution and establish the Soviet system in Russia, the peaceful nature of the transition from the old regime seems astonishing.

But while the transformation was peaceful, it brought about a grave weakening in state capacity. This occurred because many of the powerful elite groups that persisted from the Soviet period into the post-Soviet system found ways to take advantage of the new conditions for their own benefit. The political system they created left the new democratic political institutions vulnerable to authoritarian backsliding.[40] Still, the mutual adaptation of elites and institutions may have been the only way to avert a more serious social conflict during the passage from communism to democracy.

PLAN OF THE BOOK

Russia's transformation allows us to investigate the relationship between regime change and state capacity. Certainly there is no assumption here that Russia's political transition will ultimately result in a democratic state. But its political future remains open. History suggests that political systems can remain trapped in intermediate zones in which some democratic institutions coexist with strong elements of authoritarianism for decades or longer. Our question, therefore, is whether there is some overall direction to the development of Russia's political system.

The rest of the book will explore the institutions and processes of Russia's political system in greater detail. Chapters 2 and 3 provide an overview of the political history of the last two decades, when the old Soviet regime collapsed and a new political order in Russia took shape. Chapter 2 details the structures and processes of rule in the Soviet period, showing how power was exercised under the Communist Party–dominated regime. Then it discusses the Gorbachev reforms and their objectives, and the succession of schemes he advanced to reorganize the political system. The chapter shows that the reforms had unanticipated effects which resulted in Gorbachev's loss of control over political developments. When the Soviet regime collapsed in 1991, it was succeeded by newly independent successor regimes in the former republics. Already, however, the Russian Republic had initiated its own major reforms which culminated in a political crisis in 1993 and the adoption of a new constitution which is in force today. In Chapter 3, we will consider the institutions and processes of the contemporary Russian regime, analyze the trends of its development, and assess how well President Putin achieved his goal of rebuilding Russian state power by centralizing executive authority.

In Chapter 4, we look at how the public participates in the political system. The nature of political participation has greatly changed since the Soviet era. In the old regime, participation tended to be ceremonial, regimented, and controlled. Today, the prevalent pattern is one of political disengagement and mistrust of government, along with high levels of turnout at elections. Some of the "informal organizations" that sprang up during the late Soviet period evolved into political parties and interest groups, some of which fell by the wayside and others of which have survived.

The second part of Chapter 4 takes up the subject of elite recruitment. In every political system, popular participation in politics is closely related to the process of elite recruitment: through elections, organizational activism, and the exercise of influence over policy makers, some individuals get involved in politics; of them, some become full-time political professionals. Of considerable interest in this connection is the question of the relation between the old political elite in Russia and the contemporary political elite. What has happened to the old communist elite? Where do today's rulers come from, and what are the relations between big business and the political elite?

Chapter 5 assesses the findings of public opinion surveys about the values and beliefs of Russians. It observes that although typical Russian citizens value democratic rights and freedoms, they also expect the state to provide basic political order. Although many people rate the old regime favorably, not many would actually wish to restore it. Confidence in the institutions of the new order is low, but confidence in Putin is remarkably high. For the most part, Russians have accepted the new post-Soviet political regime as one that delivers basic political stability, but they are mistrustful of most institutions and feel they have little say over how they work.

In Chapter 6, we ask how Russians voice their political demands and interests through interest groups and political parties. We review several categories of actors—industrial managers, women's groups, organized labor, and the Orthodox Church—to see how the social changes of the last 20 years have altered the balance of power and interest among different kinds of social groups.

In the second part of Chapter 6, we look at the party system, focusing especially on the rise of United Russia as a dominant authoritarian party. How well do parties link different groups of the population to the national political arena? The increasingly monopolistic position of United Russia invites us to ask whether the regime is moving to some version of the old Communist Party–led state and whether United Russia can continue to maintain its power in the coming years.

Chapter 7 examines the remaking of the economy. It discusses the "shock therapy" reforms of the early 1990s and the privatization program, the depression of the 1990s, the recovery of the 2000s, and the crash of 2008–2009. It examines the effects of economic change on the lives of ordinary Russians. In particular, we will consider the importance of Russia's dependence on gas and oil exports for its economic performance and international standing. Is Russia's energy wealth in fact a "resource curse" from the standpoint of the sustainability of its economic and political development?

Chapter 8 surveys the system of judicial and law-enforcement institutions. The chapter discusses the problem of law and legal institutions at two levels: the task of putting the activity of state officials and private citizens securely under the rule of law, and the effectiveness of legal institutions in enforcing constitutional and legal rules. The chapter reviews the major institutions of the judicial system and the reforms that are being made in it. Of particular interest is the emergence of a mechanism for judicial review of the acts of other government institutions in the form of the Constitutional Court. We discuss the obstacles toward the rule of law, including organized crime, pervasive corruption, and the manipulation of the legal system by political officials.

The last chapter, Chapter 9, offers an overview of Russia's changing relationship with the international community. It emphasizes that the goal of expanding influence in the former Soviet region contradicts the goal of deepening integration with the democratic and developed world. It also examines the resources and liabilities Russia faces in its external relations, including the dynamics of "pipeline politics."

NOTES

1. Henry E. Hale. "Regime Cycles: Democracy, Autocracy and Revolution in Post-Soviet Eurasia," *World Politics* 58 (2005): 133–165.
2. Viktor Khamraev, "U rossiian rastut simpatii k prezidentu," *Kommersant*, June 1, 2010.
3. From surveys conducted by Russia's premier polling organization, the Levada Center. The "right/wrong direction" survey was posted to their Web site on April 2, 2008: http://www.levada.ru/press/2008040201.html. Results of the survey on approval of the president are available at http://www.levada.ru/press/2008061102.html.
4. Anders Aslund, *Russia's Capitalist Revolution: Why Market Reform Succeeded and Democracy Failed* (Washington, DC: Peterson Institute for International Economics, 2007).
5. Putin's address to the State Council, February 8, 2008. From the presidential Web site: http://president.kremlin.ru/text/appears/2008/02/159528.shtml.
6. President Dmitrii Medvedev, "Rossiia, vpered! [Go, Russia!]," as published on the presidential Web site on September 10, 2009: http://kremlin.ru.
7. Chapter 2 discusses Gorbachev and his reforms in more detail.
8. Larry Diamond defines civil society as "the realm of organized social life that is open, voluntary, self-generating, at least partially self-supporting, autonomous from the state, and bound by a legal order or set of shared rules. 'It' involves citizens acting collectively in a public sphere" for a variety of purposes. Diamond, *Developing Democracy*, p. 221.
9. Among the critics arguing this way is Joseph Stiglitz, formerly the World Bank's chief economist. Joseph Stiglitz, *Globalization and Its Discontents* (New York: Norton, 2002), especially the chapter "Who Lost Russia?" Other works in this vein include Stephen F. Cohen, *America's Failed Crusade*; and Peter Reddaway and Dmitri Glinski, *The Tragedy of Russia's Reforms: Market Bolshevism against Democracy* (Washington, DC: The United States Institute of Peace, 2001).
10. For example, see Minxin Pei, *From Reform to Revolution: the Demise of Communism in China and the Soviet Union* (Cambridge: Harvard University Press, 1994).
11. Barry Naughton, *Growing out of the Plan: Chinese Economic Reform, 1978–1993* (Cambridge: Cambridge University Press, 1995); Stiglitz, *Globalization and Its Discontents*, pp. 133–165.
12. Rudiger Ahrend and William Tompson, "Fifteen Years of Economic Reform in Russia: What Has Been Achieved? What Remains to be Done?" *Paris, OECD: Economics Department Working Papers* No. 430, May 13, 2005, pp. 6–8.
13. George Perkovich and James M. Acton, "Abolishing Nuclear Weapons," *Adelphi Papers* 48:396 (2008): 18–19. They estimate that the United States possesses 5,400 operational nuclear warheads (1,260 of which are inactive). Another 5,000 or so are scheduled to be dismantled.
14. Graham Allison, "How to Stop Nuclear Terror," *Foreign Affairs* 83:1 (January/February 2004): 64–75.
15. For example, despite signing the 1972 treaty banning all biological weapons, the Soviet Union pursued a large-scale program for research on and production of a number of biological weapons, including smallpox, anthrax, and plague. It is believed that this program employed some 60,000 people. A former top scientist in the Soviet bioweapons program who now lives in the United States has written a memoir of his experiences. Ken Alibek and Stephen Handelman, *Biohazard* (New York: Delta, 2000).

16. A magisterial study of Soviet foreign policy from the beginnings of the Soviet regime through the early 1970s is Adam Ulam, *Expansion and Coexistence: Soviet Foreign Policy, 1917–1973*, 2nd ed. (New York: Praeger, 1974).
17. World War II ended in 1945, and the post-war era of antagonism between the United States and its allies and the Soviet Union and its allies began in 1947–1948. Mikhail Gorbachev, the last leader of the Soviet Union, assumed power as General Secretary of the Communist Party of the Soviet Union in March 1985. In 1990, he created and assumed the position of President of the Soviet Union. He resigned formally from this position in December 1991. The USSR (Union of Soviet Socialist Republics; also known as the Soviet Union) formally dissolved as a legal entity on December 31, 1991. Since the Bolshevik Revolution in 1917, when the Soviet regime was established, the Soviet leaders and the dates of their rule are as follows:

    1. Vladimir Lenin (1917–1924)
    2. Iosif Stalin (1924–1953)
    3. Nikita Khrushchev (1953–1964)
    4. Leonid Brezhnev (1964–1982)
    5. Yuri Andropov (1982–1984)
    6. Konstantin Chernenko (1984–1985)
    7. Mikhail Gorbachev (1985–1991).

18. The treaty did not require the dismantling of all the weapons, however. It left open the possibility that either side might simply put the weapons into storage, where they might be vulnerable to theft or could be placed back into deployment.
19. For details of the treaty see the summary by the Arms Control Association at http://www.armscontrol.org/factsheets/NewSTART.
20. James M. Goldgeier and Michael McFaul, "Russians as Joiners: Realist and Liberal Conceptions of Postcommunist Europe," in Michael McFaul and Kathryn Stoner-Weiss, eds., *After the Collapse of Communism: Comparative Lessons of Transition* (Cambridge: Cambridge University Press, 2004): 232–256.
21. Jerry F. Hough, "The Russian Election of 1993: Public Attitudes Toward Economic Reform and Democratization," *Post-Soviet Affairs* 10:1 (January–March 1994): 13.
22. Results of a survey from March 2001, as cited by the RFE/RL Newsline, March 16, 2001.
23. From a survey conducted by the Levada Center in June 2008. *Nezavisimaia Gazeta*, June 11, 2008.
24. The state has made it difficult for some religious denominations to operate, however, particularly those that have not had a long-standing presence in Russia.
25. Jim Butterfield and Marcia Weigle, "Unofficial Social Groups and Regime Response in the Soviet Union," in Judith B. Sedaitis and Jim Butterfield, eds., *Perestroika from Below: Social Movements in the Soviet Union* (Boulder: Westview, 1992), pp. 175–195; Marcia A. Weigle, *Russia's Liberal Project: State-Society Relations in the Transition from Communism* (University Park, PA: Pennsylvania State University Press, 2000).
26. In Eastern Europe in the 1960s, liberal elements in the Hungarian communist regime used to frame this distinction as follows: under Stalin, the party's attitude was "he who is not with us is against us," while today "he who is not against us is with us."
27. The scope of election fraud has been estimated by three political scientists on the basis of an ingenious mathematical analysis of district-by-district election returns. The authors argue that what had been rather isolated instances of the authorities falsifying results in the 1990s have become massive and widespread in recent years.

See Mikhail Myagkov, Peter C. Ordeshook, and Dimitri Shakin, *The Forensics of Election Fraud: Russia and Ukraine* (Cambridge: Cambridge University Press, 2009). In his book *Virtual Politics*, Andrew Wilson describes a huge array of such techniques used in Russia and Ukraine and argues that these efforts to manipulate elections are so far-reaching that elections themselves are a sham. See Andrew Wilson, *Virtual Politics: Faking Democracy in the Post-Soviet World* (New Haven, CT: Yale University Press, 2005).

28. Andreas Schedler, ed., *Electoral Authoritarianism: The Dynamics of Unfree Competition* (Boulder, CO: Lynne Rienner, 2006).

29. Sarah Oates, "Television, Voters and the Development of the 'Broadcast Party,' " in Vicki L. Hesli and William M. Reisinger, eds., *The 1999–2000 Elections in Russia: Their Impact and Legacy* (New York: Cambridge University Press, 2003), pp. 29–50; also see the report on media bias in the 1999 elections on the Web site of the European Institute for the Media, www.eim.de.

30. Sarah Oates, "The Neo-Soviet Model of the Media," *Europe–Asia Studies* 59:8 (2007): 1279–1297.

31. Timothy J. Colton, *Yeltsin: A Life* (New York: Basic Books, 2008), pp. 453–454.

32. Quoted from text published on Web site on May 26, 2004: polit.ru.

33. Among the studies of the economic transformation of Russia and its consequences are Andrei Shleifer and Daniel Treisman, *Without a Map: Political Tactics and Economic Reform in Russia* (Cambridge: MIT Press, 2000); Thane Gustafson, *Capitalism Russian-Style* (Cambridge: Cambridge University Press, 1999); and Anders Aslund, *Russia's Capitalist Revolution: Why Market Reform Succeeded and Democracy Failed* (Washington, DC: Peterson Institute for International Economics, 2007).

34. A valuable analysis of the economic reform program is the book by Andrei Shleifer and Daniel Treisman, *Without a Map: Political Tactics and Economic Reform in Russia* (Cambridge, MA: MIT Press, 2000). Shleifer, a Harvard economist, helped advise the Russian government on the reforms.

35. The remainder worked in joint ventures or for public organizations or in other forms of mixed public–private enterprises. Figures drawn from *Rossiiskii statisticheskii ezhegodnik: 1999* (Moscow: Goskomstat Rossii, 1999), p. 114. This publication is the official statistical annual published by the State Statistics Committee of Russia.

36. Roman Szporluk, "The Imperial Legacy and the Soviet Nationalities," in Lubomyr Hajda and Mark Beissinger, eds., *The Nationalities Factor in Soviet Politics and Society* (Boulder: Westview, 1990), pp. 1–23; and Roman Szporluk, "Dilemmas of Russian Nationalism," in Rachel Denber, ed., *The Soviet Nationality Reader: The Disintegration in Context* (Boulder: Westview, 1992), pp. 509–543.

37. Valery Tishkov and Martha Brill Olcott, "From Ethnos to Demos: The Quest for Russia's Identity," in Anders Aslund and Martha Brill Olcott, eds., *Russia after Communism* (Washington, DC: Carnegie Endowment for International Peace, 1999), pp. 61–90.

38. Political scientist Michael McFaul has argued that we should view Russia's transformation since the end of the Soviet Union as a peaceful revolution. See Michael McFaul, *Russia's Unfinished Revolution: Political Change from Gorbachev to Putin* (Ithaca, NY: Cornell University Press, 2001). McFaul subsequently became President Obama's chief adviser on Russian affairs.

39. Gerald M. Easter, "The Russian State in the Time of Putin," *Post-Soviet Affairs* 24:3 (2008): 199–230.

40. Lilia Shevtsova, *Russia-Lost in Transition: The Yeltsin and Putin Legacies* (Washington, DC: Carnegie Endowment for International Peace, 2007).

The Soviet System and Its Demise

Russia's present-day political institutions are the product of a series of political convulsions that began in the late 1980s, when Mikhail Gorbachev first began his attempts to reform the Soviet regime. Gorbachev's reforms ultimately brought down the Soviet regime and ignited a contest within Russia itself over how the country was to be ruled. This intra-Russian struggle subsided once the 1993 constitution came into force. The adoption of the constitution settled the problem of how power should be formally organized in the Russian state, but the constitution bears the strong imprint of Yeltsin's own political objectives. In particular, the powerful presidency embodies Yeltsin's vision of a president holding paramount power to set national policy. Likewise, the design of the parliament, the Constitutional Court, and the nature of federalism all were shaped by Yeltsin's strategic imperatives, above all his determination to rid Russia of the legacies of communist rule. Although a large number of leaders and experts participated in drafting the constitution, Yeltsin had the final say on most points.[1] As president, Vladimir Putin reinforced some features of the constitution—particularly the sweeping powers of the presidency—while emptying others of all significance. But the constitution itself has been amended only once—to lengthen the term of the president from four to six years and the term of the Duma from four to five years.

In a longer-term perspective, today's political order has been shaped by a thousand-year history of Russian statehood. Both in the Soviet era and before it, Russia's rulers have sought to create the means for extending central control over a vast, cold, and thinly populated land. Before we review the basic elements of the current constitutional order, therefore, we need to know something of its historical origins. This chapter provides a summary overview of the Russian regime before the communists came to power, followed by a description of the Soviet system and its breakdown. Chapter 3 then discusses the formation of the current Russian regime.

HISTORICAL LEGACIES

The Tsarist Regime

The Russian state traces its origins to the princely state that arose around Kiev (today the capital of independent Ukraine) in the ninth century. For nearly a thousand years, the Russian state was autocratic—that is, it was ruled by a hereditary monarch whose power was unlimited by any constitution. Only in the first decade of the twentieth century did the Russian tsar agree to grant a constitution calling for an elected legislature—and even then, the tsar soon dissolved the legislature and arbitrarily revised the constitution. In addition to autocracy, the historical legacy of Russian statehood includes absolutism, patrimonialism, and Orthodox Christianity. Absolutism meant that the tsar aspired to wield absolute power over the subjects of the realm. *Patrimonialism* refers to the idea that the ruler treated his realm as property that he owned rather than as a political community consisting of individuals and groups with distinct rights and interests. This conception of power continues to influence Russian politics to this day.

The patrimonial character of the tsarist state, and the lingering elements of patrimonialism that have survived into the Soviet and post-Soviet eras, owes much to the impact of the physical environment in which Russia's state arose. As historian Richard Pipes observed, Russia might have developed as a set of decentralized political communities rather than as a mobilizing, centralizing state had it not been for the low productivity of the agrarian base of its economy. The harshness of the climate and the low productivity of the soil tended to push Russians to seek out new lands to plow rather than to increase the yield of lands already cultivated.[2] This pattern, coupled with the absence of readily defensible natural boundaries to separate Russia from neighboring peoples meant that the costs of both economic production and external security were high by comparison with European states, tending to induce a pattern of state-led mobilization of resources for economic development and military power.[3] Moreover, the Russian state's historically recurrent drive to mobilize human and natural resources for war and economic development has been far more brutal than in most Western societies owing to the immense size of the territory over which Russia's state had to maintain its lines of control and communication, its generally harsh and inhospitable climate, and its location on the borders of several European and Asian civilizations and empires. Over time, these pressures intensified Russia's rulers' demands for absolute power over their society and pushed their ideological doctrines to take on extreme and dogmatic forms. This historical legacy helps to explain why Russians place a particularly high value on state power and why their efforts to accumulate and manage state power have been so difficult.

Finally, the tsarist state identified itself with the Russian branch of the Eastern Orthodox Christian Church. In Russia, as in other countries where it is the dominant religious tradition, the Orthodox Church ties itself closely to the state, considering itself a national church. Traditionally, the Russian Orthodox Church has exhorted its adherents to show loyalty and obedience to the state in worldly matters, in return for which the state has treated it as the state church—even in those periods when the state subjected it to control and persecution. This legacy is still manifested in the postcommunist rulers' efforts to associate themselves with the heritage of Russia's church, and many Russians' impulse is to identify their state with a higher spiritual mission.

Absolutism, patrimonialism, and Orthodoxy have been recurring strains in Russian political culture. But other motifs have been influential as well. At some points in Russian history, the country's rulers have sought to modernize its economy and society. Russia imported Western practices in technology, law, state organization, and education in order to make the state competitive with other great powers. Modernizing rulers such as Peter the Great (who ruled from 1682 to 1725) and Catherine the Great (ruling from 1762 to 1796) had a powerful impact on Russian society, bringing it closer to Western European models. The imperative of building Russia's military and economic potential was all the more pressing because of Russia's constant expansion through conquest and annexation of neighboring territories and the ever-present need to defend its borders. The state's role in controlling and mobilizing society expanded with the need to govern a vast territory. By the end of the seventeenth century, Russia was territorially the largest state in the world. But for most of its history, the state's imperial reach exceeded its actual grasp.

By comparison with the other major powers of Europe, Russia's economic institutions remained backward well into the twentieth century. However, the trajectory of its development, especially in the nineteenth century, was toward that of a modern industrial society. By the time the tsarist order fell in 1917, Russia possessed a large industrial sector, although it was concentrated only in a few cities. The country's middle class was greatly outnumbered by the vast and impoverished peasantry and the radicalized industrial working class. As a result, the social basis for a peaceful democratic transition was too weak to prevent the communists from seizing power in 1917.

The thousand-year tsarist era left a contradictory legacy. The tsars attempted to legitimate their absolute power by appealing to tradition, empire, and divine right. They treated law as an instrument of rule rather than a source of authority. The doctrines that rulers should be accountable to the ruled and that sovereignty resides in the collective will of the people were alien to Russian state tradition. Throughout Russian history, state and society have been more distant from each other than in Western societies. Rulers and populace regarded one another with mistrust and suspicion. This gap has been overcome at times of great national trials such as the war against Napoleon and later World War II. Russia celebrated victory in those wars as a triumphant demonstration of the unity of state and people. But Russia's political traditions also include a yearning for equality, solidarity, and community, as well as for moral purity and sympathy for the downtrodden. And throughout the Russian heritage runs a deep strain of pride in the greatness of the country and the endurance of its people.

THE SOVIET REGIME BEFORE GORBACHEV

In October 1917, Vladimir Lenin, leader of the Russian communists, overthrew a weak parliamentary government, which itself had replaced the tsarist regime several months before.[4] From 1917 until 1991, Russia was ruled by the Communist Party, which held a monopoly on political power (see Close-up 2.1: Socialism, Communism, Marxism, Leninism). Originally, the Communist Party was a revolutionary movement aimed at overthrowing the tsarist state. Indeed, its ambitions went much further than that. The communists' long-range goal was the overthrow of capitalism throughout the world and the establishment of a worldwide socialist system. In the end, the communist movement succeeded in establishing communist regimes in Russia, Eastern Europe, much of Asia, and a few isolated countries in other regions (among them Cuba). But the worldwide communist revolution never arrived, and Russia's communists devoted most of their energies to building up the power of the Soviet state. They constantly invoked the language of class war as they sought to portray their drive for economic and military power, and for moral unity and loyalty, as a struggle against the capitalist world.

To the Russian communists, socialism meant a society without private ownership of the means of production, where the state owned and controlled all important economic assets, and where political power was exercised in the interests of the working people. *Vladimir Ilyich Lenin* (1870–1924; in power 1917–1924) formed the Russian Communist Party and headed the Soviet Russian government after the revolution.[5] In keeping with Lenin's model of the Communist Party as a "vanguard party," the Soviet regime divided power between the *soviets,* which were elective councils through which workers and peasants could voice their desires, and the Communist Party, which would lead the soviets. The communists regarded the soviets as useful channels for participation in the state by the masses, but ensured that they would be dominated by the more tightly organized and disciplined Communist Party. The party, as the bearer of the guiding vision, would direct the soviets and their executive organs, but it would remain organizationally separate from them.[6]

Lenin's successor, *Joseph Stalin* (1879–1953; in power 1924–1953), consolidated the institutional underpinnings of Lenin's model of rule, but also took its despotic impulses to extremes: Stalin's regime employed mass terror against large categories of the population, killing millions of Soviet citizens through executions, induced famine, forced labor under inhuman conditions, and deportations.[7] At least 25 million people were subjected to political repression by being executed or sent to labor camps. Stalin's regime expanded Soviet state power and defended it in World War II (although at a very high price—some 26 million people lost their lives in the war); it carried out a crash program of forced industrialization and agricultural collectivization. Stalin was a state builder, in the sense that under his rule the Soviet state extended its capacity to rule over all regions of the country and in all aspects of social life. Under Stalin, the vast state hierarchies of military and police power were built

CLOSE-UP 2.1

Socialism, Communism, Marxism, Leninism

Terms such as socialism and communism can be confusing because they have been used in a number of different ways, often by people with strongly held ideological visions of what they *want* these concepts to mean. But there is a coherent core of meaning to each of these terms, and it is helpful to recognize the distinctions.

Socialism has a broad range of meaning. Generally, it refers to the elimination of private property in some or all of the means of production of a society—that is, those forms of wealth (including land, factories, natural resources, banks, and so on) that can be used to produce more wealth. Instead, society or some agent of society such as the state would be the owner of the wealth and would use its control of resources to eliminate poverty, exploitation, and inequality in society as well as to build up the productive potential of the society to a higher level. Socialists disagree over how comprehensive state ownership of productive property should be: Some advocate that the state own only certain basic industries and natural resources, while others want to abolish private property altogether. Some link socialism with freedom and democracy, while others would allow the state to suppress some freedoms for the sake of a larger collective goal. Some advocate immediate action, while others prefer to encourage society to evolve gradually into socialism. In the twentieth century, socialists in most advanced industrial democracies adopted the program of "social democracy," a system where the state uses its power not to eliminate private property but to promote equality of opportunity and to provide basic social protection through taxation, spending, and regulatory policies. Meantime, the incentives of a market economy promote economic growth and national competitiveness. Social democratic parties are influential in a number of European countries.

Communism has a more specific meaning. It can be used either to refer to an economic system or to a type of political regime. As an economic system, communism refers to a society where there is no private property in the means of production. Most communists would subscribe to the view that the ultimate goal of communism is the elimination not only of private property but also of the state itself. They would argue that the state should take ownership and control of society's wealth from the capitalists, but should gradually give way to a system of self-organized, self-managed communal life—the kind of society that is to be found in a commune, where all share and share alike both in producing and in consuming. However, no large-scale society has ever been able to operate in the way that small communal societies operate. And even small communal societies have generally been short-lived. Communists are therefore always socialists, in that they want to do away with capitalism (the system comprising a market economy and private property rights). But not all socialists are communists, since not all socialists would want to eliminate all private property and dismantle the institutions of political democracy. In the political sense, communism refers to the

(continued)

type of regime in which a communist party—meaning a party devoted to the communist doctrine—holds power. In fact, no communist regime has ever taken any serious steps to dismantle the machinery of state power. To the contrary, communist regimes always expand the power of the state over individuals, not merely taking control of all or some of the means of production, but also intervening to different degrees in social and private life, suppressing political opposition, and sometimes putting society on a quasi-military footing. In the twentieth century, some communist regimes turned into extraordinarily violent and bloody dictatorships. Communist regimes continued to promote the vision that one day everyone would live as in a commune and that the state would at some very distant point "wither away" but in practice they placed heavy emphasis on building up the power of the state to control society, so they demanded absolute loyalty to the state, its principles and its goals. As a regime type, nearly all communist regimes have collapsed. As of this writing, North Korea remains communist, as does Cuba; Vietnam and China combine capitalism with political monopolies by their communist parties: but no serious observer now believes that communism as a regime type has a future. *Marxism* is a form of communist doctrine, developed by Karl Marx and Friedrich Engels, which holds that the end of capitalism will come about when the working class seizes control of the means of production from the capitalists and uses it to establish socialism, and eventually communism. Marxists are therefore communists. *Leninism* refers to the brand of Marxism developed by Lenin: Lenin emphasized the need for political revolution even before all the economic conditions for socialism were met, and he was especially insistent about the need for an iron dictatorship over society to be exercised by the communist party "in the name of" the working class. Through most of the Soviet period, the official doctrine taught to all citizens was called "Marxism-Leninism," because it was officially regarded as a system of thought originated by Marx and Engels and subsequently developed by Lenin and his successors. Over time, the doctrine became rigid, hollow, formulaic, and dogmatic—no longer of any relevance to Soviet leaders faced with the realities of the world in the twentieth century, where capitalism proved itself considerably more dynamic than the Soviet system.

up, together with factories, mines, power stations, highways, canals, and railroad lines; large numbers of schools, clinics, and cultural and scientific institutions were built; whole cities were constructed and Moscow itself was remade. At the same time, reflecting Stalin's compulsion to exercise absolute power, Soviet society was penetrated with networks of informers, and millions of people were arrested on charges of "anti-Soviet" activity. Yet, alongside terror, there was also a profound strain of hope and pride running through Soviet culture, as many people believed that they were building the bright socialist future.

Stalin was a state builder, but he also left a legacy of weak institutions because political authority was heavily dependent on fear, suspicion, reverence for Stalin, and a tendency of officials at all levels to refer all decisions to Stalin himself. Stalin's power was as close to being absolute as any leader in history has ever come: he set the country's priorities in every sphere and intervened in any issue he cared to take up (including deciding whether a particular movie or play should be released or forbidden, or editing the words of the new Soviet national anthem). His propaganda system fostered a quasi-religious devotion to himself personally, which his successor, Nikita Khrushchev, labeled "the cult of personality." Stalin personally approved lists of "enemies of the people," who were to be arrested and shot. His own tendency toward paranoia only intensified the climate of fear and mistrust that permeated official life. Moreover, the pattern of personal despotism was repeated in many subordinate organizations, where smaller-scale "little Stalins" ruled with an iron fist in their own organizations. Within the state, there were no checks on the power of the ruler, and the secret police were outside the control of any law or institution save the will of the supreme ruler. Little wonder that upon Stalin's death in 1953 there were neither agreed rules and procedures for transferring power to another leader nor a clear division of authority between the leader at the top, the party, and the state.

Therefore, Stalin's successors, beginning with *Nikita Khrushchev* (1894–1971; in power 1953–1964), grappled with the challenge of defining a new and more institutionalized framework for ruling the state. Lacking Stalin's unchallengeable power, they agreed on the need to make the regime less dependent on fear and more on popular consent without relinquishing their power.[8] They made the system less personalistic and more rule governed, agreeing that the system should return to the "Leninist" tradition that the Communist Party was the seat of power in the country. And within the party, they agreed, power was to be exercised collectively. They ended the use of mass terror and raised living standards somewhat, but they retained the basic Leninist tenets of state ownership of the means of production and the Communist Party's role as the source of political direction for state and society. Under Khrushchev and his successor, Leonid Brezhnev, the rules and structures of the Communist Party–governed state became more firmly defined and less subject to the caprices of a single leader.

A key to understanding the structure of the Soviet regime is the theory of the "leading role" of the Communist Party. The idea was that the Communist Party should control government without itself replacing government. The party was to set goals, resolve conflicts, and monitor all basic political processes, including political socialization, elite recruitment, and policy implementation. It would coordinate the many agencies of the state and ensure that they worked together to maintain the system and achieve its goals. But the party was not supposed to usurp the actual functions of government, such as managing the economy, policing the society, or running schools, factories, and television stations. The Soviet model was a strategy for building state power in a society at a low level of development: it created opportunities for mass participation and the recruitment of leaders, and gave ordinary working people experience in government too.

It presented a democratic facade to the Soviet population and the outside world, while concealing the enormous brutality and wastefulness of its methods. With time, the Soviet model also demonstrated its incapacity to respond to new kinds of political imperatives because the immobilism and self-interest of its powerful bureaucratic components blocked any significant institutional change.

The model incorporated a federal element. Formally, the state comprised 15 sovereign national republics, but centralized political control over them was guaranteed by the Communist Party's hierarchical chain of command that stretched across all governmental and societal organizations. Soviet citizens learned to switch back and forth in their daily lives between a world of fictions proclaimed in Soviet doctrine, taught in schools and repeated endlessly in the mass media, and a world of everyday realities: the fictions concerned the shining ideals of Soviet communism, the nominally democratic political institutions in which citizens were said to be the masters of the state, and the progress the society was making toward a life of abundance and justice. The realities reflected the stagnation in living standards, the acceptance of endless venality and cant in public life, the gap between the modest living standards of a majority of the population and those of the elite whose political status entitled them to lives of privilege.

The word "soviet" means council, and the Soviet model of government revolved around a system of soviets. These were elected bodies symbolizing the principle of democratic self-government. There were soviets in every territorial unit of the country—village, town, county, province, and so on, all the way up to the Supreme Soviet of the USSR itself. In theory, the soviets exercised all state power in the Soviet Union, but in reality, everyone understood that the soviets had no real policy-making power. The USSR Supreme Soviet, for instance, met only twice a year, and then for a few days each time, in order to hear official reports and approve motions proposed by the leadership. Generally, everyone accepted that the soviets served the function of creating a formal appearance of representative democracy, while in fact the party and the executive organs of government made all the major decisions. The only sense in which the soviets "represented" the public was descriptive, in that the candidates were selected by the party to ensure the presence of fixed quotas from each major demographic category by occupation, sex, age, ethnic group, and party status. This allowed the regime to boast that large proportions of particular groups of the population were serving as elected representatives (called deputies). Usually, only one candidate ran for a given seat, so that the elections offered voters only the opportunity to vote for or against the candidate offered. Elections were not an institution for making officials accountable to voters for their actions, but they were treated as grand national ceremonies, in which the nearly universal voter turnout demonstrated the unity of the people and their state.

Formally, the deputies of a soviet elected a set of executive officials to manage government in its territory, making the executive arm of each soviet accountable to the soviet for its actions. In reality, the soviet simply ratified a choice that had been made by the Communist Party authorities. Nonetheless, executive officials had real bureaucratic power, and together they formed an executive branch chain of command that stretched all the way from the lowest level of government up to Moscow. Meantime, the Communist Party supervised and directed—but was not supposed to usurp—the work of government executives. At the highest levels, the level of union republics and the all-union central government, there was a Supreme Soviet, which had the power to enact laws. Executive power was invested in the Council of Ministers. The USSR Council of Ministers was thus formally equivalent to the cabinet of a parliamentary government in a Western democracy, and its chairman was the functional equivalent of a Prime Minister. As the person in charge of the executive branch for the entire Soviet Union, the chairman of the Council of Ministers was in fact a very powerful figure—but never as powerful as the head of the Communist Party of the Soviet Union (CPSU).

Federalism in the Soviet state was used to give symbolic rights to ethnic minorities, especially those located on the outer perimeter of Russia's territory that had traditions of national autonomy or statehood. So, unlike federalism in the United States or Germany, the constitutional form that federalism took in the Soviet Union was linked to the goal of giving ethnic-national populations a means to maintain their national cultures but to do so without challenging the center's power. In Soviet federalism, 15 nominally sovereign republics were considered to be the constituent units of the federal union. Each republic gave a particular ethnic nationality a certain formal opportunity for representation. Most structures of power at the central level were replicated in the 15 union republics; of course, the army and the money supply were exclusively central functions.

Power was so highly centralized in the Soviet regime that the federal structure of the state was largely a formality. Yet, the effect of organizing the state around ethnic territories, each with its own trappings of statehood, proved to have powerful cumulative effects on Soviet political development. The development of "national" educational systems, cultural institutions, and the mass media reinforced ethnic-national identities in all 15 republics, even in those where there was only a weak sense of national consciousness before Soviet rule. At the same time, the centralization of political and economic power in Moscow prevented the national leaders of the federal republics from making any serious claims on the union government for greater autonomy. As time passed, members of the indigenous nationalities in the republics came to take certain rights for granted, including the right to maintain their national cultures so long as these did not directly contradict Soviet ideological doctrine. The stability of these informal rules and understandings about how far each nationality could go in preserving its national identity fostered a tendency for leaders and peoples in the republics to think of the territory and institutions of the republic as "theirs," a kind of collective national possession. Coupled with the steady rise in the population's educational levels over the decades of Soviet rule, this tacit but powerful assumption contributed to the growth of ethnic self-consciousness in each republic among the indigenous nationality.[9]

The Soviet state was federal in form, unitary in fact. Political scientists define federalism as a system in which the constituent regions of a particular state possess one or more constitutionally protected domains of power in which they are autonomous and can make policy so long as they do not violate constitutional rules, while the federal authorities also are autonomous in one or more other realms (typically national security and monetary policy).[10] In the Soviet Union, the central government (the Communist Party leadership and central executive authorities) had ultimate control over the political, economic, and cultural life of the republics, choosing how much autonomy the republics could exercise at any given time. Each jurisdictional unit was treated as subordinate to the higher-level unit within which it was located, in keeping with the chain of command principle. The union center controlled major productive resources throughout the country, including land, natural resources, industry, and human capital, while the constituent republics were given the right to manage lesser assets on their territories. Strategic decisions about economic development in the republics were determined by the center. The pattern resembled colonial imperialism in that a dominant metropolitan state developed the economies of peripheral territorial possessions for its benefit. However, the Soviet state made all it ruled into citizens and brought them under a common set of political and economic institutions. Establishing and maintaining control over so large and diverse a state was in fact a great achievement by comparison with the many failed states of the contemporary period. Yet, the political regime preserved control over the state by denying its citizens many elementary political and economic rights.

The place of the Russian Republic within the union state was anomalous. The fact that the Soviet regime was dominated by Russians did not mean that the Russian Republic benefited from the arrangement. The Russian Republic (RSFSR) was by far the largest of the 15 union republics in territory and population, and its language and culture dominated the entire union. Yet, the republic itself lacked even the weak instruments of statehood that the other republics possessed, such as its own republic-level Communist Party branch, KGB (Committee for State Security—the secret police), trade union council, Academy of Sciences, and so on. The reason, of course, is that if these organizations had had branches at the level of the Russian Republic, they would have threatened the power of the union-level structures. Union-level party and state organs thus doubled as Russian ones. One could say that Russia used the Soviet state to rule a quasi-imperial state.

Empires are costly to rule. In the USSR, the balance of trade among republics was not favorable to the Russian Republic, even though Russia dominated the union politically. Because of the deliberately low prices set for energy and other industrial inputs supplied by Russia, Russia ended up subsidizing the development of other republics. By 1991, Russia was providing the equivalent of one-tenth of its gross domestic product to other republics in the form of implicit trade subsidies.[11] Yet, the economies of the other republics were also forced to develop along the lines dictated by the central plan. Central planning and controlled prices made it impossible to judge who was exploiting whom, and within each republic, people became convinced that the union was exploiting their republic.[12] Meantime, ethnic federalism enabled republican party and state leaders to build up political machines and expand their own political control. Many of the leaders in the union republics were keen to win greater control over state resources, not necessarily to put them to better or more productive use, but to build up their own political power by distributing the stream of benefits they yielded to their favored constituents. Thus, when the political leaders in the union republics demanded the *decentralization* of economic administration, often what they wanted was to capture control over state resources for their own political benefit rather than to make more productive use of them—to transfer the *union's* bureaucratic control over the economy to control by the *republic-level* bureaucracy. Decentralization in this sense was neither democratic nor market oriented. Often, republic-level leaders played the ethnic card in behind-the-scenes bureaucratic bargaining, demanding greater economic autonomy for their territories on the grounds that the ethnic nationalities residing in those territories needed more opportunities for development.[13]

This point is a clue to the struggle for power between the union and Russian Republican levels of the Soviet system. The demand for decentralization was one on which both democratic forces and bureaucratic officials in the republics could agree: The democrats wanted to break the hold of the Communist Party and the central government over citizens' political rights, while the republic-level officials were eager to claim a share of control over Soviet state assets located in their republics. They found common cause in the desire to weaken the central government. Thus, to a large extent, the struggles over sovereignty in 1989–1991 resulting in the breakup of the union were a contest for control over state resources between elites whose institutional position was at the union level and the political forces at the next level down who sought to gain autonomy within their territorial jurisdictions. As far as the Russian Republic was concerned, this strategy meant that when the Russian leaders won sovereign power over the Russian territory, they had to give up their power over other republics.

After all, the fight for national sovereignty had a strong economic component since the state owned and controlled the means of production: land, natural resources, factories and farms, and wealth in all its forms. The struggle for power in the old regime was a struggle for the right to control the immense wealth of the country. Political and economic power was closely intertwined in the Soviet system. The relationship between these two domains is key to understanding the difference of the Soviet system from liberal democracies, even those where the state has a large ownership stake in the economy. Even the most strongly social democratic polity in Europe differs sharply from the state socialism of the Soviet-type system. In contrast to societies where there is private ownership of productive property, in the Soviet system, an individual's power, prestige, and wealth depended on his or her position in the political hierarchy. Productive wealth could not be passed on through inheritance to others.[14] State ownership of productive resources meant that political and social status derived from the same source; even the most powerful leaders depended on the favor of party officials because all lines of advancement and opportunity converged in the Communist Party. The "new class"—those who rose to power and privilege in the system—sought to use the Communist Party to protect their interests, but the absence of firm political rights or popular legitimacy created insecurity. This insecurity was compensated for by the use of propaganda and repression that fended off political challenges to their positions.[15]

In the planned economy, output growth was the standing imperative. The heads of enterprises were under intense pressure to fulfill their plan targets, and generally the authorities gave them substantial autonomy in choosing how to meet their output goals. Managers could generally get by with cutting corners, for instance reducing quality, so long as they met the basic target for physical output set by the planners. Managers had little incentive to innovate or modernize, since the risk that a new technology might fail outweighed the potential benefits of increased productivity. In short, the incentives faced by enterprise managers tended to militate against flexibility, adaptiveness, entrepreneurship, and innovation. With time, as a result, the economy tended to grow stagnant and was unable to compete in the global market. Its abundant natural resources (minerals, oil, timber, and many other goods) gave it the capacity to export and earn foreign exchange, but by the 1960s, it was experiencing chronic shortfalls in agricultural production and the quality of its manufactured goods (apart from the defense industry) was appallingly low.

Stalin's strategy of industrializing Russia rapidly brought about another important feature of the state socialist model—the reliance on the enterprise as a source of noneconomic benefits to the populace. Goods and services such as housing, child care, subsidized meals, groceries, scarce durable goods such as cars, and subsidized vacations were allocated through enterprises to their employees since they could not be purchased on the open market. Many social goods and services were provided in-kind, rather than for cash. In the late 1970s, when the economy's performance began slipping seriously and food rationing had to be introduced in many cities, enterprise channels of distribution of goods and services assumed a still greater political importance. As the supply of housing, food, and ordinary services fell ever further behind demand, enterprise managers exercised still more leverage over the state. Workers and managers were tightly bound to one another in mutual need. Managers needed a large and cheap labor force to enable them to fulfill their plan targets, and workers needed a secure position in a state enterprise in order to obtain a range of social benefits that were unavailable except through the enterprise. This created a bond of reciprocal dependence between workers and managers, which some have termed an implicit "social contract." Under the social contract, the regime committed itself to providing job security, social benefits, and relative income equality, in exchange for quiescence and compliance from workers.[16]

The social contract tended to weaken trade unions. In the Soviet model, trade unions were organized around entire economic branches, so that the managers of a firm were members of the same trade union as the engineers, the bench workers, and the cafeteria staff. Their common dependence on the state for the well-being of their workplace gave both managers and workers an incentive to pressure the state to maintain a steady stream of orders and financing regardless of whether the enterprise was profitable and productive or a wasteful drain on society's resources. Just as the economy created little incentive for entrepreneurship or innovation, it also discouraged the restructuring or closing of loss-making firms. Indeed, since the price system was set according to political criteria rather being set by the play of demand and supply, it was next to impossible to know whether a given enterprise was operating profitably or not. Some, in fact, were subtracting value from the economy by producing goods that were worth less than the materials that went into making them. The deadweight cost of inefficiency grew from year to year, as the economy stifled innovation that would have raised productivity.

Moreover, the weakness of financial constraints on enterprises' appetites for resources created a chronic syndrome of excess demand, shortages, and repressed inflation.[17] Low efficiency and failure to innovate on the part of enterprises did not incur economic penalties. To some extent, enterprises were able to conceal the facts of their performance by falsifying reports or concealing damaging information. Administrative demands from the center for improved productivity were never sufficient because managers themselves lacked incentives to take risks. The center itself was constantly pressured to satisfy the needs of powerful industrial and regional officials to protect their interests. As a result, the system settled into inertia and decay: Each year, the plan represented a modest incremental change over the previous year. Any serious attempts at reform were defeated by the combination of weak central power and inertial resistance by those who were called upon to carry out the reform. A very powerful coalition of interests—ministries, regional officials, enterprise directors, and workers—shared a latent interest in the preservation of the status quo since any serious change threatened them. (It was a latent interest because they did not organize collectively, but rather acted in concert by working to preserve the status quo.) By the beginning of the 1980s, the economy had all but stopped growing. But zero growth meant that competing with the United States on military spending placed an ever-heavier burden on the economy. By the time Gorbachev came to power, defense expenditures were running at about a quarter of gross domestic product, and the share was still increasing.[18] The heavy economic cost of high military expenditures was one of the major reasons Gorbachev undertook his program of radical reform.

The deteriorating performance of the economy in the 1960s, 1970s, and 1980s placed a greater burden on the regime's ability to meet social expectations. It meant that fewer jobs were opening up in managerial and professional positions. Yet, the stream of graduates with specialist degrees kept growing. More and more people occupied jobs below their educational qualifications. This affected both manual and specialist social strata. Many groups considered themselves underpaid and undervalued. Many of the grievances voiced in the early years of *glasnost'* centered around the low professional autonomy and esteem of managerial and professional groups, including the administrative staff of the Communist Party itself. These strains were in part the consequence of the Brezhnev leadership's policy of leveling by raising the wage levels and educational qualifications at the lower end of the social hierarchy without achieving a corresponding transformation of the structure of labor. As a result, a sizable part of the workforce occupied jobs for which they were significantly overqualified.

Economic stagnation exacerbated popular resentment of the privileges of the political elite. Crucial to understanding the explosive quality of social protest in the late 1980s is the accumulation of popular alienation, which often took nationalist forms, but which also arose from other issues, such as environmental degradation, the perception that the ruling "nomenklatura" was indifferent and parasitic, anger over shortages in the economy, and the conviction on the part of nearly every region and republic that it was being economically exploited by a distant, bureaucratized center.

In addition to the role of the soviets as the building block of the state, the principle of ethnic federalism, and the centralization of economic power, the political dominance of the Communist Party was the fourth defining characteristic of the old regime. Lenin's model of rule ensured that the organizational structure of the Communist Party maximized central control over all levels of government. The party itself was kept rather small, emphasizing that membership was a privilege and an obligation, and taking pains to admit only individuals whose political loyalties and social backgrounds passed stringent review. At its peak, the Communist Party had around 20 million members, around 9 percent of the adult population.[19] In many professions, the membership rate was higher, and generally membership was higher among the more educated strata of society. Among individuals in positions of high political and administrative responsibility, party membership was nearly obligatory. Indeed, for most individuals with high career ambitions, Communist Party membership was not just useful, it was a requirement.

The party's own organization paralleled that of the government, which it supervised and directed. In every territorial jurisdiction—district, town, province, and so on—the party maintained its own full-time organization. For instance, each city had a city CPSU organization with its own governing committee, a more powerful inner body called the "bureau," and a set of functional departments overseeing industry, agriculture, ideology, and personnel with their own full-time staff, who were overseen by managers called secretaries. The first secretary of the party organization of the city was always the city's most powerful official. The top party official was not the chief executive of the city: that was the chairman of the local executive committee of the city soviet. The first secretary of the CPSU worked closely with the chairman of the executive committee of the city, but the party official was superior in status. Directives and advice from the party secretary were binding on executive branch officials, but, by the same token, if the city government needed special help from Moscow, the party represented a direct channel of access to the highest levels of power in the country.

At the top, final power to decide policy rested in the CPSU Politburo. The Politburo was a small committee made up of the country's most powerful leaders, which made decisions in all important areas of policy at its weekly meetings. Supporting the Politburo was the powerful Secretariat of the Central Committee of the Communist Party. The Secretariat ran the party's central headquarters, which was linked to all lower party organizations. Here the party monitored the political and economic situation throughout the country and around the world, and determined which problems needed to be addressed, developing policy options for the Politburo. Here the party managed the political careers of thousands of top political officials. Here it determined the ideological line that was to be reinforced and echoed throughout the country through the channels of party propaganda and the mass media. And here it supervised the vast government bureaucracy, the army, the police, the law enforcement system, the KGB, and the governments of the republics and regions. The description of the Communist Party's political role given in the 1977 Soviet Constitution—to the effect that the party was "the leading and guiding force of Soviet society, the nucleus of its political system of [all] state and public organizations"—was reasonably accurate.[20] Three of the party's most important powers were deciding policy, recruiting officials, and policing the ideological doctrine of the country. All major policy decisions were made by the party, at every level of the political system. All responsible officials were chosen with the approval of the party. And the ideas discussed in the media, the arts, education, or any public setting had to meet with the approval of the party's ideological watchdogs.

Sweeping as the party's powers were, they were undermined by bureaucratic immobilism. This problem grew more severe in the 1970s and 1980s as a result of the growing complexity of the political system, the loss of social cohesion, and the declining capacity of the aging leaders to manage the system coherently. The role that fear of arrest had played in reinforcing central power in the Stalin era gradually diminished and gave way to the certainty on the part of many officials that they could behave incompetently or even criminally with impunity. Certainly, it is true of hierarchical organizations everywhere that overcentralization brings its own pathologies of control, through distortions of information flow, tacit resistance to the center's orders by officials at lower levels who have their own agenda, and the force of inertia.[21] By the time Mikhail Gorbachev was elected General Secretary of the CPSU in 1985, the political system of the USSR had grown top-heavy, unresponsive, and muscle bound.[22]

The old regime appeared stable, but in fact its institutions were weak. More than in political systems where legal rules and traditions govern the way power is exercised by those holding political office, Soviet politicians had to struggle for power constantly, even when they occupied an important position. Behind the surface unity and consensus of Soviet politics, Soviet political leaders were engaged in a continuous competition for power. Naturally, Soviet leaders did not advertise their moves in this game. Nonetheless, by close examination of the public record, it is possible to identify the political alliances and commitments formed by top political leaders of the CPSU. Contenders for power consolidated power by showing that they could solve policy problems: Successes in policy tended to strengthen their hand in attracting supporters and eliminate opponents, while failures weakened the incentives that other officials had for supporting them.[23] The contest was not carried out in the electoral realm since there was no electoral link between the desires of the public and the policy choices considered by the regime. Nonetheless, the contest was real and was played for high stakes. It resembled games of bureaucratic politics played out in other complex hierarchical organizations but with lower agreement over the rules and with a high risk factor: failure in the political arena could lead, at best, to forced retirement and disgrace and at worst to arrest and imprisonment—in Stalin's time, to the concentration camps.

Because there was no agreed mechanism for deciding when and how power would be transferred from one leader to another, political succession often set off an intense struggle for power. Once a leader climbed to the top, and won the office of General Secretary of the CPSU, he sought to use the powers of the office to stay in power for the rest of his life. Nikita Khrushchev was removed from power by a successful conspiracy in 1964; he spent the rest of his life as a pensioner out of the public eye.[24] The ringleader of the conspiracy, *Leonid Brezhnev* (1906–1982; in power 1964–1982), quickly consolidated his own power. He built a base of support that allowed him to remain in that office, despite obviously worsening health, until his death in November 1982. Brezhnev learned the lessons of Khrushchev's fall only too well. He owed his success at holding power for 18 years to avoiding any serious attempts at political reform that might have upset the balance of ministerial and regional power centers that dominated the regime. There was relatively little turnover of political officeholders and even less policy innovation. The result was drift in policy, worsening government performance, and a gradual aging of the entire ruling elite of the USSR, as the political system grew increasingly unresponsive to the imperative of economic and political reform.

Brezhnev was succeeded by *Yuri Andropov* (1914–1984), who had served as chairman of the KGB and as a secretary of the CPSU Central Committee. Although Andropov initially launched a policy program to reverse the decline in national economic performance, it soon turned out that he was gravely ill and could only rule from his hospital bed. When he, in turn, died in February 1984, he was succeeded by another aging, ailing member of the Brezhnev generation, *Konstantin Chernenko* (1911–1985). Chernenko had been a loyal member of Brezhnev's personal clientele and tried to hold on to power by allying himself with the remnants of the old Brezhnev political machine. This meant halting the limited reform programs launched under Andropov and returning to the conservatism and drift of the Brezhnev era. But Chernenko, too, was fatally ill and died in March 1985. At this point, the senior leadership was evidently concerned at the impression of debility and weakness created by this rapid succession of deaths and agreed to turn to a much younger, more dynamic, and open-minded figure as the new General Secretary. The youngest member of the Politburo at the time he was named its leader—born in 1931, he was only

54 when he took over—*Mikhail Gorbachev* quickly grasped the levers of power that the system granted the General Secretary and moved both to strengthen his own political base and to carry out a program of economic reform.

Gorbachev Comes to Power

One of the enduring mysteries about Gorbachev is how so radical a reformer could ever have reached the pinnacle of power under the old regime. One explanation lies in the fact that he could appeal not only to groups who wanted to liberalize the regime, but also to conservatives alarmed at the deterioration of discipline and morals in state and society. These conservatives could accept a certain amount of administrative reform in the interests of strengthening socialism. They, and pro-reform elements in the party apparatus and intelligentsia, were therefore a natural base of support for an ambitious and ingenious political leader such as Mikhail Sergeyevich Gorbachev. At the same time, probably few within the party leadership realized how radical Gorbachev was until it was too late for them to remove him: his youth, self-confidence, intelligence, exposure to the West, and personal instincts all helped fuel his drive to carry out far-reaching changes in the Soviet system, aimed at transforming it into some version of a socialist democracy. Shortly before he was made General Secretary of the CPSU, Gorbachev and his future Foreign Minister, Eduard Shevardnadze (who later became president of post-Soviet Georgia), chatted while walking along a beach at a resort on the Crimean Sea. They agreed, according to their recollections of the conversation, that "everything was rotten" and "we cannot go on living this way."[25] At that point, although he knew that the system was deeply dysfunctional, neither the model of the change he intended to bring about nor the means of achieving it was clear to Gorbachev. He possessed enormous confidence, energy, ambition, and zeal for reform, but would he have launched his reforms had he known how they would turn out?

Gorbachev's remarkable rise began in the late 1970s. In 1978, he was named Secretary of the Central Committee; in 1979, he became candidate member, and in 1980, full member of the Politburo. In March 1985, upon Chernenko's death, Gorbachev was named General Secretary of the party. He needed to build a broader base of support in the Politburo for a policy of reform. To help persuade his colleagues to embark on real reform, Gorbachev needed to generate an elite perception of impending crisis in order to overcome his colleagues' reluctance to accept the risks of major reform.

Emphasizing the need for greater openness—*glasnost'*—in relations between political leaders and the populace, Gorbachev stressed that the ultimate test of the party's effectiveness lay in improving the economic well-being of the country and its people. By highlighting such themes as the need for market relations, pragmatism in economic policy, and less secretiveness in government, he identified himself as a champion of reform.[26] The party amplified his modestly unorthodox message through its propaganda machine, disseminating to officials and citizens everywhere the new leader's appeals for "*glasnost'*," modernization, and intensification of economic development. Gorbachev called his program for reforming the Soviet system *perestroika*, which means a restructuring. He meant by this that he wanted to overhaul the entire structure of the Soviet economy and state system, but to leave its foundations intact.

Gorbachev moved rapidly to consolidate his own power using the General Secretary's power over the appointment of ranking elites. Acting cautiously at first, and then with increasing decisiveness, Gorbachev removed opponents and promoted supporters. Gorbachev not only stripped power away from the Brezhnev-era old guard but he also began transferring power away from the Communist Party altogether. Gorbachev also made use of the party's control of national policy to set new directions in domestic and foreign policy. In the economic sphere, he demanded "acceleration" of technological progress and economic growth through an infusion of capital, including stepped-up foreign investment. He also promised to loosen the suffocating bureaucratic controls that discouraged innovation on the part of enterprise managers. He called for breathing new life into the desiccated democratic forms of Soviet political life by making elections and public debate real and meaningful. In the sphere of foreign policy, he pursued a new, active diplomacy in Europe and Asia, served up a series of disarmament proposals, and promised greater flexibility in relations with the West.

Gorbachev not only called for policy reform but he also made far-reaching institutional changes in the economy and political system. He pushed through a reform bringing about the first contested elections for local soviets in many decades.[27] He sponsored a Law on State Enterprise that was intended to break the stranglehold of industrial ministries over enterprises through their powers of plan setting and resource allocation. He legalized private, market-oriented enterprise for individual and cooperative businesses and encouraged them to fill the many gaps in the economy left by the inefficiency of the state sector. He called for a "law-governed state" (*pravovoe gosudarstvo*) in which state power—including the power of the Communist Party—would be subordinate to law. He welcomed the explosion of informal social and political associations that formed. He made major concessions to the United States in the sphere of arms control, resulting in a treaty which, for the first time in history, stipulated the destruction of entire classes of nuclear missiles.

In 1988, he proposed still more far-reaching changes at an extraordinary gathering of party members from around the country, where in a nationally televised address he outlined a vision of a democratic, but still socialist, political system. In it, legislative bodies made up of deputies elected in open, contested races would exercise the main policy-making power in the country. The Supreme Soviet would become a genuine parliament, debating policy, overseeing government officials, and adopting or defeating bills. Moreover, the judiciary would be separated from party control, and at the top of the system, there would be a body called upon to adjudicate the constitutionality of legislative acts. The party conference itself was televised and treated the Soviet public to an unprecedented display of open debate among the country's top leaders. Fully exercising the General Secretary's authoritarian powers, Gorbachev quickly railroaded his proposals for democratization through the Supreme Soviet, and in 1989–1990, the vision Gorbachev laid out before that party conference was realized as elections were held, deputies elected, and new soviets formed at the center and in every region and locality. When nearly half a million coal miners went out on strike in the summer of 1989, Gorbachev declared himself sympathetic to their demands.

Gorbachev's radicalism received its most dramatic confirmation through the astonishing developments of 1989 in Eastern Europe. All the regimes making up the socialist bloc collapsed and gave way to multiparty parliamentary regimes in virtually bloodless popular revolutions (Romania was the only country where the ouster of the ruling communist elite was accompanied by widespread bloodshed)—and the Soviet Union stood by and supported the revolutions![28] The overnight dismantling of communism in Eastern Europe meant that the elaborate structure of party ties, police cooperation, economic trade, and military alliance that had developed since Stalin imposed communism on Eastern Europe after World War II vanished. Divided Germany was allowed to reunite, and, after initial reluctance, the Soviet leaders even gave their sanction to the admission of the reunited Germany to NATO. In the Soviet Union itself, meantime, the Communist Party was facing massive popular hostility and a critical loss of authority. Gorbachev forced it to renounce the principle of the "party's leading role" and to accept the legitimacy of private property and free markets. Real power in the state was being transferred to the elective and executive bodies of government—marked, above all, by the new office of state president that Gorbachev created for himself in March 1990. One by one, the newly elected governments of the national republics making up the Soviet state declared their sovereignty within the union; and the three Baltic Republics had declared their intention to secede altogether from the union. Everywhere, inside and outside the Soviet Union, Communist Party rule was breaking down.

POLITICAL INSTITUTIONS OF THE TRANSITION PERIOD: DEMISE OF THE USSR

Gorbachev's inability to overcome resistance to his economic programs by the party and state bureaucracy prompted him to push for still more radical reform by opening up channels for democratic elections and representation. He was careful not to go too far, however. His design for the democratization of the soviets had clear roots in the Leninist past, and, not incidentally, also served to reinforce his own power at the top. In introducing his political reforms in 1988, Gorbachev made it amply clear that he was not endorsing a move to a multiparty system as well. Gorbachev saw a limited role for parliamentarism as a further extension of *glasnost'*, but wanted to make sure that the power to make major decisions on domestic and national policy would still remain with the Communist Party leadership. Gorbachev sought to play the new parliamentary structures off against the party bureaucracy, bringing pressure to bear on party officials to carry out his reform policies, while ensuring that the newly elected deputies would not overstep the boundaries of their power. Gorbachev's political reforms had both direct and strategic purposes. Gorbachev did want to open up the system to more democratic participation. But he intended for the new channels of mobilization to expand his base of support for the reforms he wanted to make: He calculated that if he created new political arenas in which supporters of liberal reform could gain influence, they would pressure the bureaucracy for more *perestroika*. But by creating these new arenas of participation, including media *glasnost'*, elections, and democratized soviets, Gorbachev made it possible for a wide variety of political tendencies—radical democrats, hard-line communist conservatives, and nationalist movements—to seize the initiative. Many of these groups had entirely different aims from his own.

In retrospect, it is clear that Gorbachev underestimated the centrifugal force of demands for national sovereignty and independence in a number of the union republics. As the liberalization of political life enabled new autonomous political movements to press for changes going far beyond what he was then prepared to tolerate, he concluded that the two posts he held—General Secretary of the CPSU and Chairman of the Supreme Soviet of the USSR—did not give him enough power. Although he had initially opposed the idea of creating a state presidency, he changed his mind and declared early in 1990 that a presidency was needed in order to control the executive branch. Accordingly, in March 1990, he rammed constitutional amendments creating a presidency through the Congress of People's Deputies. He coupled this with a change in the constitution that had the effect of legalizing multiparty competition. Both of these reforms, needless to say, seriously threatened the Communist Party's power. Now Gorbachev would set policy and oversee the bureaucracy in his capacity as President, not as General Secretary; even worse from the Communist Party's standpoint was the fact that party officials would be forced to look for popular support in competitive elections.

Once again, Gorbachev's reforms had consequences he clearly did not intend. Although he was readily elected President of the Soviet Union, he was elected by the Congress of People's Deputies, not in a direct popular election (which he might have lost). Elimination of the long-standing provision that assigned the Communist Party the "leading role" in government and society authorized opposition movements to contest the party's mandate to rule. Therefore, the 1990 elections of deputies to the Supreme Soviets in all 15 republics, and for soviets in regions and towns all across the country, stimulated competition among political movements and parties. In Russia, a coalition of democratic reformers ran under the banner of a movement called "Democratic Russia," which sought to form caucuses in each soviet to which its candidates were elected. In the March 1990 elections, the Democratic Russia movement succeeded in winning a majority of seats in both the Moscow and Leningrad (a year later, the city took back its old name of "St. Petersburg") soviets. And in the races for the Russian Congress of People's Deputies, the Democratic Russia contingent claimed as many as 40 percent of the newly elected deputies as adherents. (Of course, as events later showed, many of these deputies had only a very weak, opportunistic commitment to the radical democratic tenets of its program.) A roughly equal number of the new Russian deputies identified themselves with the conservative, antireform, pro-socialist ideology of the communists of Russia. Under the influence of the democratic aspirations and national self-awareness that the electoral campaign awakened, the Congress narrowly elected Boris Yeltsin Chairman of the Russian Supreme Soviet in June 1990. As chief of state in the Russian Republic, Yeltsin was now well positioned to challenge Gorbachev for preeminence.[29]

A course of developments then followed in the Russian Republic that paralleled those occurring at the level of the USSR federation during the previous year. Like Gorbachev a year earlier, Yeltsin, too, decided in early 1991 to create a state presidency in Russia. Unlike Gorbachev, Yeltsin put the matter to a national referendum. But he did so in such a way as to challenge Gorbachev. When Gorbachev held a USSR-wide referendum in March 1991, on whether the populace desired to preserve the Soviet Union in some new, vaguely defined form, Yeltsin added a question to the ballot distributed in the Russian Republic. This asked whether voters approved the idea of instituting a national presidency for the Russian Republic. Both measures—the preservation of the union and the introduction of a Russian presidency—passed by wide margins (71 percent of Russian voters supported preservation of the union, 70 percent a Russian presidency), but the popularity of the principle of a Russian presidency effectively undercut Gorbachev's desire to win a national mandate for his efforts to defend central power.

Moreover, Yeltsin linked his power and the cause of Russian national freedom with a program of radical market-oriented economic reform. In the spring of 1990, Yeltsin had endorsed a rapid, uncompromising economic transformation program intended to dismantle the old system of state ownership and planning and set loose the forces of private enterprise. The strategy discussed by Yeltsin's economic advisors had much in common with the program of stabilization being adopted in Poland. First, the central government would relinquish many of its administrative controls over the economy, allowing prices to rise to meet demand and freeing producers to determine their own production goals. Second, the government would launch a massive effort to privatize state assets and create a broad base of property owners who would help ensure that communism would never return. Russia's program also envisioned letting the 15 union republics of the USSR claim sovereign control over the assets on their territories. This provision helped make the program palatable to the republics, but would have eliminated most remaining controls that the union center still had to regulate the economy. Little wonder that Gorbachev, pressured by conservative elements in the Politburo, military, government, and KGB, rejected the Russian plan after having initially considered it; and little wonder that Yeltsin embraced it in his struggle with Gorbachev.

The winter of 1990–1991 saw an intense political struggle between Gorbachev and Yeltsin. Gorbachev fought to hold on to his power in the central leadership while maneuvering to defeat Yeltsin. By April 1991, Yeltsin had defeated the conservative forces in the Russian parliament, and Gorbachev had failed to force Yeltsin out. Gorbachev had to accept Russia's sovereign status within the federal union. Gorbachev then sought to find terms for a new federal or confederal union that would be acceptable to Yeltsin and the Russian leadership, as well as to the leaders of the other republics. He initiated negotiations with the republic leaders aimed at drafting a new constitutional framework for the Soviet Union. In pursuing these talks, though, he was negotiating from a position of weakness: he lacked the support of the conservative, bureaucratic elements of the union government, and democratic forces were shifting their support to Yeltsin and the cause of a sovereign Russia.

Nonetheless, in April 1991, Gorbachev succeeded in reaching agreement on the outlines of a new treaty of union with nine of the 15 republics, including Russia. The agreement would have established a new balance of power between the federal union government and the constituent republics. The union government would have preserved its responsibility for defense and security and other coordinating functions. The member republics would have gained the power to make economic policy and control productive assets within their territories. Most of the power of the union bureaucracy would have been transferred to the republics. Gorbachev once again underestimated the strength of his opposition, now based in the bureaucracies of the union government. On August 19, 1991, his own vice president, prime minister, defense minister, the KGB chief, and other senior officials acted to prevent the signing ceremony of the treaty by forming the "State Committee on the State Emergency" and seizing power in what became known as the August "putsch." They put Gorbachev (then vacationing in the Crimea) under house arrest and attempted to restore the shaken power of the Soviet regime. The coup organizers made some critical errors, however. Evidently, they counted on widespread public support for their actions, but instead, the tide of public sympathy in Moscow and Leningrad was against them. Thousands of people came out to defend the "White House," the building where Russia's parliament met. The organizers failed to arrest Boris Yeltsin, who rallied mass opposition to the coup. After three days, the coup collapsed, the organizers were arrested, and Gorbachev returned again as President of the Soviet Union. But Gorbachev's power was now fatally compromised. Neither union nor Russian power structures heeded his commands. Through the fall of 1991, the Russian government took over the union government, ministry by ministry. In November 1991, President Yeltsin issued a decree formally outlawing the CPSU. In rapid succession, the union republics declared their independence and on December 9, 1991, the leaders of the Russian, Ukrainian, and Belorussian Republics met to issue a declaration that the Soviet Union was dissolved and replaced by the Commonwealth of Independent States. Gorbachev became a president without a country. On December 25, 1991, he resigned as president of the USSR and turned the powers of his office over to Boris Yeltsin.

As his nemesis Yeltsin would do eight years later, Gorbachev appeared on national television to announce his resignation. Bitterness alternated with self-justification in his speech. He explained the necessity of his attempt to reform the system, even though his efforts had led to the country's dissolution, by arguing that it would have been wrong for him simply to win office and then cling to power as long as possible (as Brezhnev, he was implying, had done). He had no alternative but to initiate major reforms:

All the attempts at partial reform—and there were any number of them—suffered failure one after the other. The country lost its vision of the future. It was impossible to live like that any longer. What was needed was a radical change. That is why I have never, ever regretted not taking advantage of the post of general secretary merely to reign for a number of years. I would have viewed that as irresponsible and amoral. I realized that it was an extremely difficult and even risky business to begin reforms on that sort of scale and in our sort of society. Even today I am convinced of the historical correctness of the democratic reforms begun in the spring of 1985.[30]

Mikhail Gorbachev's reputation stands considerably higher in the West than it does in his own country. He attempted to overcome the paralysis of the Soviet political system by introducing partial measures toward a market-oriented economy and a democratic political system while retaining the essential features of Communist Party domination, state ownership of productive property, and a centralized union state. The wave of demands that his reform awakened stimulated political leaders to make still more far-reaching demands for democratization, decentralization, and market capitalism. These demands provoked a backlash in the form of the August 1991 coup attempt, which in turn fueled a wave of independence movements in all the union republics—even Russia. With the collapse of the union itself, each former republic became a nominally independent, sovereign state. Their leaders were each faced with the challenge of finding a new basis for legitimate rule and adapting the Soviet institutional legacy to new tasks. In Russia, the struggle between the defenders of the old communist order and the advocates of a Western-oriented democratic and capitalist system now grew intense.

NOTES

1. Michael McFaul, *Russia's Unfinished Constitution: Political Change from Gorbachev to Putin* (Ithaca, NY: Cornell University Press, 2001).
2. Richard Pipes, *Russia under the Old Regime* (New York: Scribner's, 1974), p. 19.
3. Allen C. Lynch, *How Russia Is Not Ruled: Reflections on Russian Political Development* (Cambridge: Cambridge University Press, 2006), pp. 42–43.
4. Note that the communist revolution's date was October 25 under the Julian calendar then in force, but was commemorated on November 7 each year thereafter once the regime switched over to the Gregorian calendar that is used in the West. Similarly, the fall of the tsarist regime occurred in February under the old calendar, in March under the new one.

5. Vladimir Ilyich Lenin (1870–1924) was the leader of the wing of the Russian Marxist movement that insisted that socialism in Russia would only be possible if the revolutionaries seized state power and used it to construct a modern, industrial, and socialist economic base in Russia, as well as to launch similar revolutions elsewhere. This wing, which later became a separate party, was called the Bolsheviks. Still later it was renamed the Russian Communist Party, and finally the Communist Party of the Soviet Union. Lenin and his fellow Bolsheviks carried out their plan after seizing power in October 1917 in the name of the workers and peasants and established a government formed around state socialist principles. As de facto leader of the Bolshevik (later Communist) party, and chairman of the new Soviet Russian government, Lenin established the basic governing institutions of the new Soviet regime. Throughout Soviet history, Soviet citizens were taught to revere Lenin as the infallible source of guidance about ideological doctrine and his teachings were codified, systematized, and joined to official versions of Marxist theory. Together, these bodies of official teachings were given the name "Marxism-Leninism." In the Soviet Union and throughout the communist world, Marxism-Leninism had the status of dogma.

6. Two valuable historical surveys of the Soviet regime are Sheila Fitzpatrick, *The Russian Revolution: 1917–1932* (New York: Oxford University Press, 1984); Mary McAuley, *Soviet Politics: 1917–1991* (New York: Oxford University Press, 1992).

7. For an authoritative biography of Stalin that explains much of his behavior in psychological terms, see Robert C. Tucker, *Stalin as Revolutionary, 1879–1928: A Study in History and Personality* (New York: Norton, 1973); Robert C. Tucker, *Stalin in Power: The Revolution from Above, 1928–1941* (New York: Norton, 1990).

8. On Khrushchev, see William Taubman, *Khrushchev: The Man and His Era* (New York: Norton, 2003); William J. Tompson, *Khrushchev: A Political Life* (New York: St. Martin's Press, 1995).

9. Ronald Grigor Suny, *The Revenge of the Past: Nationalism, Revolution, and the Collapse of the Soviet Union* (Stanford, CA: Stanford University Press, 1993). On early Soviet policies toward ethnic nationalities aimed at building ethnic-national identities within a common multinational Soviet state, see Terry Martin, *The Affirmative Action Empire: Nations and Nationalism in the Soviet Union, 1923–1939* (Ithaca, NY: Cornell University Press, 2001).

10. Riker, William H. *Federalism: Origin, Operation, Significance* (Boston: Little, Brown & Co., 1964); Mikhail Filippov, Peter C. Ordeshook, and Olga Shvetsova, *Designing Federalism: A Theory of Self-Sustainable Federal Institutions* (Cambridge: Cambridge University Press, 2004).

11. Anders Åslund, *How Russia Became a Market Economy* (Washington, DC: Brookings Institution, 1995), p. 108.

12. Stephen White, Graeme Gill, and Darrell Slider, *The Politics of Transition: Shaping a Post-Soviet Future* (Cambridge: Cambridge University Press, 1993), p. 85.

13. On national mobilization in the republics, see Mark R. Beissinger, *Nationalist Mobilization and the Collapse of the Soviet State* (Cambridge: Cambridge University Press, 2002).

14. A person could leave "personal" property to his heirs, including money, but not property that was used to create other forms of wealth or income.

15. The famous theory of the "new class" was devised by Yugoslav dissident Milovan Djilas to explain how there could be a ruling class in a supposedly classless society.

16. Linda Cook, *The Soviet Social Contract and Why It Failed: Welfare Policy and Workers' Politics from Brezhnev to Yeltsin* (Cambridge: Harvard University Press, 1993).

17. Janos Kornai, *The Socialist System: The Political Economy of Communism* (Princeton: Princeton University Press, 1992).

18. Ibid.

19. On the Communist Party, see Ronald J. Hill and Peter Frank, *The Soviet Communist Party*, 3rd ed. (Boston: Allen & Unwin, 1986); Graeme J. Gill, *The Collapse of a Single Party System: The Disintegration of the CPSU* (Cambridge: Cambridge University Press, 1994).

20. From Article Six of the USSR constitution as given in Robert Sharlet, *The New Soviet Constitution of 1977: Analysis and Text* (Brunswick, OH: King's Court Communications, 1978), p. 78.

21. Anthony Downs, *Inside Bureaucracy* (Boston: Little-Brown, 1967).

22. Philip G. Roeder, *Red Sunset: The Failure of Soviet Politics* (Princeton: Princeton University Press, 1993).

23. George W. Breslauer, *Khrushchev and Brezhnev as Leaders: Building Authority in Soviet Politics* (Boston: Allen & Unwin, 1982).

24. He did dictate his memoirs into a tape recorder. The tapes were smuggled out and published under the title *Khrushchev Remembers* (Boston: Little-Brown, 1970) and *Khrushchev Remembers: The Last Testament* (Boston: Little-Brown, 1974). Both volumes were translated and edited by Strobe Talbott.

25. Archie Brown, *The Gorbachev Factor* (New York: Oxford University Press, 1996), p. 81.

26. Ibid.

27. Stephen White, "Reforming the Electoral System," *Journal of Communist Studies* 4:4 (1988): 1–17.

28. The eyewitness reports by Timothy Garton Ash, *The Magic Lantern* (New York: Random House, 1990), are exceptionally valuable firsthand accounts as well as a brilliant political analysis of the revolutions of 1989 in Eastern Europe. A thorough history of this period is Gale Stokes, *The Walls Came Tumbling Down: The Collapse of Communism in Eastern Europe* (New York: Oxford University Press, 1993).

29. On the 1989 and 1990 elections and the new representative bodies they formed, see Yitzhak M. Brudny, "The Dynamics of 'Democratic Russia', 1990–1993," *Post-Soviet Affairs* 9:2 (1993): 141–170; Giulietto Chiesa, with Douglas Taylor Northrop, *Transition to Democracy: Political Change in the Soviet Union, 1987–1991* (Hanover and London: Dartmouth College; University Press of New England, 1993); Robert T. Huber and Donald R. Kelley, eds., *Perestroika-Era Politics: The New Soviet Legislature and Gorbachev's Political Reforms* (Armonk: M. E. Sharpe, 1991); Brendan Kiernan, *The End of Soviet Politics: Elections, Legislatures and the Demise of the Communist Party* (Boulder: Westview, 1993); Michael E. Urban, *More Power to the Soviets: The Democratic Revolution in the USSR* (Aldershot, England and Brookfield, Vermont: Edward Elgar, 1990); and Thomas F. Remington, ed., *Parliaments in Transition: New Legislative Politics in Eastern Europe and the Former USSR* (Boulder: Westview Press, 1994).

30. "Gorbachev Resigns as USSR President," FBIS-SOV-91-248 (December 26, 1991), pp. 20–21.

Russia's Constitutional Order

THE RUSSIAN REPUBLIC IN THE TRANSITION PERIOD

The previous chapter showed that the Soviet regime established a highly centralized political order where power flowed from the center and political institutions formed a hierarchy of repeating structures. Each of the 15 union republics was a smaller-scale replica of the whole union in its political organization. Each had its own Supreme Soviet, its own government with its own ministries (even a foreign ministry!), and its own republic-level branch of the KGB and the Communist Party. A uniform, centrally planned economic system and political ideology kept the system closely knit. In each national republic, the language of the dominant ethnic nationality could be taught in schools and used in the cultural sphere, but Russian served as a lingua franca across the union and was the language of politics, science, diplomacy, and security.

As the core republic of the union, the Russian Republic comprised half the population and three quarters of the territory of the whole union. Although Russia had no republic-level branch of Communist Party, it did have a Supreme Soviet and executive branch at the republican level. When Gorbachev introduced the new two-tiered parliamentary structure consisting of a Congress of People's Deputies and Supreme Soviet for the USSR, the Russian Republic dutifully followed suit one year later and created its own Congress and Supreme Soviet. These became the political base for the radical democratic movement and gave Boris Yeltsin a platform. Over the period of 1990–1993, Yeltsin mounted his challenge to Gorbachev for preeminence in Russia by building support in the Russian legislative branch for a directly elected presidency, running for and winning the office of president, and then defying Gorbachev by demanding a program of radical economic reform. When the Soviet Union broke up at the end of 1991, these executive and legislative bodies of the Russian Republic became the supreme organs of power in a sovereign state.

Boris Yeltsin clearly understood that if he won the mantle of legitimacy that comes from being a directly elected president, he would have a political advantage over Gorbachev that he could use in dealing with the executive bureaucracy of the Russian Republic. Once he succeeded in being elected president of Russia in June 1991, he was able to outflank Gorbachev every time Gorbachev attempted to assert the power of the union government over the republics.

But Yeltsin's political strategy also had a weakness. When he ran for president in June 1991, he held the office of chairman of the Supreme Soviet. As chairman, he was effectively both the chief officer of the legislature and, because state power was constitutionally seated in the legislature rather than divided between legislative and executive branches, he was also the highest official in the state. But as soon as he was elected President of the Russian Federation, he left his position as Chairman of the Supreme Soviet to assume the new office of president. The legislature's deputy chairman, Ruslan Khasbulatov, replaced him as chairman. At that point, Yeltsin could no longer control the Supreme Soviet directly. Over the next two years, Khasbulatov and the legislature moved from a posture of support for Yeltsin and his policies to one of sharp opposition. The conflict reached a bloody climax in September and October 1993, when Yeltsin dissolved parliament by decree, and the opposition forces launched an armed uprising against him, which he suppressed. Yeltsin demanded that the legislature adopt a new constitution giving him sweeping authority as president, but the legislature refused. The growing confrontation between Yeltsin's allies and his opponents in the period between August 1991 and October 1993 very nearly resulted in civil war.

1990–1993: Deepening Constitutional Conflict

In the fall of 1991, as the union government was losing power, economic shortages spread and prices rose. Some regional authorities even put up roadblocks to prevent the sale of foodstuffs from their territories. Tax collections plummeted. Invoking the very real danger of a breakdown of state authority, Yeltsin demanded that the Russian legislature grant him extraordinary powers to cope with the country's economic crisis. Yeltsin made it clear that he believed that only a decisive program of dismantling state controls on production and prices would restore economic activity again. In October 1991, he was given the power to carry out his radical economic program by decree. The Congress also consented to his demand that he be authorized to appoint the heads of government in each region of the country, rather than holding local elections for heads of the executive branch. Yeltsin then named himself acting prime minister and proceeded to form a government led by a group of young, Western-oriented leaders determined to carry out a decisive economic transformation. Charged with planning and carrying out the program was his deputy prime minister, Egor Gaidar.

Under the program—widely called "shock therapy"—the government undertook several radical measures simultaneously that were intended to stabilize the economy by bringing government spending and revenues into balance and by letting market demand determine the prices and supply of goods. Under the reforms, the government let most prices float, raised taxes, and cut back sharply on spending in industry and construction. These policies caused widespread hardship as many state enterprises found themselves without orders or financing. The rationale of the program was to squeeze the built-in inflationary pressure out of the economy so that producers would begin making sensible decisions instead of chronically wasting resources. By letting the market rather than central planners determine prices, output levels, and the like, the reformers intended to create an incentive structure in the economy where efficiency would be rewarded and waste punished. Removing the causes of chronic inflation, the program's architects argued, was a precondition for all other reforms: hyperinflation would wreck both democracy and economic progress; only by stabilizing the state budget could the government proceed to restructure the economy. As in other economies where the financial system has broken down due to uncontrollable inflation, stabilizing prices is a difficult but essential step to persuade people to make productive investments. A similar reform program had been adopted in Poland in January 1990, with generally favorable results.

Radical economic stabilization affects many interests and causes acute hardship for society, at least in the short run. Groups that are particularly hard hit, including those dependent on state subsidies that are being cut, make their voice heard through the political process. In Russia's case, the program caused deep hardship and led to a bitter collision between the president and the parliament, each representing a powerful coalition of organized political interests. Each side claimed to represent Russia's true interests—the president backing the cause of liberal reform and the parliament demanding a return to state socialism.

The reform program took effect on January 2, 1992. The first results were immediately felt as prices skyrocketed, government spending was slashed, and heavy new taxes went into effect. A deep credit crunch shut down many industries and brought about a protracted depression. Quickly, a number of politicians began to distance themselves from the program: even Yeltsin's vice president, Alexander Rutskoi, denounced the program as "economic genocide."[1] Through 1992, opposition to the reform policies of Yeltsin and Gaidar grew stronger and more intransigent. Increasingly, the political confrontation between Yeltsin and the reformers on one side, and the opposition to radical economic reform on the other, became centered in the two branches of government. President Yeltsin expanded the powers of the presidency beyond constitutional limits in carrying out the reform program. In the Russian Congress of People's Deputies and the Supreme Soviet, the deputies refused to adopt a new constitution which would enshrine presidential power into law. They refused to allow Yeltsin to continue to serve as his own prime minister and rejected his attempt to nominate Gaidar. They demanded modifications of the economic program and directed the Central Bank, which was under parliament's control, to continue issuing credits to enterprises to keep them from shutting down. The Central Bank's liberality wrecked the regime of fiscal discipline that the government was attempting to pursue: the money supply tripled in the third quarter of 1992, and for the year, prices rose over 2,300 percent.[2] Through 1992, Yeltsin wrestled with the parliament for control over government and government policy.

In March 1993, Yeltsin threatened to declare a regime of special emergency rule in the country, and to suspend parliament, but then backed down. The Congress of People's Deputies immediately met and voted on a motion to impeach Yeltsin. The motion failed by a narrow margin. Yeltsin countered by convening a large conference to hammer out a constitution that would give him the presidential powers he demanded. On September 21, shortly before the deputies were to meet to adopt a law that would have lowered the threshold for decisions in the Congress and thus would have made it easier for them to impeach the president, Yeltsin declared the parliament dissolved and called for elections to a new parliament to be held in December. Yeltsin's enemies, who included Yeltsin's vice president, Alexander Rutskoi, and the chairman of parliament, Ruslan Khasbulatov, then barricaded themselves inside the White House, as the building where the parliament was situated was popularly known. Refusing to submit to Yeltsin's decrees, they held a rump congress that declared Rutskoi president. After ten days, during which Yeltsin shut off electric power to the building, they joined with some loosely organized paramilitary units outside the building and assaulted the building next to the White House where the Moscow mayor's offices were located. Then, they tried to take over the television tower where Russia's main national television broadcast facilities are housed, driving trucks through the entrance, smashing offices, and exchanging gunfire with police. They evidently hoped their action would set off a national revolt against Yeltsin or win the army over to their side. Finally, the army decided to back Yeltsin and suppress the uprising. Khasbulatov, Rutskoi, and the other leaders of the rebellion were arrested. The army even lobbed artillery shells against the White House, killing an unknown number of people inside.

In subsequent decrees soon afterward, Yeltsin dissolved all local soviets and called for the formation of new local representative bodies. He also called upon regional soviets to disband and hold new elections to new assemblies under guidelines that he also issued. Yeltsin was in fact ending the system of soviet power. He had made his views on this issue amply clear the previous June when, at the constitutional assembly that he convened, he declared that the system of soviet power was intrinsically undemocratic because it failed to separate legislative from executive power. In place of soviets, he decreed that there be small, deliberative bodies at the local and regional levels and a national parliament called the Federal Assembly representing Russia as a whole.

Yeltsin's plan for the parliament was embodied in the draft constitution that he put before the country for a vote in December 1993. According to it, the Federal Assembly would have two chambers. The upper house, the Federation Council, would give equal representation to each of Russia's 89 regions and republics (called "subjects of the federation").[3] As in many other parliaments, it would be weaker than the lower, or popular, chamber. The latter, called the State Duma, would be formed in a manner entirely new to Russia. It was to have 450 seats. Half were to be filled in proportion to the share of votes that parties received for their party lists.[4] The other 225 seats were to be filled in traditional single-member-district races. Each voter in December 1993 therefore cast four votes for the Federal Assembly: two for the seats from his or her region in the Federation Council, and two for the deputies of the State Duma. One of these was for a candidate running for the local district seat, and one was for a party list.[5]

In the national referendum on December 12, 1993, Yeltsin's constitution was approved. According to the official figures, turnout was 54.8 percent, and of those who voted, 58.4 percent voted in favor of the constitution.[6] The constitution therefore came into force. Figure 3.1 presents a schematic overview of the main structures of the current constitutional order.

The 1993 Constitution and the Presidency

The new constitution was designed to establish a dominant presidency: Yeltsin referred to the model as a "presidential republic." We can call the Russian system "presidential-parliamentary." In such a system, there is both a president and a prime minister. The president appoints the prime minister and other cabinet ministers, but the cabinet must also have the confidence of parliament to govern.[7] In Russia, the president does have the power to make law by decree, and to dissolve parliament, although he is subject to several specific constitutional constraints. His decrees may not violate existing law and can be superseded by laws passed by parliament. The president appoints the prime minister (who is formally termed the "chairman of the government"), subject to the approval of parliament. The Duma can refuse to confirm the president's choice, but if after three attempts, the president still fails to win the Duma's approval of his choice, he dissolves the Duma and calls for new elections. Likewise, the Duma may hold a vote of no confidence in the government. The first time a motion of no confidence carries, the president and government may ignore it, but if it passes a second time, the president must either dissolve parliament or dismiss the government. The president's power to dissolve parliament and call for new elections is also limited by the constitution. He may not dissolve parliament within one year of its election, or once it has filed impeachment charges against the president, or once the president has declared a state of emergency throughout Russia, or within six months of the expiration of the president's term.[8] The president can veto legislation passed by parliament, but parliament can override the veto by a two-thirds vote in each chamber. Thus, although the constitution gives the president the upper hand in relations with parliament, it is not an entirely free hand.

Moreover, the president cannot bypass parliament and put an issue to a popular referendum on his own authority, nor may he block one. Only once a citizens' initiative has gathered 2 million signatures can a ballot proposition be put before the country as a national referendum.

The 1993 constitution required that the president be elected by direct popular election. As in France, if no candidate receives an absolute majority of the votes in the election, a second, run-off round is held between the two candidates who received the largest number of votes. The constitution restricted the president to a four-year term and stipulated that a president could serve no

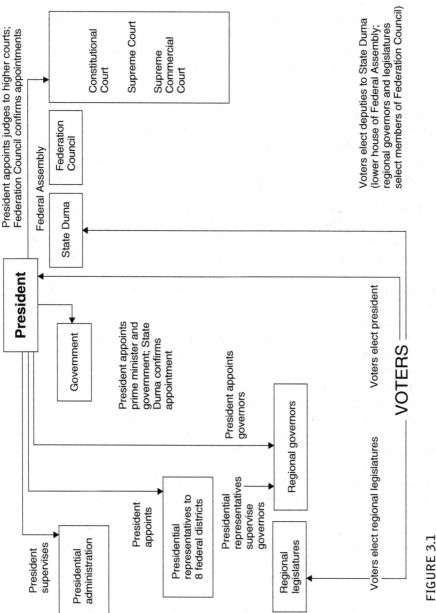

President appoints judges to higher courts;
Federation Council confirms appointments

Federal Assembly

| Federation Council |
| State Duma |

Constitutional Court

Supreme Court

Supreme Commercial Court

President

Government

President appoints prime minister and government; State Duma confirms appointment

President supervises

Presidential administration

President appoints

Presidential representatives to 8 federal districts

Presidential representatives supervise governors

President appoints governors

Regional governors

Regional legislatures

VOTERS

Voters elect deputies to State Duma (lower house of Federal Assembly; regional governors and legislatures select members of Federation Council)

Voters elect president

Voters elect regional legislatures

FIGURE 3.1
Russian Constitutional Structure

61

more than two consecutive terms. In his address to parliament in November 2008, however, Dmitrii Medvedev proposed amending the constitution so that the president would serve a six-year term (and the Duma a five-year term). A constitutional amendment must be passed by both chambers of parliament and at least two-thirds of the regional legislatures. Both the Duma and Federation Council acted with lightning speed to pass this amendment and sent it out to the country's regional legislatures, where it met immediate and universal support. For a constitutional change of this magnitude, the rapidity of the approval process was stunning: the president submitted the amendment to the Duma on November 11, which passed it 10 days later with almost no debate; the Council of the Federation followed suit on November 26; by December 16, the required two-thirds of regional legislatures had passed it. There was virtually no public debate and even less open opposition to the proposal. Although opposition parties objected to the changes, most people evidently believed that at a time of sharp economic crisis and insecurity, strengthening the president's hand made sense.[9]

The constitution calls the president "head of state" and "guarantor of the constitution." He "ensures the coordinated functioning and collaboration of bodies of state power" (Article 80, paragraphs 1 and 2). He is not made chief executive. Although the president's nominee for prime minister must be confirmed by parliament, the president can appoint and remove deputy prime ministers and other ministers without requiring parliamentary consent. These decisions are, nonetheless, to be made "on the proposal" of the prime minister.

Formally, at least, the president's power to name the government is the same as that of the French president, and the language of the relevant provisions of the two constitutions is the same.[10] However, both Yeltsin and Putin have taken liberties with their power to name the government and have directly controlled the appointment and dismissal of both the prime minister and the other members of the government. On the other hand, the constitution could also accommodate a very different relationship between president and parliament. Although a powerful and popular president is likely to dominate policy making in all spheres, with his prime minister serving as an executive in charge of formulating specific policy options and administering the machinery of government, a weaker president might find it necessary to appoint a prime minister whose base of power lay in a parliamentary majority—as happened in France during periods of "cohabitation." Some observers believe that today, Vladimir Putin is expanding the power of the prime ministership at the expense of the president's power. This could set a precedent for the future.

The major difference between Russia's semi-presidential system and that of France is that Russia's government is not formed from a party majority in parliament. The president appoints the government based on calculations about the relative power of different bureaucratic and personal factions, taking care to balance competing interests. The weakness of institutional authority is offset by the strength of the president in relation to other centers of power. As president, for example, Putin used extensive informal powers, including his near-total control over the mass media, the security organs, and a number of appointed consultative bodies, to rule with little regard to the formal structures of the constitution.

Both the formal and informal powers of the president are extensive.[11] The president exercises his power through a staff structure called the "administration of the president." This is an immense organization. The French president, for example, gets by with a staff of 40–50 people; the American president has a "White House Staff" with over 400 people and another 1,300 in the "Executive Office of the President." In Russia, the presidential administration comprises around 2,000 people, and as often as the president may try to trim it, the number keeps creeping upward. It is made up of many units, such as the press office, divisions for liaison with other bodies of power and with the regional governments, a division overseeing law making and judicial institutions, even a unit that owns and manages the properties belonging to the presidency, among which are apartment buildings, office buildings, hotels, health resorts, and other facilities—even the buildings of parliament itself.

To some extent, the presidential administration duplicates the ministries of government. Some units of it work to ensure that governments in the regions carry out federal policy. The "power ministries," that is, the state agencies directly concerned with national security, report directly to the president. These include the Foreign Ministry, Federal Security Service (formerly the Committee for State Security, or KGB), Defense Ministry, and Interior Ministry. There are, in addition, a large range of official and quasi-official commissions and administrations that are funded and directed by the president that carry out a variety of supervisory and advisory functions.

The president also directly oversees the Security Council, which consists of a full-time secretary, the heads of the power ministries and other security-related agencies, the prime minister, and, more recently, the president's representatives to the federal districts through which he keeps tabs on the territorial regions of the country. The president can appoint other officials to the Security Council as well. Its powers are broad but shadowy. President Putin sometimes used it to develop policy initiatives and appointed senior generals from the FSB (security police) and military as its top staff.[12] Since there is still no legislation establishing the rights and obligations of the Security Council, its structure, role, and power at any given time depend on the president's discretion.[13]

Both Yeltsin and Putin regularly created and dissolved new structures answering directly to the president. For example, in 2000, Putin created the *State Council*, which comprises the heads of regional governments and thus parallels the Federation Council. Five years later, he created the *Public Chamber*, which will be discussed in Chapter 6. Both the State Council and the Public Chamber duplicate some of the deliberative and representative functions of parliament and therefore weaken parliament's role. They illustrate the tendency, under both Yeltsin and Putin, for the president to create and dissolve new structures on an ad hoc basis. These improvised structures can be politically useful for the president as counterweights to constitutionally mandated bodies such as parliament, as well as providing policy advice and feedback. They help ensure that the president is always the dominant institution in the political system, but they undermine the authority of other formal institutions.

Under Putin, the presidential administration expanded its role in shaping and guiding political processes far beyond the federal executive branch. The president's staff manages relations with the parliament, the courts, big business, the media, political parties, and major interest groups. A good indication of the degree to which Putin revived Russia's traditional authoritarian style of rule is the informal rule that no political action (such as the founding of a new political party or a labor protest) in Russia should happen without prior clearance from the presidential administration.

In addition to the formal powers of the president are the symbolic resources at his disposal. The president's offices are in the Kremlin. The Kremlin—a term which means fortress or citadel—was the symbolic seat of the Russian state under Ivan the Terrible in the sixteenth century. It remained the center of Russian state power until Peter the Great moved the capital of the country to the new city of St. Petersburg, which he founded on the Baltic Sea at the beginning of the eighteenth century; the Bolsheviks moved the capital back to Moscow in 1918 and made the Kremlin once again the physical and symbolic center of the Soviet state. Today's Russian presidents deliberately identify themselves with Russian rulers of the past in order to underline the historical continuity of state power.

Far more than Yeltsin did, Vladimir Putin has quietly fostered a cult of personality through such methods as the use of portraits that officials are encouraged to hang in their offices and signals to the mass media to portray the president in a flattering light. Today Putin's portraits have been replaced with Medvedev's, but the promotion of personal leadership continues.[14] In keeping with the old tradition by which notable officials from the tsar down to local dignitaries are expected to listen to the complaints of ordinary people, the president's staff annually receives over half a million letters from Russian citizens. Putin holds periodic call-in sessions with the public where he responds to questions submitted by telephone, e-mail, text messaging, or live from broadcast sites around the country (his detailed, information-filled answers are possible because the questions have been vetted and selected beforehand.) This practice has continued even after Putin became prime minister. Putin's staff promote a media image of Putin as a straight-talking, firm, and authoritative leader. Occasional televised clips of Putin arm wrestling or engaged in a martial arts contest reinforce the official message that he is youthful, energetic, and in charge. Since he became prime minister, he has shared media attention with President Medvedev. As president, Medvedev has continued the tradition of articulating the main directions of national policy in all domains. He also makes active use of online media, such as a presidential videoblog and Twitter, to promote his image and ideas.[15]

The personalization of state power is not confined to the presidency. Many structures in the Russia's postcommunist state, such as regional governments and political parties, are closely identified with the personalities of their heads: the leader's personal priorities often define the rights and responsibilities of the office. Rules remain undeveloped and fluid. Despite efforts by Putin and Medvedev to reform the system of state administration, the bureaucracy remains inefficient, frequently corrupt, and susceptible to political manipulation. At all levels of the political system, chief executives tend to overshadow other structures of power, including courts and legislative bodies, relying as the Russian president does on a mixture of formal and informal powers.

Increasingly, the Russian authorities have adopted the practices and forms of rule used by the Soviet regime. Political scientist Gerald Easter cites four sets of resources used by the present-day Russian regime that echo Soviet and pre-Soviet patterns of rule: the reliance on the secret police to enforce political control, the tendency to grant entrepreneurs limited and reversible rights to use resources instead of establishing enforceable property rights, the personalistic and patrimonial style of public administration, and the building-up of a cult of state power.[16] There certainly are strong parallels between the organization of state power under Putin and Medvedev and that under the Soviet regime. For example, the president's role is similar to that of the old party General Secretary; his administration something like the machinery of the Central Committee.[17] The administration's far-reaching influence and coordinating role in the political system is equivalent to that of the old Secretariat of the Communist Party. Indeed, the presidential administration is located in the same offices on Old Square, adjacent to the Kremlin, that the secretariat once occupied. In the absence of other mechanisms for control, such as effective parliamentary oversight, vigorous media scrutiny, a politically independent judiciary, or a rational-legal foundation for bureaucratic authority, direct political supervision from above seems to be the only means Russian rulers know for controlling the sprawling state bureaucracy.[18] Although political centralization is an ineffective means of managing the state bureaucracy, no president wants to relinquish the enormous formal and extra-constitutional powers he can exercise over the state.

Many observers have called the Russian system "superpresidential" because the president's powers are so broad.[19] Indeed, Timothy Colton and Cindy Skach have counted the specific powers granted to the Russian president and found that he has twice as many formal, constitutionally granted powers as does the French president.[20] There are a number of dangers in superpresidentialism: the regime depends heavily on the person of the president, who may be (or become) unfit for the job; president and parliament have competing electoral mandates and so may well come into conflict; and the government is in an ambiguous position since it must serve both president and parliament.[21] Overly powerful presidencies also tend to weaken the development of robust party competition, because strong presidents often avoid lending their political authority to institutions outside their direct control; in comparative perspective, the stronger the president, the weaker the party system.[22] And of course, as both Yeltsin and Putin have shown, the Russian president may expand the use of his informal, "meta-constitutional" powers at the expense of the formal checks and balances built into the system.

One other weakness of a superpresidential system should be noted. In a system that relies so heavily on the president's power for making and carrying out policy, the president's power inevitably turns out to be inadequate to achieve large-scale policy goals that require extensive coordination, persuasion, and public support. Even a strong president soon discovers how limited the resources at his disposal are for changing the behavior of large state bureaucracies across a large range of policy issues simultaneously. The real problem with presidentialism is not that presidential power is too strong—it is that it is too *weak*.

The Government

The "government" refers to the senior echelon of leadership in the executive branch. It is charged with formulating the main lines of national policy, especially in the economic and social realms, and overseeing its implementation. (The president oversees the formulation and execution of foreign and national security policy.) It corresponds to the Cabinet in Western parliamentary systems. In the Russian system, the government answers primarily to the president and only nominally to the parliament.

Successful performance under a system featuring both a president and a prime minister requires a constructive working relationship between the two. Either this comes about through the prime minister's clear subordination to the president or they work out a mutually acceptable division of labor between them. Russia has shown examples of several different types of relationship between president and prime minister. For example, Prime Minister Chernomyrdin and President Yeltsin achieved a surprisingly harmonious working relationship that lasted over five years. First appointed by Yeltsin as head of government in December 1992 and finally dismissed in March 1998, Viktor Chernomyrdin had a comparatively long tenure as head of government. His successors as prime minister under Yeltsin did not hold on to power for so long.[23] The relationship between president and prime minister is variable. When Yeltsin was ill and removed from much day-to-day policy making, his prime minister could exercise a considerable degree of autonomy in running the government. Under President Putin, however, it was clear that the president has the major say in setting policy direction, so the prime minister was not primarily involved in formulating policy, but oversaw the implementation of policy direction from the president. Still another relation is evolving under President Medvedev and Prime Minister Putin. Medvedev lacks Putin's political resources and popularity, but he is more than a figurehead, while Putin appears to be setting the main lines of policy from his position as prime minister.[24] As in other dual executive systems, the president usually finds it convenient to be able to use the government as whipping boy for policy failures and to claim credit for successes. So long as Putin is prime minister, however, that option is no longer open to Medvedev.

An indication of the strongly presidential tilt of the system is the fact that the makeup of the government is not directly determined by the party composition of the parliament. Indeed, there is scarcely any relationship between the distribution of party forces in the Duma and the political balance of the government. For all its dominance over the Duma, United Russia has almost no presence in the government. Instead, nearly all members of the government are career managers and administrators. Generally, the government's composition reflects the president's calculations about how to balance considerations such as personal loyalty, professional competence, and the relative strength of major bureaucratic factions. The appointment of Putin as prime minister, therefore, is a major break with tradition: Not only is Putin a still powerful figure in the regime but he is also—nominally—head of the United Russia party.[25]

It is widely recognized that state administration is inefficient, corrupt, and resistant to accountability. The top leaders have attempted to reform it, but without much success. A major restructuring in 2004 reduced the number of ministries to 16. The goal was to simplify and rationalize the organization of the government by cutting down the number of ministries and state committees that were responsible for specific governmental functions and economic sectors and instead giving the other ministries broader authority to oversee specialized agencies and services. However, although the aim was to streamline the structure of government, the total number of federal-level executive bodies rose from 57 to 72.[26]

Moreover, the actual lines of control and accountability remained confusing. How much actual control ministers would have over agencies and services under their jurisdiction was unclear, and few people expected the new scheme to do away with the chronic problems of redundancy, overlap, and competition among arms of the bureaucracy that have impeded effective management and coordination for decades.

President Medvedev has initiated two other efforts to improve the quality of state administration. One is an ambitious campaign to eradicate corruption by measures such as requiring all state officials to publish annual declarations of their income and property. (Chapter 8 discusses corruption in more detail.) The other is a new program to identify a pool of promising young personnel who can be recruited to senior positions in the state administration. In effect, Putin and Medvedev are gradually restoring elements of the Soviet nomenklatura system, under which the Communist Party maintained elaborate lists of personnel available to fill positions of leadership in state and society and a list of the jobs for which the party's approval was required for the appointment to be made.

The Parliament

The parliament—Federal Assembly—is distinctly inferior to the president in power but, under Yeltsin, it sometimes succeeded in checking the president. In the 2000s, its independence has steadily diminished to the point that it serves in effect as a rubber stamp for the president's initiatives. Nonetheless, it remains a central element in the political system for several reasons. One is the fact that political parties and politicians compete hard to win seats in the State Duma, which give them opportunities to lobby the bureaucracy for their own interests and those of their constituents. Another is the role parliament plays as a forum for public debate. Pro-government and opposition parties are able to voice their positions on issues of the day even if their actual influence on legislation is limited. Moreover, interest groups work hard to shape the details of legislation (particularly when the government itself is divided over an issue). Finally, the president values the legal legitimacy that passage of legislation by parliament generates. This helps explain why the president takes the trouble of submitting bills to parliament and shepherding them through the legislative process rather than simply promulgating his policy decisions by decree.

State Duma The State Duma has the constitutional right to originate legislation except in certain categories of policy that are under the jurisdiction of the upper house, the Federation Council. Upon passage in the State Duma, a bill goes to the Federation Council. If the upper house rejects it, the bill goes back to the Duma, where a commission comprising members of both houses may seek to iron out differences. If the Duma rejects the upper house's changes, it may override the Federation Council by a two-thirds vote.

When the bill has cleared parliament, it goes to the president for signature. If the president refuses to sign the bill, he returns it to the Duma outlining his objections. The Duma may pass it with the president's proposed changes by a simple absolute majority, or override the president's veto, for which a two-thirds vote is required. The Federation Council must then also approve the bill, by a simple majority if the president's amendments are accepted, or a two-thirds vote if it chooses to override the president. Under Yeltsin, the Duma occasionally overrode the president's veto, and on several occasions it overrode Federation Council rejections. In other cases under Yeltsin, the Duma passed bills rejected by the president after accepting the president's amendments. Even when parliament and president were at odds over policy—as happened frequently during Yeltsin's presidency—the two sides avoided provoking a conflict that could trigger a major constitutional crisis. In the 1990s, around three quarters of the laws passed by parliament were eventually signed into law by Yeltsin.

Under President Putin the relationship between parliament and president became far closer. Both chambers of parliament firmly support virtually every initiative submitted to them by the president or government (sometimes extracting minor concessions as the price for their support). Following the sweeping successes of the pro-presidential party, United Russia, in the 2003 and 2007 elections, the president's followers enjoy a huge majority in the Duma and have marginalized all opposition. The number of presidential vetoes has dropped almost to zero; the Duma and Federation Council pass virtually everything submitted by the president and almost nothing the president does not support.

A distinctive feature of the State Duma is that it is organized around its party factions. Since an electoral reform went into effect with the December 2007 election, all seats have been filled by proportional representation (PR) from party lists. Every party that has won at least 7 percent of the vote is entitled to form a faction in the Duma made up of its elected deputies.[27] Factions are valuable to deputies: factions are allotted funds for staff, office space, and procedural rights. Moreover, the factions divide up all the leadership positions in the chamber, including the committee chairmanships. Party factions use the Duma to showcase their pet legislative projects, give their leaders a national forum, obtain crucial organizational support for their party work, and provide service to their constituents.[28]

The steering committee of the Duma is the Council of the Duma. The Council of the Duma makes the principal decisions in the Duma with respect to legislative agenda and proceedings. Until 2004, it was made up of the leaders of each party faction or registered deputy group regardless of size. Since the United Russia faction took control of the chamber, however, the rules and structure of the Duma have changed considerably and made it much more majoritarian. Now, the United Russia faction dominates the Council of the Duma, controlling 8 of its 11 seats.

The Duma also has a system of standing legislative committees. Each deputy is a member of one committee. Committees help sift through the amendments that are submitted once a bill has been passed in first reading. Generally, committees do not develop legislation, because most major bills are drafted by the government. But committee hearings and debates are an important channel for the articulation of expert opinion about major public policy issues, and committee deliberations often settle crucial details of particular bills before they are reported out to the full chamber for a vote.

Bills are considered in three readings. In the first reading, the Duma simply decides whether or not to approve the basic conception of a piece of legislation. If so, the bill then goes back to the committee, which then collects and evaluates the amendments that are offered to the bill by deputies. When the committee has agreed on its recommended version of the bill, it reports it out again to the floor for a second reading, and the whole chamber decides on which amendments to approve and which to reject. At that point, the floor votes on the bill in its entirety and sends it back to the committee for a final editing and polishing. The third reading then gives the Duma's final approval to the bill and it goes to the Federation Council.

The December 2003 elections gave the pro-Putin party, United Russia, a commanding position in the Duma with two-thirds of the seats. The December 2007 election widened United Russia's margin even further—since 2008, the party has held 315 of 450 seats. Since United Russia votes with a high degree of discipline, the Duma is consistently able to deliver the president legislative majorities. Other factions have very little opportunity to influence the agenda, let alone the outcomes of legislative deliberations.

The weakening of parliament's role in the political system in the 2000s was part of Putin's strategy for centralizing power. For example, after the Beslan tragedy in 2004 (see later in the chapter), Putin pushed through parliament a series of reforms that reinforce centralization both vertically and horizontally. First, in place of directly elected governors, the president now nominates governors for confirmation by regional parliaments. Second, Putin eliminated all single-member district seats from the Duma; instead all 450 seats were to be filled by national party-list proportional representation elections. Third, he called for the creation of a new "public chamber" to filter and review all legislative proposals before they were submitted formally to the Duma. Taken together, these changes severely reduced the ability of members of parliament to develop any independent local base of political support: lacking local constituencies, they now have to rely on ties to the leaders of national parties. This means that governors have less leverage over deputies from their regions.

These reforms reinforced the trend under Putin toward the suppression of independent sources of political initiative. They made both the regional governments and the federal parliament instruments for carrying out the president's will. The reforms illustrate the authoritarian tendencies that have strengthened since Putin took office. They do not eliminate all elements of political pluralism in the society, however. Although political parties face increasing obstacles, they continue to compete at the regional and federal level for representation. In the longer term, the viability of political pluralism in Russia will depend on the slow accumulation of material and organizational resources in society, the growth of political self-awareness and organizational capacity on the part of social groups and interests, and the formation of linkages between political parties and social associations.

Federation Council   The upper chamber of parliament is called the Federation Council. Constitutionally, it has some important duties. It approves presidential nominees for high courts such as the Supreme Court and the Constitutional Court. It approves presidential decrees declaring martial law or a state of emergency and any actions altering the boundaries of territorial units in Russia. It must consider any legislation dealing with taxes, budget, financial policy, treaties, customs, and declarations of war. Under Yeltsin, the Federation Council defied the president's will on a number of issues, rejecting some of his nominees for the Constitutional Court, as well as his candidates for Procurator General.[29] Putin, however, brought the chamber under the control of the executive.

On matters of ordinary legislation, where the Federation Council does not have exclusive jurisdiction, the State Duma can override a veto by the Federation Council with a two-thirds vote. The president can then choose whether to support the Duma's position and sign the law or to uphold the Federation Council and veto it.

The Federation Council was designed as an instrument of federalism in that (as in the U.S. Senate) every constituent unit of the federation is represented in it by two members. Under the constitution, they must come from the executive and legislative branches of the regional governments. As in the United States, equal representation from territories of unequal population means that the populations of small territories (which in Russia are often ethnic-national units) are greatly overrepresented compared with more populous regions. The first members of the Federation Council were elected by direct popular vote in December 1993, but under a law that was passed in

1995, the heads of the executive and legislative branches of each constituent unit of the federation were automatically given seats in the Federation Council as of 1996.

In 2000, President Putin changed this procedure as part of a package of reforms intended to strengthen the power of the federal government vis-à-vis the regions. Under the new procedure, each region's chief executive names a full-time representative to serve as a member of the Federation Council, and each regional legislature names another. It soon became clear that although the Federation Council's members were delegated by the regions, politically they were controlled by the Kremlin.[30]

In its new composition, the Federation Council has consistently supported the president and government and has passed nearly every bill they have proposed even when the legislation directly countered the interests of the regions. The members have found the credentials (and immunity from all criminal prosecution) that go with parliamentary membership to be useful to them in lobbying for the interests of the regions that delegated them. At the same time, many members and other political observers have argued that the members of the Federation Council should be popularly elected. This is difficult to reconcile with the constitutional requirement that the two members of the chamber from each of Russia's territorial subjects represent the executive and legislative branches.[31] President Medvedev has attempted to resolve this problem by pushing through a reform, to take effect in 2011, that requires all members of the chamber to have been elected to local or regional assemblies before being named to the Federation Council.

Executive–Legislative Relations

Relations between president and parliament during the Yeltsin period were often stormy. The first two Dumas, elected in 1993 and in 1995, were dominated by the communist and other leftist factions hostile to President Yeltsin and the policies of his government. This was particularly true in economic policy. On other issues, however, such as matters concerning federal relations, the Duma and the president often reached agreement—sometimes over the objections of the Federation Council, whose members fought to protect regional prerogatives. President Yeltsin sometimes replaced members of the government in response to political pressure from the Duma.[32]

The election of 1999 produced a Duma with a pro-government majority. President Putin and his government worked to build a reliable base of support in the Duma for their legislative initiatives comprising a coalition of four centrist political factions. The 2003 and 2007 elections produced a still wider margin of support for the president in the Duma and overwhelming majorities for the United Russia party. Therefore, the president does not need to expend much effort in bargaining with the Duma to win its support for his policies. Generally speaking, the pro-presidential deputies in the Duma need the Kremlin much more than the Kremlin needs them. For example, deputies rely on support from the presidential administration for their reelection campaigns. The elimination of single-member district seats in the parliament only reinforces this dependency, since all deputies now need the backing of their party leaders to gain a good place on the party list. The parties, in turn, need the favor of the Kremlin to clear the new 7 percent electoral threshold (e.g., the Kremlin will influence media coverage for the parties' electoral campaigns). As a result, for the foreseeable future, the balance of power in the political system will continue to leave the parliament in a marginalized position.

Superpresidentialism and the Separation of Powers   Article 10 of the constitution declares that: "State power in the Russian Federation is exercised on the basis of the separation of legislative, executive and judicial powers. Bodies of legislative, executive and judicial power are independent." Under President Yeltsin, there was some real separation of executive, legislative, and judicial power, both because there was effective, well-organized opposition to Yeltsin and because at crucial moments Yeltsin himself chose to respect the provisions of the constitution he had instituted.[33] But under President Putin, little remained of the separation of powers. Putin rendered parliament an ineffectual and largely ceremonial body and increased executive control over the judiciary.

The formal concentration of power in the presidency under the constitution allows the president to use informal, extraconstitutional instruments of power to strip other institutions of the ability to resist presidential authority. Once elected, a president can dominate the government and put pressure on the courts, the governors, the mass media, and business leaders to support his policies. In this respect, Russia somewhat resembles the pattern that political scientist Guillermo O'Donnell has called "delegative democracy."[34] In such a system, common in Latin America, a president may win an election and then proceed to govern as if he were the sole source of authority in the country. The president exercises so much actual power over other political structures, thanks to his control of the police and military and his access to patronage, that he can negate the nominal separation of powers written into the constitution. In such a system, parliamentarians may use their positions not to represent constituents or craft legislation but to trade favors and enrich their friends and family. Judges may deem it safer to tailor their decisions to the wishes of powerful state officials. The editors of major newspapers bury stories unfavorable to the authorities. Interest groups curry favor with officials rather than mobilizing their supporters around particular policy positions. The leaders of opposition parties learn to accept their role on the sidelines.

Under Putin, this pattern of "hollowed out democracy" became evident: without explicitly violating any constitutional limits on his power, and without abolishing elections or other democratic institutions, Putin effectively negated the constitutional limits on his power built into the constitution. Using the president's extensive powers over the executive branch, he had neutralized and marginalized most independent sources of political authority, meantime observing formal constitutional procedures. But having used his control over electoral processes to secure overwhelming majority support in both chambers, parliamentary approval of his proposed agenda was assured.[35]

The use of presidential power under Putin and Medvedev presents a sharp contrast to the Yeltsin period. Yeltsin used his presidential powers erratically and impulsively, but respected certain limits on his power: he did not suppress media criticism, and he tolerated political opposition. Faced with an opposition-led parliament, Yeltsin was willing to compromise with his opponents to enact legislation. However, Yeltsin grew dependent on a coterie of powerful financial-media-industrial tycoons (so-called "oligarchs") for support, allowing them to acquire substantial influence over policy. Likewise, Yeltsin allowed regional bosses to flout federal authority with impunity because he found it much less costly to accommodate them than to fight them.

The loss of state capacity under Yeltsin illustrates one danger of an overcentralized political system: when the president does not effectively command the powers of the office, power drifts to other centers of power. Putin's presidency illustrates the opposite danger. When Putin took over, he was faced with the task of reversing the breakdown of political control and responsibility that had accelerated under Yeltsin. Although he has repeatedly called for a system based on respect for the rule of law, he has also steadily restored authoritarian rule. Some call his model of rule "managed democracy," that is, a system where the formal trappings of democracy are preserved, but all political processes are thoroughly controlled by the president.[36] It is telling that while Putin and Medvedev rhetorically accept democracy as an ideal, they have redefined it in such a way as to rule out any limitations on the rulers' power.

THE FEDERAL DIMENSION

Many Russians feared that the breakup of the Soviet Union would lead to the breakup of the Russian Federation and many still harbor this fear.[37] Yet, apart from the two wars fought in Chechnia since 1991, Russia's path of development during the transition period has not culminated in the state's dissolution along national-territorial lines like that which ended the Soviet Union's existence. As was true of the USSR under Gorbachev, Yeltsin's government confronted the twin crises of the loss of central control over the country and of carrying out deep economic reform in the face of powerful opposition. The breakdown of the Soviet order eroded both the central government's power to enforce its power in the regions and limited the inducements it could offer regional governments to comply with federal law. Since both Gorbachev and Yeltsin had made liberal offers of autonomy to the subnational governments of Russia as part of their rivalry in 1990–1991, Russia found it difficult to reestablish the primacy of its own central authority. Through the Yeltsin period, subnational governments fought with the Russian federal authorities over their respective spheres of power. This was particularly true for several of the ethnic-national territories which enjoy a privileged constitutional status in

Russia. In several cases, the federal government even conceded to ethnic republics the right not to transmit taxes collected in the republic to the central government. Since Putin came to power, however, the center has reasserted its power over the regions.[38]

The extreme case of center-regional conflict was that of the Chechen Republic (Chechnia), whose leaders declared independence in 1991 and where the federal government intervened with massive force in 1994 and again in 1999 (see Close-Up 3.1: Security Threats in the North Caucasus). Nevertheless, Chechnia has proved to be the sole case where the federal government had to resort to force to preserve the unity of the state. Unlike the union government, the Russian state preserved itself despite centrifugal pressures from the regions. Several factors distinguishing Russia's situation from that of the USSR help to explain the different outcomes.

CLOSE-UP 3.1

Security Threats in the North Caucasus

In the region of the North Caucasus, lying between the Black and Caspian Seas, there is a belt of ethnic republics that are predominantly Muslim by religious heritage and strongly influenced by the cultural traditions of mountain tribes. Poverty, unemployment, and social discontent are high throughout the region. Post-Soviet Russia has experienced a series of security threats from groups based in these republics. The most serious of these problems arose in Chechnia, where an independence movement evolved into a radical Islamist movement using terrorist tactics. Recently, as order has been restored in Chechnia, violence—including armed assaults on federal facilities and suicide bombings—has spread to other republics of the region.

Resistance to Russian rule has a long history in Chechnia. The Chechens were subjugated by the Russian imperial army in the nineteenth century but continued to resist Russian, and later Soviet, rule. In 1944, the entire Chechen people were deported by Stalin to Kazakhstan on suspicion that the whole nation was disloyal and would collaborate with the Germans. The Chechens were allowed to return to their homeland after the war, after suffering terrible hardships, but harbored deep grievances against Moscow. In 1991, with the USSR breaking up, the leader of the republic declared independence from Russia. Yeltsin rejected the declaration as invalid but did not initially attempt to coerce the republic into rescinding it. However, in December 1994, following unsuccessful efforts to restore federal authority in Chechnia through back-channel negotiations and covert armed intervention, Russia launched a large-scale military assault, employing heavy force. Fighting between Russian federal troops and the Chechen guerrillas continued for nearly two years, punctuated by mass hostage-taking raids by Chechens on Russian soil and unsuccessful cease-fire declarations. Tens of thousands of civilians fled their homes. Finally, in October 1996, when both sides had had enough, the Chechen authorities and the federal government signed a treaty permitting the withdrawal of federal troops and granting Chechnia de facto autonomy.*

The agreement only led to a pause in the fighting. The Chechen government was unable to impose basic civil and political order. Quasi-independent paramilitary forces operated with impunity from Chechen soil. Kidnapping for ransom and drug trafficking flourished. In the summer of 1999, armed guerrilla forces (probably supported by radical international Islamist groups) crossed the border from Chechnia into the neighboring republic of Dagestan and attempted to seize power in several villages, the beginning of what they called a campaign to liberate the entire North Caucasus region. Federal forces pushed them back into Chechnia. Soon afterward, bombs exploded in apartment buildings in several Russian cities. The federal authorities immediately claimed that Chechen terrorists were responsible and began a new ground operation in Chechnia intended to destroy all the rebel units. However, neither the massive aerial bombardment of cities and suspected rebel bases nor the large-scale federal intervention succeeded in wiping out all of the resistance, and hostilities continued with hit-and-run raids and suicide car bomb attacks on federal troops. Federal forces used brutal tactics to pacify the population, including massive roundups of civilians, accompanied by interrogations and torture to identify supporters of the rebels. The harshness of the federal military tactics aroused worldwide condemnation. Although the federal government appropriated funds for rebuilding the republic, nearly all the funds were pilfered. Chechens continued to live in misery, many in squalid refugee camps outside the republic. Russian news coverage of the Chechen war was subject to drastic censorship, so most Russians received a distorted picture of the war.

As the Chechen resistance turned from independence to a radical Islamist agenda in the 1990s, it came under the control of terrorist leaders who conducted a number of highly publicized operations. For example, they seized a maternity hospital in the town of Budennovsk in June 1995, taking about 1,000 people hostage; in January 1996, they seized another hospital in the town of Kizlyar with at least 1,000 hostages; in September 1999, a series of bombings of apartment buildings in several Russian cities killed some 300 people and were believed to have been carried out by Chechen terrorists; in October 2002, a band of terrorists took over a theater in Moscow (all 41 of the terrorists and some 129 of their hostages were killed in the assault on the theater, which the special

---

*On the Chechen War, see John B. Dunlop, *Russia Confronts Chechnya: Roots of a Separatist Conflict* (Cambridge: Cambridge University Press, 1998); Carlotta Gall and Thomas de Waal, *Chechnya: Calamity in the Caucasus* (New York: New York University Press, 1998); Anatol Lieven, *Chechnya: Tombstone of Russian Power* (New Haven, CT: Yale University Press, 1998); and Matthew Evangelista, *The Chechen Wars: Will Russia Go the Way of the Soviet Union?* (Washington, DC: Brookings Institution, 2002). For a thoughtful Russian perspective, see Dmitri V. Trenin and Aleksei V. Malashenko with Anatol Lieven, *Russia's Restless Frontier: The Chechnya Factor in Post-Soviet Russia* (Washington, DC: Carnegie Endowment for International Peace, 2004).

(*continued*)

forces carried out after injecting a powerful nerve gas into the theater); in July 2003, 2 female suicide bombers killed 15 people at a rock concert in Moscow; the next month, suicide bombers killed at least 50 people at a military hospital; in December 2003, suicide bombers killed 46 people on a commuter train; in February 2004, a suicide bomb on the Moscow metro killed 39 people; in June 2004, an attack on a police headquarters in the capital of Ingushetia, which neighbors Chechnia, killed at least 92 people; in May 2004, the pro-Moscow president of Chechnia was assassinated; in August 2004, two passenger airplanes taking off from a Moscow airport were brought down by explosions detonated by female suicide bombers; and in August 2004, another suicide bomber set off an explosion outside a major market in Moscow, killing 10 people. In March 2010, two female suicide bombers detonated explosives in the Moscow metro and killed almost 40 people.

Probably the most shocking attack of all was the seizure of a school in the North Ossetian town of Beslan by a group of terrorists on September 1, 2004. As the map of Southern Russia and the Caucasus (p. xiii of the front matter) indicates, North Ossetia is an ethnic republic located between Ingushetia and Kabardino-Balkaria in the North Caucasus. September 1 is a date of particular significance because it is the first day of school each year throughout Russia. Children, accompanied by their parents, often come to school bringing flowers for their teachers. A group of around 32 heavily armed militants organized by the Chechen warlord Shamil Basaev chose September 1 to storm an elementary school and take hostage the parents, teachers, and children who were there. The terrorists crowded the captives into the school gymnasium, which they proceeded to fill with explosives to prevent any attempt at a rescue. Attempts at negotiations over the release of the hostages failed; the terrorists even refused to allow water and food to be brought into the school. Reports on the terrorists' demands varied. Some suggested that the terrorists were demanding the release of some of their comrades who had been captured earlier that summer; other reports said that the terrorists called for the withdrawal of federal troops from Chechnia.

On the third day of the siege, something triggered the detonation of one of the bombs inside the school. The roof of the gymnasium collapsed. Many of the children and adults rushed to escape. Federal forces stormed the school, trying to rescue the escaping hostages and to kill the terrorists. Many of the bombs planted by the terrorists exploded. Ultimately, around 350 of the hostages died, along with most of the terrorists and an unknown number of security troops.

The media covered the events closely. The Beslan tragedy had an impact on Russian national consciousness comparable to that of September 11 in the United States because while there had been a number of previous attacks tied to Chechen terrorists, none had cost so many innocent lives. Many Russians blamed corruption and poor organization among the police for allowing the terrorists to take over the school in the first place and for failing to prevent the destruction at the end. A parliamentary commission largely endorsed the security forces' version of events, although a civic group called "Mothers of Beslan" rejected the report as a cover-up.

In response to the crisis, Putin called for a series of measures to reinforce national security, particularly in the North Caucasus, and to improve the effectiveness of federal police, security, and military agencies. Putin has also worked hard to ensure order in Chechnia by giving a free hand to its president, Ramzan Kadyrov, who has established a personalistic and Islam-inflected authoritarian regime. However brutal his methods, he has succeeded in rebuilding Groznyi, the capital city, and suppressing the insurgency. As Chechnia has gradually stabilized, however, outbursts of popular unrest and sporadic acts of terror and violence have become more frequent in neighboring regions, such as Ingushetia. Overall, the region continues to be a source of insecurity for Russia.*

---

*A useful overview of the continuing conflict in the North Caucasus region is Charles King and Rajan Menon, "Russia's Invisible Civil War: The Kremlin's Crisis in the Caucasus," *Foreign Affairs* 89:4 (July/August 2010): 20–34.

One is the demographic factor. The Soviet population was more diverse ethnically than was the Russian Republic. Whereas half of the Soviet population was ethnically Russian, and the other half consisted of a diverse array of smaller national groups, Russia's population is 80 percent Russian. Its ethnic minorities thus form a very small proportion of the total. The Soviet population, moreover, was never an ethnic nationality, whereas Russia's national culture provided a historic identity, which encouraged (and sometimes required) other national groups to assimilate to it. Finally, the national republics of the Soviet Union were all located on the periphery of the country and thus bordered other countries. The national territories of Russia are mainly internal to the Russian Republic, and therefore have had less direct interaction with the outside world.[39]

A second factor has to do with Russia's internal administrative structure. In Russia, only around 17 percent of the population lives in territories designated as ethnic homelands.[40] In the Soviet state, by contrast, all territory was included in one or another of the ethnic-national republics. The republic of Russia took up three quarters of Soviet territory and half its population. In the Soviet state, most of the national groups giving their names to the republics had lived in the territory of their republics for centuries and had some reason to consider them "national homelands." In most cases, these peoples had a national history and had been subjugated by the Soviet Russian state. Like the USSR, the Russian Republic was also formally considered a federation and had internal ethnic-national subdivisions. But in contrast to the larger union, only some of its constituent members are ethnic-national territories. Most are pure administrative subdivisions, populated mainly by Russians. In the past, Russia's internal ethnic-national territories were classified by size and status into autonomous republics, autonomous provinces, and national districts; today, all the former autonomous republics are simply termed republics. In many, the indigenous ethnic group comprises a minority of the population. Since 1991, the names and status of some of the constituent units in Russia have changed, sometimes in order to restore an older, pre-Soviet name, and in other cases as a result of a change in their legal status in the federation.

As of 2010, Russia comprises 83 constituent territorial units; in Russian constitutional terminology, these are called the "subjects of the federation." Of these, 21 are republics, 10 are "krai's" (territories), 4 are autonomous districts (all but 1 of them located within other units), 1 is an autonomous oblast, 2 are cities, and 45 are oblasts. (See Map 1.) Republics, autonomous okrugs (districts), and the one autonomous oblast are units created specifically to give some political recognition to populations living in territories with significant ethnic minorities. Autonomous okrugs are located within larger territorial entities, although they are treated as constituent members of the federation, along with republics, the single autonomous oblast, oblasts, krais, and the two great cities of Moscow and St. Petersburg. Republics, on the other hand, have inherited certain special rights. They may adopt their own constitution so long as it does not contradict the federal constitution. They may maintain state symbols, such as a flag. In contrast, oblasts and krais are simply administrative subdivisions with no special constitutional status. Not surprisingly, therefore, between the oblasts and krais, on the one hand, and the republics on the other, there is constant rivalry. Leaders of oblasts and krais complain of the special privileges that republics are given that enable them to circumvent federal law but receive benefits such as federal subsidies.

One of the centralizing measures Putin pursued as president was the absorption of smaller ethnic districts into larger surrounding units. Six of these units have been formally dissolved as subjects of the federation and incorporated into their surrounding regions. In most of these cases, the smaller ethnic district was impoverished and the population approved the merger in the hopes of better living standards as part of a larger, richer territory.[41] Of course, the mergers also reduce the patronage rights and political voice that come with an ethnic district's status as a constituent unit of the federation.[42]

Republics, however, jealously guard their special status. During 1990–1992, all the republics adopted declarations of sovereignty and two made attempts to declare full or partial independence of Russia, Chechnia, and Tatarstan. Tatarstan, situated on the Volga, is an oil-rich and heavily industrialized region. Eventually, Russia and Tatarstan worked out a special treaty arrangement satisfactory to both sides, and the separatist movement in Tatarstan gradually subsided. This treaty then served as a precedent for subsequent bilateral agreements signed by the federal executive branch with the executives of 45 other subjects over the period from 1994 to 1998. These treaties delineated the rights and obligations of the federal government and government of the region and, in some cases, granted special privileges to individual regions under which they were exempted from certain taxes, or permitted to retain a higher share of earnings from the exploitation of regional resources, or even relieved of having to contribute soldiers to the army. In the 2000s, nearly all of these bilateral treaties have been withdrawn or have expired, corresponding to the reassertion of central power over regional government.

Republics have the constitutional power to determine their own form of state power so long as their decisions do not contradict federal law. Most have established presidencies. In many cases, the republic presidents have constructed personal power bases around appeals to ethnic solidarity and demands to preserve the cultural autonomy of the indigenous nationality. Often they have used this power to resist the expansion of political and economic rights. In the 1990s, the central government's power to enforce federal law in the republics tended to be weaker than in ordinary regions, and hence relied more on a combination of fiscal sticks and carrots. President Putin moved cautiously in his drive to reduce to the autonomy of the ethnic republics, allowing a number of the long-serving presidents to remain in power while gradually whittling away at their prerogatives. President Medvedev removed several presidents but replaced them with experienced figures from the republican political establishment rather than sending in outsiders.

Under the Soviet regime, federalism was largely nominal; it served symbolic purposes but did not provide any actual autonomy to the constituent regions of the country. In the 1990s, central and regional authorities fought over the meaning of federalism, with the territorial subjects asserting broad claims of autonomy. The contest was complicated by the fact that the 1993 constitution failed to specify the domains where the federal subjects possessed exclusive jurisdiction. Instead, after defining those domains where the federation has exclusive jurisdiction (such as providing for the national defense and a money system), the constitution defines a set of policy domains in which the federal and regional governments exercise *joint* responsibility, among them regulation of the use of natural resources. The constitution thus leaves it to subsequent legislation to define how they were to share power. Still, the new constitution went some way to make federalism real by ensuring that each of the federal subjects had an equal number of representatives in the Federation Council. In the 1990s, the Federation Council defended the prerogatives of the regions, which helped to ease some of the tensions in relations between the central government and the regions.

President Putin made recentralizing power in the federation a top priority. Among his first steps as president were several measures intended to impose greater uniformity in center–regional relations and to ensure that regional governments adhered to federal law. This reversed Yeltsin's strategy of appeasing regional leaders with grants of power and bilateral treaties as a way of obtaining their support for his battles with his communist opposition. Putin's reform of the makeup of the Federation Council was one step toward this end: by stripping the regional governors[43] and parliamentary speakers of their seats in the upper house, he was explicitly demoting them in political status. Another law that Putin pushed through parliament gave him the ability to remove a sitting governor if a court found that the governor had refused to bring his actions into line with the federal constitution and law. Needless to say, the governors strongly opposed these changes. But the Duma overrode the upper house's veto and, with some modifications, the law was passed and signed by the president.

One of the most dramatic actions taken by Putin to recentralize control over the regions was his decree on May 13, 2000, creating seven new "federal districts," each with a special presidential representative whose task was to monitor the laws and actions of the governments of a set of regions. The purpose of the new districts was to strengthen central control over the activity of federal bodies in the regions; often, in the past, local branches of federal agencies had fallen under the de facto influence of powerful governors. The new structure was intended to ensure that federal revenues were not diverted into local coffers and to supervise and coordinate federal law enforcement bodies, which had sometimes developed cozy relations with local interests. That the new presidential representatives were to rely more on military-style governance than on political methods was underscored by the fact that five of the seven individuals whom Putin appointed had made their careers in the army, the security police, or the Interior Ministry. Critics of Putin's reform complained that it was a step in the direction of creating a hypercentralized, authoritarian system of rule. Defenders argued that many regions had effectively become dictatorial fiefdoms and that decisive steps were needed to bring them back under central control. In practice, the impact of the presidential representatives has been modest. They have succeeded in bringing many regional laws into conformity with federal law and have increased federal supervision of regional government. On the other hand, they have not made the performance of regional government appreciably more efficient or transparent, and they have frequently clashed with the federal ministries whose branch offices they try to coordinate with.[44] Under President Medvedev their role has continued to be limited, although Medvedev carved out a new eighth district to concentrate specifically on the tangle of social and economic problems in the North Caucasus.

At present, the executive branch in Russia's regions is a good deal more powerful than the legislative.[45] Regional assemblies are generally weak and are dominated by regional chief executives. Most deputies work in regional assemblies on a part-time basis. Often, in fact, officials of the executive branch form the largest category of representatives. There is little separation of powers at the regional and local level, and the regional legislatures, interest groups, and mass media exert few checks on the power of governors. In most regions, governors dominate their regional legislatures and control the regional media. Usually, the only constraints on governors' powers are the presidential representatives to the federal districts, who coordinate the work of the federal agencies in their areas, and major business firms that control substantial shares of the region's employment and revenues. In some regions, the governors and the mayors of the capital cities compete for power, but usually the governors have the upper hand because of their control over most taxes.[46]

Until new legislation in 2004, regional chief executives were elected through direct popular elections in their regions. Following the Beslan terrorist incident, however, Putin enacted legislation eliminating direct elections for governors. Under the new system, the president nominates a candidate for governor to the regional legislature, which then approves the nomination. Many Russians supported this change, believing that the institution of local elections had been discredited by corruption and fraud and that elections were more often determined by the influence of wealthy insiders than by public opinion. The presidential administration had routinely intervened in gubernatorial contests to help bring about a favorable outcome for its preferred candidate. Voters had little real choice over alternative policy programs: party leanings or affiliations had little to do with how governors acted.[47] More important than partisanship were the connections between governors and powerful industrial and financial interests; the latter sometimes were able to manipulate the election process and control the winner. By appointing governors, Putin hoped to break this dependence of regional government on powerful local interests.

Under Putin, the central government also forced the republics to abandon claims to sovereignty over their territories. Several republics had declared that they had sovereign control—in effect, ownership—over the natural resources located in them. The federal procuracy demanded that regional governments revise provisions of this kind, together with thousands of other laws, that contradicted federal law. The Constitutional Court also struck down the claims to sovereignty that were asserted in the constitutions of several ethnic republics. Now no region may claim that it has "sovereignty" in any area of law, even areas that are not under federal jurisdiction.

Below the tier of regional government are incorporated municipal units that are supposed to enjoy the right of self-government. Under recent legislation, the right of local self-government has been expanded to a much larger set of units, such as urban and rural districts and small settlements. This has raised the total number of locally self-governing units to 24,000. In principle, local self-government is supposed to permit substantial policy-making autonomy in the spheres of housing, utilities, and social services (and to reduce the federal government's burden in providing such services). However, the new legislation—which is being phased in gradually—provides no fixed independent sources of revenue for these municipal entities. They, thus depend on the regional governments for most of their revenues although they have growing responsibility for the delivery of education, health, and social services to the population. For their part, regional governments resist allowing local governments to exercise any significant powers of their own. In many cases, the mayors of the capital cities of regions are political rivals of the governors of the regions. Moscow and St. Petersburg are exceptional cases because they have the status of federal territorial subjects like republics and regions. Other cities lack the power and autonomy of Moscow and St. Petersburg and must bargain with their superior regional governments for shares of power.[48]

The fears that Russia would split apart much as the Soviet Union did proved to be exaggerated despite the tragic case of Chechnia. Although Russia also underwent a wave of ethnic-national mobilization within its national republics, separatism never brought Russia itself to the brink of dissolution. The different demographic makeup of Russia, and Yeltsin's willingness to negotiate special arrangements with some of the national republics, preserved

Russia's integrity at a time when centrifugal pressures were strong. Under Putin, the much stronger economy, the institutional changes introduced by him, and his use of security structures to enforce his power have brought about a shift in the balance of power back toward centralization. Medvedev has continued Putin's policies of centralization. Nevertheless, Russia's vast size and sparse population strain the resources of the central government to keep tabs on and control state power throughout the country. The center continues to reach tacit understandings with a number of regional leaders, giving them substantial autonomy to run their regions as they see fit in return for providing the center with stability and loyalty. Thus, in many places, regional authorities wield arbitrary power much as they did both before and after the fall of the communist regime. Successful federalism requires a balancing of the demands by regional units for greater autonomy of the center and the federal government's power to enforce common legal standards throughout the country. In Russia, as in other federations, the pendulum has swung between phases of decentralization and centralization. Russia remains deficient, however, in the supply of mediating organizations, such as parties and interest groups, that would help to integrate the diverse territorial units and diffuse conflict to other arenas.[49]

NOTES

1. Celestine Bohlen, "Yeltsin Deputy Calls Reforms 'Economic Genocide,'" *New York Times*, February 9, 1992.
2. See Chapter 7, Table 7.1.
3. There were 89 subjects of the federation when the Russian Federation adopted the 1993 constitution. As a result of mergers of smaller units into larger ones, however, there are only 83 as of fall 2008.
4. To receive any seats, however, a party or an electoral association had to have been legally registered and to have won at least 5 percent of the party list votes. For the 225 proportional representation seats, the entire Russian federation was considered a single district. Votes for each party's list were added, and the sum was divided by the total number of votes cast to determine the share of PR seats that each party would receive. Certain parties further divided their lists into regional sublists to determine which of their candidates would win parliamentary mandates. As we will see later, under Putin, some of these rules have been changed.
5. On the new parliament and its formation, see Thomas F. Remington, *The Russian Parliament: Institutional Evolution in a Transitional Regime, 1989–1999* (New Haven: Yale University Press, 2001).
6. Serious charges of fraud in the vote counting were made by a team of Russian analysts. Combining individual reports of irregularities from a number of regions with statistical modeling techniques, they estimate that actual turnout may have been as low as 46 percent and that, as a result, the constitution did not pass. They also claimed that the results of the vote for parliamentary candidates were extensively falsified. Although these accusations created a stir, all sections of the political elite tacitly agreed not to challenge the validity of the referendum or the elections.
7. Matthew S. Shugart and John M. Carey, *Presidents and Assemblies: Constitutional Design and Electoral Dynamics* (New York: Cambridge University Press, 1992), Chapter 2, "Defining Regimes with Elected Presidents," pp. 18–27. An alternative

model where there are both a president and a prime minister is "premier–presidential," where the president lacks the power to appoint and dismiss cabinet ministers unilaterally.

8. The restriction on dissolving the Duma within one year of its election applies to the no-confidence procedure but not to the requirement of parliament confirmation of the president's nominee for prime minister. Thus, while the president may not dissolve the Duma twice within one year of its last election in the case where it votes no confidence in the government twice within three months or defeats a motion of confidence in the government, he is not so limited if the Duma rejects the candidates he nominates for prime minister three times in a row.

9. According to public opinion surveys by the Levada Center, 60 percent of the public approved of extending the president's term of office; only 26 percent opposed it. However, 65 percent opposed the idea of holding early presidential elections. Polit.ru, November 20, 2008; December 17, 2008.

10. The French Constitution, Article 8, says that "On the proposal of the Prime Minister, he [the president] shall appoint and dismiss the other members of the Government."

11. Vladimir Gel'man, "The Unrule of Law in the Making: The Politics of Informal Institution Building in Russia," *Europe–Asia Studies* 56:7 (2004): 1021–1040.

12. Ilia Bulavinov and Elena Tregubova, "Druz'ia, prekrasen nash Sovbez!" *Kommersant Vlast'*, June 13, 2000, pp. 14–17.

13. Article 83 of the Constitution provides that the president forms and heads the Security Council but stipulates that its powers and duties are to be prescribed by law. To date, however, no such law has been passed.

14. In one uncaptioned Russian cartoon, Putin as prime minister is sitting at his desk with a portrait of President Medvedev hanging on the wall behind him. In that portrait of Medvedev, Medvedev is sitting at his desk, with a portrait of Putin hanging on the wall behind him.

15. Medvedev's blog is at: http://blog.kremlin.ru/.

16. Gerald M. Easter, "The Russian State in the Time of Putin," *Post-Soviet Affairs* 24:3 (2008): 199–230.

17. Eugene Huskey called attention to this pattern in the 1990s, when Yeltsin was president. The restoration of Soviet methods of rule has gone considerably further since Putin took office. See Eugene Huskey, *Presidential Power in Russia* (Armonk, NY: M.E. Sharpe, 1999), p. 59.

18. The size of the Russian state bureaucracy is now estimated at around 1 million employees, which represents a doubling since the end of the Soviet era (Polit.ru, November 21, 2002.) Only about one-third of these work at the federal level, however. The rest are employed at the regional or local level. By the standards of Western capitalist democracies, the size of the Russian public administration is relatively small. See William Tompson, "The Political Implications of Russia's Resource-Based Economy," *Post-Soviet Affairs* 21:4 (2005): 335–359.

19. Steven M. Fish, *Democracy Derailed in Russia: The Failure of Open Politics* (Cambridge: Cambridge University Press, 2005). In his review of the powers of presidents in 24 postcommunist countries, Timothy Frye observes that Russia's president has the largest number of formal and residual powers of all of them. Timothy Frye, "A Politics of Institutional Choice: Post-Communist Presidencies," *Comparative Political Studies* 30:5 (October 1997): 523–552. By formal powers, he means powers exercised under a grant of authority where the exercise of power is specified by law or constitution. By residual powers, he means the right to exercise power under circumstances that the law does not specify.

20. Timothy J. Colton and Cindy Skach, "The Russian Predicament," *Journal of Democracy* 16:3 (July 2005): 119.

21. Stephen White, "Russia: Presidential Leadership under Yeltsin," in Ray Taras, ed., *Postcommunist Presidents* (Cambridge: Cambridge University Press, 1997), pp. 57–61.

22. Matthew Soberg Shugart, "The Inverse Relationship Between Party Strength and Executive Strength: A Theory of Politicians' Constitutional Choices," *British Journal of Political Science* 28 (1998): 1–29.

23. President Yeltsin appointed *Victor Chernomyrdin*, an experienced state official who had run Russia's natural gas monopoly, as prime minister in December 1992. However, as economic difficulties mounted, Yeltsin suddenly dismissed Chernomyrdin in March 1998 and appointed a young reformer named *Sergei Kirienko* in his place. Under heavy pressure from Yeltsin, the Duma confirmed the nomination on the third vote. Kirienko's government proved unable to prevent a financial collapse in August 1998. Yeltsin then dismissed Kirienko and tried to bring back Chernomyrdin again as prime minister. This time the Duma, incensed at the president's actions, balked. The president submitted Chernomyrdin's candidacy twice, and both times the Duma rejected it. Another constitutional crisis loomed. But this time, Yeltsin yielded. Instead of nominating Chernomyrdin a third time, he proposed Foreign Minister *Evgenii Primakov* to head the government. Primakov, a pragmatist with long diplomatic and foreign intelligence service experience, enjoyed good relations with both the pro-government and the opposition factions in the Duma. He was quickly confirmed, and the political crisis was, for the moment, resolved.

   Primakov did not remain in his post for long, however. Yeltsin grew suspicious that Primakov was gaining in strength and popularity and dismissed him in May 1999, after only eight months in office. Yeltsin named *Sergei Stepashin*, who had formerly been head of the FSB and later been Interior Minister, to replace him. The Duma confirmed the appointment on the first ballot by a wide margin.

   However, Stepashin's tenure was even shorter than that of Primakov. In August, 1999, Yeltsin once again abruptly dismissed the government and named *Vladimir Putin* as his candidate to head the new government (see Close-up 1.1: The Putin–Medvedev Tandem). The Duma narrowly voted to confirm Putin, and Putin quickly established himself both in public opinion and in Yeltsin's estimation as a competent and trusted head of government. After the success of the political forces close to Putin in the December 1999 parliamentary elections, Yeltsin decided to resign from the presidency in order to make Putin the acting president and thus give Putin the advantages of incumbency in running for president in his own right. Putin handily won the election in March 2000 and named *Mikhail Kas'ianov* as his prime minister. Shortly before the 2004 presidential race, Putin dismissed Kas'ianov and the rest of the government, naming *Mikhail Fradkov* as his new prime minister. In September 2007, Putin replaced Fradkov with *Viktor Zubkov*, another relatively unknown figure. After the March 2008 election, newly elected president Dmitrii Medvedev named Vladimir Putin as prime minister.

24. There is endless speculation about the "real" relation between President Medvedev and Prime Minister Putin. Perhaps some indication of the actual distribution of power between them came during the brief war between Russia and Georgia in August 2008. When the war broke out, Medvedev was on vacation, and Putin was in China for the Beijing Olympics. Putin rushed back to Russia and was shown on television conferring with Russian commanders in the town of Vladikavkaz, just north of the war zone. Normally, the prime minister would not take charge of military operations. Therefore, this television imagery may have been intended to

remind citizens of the time in August–September 1999 when Putin, as prime minister, took charge of Russia's military operation to force Chechen rebels out of Dagestan. With Boris Yeltsin physically feeble and politically a lame duck, Putin's decisive actions won him instant popularity among the populace.

25. But although he is the party's leader, he is not a member of the party! Russia is still some way from establishing party government.

26. Konstantin Smirnov, "Vse pravitel'stvo: ekonomicheskii blok," *Vlast* (28 June 2004): 63–78; and *World Bank, Russian Economic Report*, June 2004, No. 8 (from Web site: www.worldbank.org.ru).

27. Prior to 2007, half the seats were filled by plurality (first-past-the-post) elections in single-member districts, and the other half were filled by PR. A party had to receive at least 5 percent of the vote to be entitled to parliamentary seats from the party list portion of the ballot. Both before the reform and after, the parties put forward national lists in a single federal-wide district, although the parties can break down their national lists into regional sublists. For example, suppose a party takes one-third of the votes. It is entitled to one-third of the 450 seats, or 150 seats. It then fills those seats with candidates who ran on various regional sublists according to how many of its overall votes it got in each region. If it won 10 percent of its vote in Moscow, the candidates on its Moscow sublist would take 15 seats. The party lists are "closed," meaning that voters have no opportunity to express preferences for particular candidates. Party leaders thus have considerable influence in deciding the order of names on their lists. This influence allows them to keep members in line.

28. Under a recent rules change, parties that win more than 5 percent but less than 7 percent of the party list vote are entitled to obtain one or two seats and to form "microfactions" with the same rights as the big factions.

29. The Procurator General oversees the Procuracy, a branch of the legal system somewhat similar to government prosecutors in the American system, but with far broader powers. For more details, see Chapter 8.

30. Thomas F. Remington, "Majorities Without Mandates: The Federation Council Since 2000," *Europe–Asia Studies* 55:5 (July 2003): 667–691.

31. The stipulation that the two members from each region had to represent the executive and legislative branches—which creates a good deal of confusion and rigidity—was added at the last minute by President Yeltsin and sent out for publication before his aides could stop it.

32. Edward Morgan-Jones and Petra Schleiter, "Governmental Change in a President-Parliamentary Regime: The Case of Russia 1994–2003," *Post-Soviet Affairs* 20:2 (April–June 2004): 132–163.

33. Herbert J. Ellison, *Boris Yeltsin and Russia's Democratic Transformation* (Seattle: University of Washington Press, 2006).

34. Guillermo O'Donnell, "Delegative Democracy," *Journal of Democracy* 5:1 (1994): 55–69.

35. For an interpretation of Putin and his policies that sets Putin in the context of post-Soviet Russian politics, see Richard Sakwa, *Putin: Russia's Choice*, 2nd ed. (London: Routledge, 2007).

36. Harley Balzer has argued that the term "managed pluralism" better describes Putin's regime. Putin, he believes, is willing to tolerate a range of political and social interests so long as they do not directly oppose him. Rather than imposing a single ideological doctrine on society or closing off the economy to the outside world, he wants to establish a cooperative relation between state and economic, civic, religious, and other social associations. As Putin sees it, their role is to assist the state in managing society rather than to support a political opposition.

See Harley Balzer, "Managed Pluralism: Vladimir Putin's Emerging Regime," *Post-Soviet Affairs* 19:3 (2003): 189–227.

37. See Daniel S. Treisman, *After the Deluge: Regional Crises and Political Consolidation in Russia* (Ann Arbor, MI: University of Michigan Press, 1999) argues that Yeltsin used a deliberate strategy combining carrots and sticks in preventing the dissolution of the Russian Federation, averting the fate that befell the Soviet Union, Yugoslavia, and Czechoslovakia, which collapsed as states when their communist regimes fell.

38. There are a number of studies of regional government and relations between the central government and the regions, including Kathryn Stoner-Weiss, *Local Heroes: The Political Economy of Russian Regional Governance* (Princeton: Princeton University Press, 1997); Cameron Ross, *Federalism and Democratisation in Russia* (Manchester and New York: Manchester University Press, 2002); Peter Kirkow, *Russia's Provinces: Authoritarian Transformation versus Local Autonomy?* (New York: St. Martin's Press, 1998); and Camerson Ross and Adrian Campbell, eds. *Federalism and Local Politics in Russia* (London and New York: Routledge, 2009).

39. Ian Bremmer and Ray Taras, eds., *New States, New Politics: Building the Post-Soviet Nations* (Cambridge: Cambridge University Press, 1997).

40. Note that some of these territorial units are huge in physical terms: Sakha (formerly Yakutia) alone constitutes 17 percent of the territory of Russia. Altogether a little over half of Russian territory is located in ethnic republics and regions.

41. Julia Kusznir, "Russian Territorial Reform: A Centralist Project that Could End Up Fostering Decentralization?" *Russian Analytical Digest*, 43:17 (June 2008): http://www.res.ethz.ch/analysis/rad.

42. J. Paul Goode, "The Push for Regional Enlargement in Putin's Russia," *Post-Soviet Affairs* 20:3 (July–September, 2004): 219–257.

43. All the chief executives of the subjects of the federation are commonly referred to as governors, whether they are the head of a regular oblast or krai, or the president of one of the ethnic republics.

44. On the activities of the presidential envoys to the seven federal districts, see Peter Reddaway and Robert W. Orttung, eds. *The Dynamics of Russian Politics: Putin's Reform of Federal-Regional Relations* (Lanham, MD: Rowman & Littlefield, 2004).

45. Ross, *Federalism and Democratisation*; Vladimir Gel'man, Sergei Ryzhenkov, and Michael Brie, eds., *Making and Breaking Democratic Transitions: The Comparative Politics of Russia's Regions* (Lanham, MD: Rowman & Littlefield, 2003); and Mary McAuley, *Russia's Politics of Uncertainty* (Cambridge: Cambridge University Press, 1997).

46. Darrell Slider, "Governors versus Mayors: The Regional Dimension of Russian Local Government," in Alfred B. Evans, Jr. and Vladimir Gel'man, eds., *The Politics of Local Government in Russia* (Lanham, MD: Rowman & Littlefield, 2004), pp. 145–168.

47. Kathryn Stoner-Weiss, "The Limited Reach of Russia's Party System: Underinstitutionalization of Dual Transitions," *Politics and Society* 29:3 (September 2001): 385–414.

48. Alfred B. Evans, Jr. and Vladimir Gel'man, eds., *The Politics of Local Government in Russia* (Lanham, MD: Rowman & Littlefield, 2004).

49. Mikhail Filippov, Peter C. Ordeshook, and Olga Shvetsova, *Designing Federalism: A Theory of Self-Sustainable Federal Institutions* (Cambridge: Cambridge University Press, 2004), esp. pp. 301–315.

CHAPTER

4

Political Participation and Recruitment

POLITICAL PARTICIPATION AND SOCIAL CAPITAL

In communist systems, leaders make strenuous efforts to involve citizens in ceremonial displays of civic participation, such as voting in noncompetitive elections and mass membership in youth groups, trade unions, and other associations. But such participation has a ritualistic quality: it does not in fact pool demands from citizens or empower citizens to remove their leaders from power. In some authoritarian systems, regimes maintain democratic forms such as parties, elections, and legislatures to create the illusion that the rulers have been granted their power by the choice of the voters. In such systems (sometimes called "elective democracies" or "competitive authoritarian regimes"), elections do not actually confer power on the rulers or hold them accountable to the public.[1] Some authors see a tendency spreading throughout much of the modern world for nominally democratic forms of participation to coexist with authoritarian controls over political competition and accountability.[2]

Public participation in a liberal democracy enables citizens to influence government policy and to hold government to account for its consequences. The forms of democratic participation include both direct political activity, such as voting, party work, organizing for a cause, demonstrating, blogging, and the like, and indirect forms, such as membership in civic groups, churches, and voluntary associations. Both kinds of participation influence the quality of government. Through their participation in civic groups, people learn about public affairs, share and shape their views, and communicate their preferences. Collectively they influence policy. Moreover, through both direct and indirect political activity, activists rise to positions of leadership. Sometimes, they then run for office themselves. Of course, despite the legal equality of citizens in democracies, individuals' political engagement varies with differences in resources, opportunities, and motivations. The better-off and better-educated tend to be disproportionately involved in public life everywhere, but in some societies, the disproportion is much greater than in others.[3]

Political scientists have shown that the pattern of political participation in a society is structured by two factors. One is the way resources such as time, money, and civic skills are distributed among citizens. The other is the way the political system provides institutional channels for active involvement in politics.[4] In democratic societies, the tendency for policy makers to be more responsive to powerful, wealthy, and well-organized private interests than to weaker or more diffuse interests is offset, to some extent, by the ability of parties and elections to mobilize large masses of citizens into participating at the voting booth.

Parties and elections in democracies offer channels to bring politically motivated individuals into politics, including individuals from outside the established circles of wealth and privilege.[5] Parties and other civic associations such as community organizations, trade unions, and religious groups give people opportunities to gain civic skills, such as the ability to stand up in front of a group of people and persuade them to take action on an issue. In the United States, churches and other religious institutions have been an especially important setting where individuals, regardless of their income or education, have been able to acquire civic skills.[6] So have been large, national associations made up of numerous local branches, such as the Rotary Club, League of Women's Voters, and the Grange.[7] Politically relevant civic participation does not only mean direct involvement in political activities such as campaigning and voting. A growing body of scholarship confirms that the character of civic life more generally affects the quality of democracy.[8]

The Importance of Social Capital

Since de Tocqueville's time, a strong fabric of voluntary associations has been recognized as an important component of democracy. Political scientist Robert D. Putnam has offered an influential theory explaining why this should be so. Fair, honest, responsive government, Putnam argues, is a public good.[9] Everyone is interested in obtaining its benefits, but few are willing to invest much time and effort to provide it. In this dilemma, individuals are strongly tempted to let others bear the costs of informing themselves about issues, getting involved in politics, running for office, monitoring the actions of office-holders to make sure that they do not misuse their power, and so on. If everyone cooperated in getting involved, no one person would bear a disproportionate share of the costs of keeping government responsive. And no one would have a disproportionate amount of influence in government. As with other public goods, therefore, the provision of good government is a collective action problem: If everyone cooperates, everyone is better-off. But each individual is better-off individually by free-riding on others' efforts.

The stock of cooperation in a community or a society varies, Putnam shows. In some societies, people are convinced that even if they themselves are willing to act in accordance with the public interest, others will look out for their own interest at the expense of others, for instance, by cheating on their taxes, avoiding civic responsibilities, and even bribing officials to get something done.

Since no one wants to play a sucker's game, everyone is tempted to cheat first. What can induce members of a community to be willing enough to trust one another to engage in collective activity for the common good? Putnam calls this quality of a society "social capital." Social capital refers to the network of ties that keep people engaged in various kinds of cooperative endeavors. These do not need to be political. Putnam finds that one can predict the quality of government by counting how many people in the society belong to all sorts of voluntary associations—whether church choirs or bird-watching clubs or softball leagues or parent–teacher associations.[10] A key to the importance of social capital is that when there is a strong likelihood that people who have a relationship in a community also know some of the same people, they know that they have a reputation that depends on their behavior. The fact that each person's circle of acquaintance is part of a larger network of social ties reinforces the propensity for trust and cooperation in social relations.

Social capital, therefore, rests on a set of mutual understandings about the kinds of behavior that people can expect from one another and is reinforced by an actual fabric of social relations in which people encounter one another frequently—and their friends and family encounter one another as well. The denser the accumulated social capital, the likelier it is that members of society will be able to cooperate for the collective good in the public realm. This applies equally to politics and economics. Remarkably, in societies where social capital is thick, both the quality of government and the spread of economic opportunity are greater than in societies where the absence of trust, cooperativeness, and social capital impede people's ability to hold government accountable and to take advantage of opportunities for economic development.[11]

A society with a low level of social capital and correspondingly poor quality of government can persist over long periods of time, as a result of the stability of mutually reinforcing expectations. In a society where social capital is weak, people come to expect that nothing will change, at least for the better, and fall into what Richard Rose calls a "low-level equilibrium trap," where people adjust their *demand* for better conditions downward as they grow discouraged and frustrated with the quality of government. As a result, the *supply* of good government and economic development stays low:[12]

> The lowering of popular demands to the actual behaviour of government can create a low-level equilibrium trap. Citizens can adopt what the French describe as *incivisme,* a preference for government leaving people alone and a refusal to cooperate to make it better. This can be stable, in so far as reform is off the political agenda and both the people and political elites tolerate a very imperfect democracy as a lesser evil by comparison with undemocratic alternatives.

In such a case, people may prefer a "strong hand" in the form of a harsh central government to supply public order, since they cannot rely on society to provide it. They may be convinced that only an authoritarian state can prevent anarchy and that democratization will only make government vulnerable to the pressures of powerful and wealthy interests. Where there is low trust and low social capital, people are likelier to seek *private* favors through *vertical* relations with bosses and patrons rather than to work for good *public* policy through *horizontal* institutions of self-government.

The Problem of "Dual Russia"

Putnam developed his theory of the importance of social capital for effective democracy in the context of Italy, but it offers a powerful insight into many other societies, including Russia. In Russia, indeed, an enduring pattern of political life has been the social distance and political alienation between state and society: State authorities have rarely been integrated into the fabric of social relations, but rather have stood above society, extracting what resources they needed from society but not cultivating ties of reciprocity or obligation to it. In a famous essay, Robert C. Tucker characterized this problem as the "image of dual Russia." He quotes the Russian liberal statesman and historian Pavel Miliukov, who wrote that in Russia the state had traditionally been[13]

> an outsider to whom allegiance was won only in the measure of [its] utility. The people were not willing to assimilate themselves to the state, to feel a part of it, responsible for the whole. The country continued to feel and to live independently of the state authorities.

To a large extent, the gap between state and society still remains today, both in Russians' attitudes and behavior. Mass participation in voting is at a high level. But participation in other forms of political activity is very low. Public opinion polls show that most people believe that their involvement in political activity is futile and few believe that government serves their interests.[14]

Political participation in Russia saw a brief, intense surge in the late 1980s, followed by a protracted ebb in the 1990s. But tens of thousands of voluntary associations do exist, reflecting a wide range of interests and causes. Although participation in public life is low compared with European or North American societies, it is higher than in most periods of Russian history. Certainly, there is more participation in voluntary associations today than there was in the Soviet period despite what appeared to be extremely high levels of mass participation in state-sponsored political organizations.

In the Soviet period, the authorities devoted tremendous efforts to urging people to take part in the regime-sponsored forms of mass participation. For instance, they placed huge emphasis on achieving extremely high turnout levels in the uncontested, single-candidate elections of deputies to the soviets. The façade of mass participation served the needs of Soviet propaganda, which promoted the idea that the state was the instrument of the people's collective will. But most mass participation in Soviet times was purely nominal. People joined mass organizations because it took an active effort *not* to be a member. Today, few Russians are members of civic organizations, partly out of an aversion to having been pressured into joining state-sponsored associations in the Soviet period.[15]

Yet, although Russians are skeptical about their ability to influence government through political participation, all the evidence suggests that Russians today *do* take elections seriously. There are about a quarter-million nongovernmental organizations (NGOs), many of them involved in civic and social issues. And certainly most Russians maintain a dense set of social networks with family and friends. But these networks are only weakly tied to civic associations; often, in fact, they reinforce antidemocratic patterns of behavior. The persistence of close networks of family and friendship seems to come at the expense of a wider web of civic life.[16]

Surveys show that the proportion of the population active in participation is low. A Russian survey in the fall of 2007 found that only about 7.7 percent of the adult population belonged to a civic organization and volunteered time to it. On average, these activists belonged to 2 organizations, although some were members of as many as 10.[17] Compare these figures with the United States: In the 1990s, even after several decades of steadily declining civic involvement, around 70 percent of Americans belonged to one or more voluntary associations and half consider themselves *active* members.[18] To be sure, the United States is still distinctive in the world for the high degree to which citizens actively take part in voluntary associations. But Russia stands out for the pronounced disengagement of its citizens.

This is not to say that Russian citizens are *psychologically* disengaged from public life. Half of the Russian adult population reports reading national newspapers "regularly" or "sometimes," and almost everyone watches national television "regularly" (81 percent) or "sometimes" (14 percent). Sixty-nine percent read local newspapers regularly or sometimes. Sixty-four percent discuss the problems of the country with friends regularly or sometimes, and 48 percent say that people ask them their opinions about what is happening in the country. A similar percentage of people discuss the problems of the city with their friends.[19] Moreover, Russians accept that voting is a civic duty. On the eve of the 2007 Duma election, over two-thirds of the voters told surveyors that democratic elections are important for Russia, and almost 40 percent of those intending to vote said that they were doing so out of a sense of duty.[20] Indeed, Russians do vote in high proportions in national elections—higher, in fact, than their American counterparts.[21]

Increasingly, however, Russian elections are coming to resemble those that took place in the Soviet system, where the regime manages the process to ensure a predetermined result, rather than giving citizens an actual choice over competing visions of public policy. The authorities go to great lengths to get voters to go to the polls, treating high turnout in itself as a sign that the populace supports the regime. In the Soviet era, the Communist Party was the only party allowed to participate in public life. Today, however, the authorities ensure that elections are at least nominally contested and let other parties besides United Russia appear on the ballot. Those parties, however, are kept on a short leash. Many Russians accept that voting in elections is a ceremonial demonstration of loyalty to the regime and accept the fact that elections do not choose leaders or policies.

Another similarity between participation under the Soviet regime and today is the prevalence of what political scientists call "particularized contacting." In the Soviet system, citizens who had a problem often sought the intercession of an influential individual, someone placed high in the hierarchy of power. They turned to party and government officials, newspaper editors, soviet deputies, managers at their workplace, or other influential individuals. They wrote letters to the General Secretary of the Communist Party of the Soviet Union or to cosmonauts. Party and government offices had elaborate mechanisms for analyzing and responding to the letters and complaints that poured in.

Today, officials continue to encourage these individualized, particularistic contacts between citizens and the state. For example, the United Russia party has set up "Putin reception offices"—storefront offices where citizens can go to get help with their problems. These offices are a source of information for higher authorities about patterns of problems that need to be addressed. From the officials' standpoint, the stream of information that comes in through these particularized contacts, via questions, complaints and ideas, is valuable. First, it gives them a rough idea of the level of satisfaction or dissatisfaction among the populace and lets them monitor how effective or ineffective local leaders are, as well as allowing them to show that they are responsive to the citizens' problems. Second, it serves as an alternative to more aggregate forms of public pressure, as would exist if there were open electoral and party competition.

Since participation and recruitment are closely related processes, it is not surprising that the breakdown of the old system of participation has been accompanied by the breakdown of the old system's mechanism for elite recruitment. Elite recruitment refers to the process by which individuals enter careers giving them access to influence and responsibility. Educational institutions, voluntary associations, civil service examinations, political party work, and elections are all means by which society's need for officials and leaders are met. In the Soviet system, the formal channels of mass participation were closely linked to its method for grooming officials and placing them in positions of responsibility. The old system has not been replaced by a competitive, democratic system of participation and recruitment. Instead, the authorities are working to create a new administrative structure under presidential control for identifying and training future leaders.

PARTICIPATION AND RECRUITMENT UNDER THE SOVIET REGIME

Channels of Mass Participation

For most rank-and-file citizens of the old Soviet regime, participation in membership organizations was mainly pro forma—a matter of attending required meetings, paying the monthly dues, and obtaining the benefits these organizations distributed. Virtually everyone who had a job belonged to a trade union, if only because trade unions administered social insurance funds and subsidized vacations. Youth groups provided recreational opportunities as well as political indoctrination, and nearly all youth belonged to the organization appropriate for their age group. Millions of people were members of voluntary public associations. For most people, membership in such organizations was largely nominal. Mass organizations were an essential rung on a career ladder through which energetic activism, coupled with political reliability, could bring ambitious individuals keen on making political careers to the attention of the party's personnel managers, who in turn could ensure that the individual received the right combination of political education, volunteer assignments, and job opportunities to allow him or her to rise through the ladder of promotions.

A good example of mass participation was the soviets, the elected councils that served as representative and law-making bodies. Elected deputies were expected to help their constituents with various individual problems, but they were not able to make policy decisions in their jurisdictions without the guidance of the Communist Party. In every territorial subdivision of the state—every town, village, rural district, city, province, ethno-territory, and republic—there was a corresponding soviet. (In the case of the union and autonomous republics, and at the level of the union government itself, it was called Supreme Soviet.) Soviets tended to be quite large: In 1987, 2.3 million deputies were elected to 52,000 soviets across the country. A deputy's calling was not full time; soviets usually met on a quarterly or biannual basis, for a day or two at a time, hearing reports and approving the proposed budget and plan. Soviets were not deliberative, policy-making bodies, but were means of acquainting deputies and citizens with the policies and priorities of the regime at each level of the state, for giving deputies a feeling of personal responsibility for the well-being of the system, and for showcasing the democratic character of the state. This last function was particularly evident in the care taken to ensure a high level of participation by women, blue-collar workers, youth, nonparty members, and other categories of the populace who were severely underrepresented in more powerful organs. To this end, the party employed a quota system to select candidates to run, controlling the outcome of the nomination process to obtain the desired mix of social characteristics among the elected deputies.[22] Generally speaking, the party tried to select as candidates people who could serve as role models to society, leading citizens from all walks of life who were politically reliable and socially respectable. Virtually all prominent Soviet citizens were deputies to soviets at one level or another.

In addition to service as deputies, Soviet citizens were brought into the work of local government and administration in other ways as well. Many served as volunteer members of the standing committees of local soviets monitoring government's performance in housing, education, trade, catering, public amenities, and other sectors of community life. Still others joined residential committees and neighborhood self-help groups. These activities were not entirely ceremonial. Often, they gave public-spirited citizens an outlet for community service.[23]

Party Control of Social Organizations   As time went on, the growth of repressed popular grievances far exceeded the small number of approved channels for collective action. The gap between the façade of mass participation and the actual realities of power widened. Those new public organizations that formed with official approval quickly grew into branches of the state rather than autonomous expressions of a public interest.[24] Even the Russian Orthodox Church had a quasi-official status, despite the constitution's declared separation of church and state. The KGB had a large network of informers and agents working within the Church for surveillance of believers and to guide the Church's social and political activity in directions congruent with the regime's purposes.[25] The party exercised, in effect, a "licensing" power over organized social bodies through which it ensured control over their choice of leaders and the direction of their activity.[26] Because the nominally public (*obshchestvennye*—meaning formally nonstate) organizations in fact carried out state-set goals and operated under close political control, the boundary lines between state and society were never distinct. However, precisely because social organizations were so heavily controlled by the party, they did not foster much usable social capital in the form of generalized social trust and autonomous collective action. Until the end of the Soviet regime, people continued to rely much more heavily on personal networks of family and friends to exchange information and favors than in democratic societies and much less on voluntary participation in public life.[27] At home and at work, in the intimate company of trusted family and friends, Soviet citizens swapped information and opinion. Such networks were necessary for coping with the bureaucratized Soviet system, but at the same time, they undermined both its basic ideological premise—that the people and the state were one—and its centralized control over resources.[28]

Dissent and the Intelligentsia   During the Soviet period, some people operated outside the boundaries of acceptable participation and, as a result, risked being repressed. Overt dissent from the official doctrines was treated by the authorities as a criminal offense. Beginning in the mid-1960s, various small, unofficial groups pressed the regime to respect the civic and political rights that were granted by the Soviet constitution but were denied whenever the authorities found that a particular act violated the limits of permitted expression.[29] Those individuals who stepped outside the limits of permissible public expression—called dissenters or dissidents—were harassed, arrested, or even incarcerated in mental hospitals; a few were forced to emigrate. Many more people, particularly members of the cultural and scientific intelligentsia, chose not to take actions that could provoke their arrest, but shared similar democratic values. Working in institutions such as theaters, labs, research institutes, universities, the mass media, and professional bodies, many of these individuals formed strong ties of mutual trust. Some of them later came to lead the movements for democratic, national, and religious rights that blossomed in the Gorbachev period.

Some prominent dissident and nondissident intellectuals became leaders and symbols of new political movements in the late 1980s and 1990s. One such figure was Andrei Sakharov, the most famous of the democratic dissidents. Sakharov, known as the father of the Soviet hydrogen bomb, was a brilliant nuclear physicist who became a champion of human rights and democratic reform in 1960s. Sent into internal exile in 1980 after protesting the Soviet invasion of Afghanistan, he was invited to return to Moscow by Gorbachev in 1986. Soon he became the moral leader of the democratic movement in the 1989 elections to the new, expanded and democratized Soviet parliament. His participation in parliamentary politics was short-lived, however. He died, at the age of 68, in December 1989, shortly after warning the group of democratic deputies elected to the Soviet parliament that to be effective in the new political arena established under Gorbachev, they would have to learn what it meant to become a "loyal opposition."

Another famous dissident was the writer Alexander Solzhenitsyn. Imprisoned under Stalin, he wrote short stories in the late 1950s and early 1960s while working on a monumental study of the Soviet prison camp system, which became known as the *GULAG Archipelago*.[30] The Soviet authorities expelled Solzhenitsyn from Russia in 1974. In 1994, after the collapse of the Soviet regime, he returned to Russia, widely honored for his principled opposition to the communist regime. He never entered the political arena, however. Solzhenitsyn opposed communism on the grounds that it had destroyed Russian national traditions of morality and community but never embraced democracy as an alternative; indeed, he considered Western-style democracy an abomination. Although he was contemptuous of Yeltsin, he admired Putin for restoring Russian state power, and Putin publicly honored him. After he died in August 2008, at the age of 89, Putin ordered that Solzhenitsyn's works—particularly the *GULAG Archipelago*—should be studied in Russian history classes in lessons on the Stalin period.

A third intellectual—a nondissident and academic who always remained within the system and who entered politics in 1989—was Anatolii Sobchak. Sobchak was a law professor at Leningrad State University, where Vladimir Putin was a student of his. Sobchak joined the democratic movement and won election to the Leningrad city soviet in 1990 and then went on to become mayor of Leningrad (later St. Petersburg), where Putin worked with him as deputy mayor. Sobchak, who died in 2000, was characteristic of the first generation of post-Soviet Russian political leaders. Many of the intellectuals who entered politics at that time had forged democratic ideals in the academic and research institutes where they worked and had broad networks of friends and associates who supported them in their election campaigns for the new reformed soviets of the Gorbachev era. Often their belief in ideals such as liberal democracy and an open, market-oriented economy were linked to a desire to see Russia break free of the Soviet system (even if they were ambivalent about giving up the Soviet Union as a country). Similar amalgams of national and democratic ideals were typical of the political movements headed by intellectuals in a number of the other republics in 1988–1991.

Still, although the forms of public association that were allowed in the Soviet regime did foster some capacity for collective action among intellectuals, artists, ethnic groups, and other groups, most civic associations in the Soviet period operated as extensions of the state's power. Elimination of most forms of private property, the suppression of opposition, and the spread of state control over social organizations left a vacuum of nonstate structures when the political regime fell apart. This vacuum in turn created opportunities for a surge of radical politics, particularly radical ethno-nationalism, because of the destruction of class and other cleavages that cut across national divisions.[31] The most widespread type of such political activity was the drive for national independence in the union republics.

Participation and Recruitment in the Old Regime: Interlocking Directorates

The close link between mass participation and elite recruitment in the Soviet regime thus helps explain the explosive quality of political activity in the late 1980s and early 1990s and the sudden emergence of new kinds of elites to lead it. Lacking a system of open, competitive parties and interest groups, the state had no institutional channels for the articulation and aggregation of demands and for the resolution of conflicts apart from the party-state bureaucracy. The old leadership was skilled at operating within a bureaucratic, authoritarian environment, but most officials who had made their careers in the old regime were ill equipped to manage in the new competitive political arena.

One reason the communist regime placed such emphasis on mass participation was that it contributed directly to the recruitment of leaders.[32] The numerous governing bodies of social organizations created positions for activists and leaders who directed mass participation. Leaders in these organizations, in turn, belonged to the governing bodies of other organizations. The Communist Party likewise formed its own party committees at every level: Its members always included the ranking full-time party officials in the given jurisdiction, as well as the heads of government and social organizations. Serving as the hub from which a series of membership ties extended into a locality's organized institutions, the party committee at each level of the hierarchy was a vehicle for the *horizontal integration* of elites by drawing together the key government and societal leaders in any given jurisdiction. At the same time, such channels provided for the *vertical integration* of elites through the inclusion of heads of subordinate organizations on nominally elective collective bodies at higher levels. For example, the first secretaries of the most important regional party committees were members of the Central Committee of the Communist Party of the Soviet Union (CPSU). This helped maintain political unity across the vast and diverse expanse of the country.

Integration of elites through organizational cross-representation helped cement ties among the members of different elite groups in the Soviet system and thus facilitated central control and coordination throughout the political system. Although in practice, the old regime vested actual decision-making authority in administrative bodies, it also preserved elements of the old Bolshevik model of "democratic centralism" and "soviet democracy." These were embedded in the system of soviet elections as well as within the party.

Party members cast ballots for representatives to governing bodies that were supposed to oversee the work of its own executive organs. These governing bodies included the Central Committee at the summit of the party hierarchy, as well as party committees at each level of the party's organizational ladder. But, as in elections of deputies to soviets, elections within the party were noncompetitive, and the act of voting was purely ceremonial. Likewise, the authority of party committees that were "democratically elected" in this way was understood by everyone to be a formality. The entire system was regarded as lip service to the party's claim to be democratic and representative. It was considered unthinkable to demand that the party actually behave as if it were democratically accountable to its members.[33]

By comparison with many present-day failed states, the Soviet system had a high level of organizational capacity. It had well-defined procedures for the recruitment of elites, the coordination of policy makers, and the participation of the population in political routines that acquainted them with the basic institutions of the state. It enabled central policy makers to communicate their goals and priorities down to lower-level elites and provided political leadership throughout the state. By comparison with more developed political systems, however, the Soviet state demonstrated serious failings. It did a poor job of holding officials accountable either to central authorities or to the citizens at large. Its reliance on self-nominating, closed procedures for appointing and "electing" officials made it vulnerable to pathologies such as corruption, favoritism, and incompetence. Perhaps most fatally, the system became rigid and immobile, so that it could not modernize the economy without upsetting powerful and well-entrenched political interests. Ultimately, the system proved incapable of adapting itself to pressures for better performance and greater international competitiveness.

Participation and Recruitment in the Old Regime: Conclusions

Reviewing the patterns of state-sponsored mass political participation and elite recruitment under the old regime, we can draw three conclusions. First, the high volume of formal civic involvement reflected the mobilizing impulses of a political regime that was born in revolution and that sought to impose comprehensive controls on public attitudes and behavior. However ritualized and formalistic these forms of participation became, they demonstrated a massive effort by the regime to control society. Second, they generated little social capital that could be made the basis for a democratic regime following the collapse of communism. For the most part, citizens continued to rely heavily on networks of family, friends, and coworkers for communication and on parochial contacting in their dealings with state authorities; these, as we saw, tended to counteract wider civic involvement. The webs of voluntary, overlapping social association that are the base of support for democratic societies were replaced in the Soviet system by a series of interlocking state hierarchies. As a result, officials were accountable to their superiors rather than to their constituents, and there was a wide gap between the political elite and ordinary citizens.

Finally, there were some important exceptions to this generalization. Some arts organizations, research institutes, universities, and other institutions fostered ties of generalized trust and social cooperation through the long decades after Stalin's death. When Gorbachev finally opened the doors to freer public communication and political action, intellectuals based in these institutions initiated new forms of collective action. In some republics, these movements were aimed at winning national independence for their republics. In several major cities of Russia, these groups spearheaded political movements for democratic reform and became the nucleus of new democratic coalitions and parties, which competed in the elections of 1989 and 1991. Intellectuals, in alliance with some radicalized members of the ruling elite, mobilized popular pressure for democratization, linking populist demands for an end to elite power and privilege with the longing for a more prosperous, open, "civilized" way of life. These aspirations were soon succeeded, however, by disillusionment with the outcome of the transition.

SURGE AND EBB IN POLITICAL PARTICIPATION
The Mobilization of Discontent

In a famous comment on the fact that the minor reforms under Louis XVI in France not only failed to relieve the revolutionary pressure of mass discontent but actually seemed to stimulate it, Alexis de Tocqueville noted that "the most dangerous time for a bad government is when it starts to reform itself." In our time, there have been many examples when authoritarian regimes attempted to release the pressure of popular discontent by holding elections or by legalizing opposition groups, only to find that the public's desire for radical, fundamental change was more powerful than they calculated. If the leadership is willing to concede power peacefully to its opponents in the face of massive public pressure, a democratic transition may occur. Both the old regime and its supporters (such as the military and the security forces) and the popular opposition must be committed to a nonviolent turnover of power for that to occur. In much of Eastern Europe, regime transitions were peaceful and resulted in new democracies.

The Soviet Union did not undergo a full transition of this kind. Although new channels of participation and recruitment quickly sprang up in response to the opening that Gorbachev's democratic reforms provided, few organizations spanned the entire territory of the country: Most of the new organizations were based in particular cities or national republics. Some were not explicitly political in character and took the form of rock music groups, body building and martial arts clubs, loose associations of pacifists, hippies, religious mystics, and cultural and environmental preservation movements. But even many groups without an explicit political agenda were *implicitly* political, because they challenged party controls over ideology and personnel selection. With time, therefore, as opportunities opened up for forms of political expression, more and more groups were drawn into politics. This process of politicization of the informal groups reached a peak in the 1988–1989 period, as society was drawn into the debate over democratization.[34] In Russia, many of the informal groups became supporters of Boris Yeltsin and the democratic cause, which they considered to be the only way of defeating the stultifying control exercised by the communist regime over society.

In several national republics, organized political activity in the 1988–1989 period took the form of a popular front. Typically, the popular front was a broad popular movement with a democratic orientation that sought greater autonomy for the national homeland. Another important form of spontaneous collective action was strikes. Usually strikes by industrial workers were motivated by a set of grievances revolving around degrading living and working conditions, demands for meaningful workplace and regional autonomy, and resentment at the privilege and power of the ruling elite. In many regions, however, strikes were vehicles of ethnic-national protest, beginning in 1988 with strikes in Transcaucasia and the Baltic Republics.[35] The largest labor action was the strike by coal miners in July 1989, when at its peak, the strike was joined by 300,000–400,000 workers. Generally, nationalism mobilized more strikes than did the labor movement. The evidence from the count of workdays lost to strikes and protest in 1989 indicates that far more downtime was caused by ethnically related movements than from economically inspired protest.[36] The national fronts, strikes, and other political movements that sprang up were not only vehicles for popular participation; they also created opportunities for grassroots leaders to enter politics and for figures from the cultural and scientific intelligentsia to frame demands and plot strategy. Gorbachev's call for open elections in 1989 caused many of the new activists to enter electoral politics, thus opening a new channel of elite recruitment.

The spontaneous character of much popular political participation in the late Gorbachev period had important effects on the subsequent development of Russian politics. The explosiveness of demands for decent living conditions, ending bureaucratic privilege, autonomy for the national culture, and redress of other broad popular grievances substantially raised the costs to the regime of using force to suppress protest. They therefore helped to bring about radical change, such as the acknowledgement of the right to strike, the legalization of opposition parties, and ultimately the breakup of the union. Since the Soviet regime had suppressed almost all forms of organized participation except those it controlled and directed, there were few independent associations able to channel popular protest in the *perestroika* period. In contrast to Central Europe, Soviet society lacked a network of civic associations that could assume responsibility for mobilizing and managing popular pressure for democratic change. In the Soviet case, the mass outpouring of popular protest in 1989–1991 therefore gave way to a rapid demobilization after 1991. Still, the surge of popular participation in this period left two lasting institutional changes: regular democratic elections and the nuclei of a number of political parties and interest groups. In the following section, we will discuss electoral participation before turning to the relationship between participation and the formation of the political elite. Then in the next chapter, we will take a closer look at the dynamics of Russians' attitudes and values.

Electoral Participation

Yeltsin and Electoral Politics   The mobilization of popular political participation had the effect of generating new leadership and new organizations voicing a variety of populist, democratic, and nationalist demands. In many areas, it forced former Communist Party and government executives to adapt themselves to a pluralized political environment that they could no longer control. Some were swept away, but most managed to hold on to their power, and a few emerged as champions of reform. A prominent example of the latter was Boris Yeltsin (see Close-up 4.1: Boris Yeltsin—Russia's First President).

◥ CLOSE-UP 4.1

Boris Yeltsin—Russia's First President

Boris Yeltsin was Russia's first president and the architect of its breakaway from the USSR. As a leader, he embodied all the contradictions of the stormy passage from the communist to postcommunist era. He alternated between taking radical steps toward democracy and retreating toward opportunistic alliances with wealthy and powerful interests that could keep him in power. Gifted with a brilliant instinct for political strategy, he was also prone to fits of depression, heavy drinking, and passivity. Ill for much of his presidency with serious heart disease, he was also capable of summoning enormous energy when battling against his enemies. Most of the breakthroughs as well as the fatal compromises of Russia's transition are the direct result of decisions he made.

Yeltsin rose through the ranks as a Communist Party leader in the heartland industrial region of the Urals. Born in 1931, he graduated from the Urals Polytechnic Institute in 1955 with a diploma in civil engineering and worked for a long time in construction. From 1976 to 1985, he served as first secretary of the Sverdlovsk oblast (provincial) Communist Party organization. He was known there as a hard-driving, imperious leader, blunt and impatient with subordinates who failed to measure up to his standards, but genuinely devoted to improving the well-being of his region.

Early in 1986, he became first secretary of the Moscow city party organization but was removed in November 1987 for speaking out against Gorbachev. Positioning himself as a victim of the party establishment, Yeltsin made a remarkable political comeback. In the 1989 elections to the Congress of People's Deputies, he won a Moscow at-large seat with almost 90 percent of the vote. The following year, he was elected to the Russian Republic's parliament with over 80 percent of the vote. He was then elected its chairman in June 1990. In 1991, he was elected president of Russia, receiving 57 percent of the vote. Thus, he had won three major races in three successive years. He was reelected as president in 1996 in a dramatic, come-from-behind race against the leader of the Communist Party.

In foreign policy, Yeltsin generally regarded maintaining good relations with the United States as being of paramount importance, despite a growing set of serious policy differences over issues such as Russia's brutal war in Chechnia, the admission of new members to NATO, American military actions against Serbian aggression in Bosnia and in Kosovo, and Russia's squandering of IMF loans and credits through corruption. It was extremely important to Yeltsin that the West grant Russia the status of an equal partner in great-power deliberations, and he recognized how important Western trade and investment were for the future revival of the economy. Russia's methods for fighting Chechen rebel forces provoked worldwide condemnation because of the massive civilian destruction and refugee flight they brought about, but it was also Yeltsin who, in 1996, accepted the need for a peaceful political resolution of the conflict and signed a truce agreement with the Chechen leadership providing for a withdrawal of federal forces.[1]

Yeltsin's last years in office were notable for his lengthy spells of illness and for the carousel of prime ministerial appointments he made. The entourage of family members and advisors around him, dubbed colloquially "the Family," seemed to exercise undue influence over him on behalf of a clique of powerful state bureaucrats and financial tycoons. He became preoccupied with finding a successor who would protect his security and his political legacy and in 1999 settled on Vladimir Putin as the right candidate. Following the success of the hastily concocted pro-Kremlin party, Unity, in the Duma elections of December 1999, Yeltsin decided to resign six months ahead of the expiration of his term in order to give Putin an edge in running for president. Upon his retirement, Yeltsin became a private citizen and stayed out of the public eye.

Yeltsin died of heart failure on April 23, 2007. His funeral at the Cathedral of Christ the Savior in Moscow was attended by dignitaries from Russia and around the world. President Putin eulogized him by saying, "To very few is it given to become free themselves and to lead millions behind them, to arouse the Fatherland to truly historic changes and thus to transform the world. Boris Nikolaevich Yeltsin was able to do that—never turning back, never wavering, never betraying the people's choice and his own conscience. Such personalities do not leave us. They continue to live in the ideas and aspirations of people, in the successes and achievements of the Motherland."

---

[1] For a firsthand account of U.S.–Russian relations during the 1990s, see Strobe Talbott, *The Russia Hand* (New York: Random House, 2002). Talbott was President Clinton's senior policy advisor on Russian policy and offers fascinating firsthand accounts of meetings with Yeltsin. For a detailed biography of Yeltsin, see Timothy J. Colton, *Yeltsin: A Life* (New York: Basic Books, 2008). George Breslauer, *Gorbachev and Yeltsin as Leaders* (Cambridge: Cambridge University Press, 2002), provides a systematic comparison of the leadership styles of Gorbachev and Yeltsin.

Radical Democratic Populism   The elections to the all-union Congress of People's Deputies in 1989 and the republican and local soviets in 1990 illustrate the turn from the directed political participation characteristic of the old system to the new politics of competitive elections. The 1989 and 1990 elections were conceived by Gorbachev as ways of giving the wave of popular political participation stimulated by *glasnost'* a constructive outlet, one that would help weaken Gorbachev's conservative opposition while also enabling him to continue to set the country's basic policy direction. But the elections had much more far-reaching effects than he anticipated, by activating popular movements and generating new opposition leaders with large popular followings. Although the elections of 1989, 1990, and 1991 were not for the most part organized around competing parties, party-like contests formed as candidates aligned themselves with competing political causes—some emphasizing liberal democracy, others hard-line communism, and still others ethnic nationalism.

The elections of 1989–1990 had a strongly populist flavor. Campaigns focused on antiestablishment causes and personalities. In many cases, they were a referendum on the system rather than a choice between alternative political programs. The 1989 elections to the USSR Congress of People's Deputies enabled the populace to register their opposition to the old party and government elites, resulting in some dramatic upsets. Dozens of leading party and government officials were defeated, and a group of 300–400 deputies identified with liberal democratic views were elected to the Congress. In some republics, however, particularly in Central Asia, the entrenched political elite was able to maintain its control in much the same way as it had done in the past. The same pattern was apparent in the 1990 elections as well: Candidates who were state officials managed for the most part to win their races by avoiding direct confrontation with well-organized opposition movements, but, especially in major cities, new political movements succeeded in electing democratically minded candidates to the republican and local soviets.

Democracy and the End of "Descriptive Representation" The results of the new, open elections differed considerably from the old system in social makeup of the elected deputies. For one thing, voters generally rejected the social tokenism of the old system. This is reflected most dramatically in the sharp decline in the number of women, workers, and collective farm workers among the new deputies. Second, these early elections were not structured by party. Broad political coalitions with ideological identities did form, but they were informal, loose movements based on shared ideological outlooks rather than on organized parties capable of turning out loyal followers. Only in the 1993 and 1995 parliamentary elections did voters have an actual choice among parties. Only slowly and partially did parties begin to link the preferences of segments of the electorate with the policy-making processes of the state. By the 2000s, the formation of a national system of competitive parties was reversed as United Russia came to dominate all aspects of elections.

In the early elections, members of the "prestige" elite—intellectuals, scientists, professionals—comprised a large share of the newly elected officials as citizens voted to turn out the existing political establishment.[37] Candidates' prior political experience was often a liability in the voters' eyes. Later elections, however, witnessed a backlash against the antiestablishment politics of the 1989–1990 period. This is because of the sharp disappointment that most people felt over the results of the change of regime. The very label of "democrat" became a pejorative name, often coupled with the term "so-called." The intellectuals who entered politics in 1989–1991 either turned into career politicians or left the political arena.

Disillusionment with the early wave of democratic populism resulted in a sharp decline in electoral turnout. In 1989, total turnout for elections of deputies to the new all-union Congress of People's Deputies was 90 percent. In 1990, turnout for the elections of deputies to the new Russian Congress of People's Deputies was 76 percent. Seventy-four percent of the electorate took part in the 1991 presidential election in Russia. Sixty-nine percent voted in the Russian referendum of April 1993 on approval of President Yeltsin and his government.

At the end of 1993, after Yeltsin forcibly dissolved the parliament and demanded new elections to a parliament whose structure he instituted by decree, turnout fell further. Anticipating that turnout would be low, Yeltsin decreed that elections of representatives to the parliament would be valid if turnout in a district was at least 25 percent and that a candidate would be elected if he or she received more votes than any other candidate. For passage of the constitutional referendum, however, Yeltsin decreed that at least half of the registered voters in the country would have to take part in the voting and that at least half of them would have to have approved it. President Yeltsin and his administration went to considerable lengths to ensure the constitution's passage. Regional heads of administration were placed under heavy pressure by President Yeltsin to achieve a 50 percent turnout and a majority for the constitution. In the end, the government declared that some 54.8 percent of the electorate had voted and that of these, 58.4 percent cast their ballots in favor of the constitution. However, these official figures may overstate the actual level of turnout. According to estimates by a respected team of researchers, actual turnout was probably closer to 46 percent, which implied that the constitution had, in fact, not been adopted.[38] While these charges were stoutly refuted by election officials,[39] the precipitous decline in electoral participation was a warning to all sides that many citizens no longer considered voting worth the effort. Turnout in many regional and local races was still lower in the 1990s.

However, turnout, at least in national elections, began to rise again in the mid-1990s. Perhaps because of the efforts by parties to mobilize voters for their leaders, voter turnout in the December 1995 parliamentary elections was almost 65 percent and it was still higher for the two rounds of the presidential election in 1996. Table 4.1 shows the figures for electoral participation in parliamentary and presidential elections from 1991 to 2008.[40]

It may be that the vigorous campaigns mounted by the parties in the elections, including heavy—but heavily biased—television news coverage and advertising, have had the effect of persuading voters that their interests were at

TABLE 4.1

Voter Turnout in Russian Parliamentary and Presidential Elections (Official Figures)

Election	Turnout (%)
Presidential election 1991	74.7
Duma election 1993	54.8
Duma election 1995	64.8
Presidential election 1996	
First round	69.8
Second round	68.9
Duma election 1999	60.4
Presidential election 2000	68.8
Duma election 2003	55.7
Presidential election 2004	64.4
Duma election 2007[*]	63.0
Presidential election 2008[*]	69.8

[*]Observers believe that turnout figures for the 2007–2008 election cycle were significantly inflated by officials.

stake in these elections.[41] Evidently, no matter how disillusioned voters may feel with democratic politics, they see a link between their participation in the electoral process and the country's future.

The low level of attachment between voters and parties helps explain the fact that small but significant shares of the electorate choose the "against all" box on the ballot form or cast an "invalid ballot" (see Table 4.2). It is a telling indication of the desire by the Putin regime to limit opportunities for the expression of opposition as much as possible that it enacted legislation in the summer of 2006 eliminating the "against all" option from ballots. Dropping it removed the last vestige of the populist, antiestablishment voting of the late 1980s.[42]

Backlash Against Democratic Populism Besides the ebbing turnout in elections in the early to mid-1990s, another effect of the disillusionment with radical democratic expectations was a backlash against democratic candidates and parties. This trend strengthened the hand of Yeltsin's political opponents. Yeltsin's political successes had always come about through his ability to appeal to the public at large for support. Yeltsin appealed to the fear that the communists would come back in his presidential reelection bid in 1996, but by the end of the 1990s, the very term "democrat" had been badly discredited by association with the excesses of the Yeltsin era—the widespread corruption, venality, cynicism of many politicians, the apparent giveaways of state property to manipulative tycoons, and the weakening of the fabric of public order and morality. Disillusionment with the promise

TABLE 4.2

"Against All" Votes and Invalid Ballots

Election	Against All (%) (as percentage of all valid ballots cast)	Invalid Ballots (%) (as percentage of all ballots cast)
1993 Duma election (party list vote)	4.36	3.10
1995 Duma election (party list vote)	2.8	1.9
1996 Presidential election		
First round	1.5	1.4
Second round	4.8	0.7
1999 Duma election (party list vote)	3.3	1.29
2000 Presidential election	1.99	0.94
2003 Duma election (party list vote)	4.77	1.56
2004 Presidential election	3.45	0.83
2007 Duma election	(option not available)	1.1
2008 Presidential election	(option not available)	1.35

Source: Reports of the Central Election Commission; http://cikrf.ru/.

of democracy to a large extent fostered a massive retreat from public political participation and a return to the more immediate day-to-day tasks of private life.

Thus, from the late 1980s to the late 1990s, political participation in Russia underwent enormous change. *Perestroika* upset the old model of directed participation—where the rituals of lip-service to communist ideals were complemented by a modest undercurrent of unlicensed activity and a great deal of parochial contacting between citizens and state. Initially, Gorbachev's reforms stimulated a great surge of popular involvement in new forms of participation. This wave of activism brought a generation of democratic political leaders to power—some of them intellectuals from outside the political establishment, others young and ambitious politicians. A few, like Yeltsin, were ranking officials of the old regime who became champions of change. Then this surge of mass participation passed and many informal organizations faded away, although citizens still had numerous opportunities to cast ballots in local and national elections. In its wake was widespread disillusionment with the promise of reform and a broad withdrawal of the populace from political participation except for voting in elections.

Still, although participation in public life is far lower than it was at its peak in the late 1980s and early 1990s, what participation there is today is voluntary. Voting still provides some opportunity for citizens to express their preferences over candidates and parties, and involvement in social associations, although much less widespread than in the West, nonetheless gives many citizens an opportunity to become engaged in the larger public life of their communities. As we shall see in Chapter 6, these forms of involvement more often concern social and cultural interests than directly political ones. But throughout the country, the upheavals of the 1980s and 1990s have left a small but durable residual core of civic life outside the state's direct control.

The very limited scope of participation in civic life, however, compared with Western societies, replicates a much older pattern of political disengagement by the Russian people from the authorities. This pattern may even have been reinforced by the Soviet regime's strenuous efforts to turn the masses out in a variety of forms of state-sponsored channels of activity, which triggered the surge of informal, extra-systemic participation of the late 1980s, followed by the ebbing of such involvement over the course of the 1990s. The low expectations that people held of the government were matched by government's poor performance, forming a "low-level equilibrium trap" in which the low level of actual demand for good government is matched by an equally meager supply of it.[43]

The alienation of the populace from public life is reinforced by the high level of inequality in income and wealth, which widened sharply as a result of the economic changes occurring in Russia since 1991. Many feel that the dramatic gap in living standards that has arisen between the newly rich and the rest of society has reduced the sense of community.[44] As in other societies with high disparities in economic resources, the political system may act so as to deepen inequality rather than to offset it.[45] As we saw, in most countries, people with higher levels of education and income tend to be more active in politics.[46] However, *voting* usually reflects a different pattern than other forms of participation, such as joining political associations or taking part in campaigns. Voting requires much less effort than many other forms of political activity and so tends to be more readily accessible to poorer, less mobile strata of a society. In a democracy, therefore, the participation of individuals with low education and income levels depends on the success of parties and interest groups in motivating them to turn out. A competitive party system can offset some of the effects of inequality that bias other forms of political participation. In an authoritarian system such as Russia, by contrast, electoral participation replicates existing patterns in the distribution of wealth and power.

ELITE ADAPTATION AND REPLACEMENT

Political Recruitment, Old and New

To understand how elite recruitment works today, we have to go back again to the Soviet system, since so much of the present-day elite was shaped under it. Like other features of the pre-Gorbachev Soviet political system, the method by which political elites were chosen was carefully regulated by the Communist Party. Party approval was needed to fill any position that carried important administrative responsibility or that was likely to affect the formation of public attitudes. The system for recruiting, training, and appointing individuals for positions of leadership was called the *nomenklatura* system, and those individuals who were approved for the positions on *nomenklatura* lists were informally called "the *nomenklatura*." Many citizens thought of them as the true ruling class in Soviet society.

Members of the *nomenklatura* did enjoy certain privileges, minor ones in the case of lesser posts and substantial ones for positions carrying greater status and authority. For much of the post-Stalin era, their careers were relatively secure: Only in cases of severe incompetence or malfeasance were they likely to be removed entirely from the ranks of the privileged. Some organizations, such as the trade unions, were considered "retirement homes" for older or less able officials, while postings to others were considered necessary stepping stones for political advancement. Many officials, for instance, spent a tour of duty as a full-time functionary for the Communist Party itself before reentering jobs in government or economic management.

The party used the *nomenklatura* system to keep lower officials accountable for their actions, although it was a relatively inefficient mechanism. Among other effects, the *nomenklatura* system fostered the formation of patron–client relationships: A leader was often more interested in subordinates' political loyalty in party power struggles than in their merits as administrators. Personal networks no doubt contributed to elite cohesion and coordination and thus helped stabilize the political regime in much the same way that corruption, to which patronage was often linked, helped to redistribute resources and therefore iron out certain rigidities in the centrally planned economy. But this flexibility came at a very high price, which was ultimately paid by the political regime as a whole. The undermining of party policy and principles by the pursuit of private ends, the ubiquity of mediocrity and incompetence, and the impunity of corruption all corroded the foundations of the regime. Finally, as the entire Brezhnev-era political elite entrenched itself into power, growing older and older through the 1960s, 1970s, and 1980s, upward mobility ground to a near-halt, blocking the opportunities for advancement by succeeding cohorts of elites. Not the least of the reasons for the collapse of the Soviet system was the frustration of their aspirations for a larger share of power.[47]

Changing Patterns of Elite Recruitment   The democratizing reforms of the late 1980s and early 1990s made two important changes in the process of elite recruitment. First, the old *nomenklatura* system crumbled along with other Communist Party controls over society. Second, although most members of the old ruling elites adapted themselves to the new circumstances and stayed on in various official capacities, the wave of new informal organizations, popular elections, and business entrepreneurship brought about an infusion of new people into elite positions. Thus, the contemporary Russian political elite consists of some people who were originally recruited under the old *nomenklatura* system and have stayed on in high positions, a smaller number of individuals who have entered politics through new channels such as elections and business, and a growing proportion who have been recruited since the end of the Soviet regime. In numerous cases, the old guard successfully adapted themselves to the new conditions and, drawing upon their experience and contacts, have found different high-status jobs for themselves. Some officials have entered politics through elections to local legislative bodies or after experience managing private businesses. Some have been recruited from the military or the security structures. The overall pattern is one of gradual, incremental turnover in the composition of the political elite rather than a wholesale, revolutionary replacement.

In the mid-1990s the Russian public opinion research institute, the Levada Center (formerly known as VTsIOM) conducted a survey of Russia's social and political elite.[48] The center compared a sample of over a thousand people who had held senior *nomenklatura* jobs in 1988 with an equivalent group holding leading positions in the state administration, politics, science, culture, and economic management in 1993. The results showed that the great majority of the 1993 elite had either held *nomenklatura* jobs in 1988 or came from positions that were in the "reserve *nomenklatura*"—positions such as deputy director of important institutions rather than director. Only 16 percent had entered elite positions without having had any administrative experience at all. By the same token, 57 percent of the old *nomenklatura* group had been able to stay in administrative positions in the state or economy; another 18 percent found reasonably high but not top-level positions. Most of those who failed to stay in the elite were over 60 years of age. Clearly, the old elite managed to survive in positions of power and influence.

Continuity through adaptation thus accounts for a larger share of the members of the new Russian political elite than does turnover through democratic renewal. Strikingly, few of the old elite were displaced, one reason for the largely peaceful nature of the transition from communist rule in Russia.[49] Quite clearly, the old *nomenklatura*—which comprised most of the people who possessed leadership and administrative experience at the time that the old system fell apart—had to be the principal pool from which political and bureaucratic officials in the post-1991 period were drawn.

As in other areas of political life, old Soviet institutional mechanisms for recruitment were restored after the change of regime, including elements of the old nomenklatura system. In the communist regime, the party maintained schools for training political leaders, where rising officials were given a combination of management education and political indoctrination. Today, most of those schools serve a similar function as academies for training civil servants and are overseen by the presidential administration. Putin initiated a system for identifying, training, and promoting "reserve cadres" with a view to ensuring that competent and politically reliable cadres are available for recruitment not only to state bureaucratic positions but also for management positions in major firms.[50]

Dmitrii Medvedev has made the establishment of a "reserve cadre" system a high priority for his administration as well. Medvedev has called the shortage of well-qualified cadres a major problem: "Every time we have to scratch our heads over where to find the people for placement to high official positions in the regions," he said in a televised speech in July 2008. He noted, "decisions on placing people to official positions are sometimes taken through the buddy system—along the principle of personal loyalty or, what's more distressing, for money when positions are kind of sold."[51] Medvedev called for the creation of a database of competent specialists, with those rated as being most highly qualified entered into a "presidential reserve." Since then, the Kremlin has periodically announced the formation of a "cadre reserve" of 1000 people ("the golden thousand") who would be given special training and career counseling. Medvedev has also urged regional governors to form their own "cadre reserves" of young and promising officials. But so far observers believe that these efforts have not changed the traditional, personalistic methods for recruiting officials. They reflect the president's desire to build a merito-cratic system for forming the bureaucracy, borrowing elements of the old Soviet nomenklatura system, but without making any serious effort to replace the existing procedures for hiring and promoting officials.

Thus, there are some significant differences between elite recruitment in the Soviet era and today. The *nomenklatura* system of the Soviet regime ensured that in every walk of life—government, education, science, culture, economic management, the judiciary, law enforcement, and the media—the appointment of people to positions of power and responsibility was managed by the party. All officials thus formed different sections of a single political elite and owed their positions to their political loyalty and usefulness. Today, however, there are multiple elites (political, business, scientific, cultural, etc.), reflecting the greater degree of pluralism in post-Soviet society. Second, there are more channels for recruitment to today's *political* elite. Many of its members come from positions in the federal and regional executive agencies; Putin in particular recruited officials for his administration heavily from among the police (the regular police and the security services) and from the military.[52] But other prominent political personalities climbed the ladder by winning local or national elections or after making successful business careers. Overall, however, there is much less turnover of elites today than there was in the 1990s.[53] In the absence of continuous party competition and of a meritocracy-based civil service, the entrenchment of the new political elite has allowed patron–client ties to flourish, as they did in the mature Soviet system.

One of the most marked changes since the fall of the Soviet regime has been the formation of a new business class. To be sure, many of its members come out of the old Soviet *nomenklatura,* as old-guard bureaucrats discovered ways to cash in on their political contacts. As early as 1987 and 1988, officials of the Communist Youth League (Komsomol) began to see the possibilities of cashing in the assets of the organization and started liquidating the assets of the organization in order to set up lucrative business ventures, such as video salons, banks, discos, tour agencies, and publishing houses.[54] They benefitted from their insider contacts, obtaining business licenses, office space, and exclu-sive contracts with little difficulty.

But many other members of the new business elite rose through channels outside the state. Many, in fact, entered business in the late 1980s, as new opportunities for legal and quasi-legal commercial activity opened up. A strikingly high proportion of the first generation of the new business elite comprised young scientists and mathematicians working in research institutes and universities.[55] The new commercial sector sprang up very quickly: By the end of 1992, there were nearly 1 million private businesses registered, with some 16 million people working in them.[56] Since then, however there has been no net growth in the number of small enterprises.

Much of the business elite maintains close and often collusive relations with ranking state administrators and legislators. The same pattern is evident at the regional and local levels as well, as political leaders and business elites form close relations of mutual dependence. Businesses need licenses, permits, contracts, exemptions, and other benefits from government; political officials in turn need financial contributions to their campaigns, political support, favorable media coverage, and other benefits that business can provide. In the 1990s, the climate of close and collusive insider relations between many businesses and political leaders nurtured widespread corruption and the ascendancy of the oligarchs. Under Putin, the regime reasserted its dominance over big business. Now businesses depend on the political favor of state officials for their continued success. Often in the Yeltsin period, business interests sought to "capture" state power for their benefit, for instance, to protect themselves from arbitrary treatment or a predatory state. In other cases, state officials and businesses "colluded" to share the benefits from privileged treatment.[57] Since Putin came to power, however, the top echelons of the business elite no longer have had the upper hand in dealing with the state but are increasingly being forced to accept a subordinate role.[58] For example, Putin appointed a number of his close associates to top positions in Russia's largest firms.[59] Russian authorities see no problem stemming from a conflict of interest between these officials' loyalty to the state and their role in managing and overseeing state firms. Quite the contrary: Their view is that they need trusted, senior state officials looking out for the state's interests in the activity of these companies. Moreover, far from suppressing the power of oligarchs, Putin has encouraged a number of new oligarchs with close ties to him and his associates. Unlike the oligarchs of the 1990s, however, today's tycoons take pains to avoid crossing swords with the authorities.

President Medvedev has publicly demanded that state officials put the public interest ahead of their private material interest. He has demanded that officials be barred from holding jobs in the private sector while serving as state employees. He has also prohibited state officials from taking up a job with a commercial firm within two years of leaving their government job if they had extensive dealings with that company as part of their job. Enforcement of these provisions will be difficult, but establishing the norm is a step in fighting government–business collusion. It will take an enormous enforcement effort to ensure that these norms are more than pious lip-service, however, and so far there has been little evidence that they have reduced corruption or improved the quality of state administration.

As in other areas of the political system, therefore, there has been some significant change since the fall of communism, while in other respects, elements of the old system are being restored. Certainly, a major shift occurred in the pattern of recruitment of political elites in the 1990s, as the old comprehensive system for developing politically loyal cadres ended. Today's political elite is relatively diverse in its origins, with considerable movement between government and business. Still, although there is no longer a single unified system for controlling the selection of elites to all corners of the state and society, today's regime is seeking to reestablish control by the executive branch over the recruitment of elites for many state positions. This has not prevented traditional practices such as patron–client networks, bureaucratic parochialism, and corruption from flourishing. The stifling of party competition and the demobilization of society have also meant that there is little recruitment into politics from parties and interest groups.

Summing Up   In this chapter, we have seen that the pattern of political disengagement that characterizes Russia today followed a surge of popular mobilization in the late 1980s and early 1990s, much of it motivated by radical democratic, populist, and nationalist aims. This wave then ebbed and left widespread disillusionment and mistrust toward government in its wake. At the same time, survey research consistently finds that Russians value their democratic freedoms, including the freedom to vote (or *not* to vote), to practice religion, and to criticize the regime. Turnout in national elections is reasonably high, but involvement in other forms of public life is meager.

We noted that the current alienation of citizens from the state echoes an older model of Russian political life, which some have called the image of "dual Russia," although looking very different—on the surface, at any rate— from the picture of mass participation in public life that the Soviet regime presented. In the Soviet period, everyone belonged to a trade union; participation in youth activities was nearly universal; a massive vote turnout effort got nearly all citizens to the polls to elect deputies to soviets in uncontested elections; 2 million people served on a part-time basis as deputies to soviets at different levels; and membership figures in huge, state-directed public associations were enormous.

Yet, actual participation in the Soviet period was much lower than the reported figures suggested, and public associations did not result in the formation of much usable social capital that could help people cooperate in bearing the burden of providing good government. In today's Russia, political participation is voluntary. However, there is so little active involvement in civic or directly political activity that social capital is low, by comparison with Western societies. Political rights such as the right of association and expression are not coupled with the habits of civic cooperation for collective goods. The stark inequalities in income and wealth within society further reinforce the pattern of detachment from and mistrust of public institutions. Still, as we shall see in Chapter 6, there are more forms of autonomous civic participation than there were under the Soviet regime.

The pattern of elite recruitment also shows major differences with the old regime as well as some continuities with it. In the Soviet regime, the selection, grooming, and appointment of officials were tightly regulated by the Communist Party, which used the nomenklatura system to ensure that the political elite was loyal and dependent on the party. No matter what sphere of state or society responsible officials worked in, they owed their positions and future careers to the party's favor. Nomenklatura officials came up through the ranks of mass organizations such as the party, youth leagues, trade unions, and so on, so the breakdown of party control over mass participation meant that elites today are more diverse in their origins. Some enter politics through elections, some come from business, and others come from posts in the military or security services. The largest number enter from lower rungs on the ladder of the state bureaucracy. And although the authorities have made some effort to create a merit-based system for appointing top officials, it has not yet had any appreciable impact on the character of the political elite.

NOTES

1. Cf. Steven Levitsky and Lucan A. Way, "Elections Without Democracy: The Rise of Competitive Authoritarianism," *Journal of Democracy* 13:2 (2002): 52–65.
2. Fareed Zakaria, *The Future of Freedom: Illiberal Democracy at Home and Abroad* (New York: Norton, 2004); Andreas Schedler, ed., *Electoral Authoritarianism* (Boulder, CO: Lynne Rienner, 2006).
3. Sidney Verba, Norman H. Nie, and Jae-on Kim, *Participation and Political Equality: A Seven-Nation Comparison* (Cambridge: Cambridge University Press, 1978); Arend Lijphart, "Unequal Participation: Democracy's Unresolved Dilemma," *American Political Science Review* 91 (1997): 1–14.
4. Sidney Verba, Kay Lehman Schlozman, and Henry E. Brady, *Voice and Equality: Civic Voluntarism in American Politics* (Cambridge, MA: Harvard University Press, 1995). This volume presents a detailed examination of the way time, money, and civic skills affect patterns of political participation in the United States.
5. Joel D. Aberbach, Robert D. Putnam, and Bert A. Rockman, *Bureaucrats and Politicians in Western Democracies* (Cambridge, MA: Harvard University Press, 1981).
6. Verba, et al., *Voice and Equality*, pp. 313–333; Brady, Henry, Sidney Verba, and Kay Lehman Schlozman, "Beyond SES: A Resource Model of Political Participation," *American Political Science Review* 89:2 (1995): 271–294.
7. Theda Skocpol, *Diminished Democracy: From Membership to Management in American Civic Life* (Norman, OK: University of Oklahoma Press, 2003); Theda Skocpol, "Advocates Without Members: The Recent Transformation of American Civic Life," in Theda Skocpol and Morris P. Fiorina, eds., *Civic Engagement in American Democracy* (Washington, DC: Brookings Institution Press, 1999), pp. 461–509; Douglas Rae, *City* (Yale University Press, 2003).
8. Robert D. Putnam, *Bowling Alone: The Collapse and Revival of American Community* (New York: Simon & Schuster, 2000).
9. A public good, as opposed to a private good, is *nonrivalrous;* that is, it cannot be diminished in quantity as individuals consume it; one person's enjoyment of it does not lessen another's person's opportunity to enjoy it. And it is *nonexcludable,* that is, one person cannot keep another from enjoying it. So, public goods typically tempt people to "free ride" on the efforts of others, since those who produce them cannot measure or meter others' use of them.
10. Robert D. Putnam, with Robert Leonardi, et al., *Making Democracy Work: Civic Traditions in Modern Italy* (Princeton, NJ: Princeton University Press, 1993);

Robert D. Putnam, *Bowling Alone: The Collapse and Revival of American Community* (New York: Simon and Schuster, 2000).

11. As Putnam and other scholars have pointed out, social capital can divide groups as well as unite them. The members of an ethnic minority or religious cult may have dense social ties with one another, but these may serve more to isolate them from the rest of society than to integrate them. At their most extreme, divisive forms of social capital can foster extremism, intolerance, and exclusion.

12. Richard Rose, William Mishler, and Christian Haerpfer, *Democracy and Its Alternatives: Understanding Post-Communist Societies* (Baltimore: Johns Hopkins University Press, 1998), p. 14.

13. Quoted from Robert C. Tucker, "The Image of Dual Russia," in Robert C. Tucker, ed., *The Soviet Political Mind: Stalinism and Post-Stalin Change*, rev. ed. (New York: W. W. Norton & Co., 1971), p. 122. Miliukov was a political leader in the late tsarist period, who went into exile after the Bolshevik Revolution.

14. A study by Political scientist Marc Morje Howard has shown that not only Russia, but all the postcommunist societies are low in levels of civic participation. Even controlling for other factors associated with involvement in public life, such as age, income, and education, citizens of the entire postcommunist sphere are far more disengaged than are their counterparts in other postauthoritarian societies, let alone established democracies.

    Marc Morje Howard, *The Weakness of Civil Society in Post-Communist Europe* (Cambridge: Cambridge University Press, 2003).

15. Marc Howard finds that three factors in particular—distaste for the mobilized participation of the old regime, the continuing strength of family and friendship ties, and disappointment with the results of the regime change—are most closely associated with individuals' decisions about whether to join civic organizations, both in Russia and East Germany. Howard, *Weakness*, pp. 105–145.

16. Howard finds that (although more in East Germany than in Russia), "the vibrant private networks that developed under communism remain an impediment or an alternative to organizational membership today" (*Weakness*, p. 109.) In Russia, more than in East Germany, the close ties among friends and family continue to help buffer people from the hardships of the transformation, so there has been less change to observe.

17. I. Mersiianova, "Sotsial'naia baza rossiiskogo grazhdanskogo obshchestva," in E. S. Petrenko, ed., *Grazhdanskoe obshchestvo sovremennoi Rossii. Sotsiologicheskie zarisovki s natury* (Moscow: Institute Fonda "Obshchestvennoe mnenie," 2008), pp. 127–150.

18. Robert D. Putnam, *Bowling Alone: The Collapse and Revival of American Community* (New York: Simon & Schuster, 2000), p. 59.

19. Richard Rose, *Getting Things Done with Social Capital: New Russia Barometer VII*, Paper no. 303, Studies in Public Policy (Glasgow, UK: Centre for the Study of Public Policy, University of Strathclyde, 1998), pp. 32–33.

20. Brian Whitmore, "RFE/RL Poll Finds Russians Skeptical About Elections, Hopeful for future," *RFE/RL Newsline*, November 16, 2007.

21. Turnout in U.S. presidential elections (as a proportion of citizens eligible to vote) was 54.2 percent in 2000 and rose to 60.1 percent in 2004 and 61.6 percent in 2008. Turnout for congressional elections was much lower. In Russia, officially reported turnout in presidential elections from 1991 to 2008 averaged 69.5 percent and for Duma elections from 1993 to 2007 averaged 58.9 percent.

22. See Stephen White's discussion of this process in *Gorbachev and After* (Cambridge: Cambridge University Press, 1991), pp. 27–29.

23. Theodore H. Friedgut, *Political Participation in the USSR* (Princeton: Princeton University Press, 1979); L. G. Churchward, "Public Participation in the USSR," in Everett M. Jacobs, ed., *Soviet Local Politics and Government* (London: Allen & Unwin, 1983), pp. 38–39; Jeffrey W. Hahn, *Soviet Grassroots: Citizen Participation in Local Soviet Government* (Princeton: Princeton University Press, 1988).

24. On the Rodina Society, see John B. Dunlop, *The Faces of Contemporary Russian Nationalism* (Princeton: Princeton University Press, 1983), p. 38. See also the article, published posthumously, by the great Soviet journalist Anatolii Agranovskii, "Sokrashchenie apparata," *Izvestiia*, May 13, 1984, which discusses the bureaucratization of the Rodina and other nominally public organizations.

25. On the politics of the Church, see John Dunlop, "The Russian Orthodox Church as an 'Empire Saving' Institution," in Michael Bourdeaux, ed., *The Politics of Religion in Russia and the New States of Eurasia* (Armonk, NY: M. E. Sharpe, 1995), pp. 15–40; and Dimitry V. Pospielovsky, "The Russian Orthodox Church in the Postcommunist CIS," in Michael Bourdeaux, ed., *The Politics of Religion in Russia and the New States of Eurasia* (Armonk, NY: M. E. Sharpe, 1995), pp. 41–74.

26. John H. Miller, "The Communist Party: Trends and Problems," in Archie Brown and Michael Kaser, eds., *Soviet Policy for the 1980s* (Bloomington: Indiana University Press, 1982), p. 2.

27. Soviet sociologists worked under severe political constraints, but were able to shed some light on how social communication and the formation of public opinion actually worked. One major study found that despite the fact that the vast majority of the population watched Soviet television and read Soviet newspapers, half or more of the population still relied heavily on conversations with friends, family members and coworkers for basic information and opinion. Until Gorbachev introduced *glasnost'*, the relative lack of credibility of the mass media meant that people depended heavily on contacts with individuals whom they trusted for acquiring information and shaping opinion.

    See Thomas Remington, "The Mass Media and Public Communication in the USSR," *Journal of Politics* 43:3 (August 1981): 804.

28. This point is extensively documented in Alena V. Ledeneva, *Russia's Economy of Favours: Blat, Networking and Information Exchange* (Cambridge: Cambridge University Press, 1998), p. 103 and passim.

29. A comprehensive chronicle of such movements is Ludmilla Alexeyeva, *Soviet Dissent: Contemporary Movements for National-Religious, and Human Rights* (Middletown, CT: Wesleyan University Press, 1987). See also Frederick C. Barghoorn, *Detente and the Democratic Movement in the USSR* (New York: Free Press, 1976).

30. GULAG was the official acronym for "Main Administration of Camps," the state organization in charge of running the labor camps. Solzhenitsyn's three-volume book was published in the West beginning in 1973, but was only published in Russia in the 1990s, after communism fell. The book had an enormous impact on public understanding of the nature of terrorism and repression in the Lenin and Stalin eras.

31. Zbigniew Brzezinski, "Post-Communist Nationalism," *Foreign Affairs*, Winter 1989/1990, pp. 1–2. A comprehensive study of nationalist mobilization in the last years of the Soviet Union is Mark R. Beissinger, *Nationalist Mobilization and the Collapse of the Soviet State* (Cambridge: Cambridge University Press, 2002).

32. See Bohdan Harasymiw, *Political Elite Recruitment in the Soviet Union* (New York: St. Martin's Press, 1984).
33. In a similar vein, Stalin once supposedly commented that every republic of the Soviet Union had the right to secede from the union under the 1936 Constitution. But, he added, no republic had the right to exercise that right.
34. Vladimir Brovkin, "Revolution from Below: Informal Political Associations in Russia, 1988-1989," *Soviet Studies* 42:2 (April 1990), p. 234.
35. Peter Rutland, "Labor Unrest and Movements in 1989 and 1990," in A. Hewett and Victor H. Winston, eds., *Milestones in Glasnost and Perestroika: Politics and People* (Washington, DC: The Brookings Institution, 1991), p. 290.
36. Elizabeth Teague, "Soviet Workers Find a Voice," *Report on the USSR*, Radio Liberty 302/90, July 13, 1990, pp. 13–17.
37. Gerhard Loewenberg, "The New Political Leadership of Central Europe: The Example of the New Hungarian National Assembly," in Thomas F. Remington, ed., *Parliaments in Transition: The New Legislative Politics in the Former USSR and Eastern Europe* (Boulder: Westview Press, 1994), pp. 29–53.
38. V. Vyzhutovich, "Tsentrizbirkom prevrashchaetsiia v politicheskoe vedomstvo," [The Central Electoral Commission is Turning into a Political Agency] *Izvestiia*, May 4, 1994. While it is impossible to assess the validity of the researchers' charges, it is worth noting that the Central Electoral Commission reported that the total number of voters on the registration rolls in December 1993 was lower by 1.14 million voters than the number in April 1993. The lower figure, of course, eased the task of declaring that a majority of voters had turned out for the election. How a million voters had vanished between April and December was not indicated. Moreover, the Central Electoral Commission refused to publish a full tally of election results by electoral district, confining itself only to publishing a list of winners. No independent verification of the CEC's own conclusions was thus possible.
    See Vera Tolz and Julia Wishnevsky, "Election Queries Make Russians Doubt Democratic Process," *RFE/RL Research Report* 3:13 (1 April 1994): 3.
39. Iu. Vedeneev and V. I. Lysenko, "Vybory-93: Uroki i al'ternativy," *Nezavisimaia gazeta*, June 28, 1994.
40. Note that the Duma elections in 1993, 1995, and 1999 were held in December—when days are shortest and the weather cold. The 1991 presidential election was held on June 12 and required only one round. The 1996 presidential election required two rounds because no candidate won an outright majority in the first round. These were held on June 16 and July 3, respectively. The presidential election in 2000 did not require a second round because Vladimir Putin won an absolute majority of votes in the first round. It was held on March 26 rather than in June, because President Yeltsin's premature resignation forced a new election within three months of the resignation.
41. Regarding the role of the media in the parliamentary elections of 1995 and 1999, see Sarah Oates, "Vying for Votes on a Crowded Campaign Trail," *Transition 2* (1996): 26–29; and Sarah Oates, "The 1999 Russian Duma Elections," *Problems of Post-Communism* 47:3 (May/June 2000): 3–14.
42. One survey found that a majority of Russian citizens opposed dropping the "against all" option from Russian elections and that over 30 percent of respondents had availed themselves of it at some point. *RFE/RL Newsline*, 10:121 (July 3, 2006) at http://www.rferl.org/newsline/.
43. Richard Rose, William Mishler, and Neil Munro, *Russia Transformed: Developing Popular Support for a New Regime* (Cambridge: Cambridge University Press, 2006).

44. Howard, *Weakness of Civil Society*, pp. 130–136.
45. Carles Boix, *Democracy and Redistribution* (Cambridge: Cambridge University Press, 2003).
46. Sidney Verba, Norman H. Nie, and Jae-on Kim, *Participation and Political Equality: A Seven-Nation Comparison* (Cambridge, Cambridge University Press, 1978); Samuel H. Barnes and Max Kaase, eds., *Political Action: Mass Participation in Five Western Democracies* (Beverly Hills, CA: Sage Publications, 1979).
47. Boris Golovachev, Larisa Kosova, and Liudmila Khakhulina, <<*Novaia*>> *rossiiskaia elita: starye igroki na novom pole? Segodnia*, February 14, 1996.
48. Ibid.
49. Olga V. Kryshtanovskaia, "Has-Beens: Trends of Downward Mobility of the Russian Elite," *Russian Social Science Review* 46:2 (2005): 4–51.
50. Eugene Huskey, "Nomenklatura Lite? The Cadres Reserve *(Kadrovyi reserv)* in Russian Public Administration," *NCEEER Working Paper*, October 24, 2003, Washington, DC, National Council for Eurasian and East European Research.
51. From a speech to a conference on July 24, 2008, translated by the press agency ITAR-TASS. World News Connection, Document Number: 200807241477.1_0542018c80932b33.
52. Olga Kryshtanovskaya and Stephen White, "Putin's Militocracy," *Post-Soviet Affairs* 19:4 (2003): 289–306.
53. Kryshtanovskaia, "Has-Beens," pp. 47–50.
54. Steven L. Solnick, *Stealing the State: Control and Collapse in Soviet Institutions* (Cambridge, MA: Harvard University Press, 1998), pp. 112–124.
55. I. M. Bunin, *Biznesmeny Rossii: 40 istorii uspekha* (Moscow: OKO, 1994), p. 386.
56. Ibid., p. 366.
57. Joel S. Hellman, Geraint Jones, and Daniel Kaufmann, *"Seize the State, Seize the Day": State Capture, Corruption, and Influence in Transition* (Washington, DC: World Bank Institute, 2000).
58. Harley Balzer, "Managed Pluralism: Vladimir Putin's Emerging Regime," *Post-Soviet Affairs* 19:3 (2003): 189–227.
59. A few examples: Dmitrii Medvedev, before becoming president, was simultaneously first deputy prime minister and chairman of the board of Russia's natural gas monopoly, Gazprom; Igor Sechin, deputy chief of the presidential administration under Putin and now a deputy prime minister under Putin, is chairman of the state-owned oil firm, Rosneft; Vladislav Surkov, the president's chief political strategist and a deputy chief of the presidential administration, is chairman of the board of the state-owned firm, Transnefteprodukt, which manufactures oil pipeline equipment; Igor Shuvalov, first deputy prime minister under Putin, is a member of the board of the state railroad monopoly. Many of these officials have backgrounds in the security services. See Marshall I. Goldman, *Petrostate: Putin, Power, and the New Russia* (New York: Oxford University Press, 2008), p. 193.

Political Culture and Public Opinion

Contemporary Russian political culture is the product of many influences, some accumulated over the long and turbulent history of Russian statehood, others reflecting the change in political and economic institutions since the end of the Soviet regime. The values and beliefs of the populace have been shaped and reshaped again and again by war, revolution, and regime change. The very identity of the state—whether Russia was to be a nation-state, an empire, a communist republic, a crusade, or a democracy—has been bitterly contested and is only beginning to be settled today. Many Russians believe that their country needs a national idea to define its institutions and goals, which some still find in communism and others in the country's Russian Orthodox religious heritage. Today's leaders have not tried to promulgate a new master ideology but they have tried to replace Marxist-Leninist values with patriotism and national pride.[1] Russia's citizens are deeply conscious of being part of a cultural tradition that is neither entirely Western nor Asian, but that has absorbed elements of a number of neighboring civilizations with which it has come into contact.[2] President Medvedev has repeatedly insisted that Russia is a part of European civilization but that it can only develop European values and institutions at its own pace.

Historically, Russia's political culture has been shaped by four factors: the country's geographic location, climate, and territorial expanse; the tradition of autocratic and patrimonial rule; the Orthodox Christian heritage; and the recurrent pattern of state-directed modernization. These elements of Russia's development as a political community have influenced the values and beliefs of the population as well as the mutual expectations between rulers and populace.

The Russian state became the largest state in the world in territorial terms by the end of the seventeenth century through the centralization of the rule of the Muscovite princes and the expansion of their dominion southward and eastward. Wars, both of defense and for conquest of new lands, strongly influenced the way the state structured its relations with the people.

The challenge of ruling so large a domain with a relatively small population and an extremely meager foundation of productive economic resources always strained the resources of the state. As a result, historically, the state was organized around the imperative of creating a capacity for extracting human and material resources from the populace.[3]

A distinctive feature of Russia's development has been that, much more than in other societies, patterns of human settlement have been planned. In their drive to acquire and assimilate new lands through territorial expansion, make the country's borders secure, and exploit its immense natural resource wealth, Russian and Soviet leaders built great cities in remote and inhospitable regions in order to exploit natural resources such as coal, oil, gas, gold, diamonds, and hydropower and to defend the country's territorial frontiers. But this pattern of planned spatial development has taken a huge toll on Russia's economy because of the necessity of overcoming the obstacles of cold temperatures and long distances. As Allen Lynch puts it, compared with other states in the world, Russia's geography makes both the costs of security and the costs of production high. In the Soviet period, when prices were set administratively and resources were allocated by the planning mechanism, leaders could act as though these costs were irrelevant. Of course, they were not irrelevant: Ultimately, the tremendous cost of maintaining the system exceeded its capacity. Today, as Russia struggles to free itself of the legacy of the failed socialist experiment and to integrate itself into the international economy, it cannot ignore the costs geography imposes on social development and national security any longer.[4] But because of the huge investment made in the human, military, and economic assets it has inherited, the state is forced to play a much larger role in redistributing economic resources than it would in other economies.[5]

The political legacy of autocratic, patrimonial rule is also critical. By comparison with European states, Russia's state was more absolutist and centralized, and its society weaker in independent resources for self-expression and organization. Russia did not experience the Enlightenment; doctrines of civic and human rights penetrated Russian intellectual culture long after they had been absorbed in Europe. As of the beginning of the twentieth century, four-fifths of Russia's population was still rural and illiterate. The growth of urban property-holding classes was very limited and late in comparison to that of Western Europe. The ideology of liberal democracy had a negligible following among Russians in the nineteenth century; much more widespread, particularly among workers and peasants, were radical doctrines of revolutionary socialism. The rise of revolutionary ideologies focusing on the overthrow of the state reflected the long heritage of "dual Russia." For many Russians, the state was an alien and intrusive power that conscripted their young men into the army, enforced the institution of serfdom, rendered arbitrary justice, and sent opponents into exile or hard labor.

For centuries, the tsars embodied the aspirations of state power and glory. Tsarism also provided a focal point for a patrimonial pattern of rule that pervaded Russian political culture. In patrimonialism, the ruler considers his domain to be his private property rather than a community with sovereign rights and interests. A patrimonial ruler is not accountable to his subjects, but treats them as a landowner treats an estate—neglecting it or developing it, as the case might be, but never conceiving it as lieing outside his control or enjoying independent rights. Some tsars sought to expand the state, others to rationalize their rule, but none until the twentieth century thought it necessary to grant the country a constitution. The bureaucracy was secretive, riddled with corruption, and averse to change. Neither in the tsarist era nor in the Soviet period were there institutions providing for the control of the bureaucracy by elected representatives or by courts of law: State officials were accountable to their superiors and ultimately to the tsar, but not to the people.

In turn, the tsar was considered to be subordinate only to God; the people—nobles and commoners alike—were expected to submit to the tsar's absolute authority. The tsar sought to maintain an equal distance from all his subjects, because all classes and estates were equally bound in service obligations to the state. There was no conception of a public sphere or a nation outside the state until late in the history of the empire. The idea that a strong state required a strong civil society was largely alien to Russian political culture until the late 1980s and the 1990s. Even when the tsar finally granted a constitution, following the 1905 revolution, the state did not evolve into a constitutional monarchy. Soon afterward, World War I, which imposed insuperable strains on Russia's capacity to mobilize and supply a huge army, overwhelmed tsarism in the revolutions of 1917. First, the tsar abdicated and was replaced by a short-lived provisional government. A half year later, that government was pushed aside by the Bolsheviks in the October Revolution.

Today, the legacy of patrimonialism and absolutism continues to be reflected in the pattern in which civic associations depend on the state for many of the resources they need to organize—including office premises, communications infrastructure, and access to the public. Even big business, which is the most effectively organized sector of society, cannot operate independently of the state's patronage. Labor, the professions, the mass media, and religious bodies, all turn to the state for organizational support. Although it is customary to regard Russia's state as chronically usurping power from society, in many ways, it is society that turns to the state for help in resolving its own dilemmas of collective action.

Besides patrimonialism, Russia's cultural heritage is also marked by the close alliance between church and state. Tradition holds that Grand Prince Vladimir of the Kievan city-state called Rus' (officially regarded by Russian historians as the predecessor of the contemporary Russian state), was baptized into the Eastern Orthodox faith in 988. By choosing the Byzantine or Eastern branch of Christianity for the spiritual ideology of his rule, Vladimir linked Russia with the Byzantine Empire for trade and political relations. The impact of Orthodoxy has been strongly felt in Russian political culture, much as Roman Catholicism and Protestant Christianity have shaped West European legal and political traditions. Orthodox Christianity is organized into national churches, which are regarded as the spiritual patrimony of particular national communities, and in worldly matters, each national church practices accommodation to the state authorities. In religious doctrine, Orthodoxy values faithfulness to changeless forms of worship and resists new practices or ideas. Its doctrine emphasizes the distance separating the kingdom of heaven from the sinful world.

Some scholars see elements of democratic values in the spiritual heritage of Orthodoxy. These include the church's traditional concern with social equality and community, as well as the ideal of an organic harmony—rather than separation or conflict—between civil and religious authorities. They believe that it is possible for Russia today to recover these elements and to incorporate them into a new and distinctive model of Russian democracy.[6] However, other scholars point out that Russia's history lacks a tradition of natural law or right, such as developed early in the Middle Ages in Europe and lent itself to the development of a doctrine of popular sovereignty. Instead, Russia's Orthodox thought reinforced the doctrine of unlimited power in the autocracy and undivided power in the state.[7] Certainly, there is little in the Russian Orthodox tradition that could nurture political doctrines of liberal democracy. "Heaven," church officials sometimes say, "has a kingdom, while hell has democracy."[8]

Orthodoxy in Russia not only reinforced the values of collectivism and communal harmony but also opposed the West's individualism and materialism. It also fostered a sense of a special mission for Russia. In the sixteenth century, some writers went so far as to proclaim Russia the "Third Rome," arguing that with the fall of the two previous seats of Christianity's political power, Rome and Constantinople, Moscow was now destined to become the source of the message that would bring salvation to the world. The great nineteenth-century writer Fedor Dostoevsky had a similar conception of Russia's destiny, and echoes of this idea reappeared in the messianic ideology of Russian communism, which claimed to be a doctrine of universal force.

Russia's Orthodox heritage has also left its stamp on organizational patterns in state and society. The rulers of the Byzantine Empire saw the cosmos as ordered hierarchically and the empire as an imperfect copy of the perfect original. In the hierarchy of ranks in the empire, the emperor was the equivalent of the almighty, next to him in honor and glory were the members of the court, and so on down to the lowest strata of society. A way of thinking that identifies hierarchies of rank and status in all organizational relations continues to be a prevalent pattern in Russia today, as seen, for example, in the closely prescribed rights and privileges that state officials may enjoy depending on their rank in the bureaucracy. This pattern of thought and perception differs considerably from one that proceeds from an assumption of the equality and independence of individual citizens.

The fourth element of Russia's legacy that shapes contemporary political development is the recurring pattern of state-led modernization. Over and over in Russian history, technological and organizational changes designed to raise efficiency and productivity have been imposed on society by autocratic rulers, generally with highly uneven effects on society. Tsars such as Peter the Great and Catherine the Great had pressed for adopting some features of European industrial technology in order to increase Russia's productivity and competitiveness in the international environment. The late nineteenth century saw an intense spurt of industrialization. By the beginning of World War I, Russia was one of the leading producers in the world of steel, oil, cotton, and other goods, and its railroad network was second only to that of the United States in total length.[9] But modernization affected different regions and strata differently, exacerbating inequality in living standards and widening the gap in values and beliefs between social elites and the mass of the population.

For their part, the founders of the Soviet regime identified socialism with modernity and worked to transform society by creating an urbanized industrial economy, a comprehensive educational system, and a powerful scientific–technical infrastructure. The Soviet leaders suppressed cultural traditions in many parts of the country that were antithetical to modern values, such as the veiling of women in Central Asia, and imposed the Soviet system of values, including secularism and the equality of the sexes.[10] They regarded modernization as critical to state building: A state that could accomplish its long-term goals, defeat its enemies on the battlefield and its ideological rivals in the Cold War required, Soviet leaders believed, a dynamic industrial economy. However, the Soviet model for industrial development had exhausted its capacity for further growth by the early 1980s. Factor productivity was declining, and the economy lacked the human and material resources needed to stimulate continuous technological improvement. To a large degree, the economy was locked into a model of modernization that was wasteful, costly, and increasingly obsolete.

This inheritance of stalled development in turn has shaped the post-Soviet policy agenda. Presidents Putin and Medvedev have made a top priority the reinvigoration of Russian economic growth in order to restore Russia's power and greatness in the world and to raise the living standards of its populace. Yet, like Russian rulers before him, both Putin and Medvedev have looked for forms of modernity that do not threaten the state's control over society.

These factors—geography, patrimonialism, Orthodoxy, and state-led modernization—continue to shape Russian political culture. Although contemporary Russians are deeply conscious of their distinctive political heritage, they differ over what this legacy means for the future. In this chapter, we will explore some of the attitudes and values that underpin Russians' attitudes about the state and their place in it. We will look at some of the enduring features of Russian political culture as well as ask what long-term and short-term forces are affecting it. Also, we will ask how political values and beliefs differ across social groups, by age, education, gender, and ethnicity. Before we look at Russia's political culture more closely, however, let us ask what we mean by political culture and why we study it.

THE CONCEPT OF POLITICAL CULTURE

Political scientists define political culture as the distribution of people's values, beliefs, and feelings about politics in a particular society. Values are views about what is right or wrong, good or bad. Beliefs are conceptions of the state of the world. Emotions include pride, shame, desire, anger, or resentment felt toward objects in the political environment. A political culture is the totality of the values, beliefs, and emotions of the members of a society expressed about the political regime and about their roles in it.[11]

The subject of political culture has been the source of lively controversy in political science and in the study of Russia and the Soviet Union.[12] A major point of contention is how political culture is related to the structures and institutions of a political system. Political culture is never static; culture tends to change gradually and incrementally, whereas political regimes sometimes undergo drastic and discontinuous changes. Therefore, if political culture *directly* determined how a national political system operates, we could not explain some of the startling transformations in regimes that we have observed in our time. Some countries that were formerly considered to have deeply conservative, authoritarian political cultures have succeeded in sustaining viable and successful democratic polities after a major constitutional transition. Other countries considered to have had democratic political cultures have experienced spells of authoritarian rule. Clearly, there can be no simple causal path leading from the distribution of values and beliefs in a society to its form of government at any given point in time. Likewise, we should not expect that any particular set of political and social institutions will transform the nature of a country's political culture. If so, we could not explain why so many regimes that have poured resources into shaping their populace's hearts and minds have had so little to show for their effort. Political culture may be malleable, but only up to a point. A country's institutions and its political culture interact and shape one another over time. Where institutions and culture stand in mutually reinforcing equilibrium, we expect change to occur without major ruptures. But in cases where institutions and culture are not congruent, the chances are stronger that there will be abrupt, discontinuous changes in the political regime.

Differences across countries in the composition of political cultures are stable over time, but certainly not static. "Culture," political scientist Ronald Inglehart writes, "is not a constant. It is a system through which a society adapts to its environment: Given a changing environment, in the long run it is likely to change."[13] He provides evidence that the political culture of a country does influence its political and economic performance. In turn, the country's performance has a feedback effect on its political culture. For instance, where democracy is successful, its operation is likely to reinforce people's belief that democracy works better than the alternatives. A country may remain stuck in an equilibrium between poor quality government and its population's low expectations of government for long periods of time because people have no faith that a different regime could work any better.

Still, political cultures can evolve, sometimes changing in significant ways. The succession of generations can bring about deep and lasting changes in the values and beliefs of a society. People in their late teens and early twenties are especially susceptible to formative influences in their political and economic environment. At that age, people often come to adhere to orientations which continue to shape their outlook on politics and society for the rest of their lives. We can see evidence of this phenomenon in Russia.

Political scientists believe that a country's political culture has an impact on the development of its political system through both direct and indirect pathways. The direct path is through the influence of people's values and beliefs on their political behavior, including their voting choices at election time. The second is the indirect influence of people's everyday habits, expectations and values on their relations with the political environment. As we saw in the last chapter, to the extent that people are able to sustain ties of mutual trust and cooperation in settings outside their immediate circles of family and friends, they are much likelier to be able to solve collective dilemmas, such as how to keep government honest, fair, and responsive. The direct and indirect pathways by which political culture affects political life therefore parallel the kinds of political participation discussed in the previous chapter: the participation that takes place directly in the political sphere, such as through voting and campaigning, and people's involvement in public life more generally.

The *direct* influence of political culture on the political system by means of voting can be compared to the relationship between consumers and producers in a market economy. In the abstract, consumer demand is supposed to guide the decisions of producers to offer the desired mixture of goods and services at competitive prices. But in the real world, individual consumers have little actual control over the economy because information about what consumers want and need may be hidden to producers and because consumers' knowledge about the quality and availability of what producers offer is never perfect. In a perfect market economy, consumers in the aggregate are sovereign, but no one consumer has much influence over what is produced or the price at which goods are sold. Matching demand and supply is a complex process that over time tends toward a hypothetical equilibrium point between price and quantity that may never be reached. But at any one moment, there is likely to be a gap between what people want and what the economy provides.

The analogy between economic demand and supply and the relationship between political culture and political institutions is useful up to a point. A democracy usually will do a better job of matching what people demand and what politicians provide them than would a dictatorship, just as a market economy usually matches demand and supply for goods more efficiently than would a centrally planned economy. In a democracy, the distribution of people's preferences will influence the way parties and candidates compete for votes. Over time, as people's values and expectations change, leaders offer new policies that match the shifts in voter demand, moving the demand for and supply of policies toward equilibrium.

But, just as there are many obstacles to the smooth matching of demand and supply in real-world economies, so may political systems suffer from a gap between the policies and institutions that people want and those that the political leaders offer them. In some societies, people give up expecting that government will supply them with honest, fair and efficient administration, effective public order, or simple justice in the courts. The few brave souls who try to fight for an improvement may quit in dissatisfaction when they fail to stir up their discouraged fellow citizens to join them in the cause.

Observing the low demand for good government, rulers do not supply it, and instead treat the state as a source of private plunder. Such situations can also become stable and last for long periods of time. In extreme cases, central government disappears altogether and is replaced by warlords or criminal rackets.

Although the influence of political values and beliefs on voting and other kinds of political action is important in guiding political elites about what sorts of promises to make at election time, probably the indirect path by which political culture influences the political system is still more important. Through their daily interactions, members of a society shape one another's values and expectations, including their expectations about government. The patterns of behavior that influence how government operates are established through these channels of association, many of them entirely outside the government sphere. In political cultures in which individuals harbor mistrust for one another, they fear that combining for the common good is a sucker's game: reasoning that others will take advantage of them if they do not look out for themselves, they avoid committing themselves to any collective effort where the cost is known and immediate, and the payoff distant and uncertain— and dependent on the collective effort. Since good government requires collective effort on the part of citizens to keep officials honest, responsive, and effective, societies pervaded by norms of mistrust for those outside the immediate circles of family and friends are likely to be poorly governed. Where people discount the common interest in favor of private benefit, government is likelier to be both more oppressive and more corrupt. Therefore, in studying political culture, we need to look both at people's values and beliefs about government and at their expectations about social life more generally.

RUSSIAN POLITICAL CULTURE IN THE POST-SOVIET PERIOD

A good deal of public opinion research has been devoted to analyzing the dynamics of Russian political culture. On some points, the findings of a large number of recent opinion studies converge. Surveyors have found that there is a high level of support for principles associated with liberal democracy, including support for the values of political liberty and individual rights, rights of opposition and dissent, independence of the communications media, and competitive elections.[14] In a 2005 survey, 66 percent of Russians agreed that "Russia needs democracy," but 45 percent said that the kind of democracy Russia needs is "a completely special kind corresponding to Russian specifics."[15] Surveys in late 2007 found that two-thirds of Russians believed that Russia needs a political opposition.[16] By a similar margin, Russians say that there should be a multi-party system.[17] On the eve of the December 2007 Duma election, almost two-thirds of the public did not believe the elections would be free or fair, yet a majority believed that their lives would improve, thanks to the elections.[18] Asked whether they believed they could have any influence on policy decisions in the country, 83 percent said no.[19] But two-thirds of voters thought that democratic elections are at least somewhat important to the country.

Political scientist James Gibson summed up the findings of a number of studies of Russian public opinion in the 1990s by drawing three conclusions: there is fairly wide support in Russia for democratic institutions and processes so long as people see these as rights for themselves; there is much less support for extending rights to unpopular minorities; and the segments of the population who are the most exposed to the influences of modern civilization (younger people, more educated people, and residents of big cities) are also those most likely to support democratic values.[20]

However, Russians' support for democratic rights is tempered by a pragmatic recognition that freedoms are beneficial only to the extent that they improve living conditions. Russians are more willing to trade off democratic rights for political order and stability than are their counterparts in many other countries. Nearly half said, in a 2005 poll, that things would have been better if they had stayed the way they were before "perestroika."[21] More than citizens in many other countries, Russians tend to rank social stability higher in the hierarchy of values than freedom of the press. Asked which they think is more important, press freedom or social stability, 47 percent of Russians chose social stability (compared to an average of 40 percent in other countries) and 39 percent put press freedom first (as opposed to 56 percent globally).[22] A majority believe that Russia can have both democracy and a strong state.[23] This belief that both democracy and a strong state are valuable and, in principle, compatible—but that if they are not compatible, a strong state is preferable—helps explain the fact that 50 percent of the public regard Stalin as a positive figure in Russian history; only 36 percent assess him negatively.[24]

Democracy is also judged by its ability to benefit individuals materially. Asked in a recent survey what freedoms were most important to them *personally*, over half the respondents named the "freedom to be protected by the state in case of illness, loss of work or poverty" and the "freedom to purchase what I want" as the most important; freedoms such as the right to vote for competing political parties or to participate in political demonstrations were named by only 13 and 10 percent, respectively.[25] While 46 percent named the freedom to choose their job as being important to them personally, only 30 percent named freedom of religion as personally important and 38 percent named the freedom to acquire property such as real estate and a car as important (see Figure 5.1).

This pragmatic view of democracy helps explain why many Russians praise both Putin for strengthening democracy and Medvedev for continuing his policies. Far from seeing "freedom" and "order" as necessary enemies, many recognize that freedom is only possible in an ordered society. Similarly, it is not surprising to find a rather high degree of continuity in the level of support for values concerning the state's responsibility for ensuring society's prosperity and for providing individuals with material security.[26] One cross-national poll found that 40 percent of Russians would favor a planned economy.[27] More than in Western Europe or the United States, Russians continue to believe that the state is

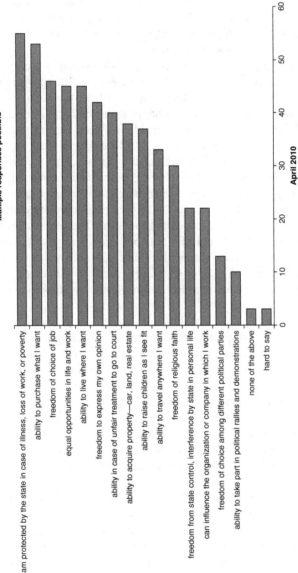

Russia: Which freedoms on this list are especially important to you personally?
Multiple responses possible

am protected by the state in case of illness, loss of work, or poverty
ability to purchase what I want
freedom of choice of job
equal opportunities in life and work
ability to live where I want
freedom to express my own opinion
ability in case of unfair treatment to go to court
ability to acquire property—car, land, real estate
ability to raise children as I see fit
ability to travel anywhere I want
freedom of religious faith
freedom from state control, interference by state in personal life
can influence the organization or company in which I work
freedom of choice among different political parties
ability to take part in political rallies and demonstrations
none of the above
hard to say

April 2010

FIGURE 5.1
Rating Importance of Freedoms.

Respondents were asked to rate a series of freedoms according to their importance to the respondent personally. Respondents could choose multiple freedoms. They are listed here in order of how many individuals cited them as personally important.

Source: Levada Center. http://www.levada.ru/press/2010052618.html (accessed December 1, 2010)

responsible for providing a just moral and social order, with justice being understood as social equality more than as equality before the law.[28] This pattern reflects the impact of traditional conceptions of state and society in Russian political culture. Older patterns of collectivism and statism in Russian political culture remain prevalent. A number of surveys find that there is broad support for the idea that the state has a responsibility for maintaining basic equality, cohesion, and security for members of society, while guaranteeing economic and political freedom to individuals to the extent consistent with society's well-being.

Putin and Medvedev reinforce the idea that democracy is valuable, but that public order is fragile and the outside world threatening: therefore, the state must be strong enough to defend against threats from inside and out. Putin in particular has emphasized that Russia must create its own form of democracy rather than mechanically adopting Western models. This is the implication of the phrase that he and his aides sometimes use to describe their vision for Russia: "sovereign democracy." Kremlin strategist Vladislav Surkov is in charge of formulating and popularizing this concept. Surkov argues that Russian society was not ready for democracy when the Soviet regime fell. As a result, a handful of corrupt oligarchs were able to enrich themselves at the expense of the state. The state must restore its sovereignty at home (where it has to reclaim power from the oligarchs) and abroad (where it has to fight against the dominance of the United States), he argues. Then, Russia can build its own form of democracy—part of the community of nations in the world but not dependent on any of them. Thus, the state must take the lead in reconstructing a strong and self-aware middle class, a competent and honest bureaucracy, an effective military, and a productive flourishing economy. And for this to happen, Surkov argues, the United Russia party should rule the country for 15 or 20 years, much as the PRI ruled Mexico for decades and the LDP ruled Japan.[29]

Surkov's belief that the state needs to create the social foundation for its own future echoes the historical pattern of state-led modernization in Russia. A widespread tacit acceptance of this idea may also help explain why many Russians associate Putin and Medvedev with democracy. Over half of the population (55 percent) thought that following Putin's reelection as president in 2004, the country would develop as a democracy; the comparable figure in 2000 was only 35 percent. Likewise, a survey at the time of the March 2008 elections found that a majority of Russians believed that the newly elected President Medvedev would pursue policies that "strengthened democracy."[30] Clearly, in the minds of many Russians, the strength and competence of the president are associated with political order in the state, and thus with democracy.

SOVIET POLITICAL SOCIALIZATION

In order to understand how contemporary Russian values and beliefs are shaped, let us briefly review the old regime's system of political socialization. The Soviet regime made a remarkable effort to inculcate a faithful commitment to regime doctrine among the population. The system of formal political socialization extended throughout to virtually every setting of education and communication in society—from schools and youth activity, to the mass media, the arts, and popular culture, and to collective activity in the workplace, place of residence, and avocational groups. As much as possible, influences that contradicted Marxist-Leninist doctrine were suppressed, while official rhetoric constantly reaffirmed the doctrine of the leading role of the Communist Party, the superiority of socialism, devotion to the Soviet fatherland, and the correctness of the party's general policies at home and abroad. Because the regime assigned viewed mass communications as crucial agencies of political socialization and mass mobilization, it saturated Soviet society with multiple channels of print and broadcast communications.[31]

The doctrine that guided political socialization—the doctrine called Marxism-Leninism—was based on the ideas of Karl Marx and Friedrich Engels as interpreted and applied by Vladimir Lenin and by the Soviet Communist Party's leaders. Each new group of leaders that came to power reinterpreted Marxist-Leninist ideas to serve their policy interests, often discarding concepts promulgated by the preceding leaders. The doctrine was flexible (although not on core issues—such as the idea that capitalism was incompatible with socialism) and was regularly revised to justify the current preferences and decisions of the party leadership. Ideological doctrine and political authority were always closely linked, because power and ideology legitimated one another. Ideology was a source of strength for the Soviet state so long as there was no serious challenge to it. But the state's reliance on the ideology also produced rigidity and dogmatism. The close control over communications stifled innovation and serious discussion of the trends affecting society. The rulers became blind to the real state of the system and wedded to an increasingly obsolete model of rule.

The party's demand for political loyalty meant that no alternative political ideologies could be propagated publicly. Soviet leaders acknowledged that the two great ideological alternatives in the world, socialism and capitalism, might be able to coexist and even cooperate at the level of diplomacy, trade, and cultural and scientific contacts, but that at the fundamental level of ideas, the two ideologies were ultimately incompatible, and that in the end, socialism would triumph over capitalism because of its intrinsic superiority. Soviet leaders, especially the more conservative of them, were always hostile to any notion that the struggle between the world system of capitalism and the world system of socialism could or should be ended in favor of a convergence of ideologies. Soviet leaders often quoted Lenin to the effect that any weakening of socialist ideology would inevitably lead to a strengthening of bourgeois ideology. The state's propaganda system thus had a twofold purpose: to persuade Soviet people of the correctness of party doctrine and to prevent hostile ideologies from winning adherents.

The elaborate machinery for propagating and defending ideology included the following features:

1. *Family.* The regime sought to persuade parents to raise children steeped in communist morality, firm faith in the party and its leadership, a positive attitude toward labor, confidence in the socialist future, and intolerance toward hostile

worldviews such as religion. But because the family was the least amenable to control by the party authorities and because it tended to protect value systems at odds with the official ideology, the family was the most important agency of transmission of liberal democratic values, national awareness, and religious faith.

2. *School.* Schooling contributed to political socialization both through the curriculum, where lessons in history, social studies, literature, and other subjects were used to reinforce political doctrines, and through a system of youth groups that organized school-time and after-school activities.

3. *Youth groups.* The regime maintained a set of organized youth leagues for different age categories that combined political indoctrination with organized activities such as field trips, hobby clubs, service activities, summer camps, and study circles. The system of organized youth activities was divided into three age-specific groups: Octobrists, for 7–9-year-olds; Pioneers, for 10–14-year-olds, and Komsomol (the acronym for the Communist Youth League) for 15–28-year-olds. Each group combined play, recreation, and basic socialization with political indoctrination appropriate to the age level. Many youths who remained active in Komsomol into their twenties were admitted directly to the Communist Party from Komsomol on the strength of their good records as Komsomol members.

4. *Mass media.* Officially, the broadcast and print media were to serve as instruments of political socialization in addition to their roles as conduits of needed information, exhortation to work hard and well, criticism of problems, and some feedback from the public through letters. They were thus called upon to mold the consciousness of the population while also combating the system's inefficiencies. All mass media organizations were under the ideological authority of the party through its department of propaganda and similar departments charged with ideological oversight in every lower party committee.

5. *Adult political education.* The party oversaw a system of workplace talks and political study groups for various categories of the population—workers, managers, political executives, and so on. Party-run schools gave local party staff members up-to-date instruction on current party doctrine and policy and even gave graduate degrees in such topics as the theory of scientific communism.

Despite its immense scope, the Soviet political socialization machine never possessed, or even claimed, full control over all possible influences on citizens. Even in the darkest years of Stalinist tyranny, a sphere of private life survived, formed through powerful family and friendship links. So too did something of the legacy of Russian and Western humanism through the great classic works of prerevolutionary literature and art, which generations of Soviet schoolchildren were taught to know and respect. Throughout the Soviet Union, intellectuals, artists, and teachers preserved over a hundred different cultural legacies and national languages. The imperative of providing the Soviet regime with a powerful scientific and technological capability required the regime to accept a certain level of openness to outside influences: scientific and cultural exchanges of people and ideas, though closely monitored and directed, nonetheless kept open channels through which the diverse influences of the world society filtered in and out of the Soviet Union. As the regime's own ideological machinery grew increasingly ossified and ineffectual in the 1970s and 1980s, these internal and external cultural influences assumed an ever greater importance in shaping Soviet political culture and public opinion.

A second point to remember is that the discrepancy between the beliefs and values that the regime preached and the actual behavior of officials and citizens tended to weaken the credibility of regime propaganda. Everyone understood that in public, certain ritualistic words needed to be uttered and gestures made—it was appropriate to quote Lenin and the current party General Secretary and to pay tribute to the wisdom of the party. The vote taken at a meeting was to be unanimous; citizens would dutifully go to the polls to cast a ballot or attend a ceremony celebrating some official event. But these forms and observances had little bearing on people's everyday lives. They provided a certain stability and predictability in the forms of social interaction, which might have been comforting to people who had undergone the horrors of revolution, war, and terror in previous decades. These rituals also gave the authorities a convenient way to see whether anyone was bold enough to deviate from the accepted patterns.

But few actually believed in the conventional pieties that were constantly echoed throughout the public domain. Behind the ritual obeisances to Marxist-Leninist dogmas, Soviet political culture was extremely diverse. For example, dreams of national independence stayed alive in a number of national republics. Youth followed the latest trends in Western popular culture. Intellectuals preserved humanistic values, while religious communities maintained their adherence to their traditional faiths. The incompleteness of the political socialization effort, combined with the sharp divergence between what was preached and what was practiced, meant that actual Soviet political culture was being shaped by a variety of home-grown and international influences.

Thus, while the state expended substantial effort in the 1960s and 1970s to inculcate its increasingly hollow Marxist-Leninist doctrine, intellectuals in the arts, the sciences, the professions, and even in policy institutes of the party and state were coming to abandon many tenets of Soviet ideology. Elements of social–democratic and liberal–democratic thought, ethnic nationalism, and secular humanism gained strength. Some thinkers explicitly rejected Soviet doctrine and clandestinely shared with friends their writings or those of other authors whose writings had been suppressed.[32] Others tempered their dissent and stayed inside the system, while discussing their heterodox views in the intimate company of colleagues and friends.

By the time Gorbachev came to power, many intellectuals, including some in senior positions, were privately convinced that the old theory of an international "class struggle" between rival socialist and capitalist camps was leading the Soviet Union into a developmental dead end. The only way for the country to regain its economic and political strength was to adopt universal values of human rights and freedoms and to join in finding solutions to the challenges facing mankind as a whole. This was a shift in the very conception of Russian national identity. Instead of seeing Russia as being defined by an ideological confrontation with the West, or even arguing that Russia must *cooperate* with the West, an influential body of intellectuals came to believe that Russia must become *part* of the liberal international community.[33] The philosophical ground was thus prepared for the leadership of Mikhail Gorbachev, who, remarkably, proved willing to embrace the radical new thinking that transformed Russia and the world.[34]

Why did the party persist in keeping its program of mass political indoctrination going despite the fact that its efforts were so unsuccessful? Various reasons have been proposed. One is inertia. The section of the party concerned with ideological propaganda and control justified its existence by ever greater quantitative displays of success, increasing the number of people reached and activists recruited. Another is fear. The leadership acted on the premise that ideology was a zero-sum game: if socialism weakened, hostile counter-ideologies would take its place. However ineffective the party's ideological effort may have been, it helped to combat the spread of ideas and values opposed to Marxism-Leninism. Ultimately, the reason ideological control over society was important to the party was that it checked the formation of opposition movements. In any event, no Soviet leader until Gorbachev was willing to relinquish the party's monopoly upon ideology. Even Gorbachev, when he first came to office, used the traditional powers of the general secretary to reprogram and redirect party propaganda, rather than to dismantle the system itself.

At first, Gorbachev's attempt to reform the Soviet economy and to introduce an element of freer debate under the slogan of *"glasnost'"* (openness) hardly affected either the forms or the content of "communist upbringing." But gradually, the *glasnost'* campaign gained momentum.[35] Eventually, it produced a significant feedback effect on the party's socialization program itself by revealing to people how widespread was the rejection of Marxism-Leninism. A poll of nearly 2,700 people throughout the Soviet Union in December 1989 found that 48 percent considered themselves religious believers, and only 6 percent thought that Marxism-Leninism had the answers to the country's problems.[36] Another countrywide survey in 1989 found that 61 percent of the respondents supported the principle of legalizing private property and only 11 percent opposed it.[37] Over 1989 and 1990, there were many other indications of the power and speed of popular rejection of communist ideology. Close to 2 million members—one-tenth of the membership—quit the Communist Party before Yeltsin banned it in September 1991. A radical reform wing of the Communist Party itself threatened to break away from the party and form an alternative party.

At the same time, the policy positions taken by Gorbachev and the party leadership grew progressively more unorthodox, until by 1990 almost nothing of the old Marxist-Leninist doctrine remained. The theory of the international class struggle between capitalism and socialism was gone; the party's leading role had been abandoned in favor of support for multiparty competition and parliamentary politics; and Gorbachev called his domestic program a transition to a "social market economy." In a 1990 document adopted as a basis for economic policy, Gorbachev himself declared that "there is no alternative to switching to a market. All world experience has shown the viability and effectiveness of the market economy."[38] This was an admission that Marxism-Leninism had failed. The doctrine had been abandoned in all essential points by the Communist Party, and the party itself had lost its power to rule the country's ideological life. Both among the leadership and among the populace, only a small minority remained willing to defend communist ideology. Both democratic and antidemocratic ideologies arose to take its place.

SUPPORT FOR DEMOCRATIC VALUES

As soon as survey researchers were able to start conducting objective, scientifically structured opinion surveys in Russia, beginning in 1989–1990, they reported surprisingly high levels of support for democratic rights. For instance, in 1990, James Gibson and a team of American and Soviet researchers conducted a survey of 504 residents of the Moscow *oblast*—that is, the region around the city of Moscow—to determine support for important values associated with liberal democracy. They found strong support for liberal values. For instance, on such issues as whether freedom of speech should always be respected, they found that Soviet respondents expressed support for democratic values at about the same levels as did the citizens of West European countries (77 percent in agreement for the Moscow province population, 78 percent for the West Europeans). On a series of items, measured by the percentage agreeing that a particular right ought always to be respected, the views of Soviet citizens resembled those of West Europeans.

In addition, Gibson et al. found that education was positively associated with rights consciousness, much as age (and being female) was negatively correlated with it; these were the only demographic factors significantly predicting the likelihood of support for democratic rights. The more educated a person was, all else being equal, and the younger, the greater the probability that a person would support democratic rights. On the whole, women were slightly less supportive of individual rights than were men, even after controlling for the effects of education and age.

However, Russians quickly lost faith in the ability of the new political institutions of the state to deliver the hoped-for benefits of democracy. Surveys conducted by Russian survey research firms have asked how much confidence Russians place in various institutions. Consistently, Russians report much higher levels of confidence in nonelected institutions such as the Church and the army than in elective institutions. They also report much higher confidence in Putin than in other institutions—and least of all in representative institutions such as parties and parliament.[39] Table 5.1 reports the results of surveys conducted in 2001 and 2007. The results show that while Putin's level of popular trust went up significantly, trust in most other institutions hardly changed at all. The gap between Putin's rating and that of other elective

TABLE 5.1

Trust in Institutions, 2001 and 2007 "To What Degree, in Your View, Does . . . Deserve Trust or Mistrust?"

	Fully Deserves Trust		Does Not Fully Deserve Trust		Completely Does Not Deserve Trust	
	2001	2007	2001	2007	2001	2007
President of Russia	52	64	31	23	7	7
Church, religious organizations	41	42	21	17	12	12
Army	33	31	31	30	18	20
Press, radio, television	28	27	43	35	18	14
State security organs	22	24	32	27	19	18
Government of Russia	21	19	41	40	22	26
Regional bodies of power	21	18	36	35	27	33
Courts	13	17	34	28	26	27
Procuracy	11	16	32	28	30	26
Local bodies of power	20	16	36	31	31	41
State Duma	10	13	41	41	35	33
Federation Council	12	12	36	37	21	22
Police	12	12	36	35	38	38
Trade unions	14	9	25	21	31	28
Political parties	7	7	28	27	36	36

Source: Levada Center.

institutions is striking. Skepticism about most institutions of power is evidently deeply rooted.[40]

For the most part, Russians feel distant from the state. Few have any interest in participating in political life (34 percent definitely would not want to, 28 percent are more inclined not to participate than to participate). Even fewer think they could have any influence on political processes in the country: only three percent say "yes, definitely" they could have an effect, and seven percent say "more yes than no." Eighty-four percent say they could not exercise any influence. And they are skeptical and suspicious of those who do get involved in public affairs. Only 13 percent believe that most public movements and initiatives are organized from the grass roots; over half think that they are mobilized by the government or by opposition forces.[41] This mistrust of the state and of other citizens impedes the leadership's efforts to inspire commitment to its drive to encourage innovation and entrepreneurship. Asked their opinion on President Medvedev's modernization program, 16 percent of respondents said that it is simply another effort to steal resources from the state and 17 percent consider it to be no more than talk. Only 11 percent expect it to result in the formation of a law-governed state with a free market economy.[42]

Overall, Richard Rose and his collaborators conclude that Russia today reflects "resigned acceptance of an incomplete democracy." That is, their approval of the current regime is based on a pragmatic view of how their lives have been affected by the changes of the 1990s and 2000s and what they consider to be possible in the future. They tend to approve of the current political system, and majorities reject alternatives (such as restoring communism, suspending parliament, installing a harsh dictatorship, or army rule). They see little chance of significant change in the regime, and they credit Putin with improving economic conditions in the country. Their support for the current regime is thus contingent on their judgment as to what has been achieved in light of what is possible. They are highly critical of the corruption and ineffectiveness in the state, but believe themselves to have little ability to make a difference—in part because of the widespread mistrust of parties and parliament as institutions affording ordinary people any real influence. Thus, they may regard the current regime as less than ideal, but far better than many of the alternatives that are available.[43]

INFLUENCES ON RUSSIAN POLITICAL CULTURE IN THE SOVIET PERIOD

Both long- and short-term forces act on Russian political culture. Modernization, including the rise in individual educational opportunities, geographical and career mobility, and economic productivity, has had a significant impact on political culture in Russia over time. Indeed, one of the major reasons that the Soviet regime collapsed was its inability to meet the demands posed by a society that was far more educated and informed than had been the case when the Bolsheviks took power in 1917—thanks to the enormous efforts by the Soviet regime to educate and inform the populace. By the end of the 1980s, over 60 percent of the Soviet population over 15 years of age had attained at least a complete secondary education and over 10 percent had higher educational degrees.[44] As many studies showed, education had the effect of reinforcing more critical and more demanding outlooks on the part of Soviet citizens.[45] Education, moreover, is closely linked to support for democratic principles: the more highly educated, the more likely an individual is to support values and principles associated with liberal democracy.[46] Consequently, over time, as Russian society comprised more and more people with secondary and higher educational degrees, levels of support for democratic principles grew.

The opening of career and geographic mobility (and particularly the industrialization drive) by the Soviet regime led rapidly to the urbanization of society. Although old village mentalities and habits retreated only slowly, Russian society became predominantly urban in a relatively short span of time. By the late 1970s, more than two-thirds of the Russian population lived in cities; as of 2008, 73 percent of the population of Russia was classified as urban. But as recently as the late 1950s, the society was half urban, half rural. From 1950 to 1980, the urban population of the Soviet Union increased by nearly 100 million people—most of them immigrants from the countryside. Urbanization was in many respects driven by the imperatives of Soviet industrialization and many Soviet cities are little more than glorified dormitories serving major industrial enterprises. Yet, urban life fostered new forms of interchange among people, new social identities, and, ultimately, new aspirations and expectations of government.

Generational Change

The effects of rising educational levels and of urbanization have been particularly important because each new generation of Soviet and Russian citizens has been more educated and urbanized than that of their parents. Political scientist Donna Bahry has compared surveys taken at different times to see how public opinion has evolved and found that the single largest factor in the gradual change in political culture was the *turnover of political generations.*[47] The generation gap widened substantially by the time of the Brezhnev- and Gorbachev-era studies. Those of the older generation might be critical of some features of the Soviet system, such as collectivized agriculture, but were more inclined to accept some of the political and economic values associated with state socialism. Not so the younger generations, which were significantly more critical of living conditions in the society and sympathetic to the loosening of political and economic controls. Thus, not age (and hence life-cycle effects) but generation, Bahry finds, affects the shift in public opinion: "Those born after World War II, and especially after 1950, had fundamentally different values from their elders."[48]

Generational change continues. Those who are in their twenties today were born in a period of intense turmoil as the post-Soviet regime took shape, opening unprecedented opportunities for individual freedom and prosperity, but at the same time producing widespread disillusionment, even cynicism, with the actual results of the regime transition. As expectations for rapid improvement in social conditions as a result of the regime change failed to materialize, nationalism and xenophobia found a sympathetic following among many youth who embraced a simple division of the world into "us" and "them."[49] Many more simply reject all ideologies and focus instead on getting rich or getting by. Those who are in their twenties today have little personal memory of the Soviet period, but witnessed the explosive growth in criminality, corruption, inequality, and materialism that followed its breakdown. They also benefitted from the new opportunities to share in the tastes and aspirations of the global youth culture, the spread of digital communication technologies, and the new freedom to enter the worlds of commerce and finance.

In the mid-2000s, the authorities grew anxious that an uncontrollable youth movement might be organized against the authorities, as occurred in Serbia, Georgia, and Ukraine's "colored revolutions" (see Close-up 9.1).

In each of these episodes, mass protests—led by youth groups—forced out corrupt, authoritarian leaders who had attempted to rig the results of elections. To prevent a "colored revolution" from breaking out in Russia, the Kremlin created pro-regime youth groups (recruiting members, for example, from soccer fan clubs) prepared for street fights against antiregime protesters. These pro-regime groups used belligerent anti-Western nationalist rhetoric and professed loyalty to Putin. The largest of these groups, called "Ours" (*Nashi*), held annual summer camps at Lake Seliger in central Russia for thousands of followers, where they practiced military-style drills and held seminars on the current political situation. At the first three of these (held in 2005, 2006, and 2007), the message was militant and xenophobic. Instructors warned that the West was trying to subvert Russia from outside, while oligarchs, liberals, and other "fascist" elements were seeking to undermine it from within, so that patriotic youth must be ready to defend the country, by force if necessary, against both external and internal enemies.[50]

After the December 2007 Duma election, however, the Kremlin evidently decided that the threat of a revolution had passed and it began to withdraw support from Nashi (three of whose leaders were elected to the Duma). Instead, the authorities worked to depoliticize and downsize the youth movement they had conjured up. The 2008 and 2009 Lake Seliger summer camps were devoted to promoting innovation and entrepreneurship. The organizers of the 2010 camp attempted to internationalize the program by recruiting a thousand foreign students to join their Russians peers for "an intensive educational forum consisting of six modules": international politics, business and innovation, the media, civil society, art and design, and sustainable development.[51] Gone are the boot camp-style physical training and the anti-Western message. Nashi itself has grown less active. The ease with which the Kremlin can create and then dispose of such youth movements is a telling indication of how shallow their roots are.

Political Socialization in Contemporary Russia

Whereas the Soviet regime devoted enormous effort to political indoctrination and propaganda, controlling the content of school curricula, the mass media, popular culture, political education, and nearly every other channel by which values and attitudes were formed, today both the forms and content of political socialization have changed substantially. Gone is the comprehensive control over all forms of socialization by the ruling party. Citizens are exposed to a much broader array of values and beliefs. The regime uses the media and the education system to promote a more minimal set of messages revolving around patriotism, national identification, and loyalty to the regime. In place of the old Soviet doctrine of the class struggle and the international solidarity of the working class, today school textbooks emphasize love for the Russian national heritage and the importance of state sovereignty. Historical figures who in the communist era were honored as heroes of the struggle of ordinary people against feudal or capitalist masters are now held up as great representatives of

Russia's national culture.[52] Patriotic education aims to build loyalty to Russia as a state as well as to Russia as a nation. This is logical, in view of Russia's effort to create a sense of national community within the new post-Soviet state boundaries.

But because building patriotic loyalty to the state means inculcating identification with aspects of both the pre-Soviet and the Soviet regimes, as well as acceptance of the transition to a post-Soviet, ostensibly democratic, political order, the message conveyed by Russian history textbooks can be somewhat self-contradictory. Past regimes and periods of history tend to be evaluated according to two general criteria—whether they contributed toward the strengthening of the state and whether they built up the economy. The Yeltsin years, for instance, are officially praised for breaking down the communist regime and laying the foundations of a market economy, but are condemned for bringing about a weakening of state power. The Brezhnev regime is criticized for allowing stagnation both in the state and in the economy.[53]

The Stalin period is the most controversial and sensitive topic for political education. Stalin is given credit for increasing state power and capacity and for defending the state in World War II. At the same time, the current regime officially condemns the enormous scale of terror and repression under Stalin. At a religious ceremony in October 2007 remembering Stalin's victims, then president Putin called the terror "a particular tragedy for our nation."[54] Moreover, after Alexander Solzhenitsyn died, Putin instructed the Ministry of Education to incorporate Solzhenitsyn's works into both history and literature courses in schools. The Ministry of Education duly prepared instructions to teachers: "Paying attention to this work permits us to raise the theme of the tragic fate of an individual in a totalitarian state and the responsibility of a people and its leaders for the present and future of the country," according to the ministry's memorandum.[55] But one member of the Federal Expert Council on Education commented that as a result of adding Solzhenitsyn to the curriculum, "schoolchildren might develop schizophrenia: on the one hand they are reading *Archipelago Gulag* and on the other in their history class they are telling them that Stalin was an effective manager. And since as a writer Solzhenitsyn is substantially stronger than the author of the history textbook, probably it is his assessment of Stalin's repressions that will linger in the minds of the pupils."[56]

Contemporary political culture also reflects a strong undercurrent of desire for some sort of restored union among at least some of the former Soviet republics. Russian television broadcasts pay a considerable amount of attention to activities in the "near abroad," as Russians term the other former Soviet republics. Russians continue to feel tied to the other republics by decades of shared social, economic, cultural, and political experience. Asked in a 2008 survey whether Russia's future lies with the countries of Western Europe or with the countries of the Commonwealth of Independent States (CIS), two-thirds of Russians responded that it lay with the CIS.

Only one-third were willing to say that it lay more with Western Europe.[57] A 2007 survey found that (despite what Presidents Putin and Medvedev have declared) 71 percent of Russians do not consider themselves Europeans.[58]

Seeking to reinforce their political legitimacy as well as to replace communist doctrine with a solid foundation of ethics, the authorities treat the Russian Orthodox Church as an ally in political socialization. The Church helps instill patriotic loyalty, national pride, and principles of ethical behavior in society. Organizationally, the Church benefits from its ties to the state as it seeks to expand its reach, to protect its traditional status as Russia's state church, and to block other Christian denominations from proselytizing in Russia. There has been an ongoing debate over whether to make Russian Orthodoxy the foundation for ethics instruction in the schools. As of the spring of 2010, for example, a new course was introduced into the curriculum of 19 regions. All fourth- and fifth-graders must take a course on "the fundamentals of religious culture and ethics," but their families may choose among six different versions of the course, depending on which textbook is used: Orthodox Christian, Muslim, Buddhist, or Jewish, or one on world religions, or one on secular ethics. According to the Ministry of Education, by far the largest number of requests were submitted for the secular ethics book and that only 20 percent of families requested the Orthodox Christian version. The Orthodox Church, however, disputes the government's figures.[59] Many intellectuals fear that the Church's rising influence in educational and social policy threatens the constitutional principle of the separation of church and state. But many people, whether religious or not, deplore the decay of morals in society and the relentless rise of consumerism and materialism as Russia opens itself to the global capitalist system. They see the Church, with its long history of partnership with the state, as a force for restoring traditional moral values in society.

The regime has imposed far-reaching political controls over the mass media, not to impose a comprehensive political ideology on society but to prevent opposition movements from arising.[60] Media control is stratified: central television programs present a view of the world that is faithful to the Kremlin's positions, while the main business-oriented print media, which reach a much smaller audience, present a fairly wide spectrum of information and opinion. Throughout the media realm, regime controls take three main forms. First, journalists and editors are subject to a variety of carrots and sticks. Friendly writers are given privileged access to the authorities, while the independent-minded journalists and editors who defy the authorities with their investigative reports are subject to harassment and intimidation.[61]

Second, the regime works through indirect control, in effect delegating responsibility for political control to major companies that own media properties. Most private media outlets are owned by business firms that maintain close relations with the regime. For example, the natural gas giant Gazprom owns many media properties. The regime lets the owners of the companies take the lead in deciding how much editorial independence their media organizations may have. The private oil company Lukoil is one of several commercial owners of a media organization called the Russian News Service, which supplies news content to a network of radio stations around the country. In April 2007, the owners brought in new managers, who laid down the new line for journalists. Henceforth, they said, at least 50 percent of the content of broadcasts had to be "positive." This meant accentuating reports of favorable developments in the country and downplaying stories about violence, poverty, bad weather, and other depressing topics. Moreover, the new managers demanded that the news reports treat the United States as an enemy and that there be no coverage of opposition leaders.[62] Several journalists working for the service resigned in protest.

Finally, the Kremlin provides direct editorial instruction to editors. Reportedly, Vladislav Surkov, the presidential advisor in charge of political strategy, meets weekly with the editors of the major media organizations to provide guidance. For example, according to some reports, the Kremlin gave broadcasters a list of opposition leaders who are not to be given any media coverage.[63] The former world chess champion Garry Kasparov, who has become an outspoken critic of the regime, is on such a "stop list." Likewise, media are advised how to cover certain events. During the worldwide financial crisis in the fall of 2008, when Russian financial markets saw massive panic selling so that trading had to be stopped repeatedly, the major television evening news broadcasts confined themselves to reporting that Russia had experienced some "echoes of the world crisis" and did not report the actual situation on the Russian markets.[64] Only later did the media begin to report on the full extent of the crisis.

Therefore, although there is no formal censorship agency as there was in Soviet times, most journalists are careful to avoid offending the authorities. Moreover, similar methods are used by regional authorities to keep the media in their regions in line. Regional media are even more vulnerable to pressure from the regional political authorities than the central media are to the federal-level influence.[65]

At the same time, the Internet is largely free of direct political control. Periodically the authorities warn Internet service providers and Web site hosts that those who use the Internet improperly—for instance, to spread "extremist materials"—are subject to prosecution. There have been regular efforts by the government and the Duma to draft legislation to regulate the Internet. The proposed legislation would require providers to turn over information to law enforcement bodies about their users upon request.[66]

Internet use is growing, although it is well behind the levels of Western Europe or North America. Around a third of Russians use the Internet, with much higher use in the large cities and among younger age groups.[67] There are some 5 million blogs, of which about 11,000 are active in commenting on public affairs; sometimes they spur active public mobilization around specific events.[68] Most Russians rely on central television channels for news, however, and the great majority of those who do go online do so for social networking purposes.[69] The relative freedom enjoyed by Internet-based news organizations allows a small part of the population to live in an environment where relatively bias-free information is available. Meantime, the main conduits of news and opinion that reach mass audiences are under the control of the authorities and their allies in big business.

CULTURAL DIVERSITY WITHIN RUSSIA

The opening of political activity in the late 1980s and early 1990s stimulated a surge of ethnic-national consciousness among ethnic minorities living in Russia's national republics and autonomous territories. Cultural centers, language revival movements, and political associations sprang up in many regions of Russia, including Tatarstan, Bashkortostan, Chechnia, Udmurtia, Tuva, and elsewhere.[70] For the most part—with Chechnia serving as a tragic but isolated example—post-Soviet Russia has succeeded in accommodating the demands of ethnic-national groups for cultural expression within a framework of civic nationalism and Russia-centered patriotism. Although there are some ultranationalist Russian politicians who call for "Russia for the Russians," most people recognize that Russia historically has been and will continue to be a multinational state, consisting of peoples who historically have coexisted for hundreds of years. Russia's ethnic diversity is, in fact, a source of pride for many Russians.

As noted in Chapter 3, Russia inherited the institutional subdivisions of the Soviet regime, many of which assigned specific territorial units to individual ethnic nationalities. Those that were larger in size were granted the status of a republic; some less populous groups were given an autonomous district. Most ethnic nationalities lack a specific territorial unit of their own, but are officially recognized in census and other civil registries. Official policy is to protect the rights of cultural autonomy of ethnic minorities. The political challenge that might otherwise be posed by dividing the country into territorial units designated for particular ethnic nationalities is mitigated by the fact that ethnic Russians constitute 80 percent of the total population of the country and by the fact that in most republics and districts, ethnic Russians are the largest ethnic group. Where they are not the majority or plurality, they are usually a sizable minority.

Russia has over 100 recognized ethnic nationalities, some of them numbering no more than a few thousand people. They represent several different ethnic-language groups. These include the Finno-Ugric groups (such as the Komi, Udmurt, Mari, and Mordvin), who share a common ethnic and cultural heritage with Finns, Estonians, and Hungarians; Turkic groups such as the Tatar, Yakut, Bashkir, and Chuvash peoples; and Caucasian (i.e., from the Caucasus) groups, such as the Chechen, Ingush, Cherkess, and many others residing in the North Caucasus region. In addition, there are a number of Siberian groups, including a few peoples indigenous to the Far North and Far East, as well as nationalities living farther south in Siberia.

Culturally, the non-Russian nationalities are enormously diverse. For many, religion is a defining feature of their ethnic-national identity. Many groups are Muslim by religious heritage; among some of these, particularly the peoples of the North Caucasus, radical forms of Islam have become potent. The Muslims living farther north along the Volga (such as the Tatars and the Bashkir) tend not to be militant in their religious practice, although, as with many other nationalities, the revival of religion tends to reinforce their sense of national distinctiveness. A number of nationalities practice forms of shamanism[71] (especially among Siberian groups), others have converted to Russian Orthodoxy, and in two cases (the Kalmyk and the Buryat), Buddhism continues to be practiced. The Jews are regarded as a distinct ethnic group, in fact one of the four traditional religions of Russia. The close link between religion and nationality helps explain why Russia's law on religion gives blanket recognition to four "traditional" religions that have been practiced on Russian soil since well before Soviet times: Russian Orthodox Christianity; Islam; Buddhism; and Judaism. In the next chapter, we will discuss this law and the concept underlying it in more detail.

An ethnic revival fueled separatist movements in the early 1990s, but for the most part, these have subsided. In the case of Tatarstan, for example, Tatar (who constitute Russia's largest ethnic minority, with 5.5 million or 3.7 percent of the population) nationalist groups demanded sovereignty and even independence in the early 1990s. Tatars trace their ancestry to Genghis Khan, who at one time had conquered much of Russia. The national movement demanded an end to Russification and called for switching from the Cyrillic alphabet to Latin. In 1994, Tatarstan's long time president, Mintimir Shaimiev, signed a treaty with President Yeltsin that the Tatarstan authorities interpreted as an act of mutual recognition of sovereignty that acknowledged Tatarstan's "special relationship" with the federal government. The treaty was renewed in 1999 and again in 2005 despite Putin's hostility to such bilateral agreements with individual subjects of the federation. Putin also reappointed President Shaimiev to another term as president in 2005. Thus, even Putin, who reversed the decentralizing trends of the 1990s in almost every area, deemed it wise to keep Shaimiev in power in view of Shaimiev's singular skill at balancing Moscow's demand for loyalty against local demands for the assertion of Tatar ethnic nationalism. In 2010, as his fourth term ended, Shaimiev announced that he did not want to be appointed to another term, and stepped down after more than 20 years running the republic. His successor as president, the republic's prime minister, kept Shaimiev on as a special advisor and gave him an office in the Kremlin of the republic.

Tatarstan's ethnic revival has been reinforced by the resurgence of Islam in the republic. One of Shaimiev's major public acts was to rebuild the great mosque in the Kremlin of the capital city of Tatarstan, Kazan', which is the largest mosque in Russia. At its opening in 2005, Shaimiev observed that the fact that the mosque and the Orthodox Cathedral stood side by side at the symbolic center of the city symbolized the multiethnic character of the republic. According to local officials, Shaimiev took pains to attend services at both the mosque and the cathedral. Shaimiev tolerated (and in fact encouraged) a certain level of ethnic-national political consciousness and Muslim religious activity, while keeping both well within safely defined boundaries. In turn, he was able to use the existence of ethnic-national and Islamic religious movements in the republic as implicit threats to Moscow that too much centralization could trigger a nationalist or religious backlash movement that could spiral out of control.

Tatarstan is characteristic of a number of ethnic republics in Russia in that demands for cultural autonomy and a greater share of economic sovereignty have been granted by the federal government in return for the preservation of Russia as a multicultural federal state. Even under Putin, the center has shown a striking degree of flexibility, in fact, in handling the political implications of Russia's ethnic-cultural diversity. In all the republics except for Chechnia, both under Yeltsin and Putin, the central government has been able to find the necessary mix of concessions to demands for cultural and political autonomy and threats sufficient to satisfy all but the most irreconcilable separatists. But under Putin and Medvedev, there has been much less room for maneuver for ethnic nationalists than there was under Yeltsin.[72]

Contemporary Russian political culture has been influenced both by slow-acting, long-term forces, including the impact of modernization, and by more immediate events such as the abrupt change in regime that occurred at the beginning of the 1990s. Through modernization, urbanization, and the turnover of generations, the Russian people gradually came to aspire to a freer and more prosperous standard of living than they had enjoyed under communism. But the disappointments caused by the breakdown of the old Soviet social safety net and the chaotic processes of marketization and privatization that led to extremes of wealth and poverty led many to accept a heavier hand of state control as a necessary condition for order. Vladimir Putin's highly personalized and centralized regime, coupled with steady economic growth since 1999, restored confidence in the regime after a decade of sharp disillusionment with the results of the regime change. But while Russians tend to approve of Putin and Medvedev as leaders who are preserving order and predictability in society, they remain mistrustful of other political institutions and doubtful of their own capacity to influence them.

The leadership has not attempted to impose a comprehensive new ideological doctrine on society, concentrating instead on promoting basic values of patriotic loyalty and national pride. Putin and Medvedev have emphasized, however, that Russia must modernize its economic and social institutions and overcome its dependence on the export of raw materials if it is to compete successfully in the global economy. The modernization agenda clashes, however, with the conservatism of its political institutions, the inertia of the bureaucracy, and the skepticism of the populace about change. The demobilization of society and the weakness of civic institutions encourage people to prefer leaders who can check the power of rapacious bureaucrats and businessmen, but make it difficult for leaders to build support for new initiatives that require long time horizons and upset entrenched interests. Preserving political control in a country as large and diverse as Russia poses a huge challenge for state leaders and reinforces historical patterns of authoritarian rule and reliance on the state to provide the impetus for modernizing change. In this political culture, individuals regard the value of democratic rights pragmatically, welcoming freedoms when they expand prosperity and security but treating them as secondary to more basic values of order and stability.

NOTES

1. Speaking to a group of university professors who were complaining about the widespread immorality portrayed in the media, Prime Minister Putin said that the state can no longer issue commands to the media as it did in the Soviet era. Instead, he said that patriotism—"in the good sense of the word"—should be the universal principle for national unity, much as Russian Orthodoxy was in the tsarist era and communism in the Soviet time. "People," he commented, "used to underestimate it [patriotism], did not understand that by itself it is de-ideologized and has a particular value. It must be ably and intelligently inculcated into the consciousness of society." Alexandra Samarina, "Goszakaz na patriotov," *Nezavisimaia gazeta*, October 8, 2008.

2. There is a vast literature on the history of Russian national identity. For a recent contribution, see Marlene Laruelle, *In the Name of the Nation: Nationalism and Politics in Contemporary Russia* (New York: Palgrave Macmillan, 2009). One strain of thought about Russian national identity emphasizes Russia's geographic location at the intersection of Europe and Asia, where European and Asian cultures and peoples have mingled. They argue that Russia's "Eurasian" character affects its political and social institutions. Mark Bassin, "Russia Between Europe and Asia: The Ideological Construction of Geographical Space," *Slavic Review* 50:1 (1991): 1–17; Marlene Laruelle, *Russian Eurasianism: An Ideology of Empire* (Washington, DC; Baltimore, MD: Woodrow Wilson Center; Johns Hopkins University Press, 2008).

3. Allen C. Lynch, *How Russia Is Not Ruled: Reflections on Russian Political Development* (Cambridge: Cambridge University Press, 2005).

4. An insightful book on this subject is Fiona Hill and Clifford Gaddy, *The Siberian Curse: How Communist Planners Left Russia Out in the Cold* (Washington, DC: Brookings Institution Press, 2003). They emphasize the factor of Russia's cold climate in particular, but note that the general problem of finding a suitable model of economic development in a country as large as Russia is a multidimensional challenge.

5. Lynch, *How Russia Is Not Ruled*, pp. 236–238.

6. For example, Nicolai N. Petro, *Crafting Democracy: How Novgorod Has Coped with Rapid Social Change* (Ithaca, NY: Cornell University Press, 2004); Nikolas K. Gvosdev, "'Managed Pluralism' and Civil Religion in Post-Soviet Russia," in Christopher Marsh and Nikolas K. Gvosdev, eds., *Civil Society and the Search for Justice in Russia* (Lanham, MD: Lexington Books, 2002), pp. 75–88.

7. James W. Warhola, "Revisiting the Russian 'Constrained Autocracy': 'Absolutism' and Natural Rights Theories in Russia and the West," in Christopher Marsh and

Nikolas K. Gvosdev, eds., *Civil Society and the Search for Justice in Russia* (Lanham, MD: Lexington Books, 2002), pp. 19–40.

8. *Nezavisimaia gazeta*, November 27, 2008.

9. George Vernadsky, *A History of Russia* (New Haven, CT: Yale University Press, 1961), p. 244.

10. On the campaign against women's veiling in Central Asia, see Douglas Northrop, *Veiled Emprire: Gender and Power in Stalinist Central Asia* (Ithaca, NY: Cornell University Press, 2003).

11. Gabriel A. Almond and Sidney Verba, *The Civic Culture: Political Attitudes and Democracy in Five Nations* (Boston: Little-Brown, 1965).

12. Gabriel A. Almond and Sidney Verba, eds., *The Civic Culture Revisited* (Boston: Little-Brown, 1980); Stephen White, *Political Culture and Soviet Politics* (London: Macmillan, 1979); Frederic J. Fleron, Jr., "Post-Soviet Political Culture in Russia: An Assessment of Recent Empirical Investigations," *Europe–Asia Studies* 48:2 (1996): 225–260; Harry Eckstein, Frederic J. Fleron, Erik P. Hoffmann, and William M. Reisinger, eds., *Can Democracy Take Root in Post-Soviet Russia? Explorations in State–Society Relations* (Lanham, MD: Rowman & Littlefield, 1998); James Alexander, *Political Culture in Post-Communist Russia* (New York: Macmillan, 2000).

13. Ronald Inglehart, *Culture Shift in Advanced Industrial Society* (Princeton: Princeton University Press, 1990), p. 55.

14. James L. Gibson and Raymond M. Duch, "Emerging Democratic Values in Soviet Political Culture," in Arthur H. Miller, William M. Reisinger, and Vicki L. Hesli, eds., *Public Opinion and Regime Change* (Boulder, CO: Westview, 1993), pp. 69–94; William M. Reisinger, Arthur H. Miller, and Vicki L. Hesli, "Political Values in Russia, Ukraine and Lithuania: Sources and Implications for Democracy," *British Journal of Political Science* 24 (1994): 183–223; and Jeffrey W. Hahn, "Continuity and Change in Russian Political Culture," *British Journal of Political Science* 21:4 (1991): 393–421.

15. From a survey conducted by the Levada Center in June 2005 and posted to its Web site: http://www.levada.ru/press/2005070410.html.
The Levada Center is a widely respected independent public opinion survey firm.

16. From a Levada Center survey reported by *RFE/RL Newsline*, November 9, 2007.

17. Ibid., November 13, 2007.

18. Brian Whitmore, "RFE/RL Poll Finds Russians Skeptical About Elections, Hopeful for Future," *RFE/RL Newsline*, November 16, 2007.

19. L. D. Gudkov, B. V. Dubin, and Yu. A. Levada, *Problema <<elity>> v segodniashnei Rossii: Razmyshleniia nad rezul'tatami sotsiologicheskogo issledovaniia* (Moscow: Fond Liberal'naia missiia, 2007), p. 136.

20. James L. Gibson, "The Resilience of Support for Democratic Institutions and Processes in the Nascent Russian and Ukrainian Democracies," in Vladimir Tismaneanu, ed., *Political Culture and Civil Society in Russia and the New States of Eurasia* (Armonk, NY: M. E. Sharpe, 1995), p. 57.

21. From a survey conducted by the Levada Center, http://www.levada.ru/press/2005031100.html.

22. From a survey conducted in the United States, United Kingdom, Germany, Russia, India, Kenya, Brazil, Venezuela, Egypt, Mexico, Nigeria, Singapore, the United Arab Emirates, and South Africa by the organization Globescan, sponsored by the British Broadcasting Corporation. Reported by Polit.ru, December 10, 2007.

23. Timothy J. Colton and Michael McFaul, *Popular Choice and Managed Democracy: The Russian Elections of 1999 and 2000* (Washington, DC: Brookings Institution, 2003), p. 222.

24. From a survey in 2005 by the All-Russia Center for the Study of Public Opinion (VTsIOM) and reported by *RFE/RL Newsline*, March 7, 2005. The highest percentage of positive assessments of Stalin was found among the oldest and youngest generations.

25. Levada. ru, May 26, 2010, http://www.levada.ru/press/2010052618.html, accessed May 30, 2010.

26. James R. Millar and Sharon L. Wolchik, "Introduction: The Social Legacies and the Aftermath of Communism," in James R. Millar and Sharon L. Wolchik, eds., *The Social Legacy of Communism* (Washington, DC and Cambridge: Woodrow Wilson Press and Cambridge University Press, 1994), p. 16.

27. From a survey sponsored by the European Bank for Reconstruction and Development, as reported by *RFE/RL Newsline*, November 9, 2007.

28. Marcia A. Weigle, *Russia's Liberal Project: State–Society Relations in the Transition from Communism* (University Park, PA: Pennsylvania State University Press, 2000), pp. 432–441.

29. See the speech Surkov gave to a group of United Russia party activists on February 22, 2006. The text (in Russian) may be found on the United Russia Web site at http://www.edinros.ru/news.html?id=111148, accessed March 13, 2006. For an overview of Surkov's political views, influence, and career, see Gregory L. White and Alan Cullison, "Putin's Pitchman: Inside Kremlin as it Tightens Its Grip: Ex-Aide to Tycoons; Domestic Adviser Surkov Hails Concentration of Power as 'Sovereign Democracy'; 'There'll Be No Uprisings Here,'" *Wall Street Journal*, December 19, 2006.

30. From a survey conducted by a state-controlled survey organization, All-Russia Center for the Study of Public Opinion (VTsIOM), as reported by *RFE/RL Newsline*, March 14, 2008.

31. On the impact of television in Soviet society, see Ellen Mickiewicz, *Split Signals: Television and Politics in the Soviet Union* (New York and Oxford: Oxford University Press, 1988); on propaganda and mass communications more generally, see Stephen White, *Political Culture and Soviet Politics* (London: Macmillan, 1979); and Thomas F. Remington, *The Truth of Authority: Ideology and Communication in the Soviet Union* (Pittsburgh: University of Pittsburgh Press, 1988).

32. Comprehensive studies of Soviet dissent include Ludmilla Alexeeyeva, *Soviet Dissent: Contemporary Movements for National, Religious, and Human Rights* (Middletown, CT: Wesleyan University Press, 1987); Frederick C. Barghoorn, *Detente and the Democratic Movement in the USSR* (New York: Free Press, 1976).

33. Robert D. English, *Russia and the Idea of the West: Gorbachev, Intellectuals, and the End of the Cold War* (New York: Columbia University Press, 2000), pp. 5–8.

34. Mikhail Gorbachev himself portrayed his reform program as applying to not merely Russia but also as a doctrine for the whole world, as the title of the book he published in 1987 indicates: *Perestroika: New Thinking for Our Country and the World* (New York: Harper & Row, 1987).

35. Thomas Remington, "A Socialist Pluralism of Opinions: Glasnost' and Policy-Making Under Gorbachev," *Russian Review* 48 (1989): 271–304.

36. Yu. Levada et al., "Homo Sovieticus: A Rough Sketch," *Moscow News* 11 (1990): 11.

37. Tatiana Zaslavskaia, "Vesti dialog s liud'mi," *Narodnyi deputat* 2 (1990): 25–27. Zaslavskaia was a distinguished sociologist who was one of the most important

theorists of reform in the pre-Gorbachev and early Gorbachev periods. A member of the Academy of Sciences and a deputy to the Congress of People's Deputies, she founded a new institute to conduct public opinion surveys throughout the Soviet Union.

38. "Main Directions for the Stabilization of the National Economy and the Transition to a Market Economy," as published in the British Broadcasting System Summary of World Broadcasts (BBC SWB), SU/0900, 20 October 1990, p. C/1. This policy statement was adopted as the basis of national economic policy by the USSR Supreme Soviet on October 19, 1990. It is important mainly as a statement of goals and principles rather than as a working program of action.

39. Survey conducted by the Levada Center, released April 9, 2007. Based on a survey of 2,107 adults, March 1–18, 2007. Taken from Web site: http://www.levada.ru/press/2007040901.html.

40. Levada Center, http://www.levada.ru/press/2007040901.html, released April 9, 2007. Based on survey of nationally representative sample of 2107 adults, conducted March 1–18, 2007.

41. From a survey by the Levada Center, reported in Polit.ru, June 25, 2010.

42. Vera Kholmogorova, "Reformy bez podderzhki," *Vedomosti*, March 5, 2010.

43. Richard Rose, William Mishler, and Neil Munro, *Russia Transformed: Developing Popular Support for a New Regime* (Cambridge: Cambridge University Press, 2006); Richard Rose and Neil Munro, *Elections without Order: Russia's Challenge to Vladimir Putin* (Cambridge: Cambridge University Press, 2002); Richard Rose, Neil Munro, and William Mishler, "Resigned Acceptance of an Incomplete Democracy: Russia's Political Equilibrium," *Post-Soviet Affairs* 20:3 (2004): 195–218.

44. In the United States, according to the U.S. Census Bureau, as of 2005, 85 percent of Americans 25 years old and older had completed high school and 28 percent had completed college. See http://www.census.gov/Press-Release/www/releases/archives/education/007660.html, accessed January 28, 2007.

45. Brian Silver, "Political Beliefs of the Soviet Citizen," in James R. Millar, ed., *Politics, Work, and Daily Life in the USSR* (Cambridge: Cambridge University Press, 1987), p. 127.

46. Gibson and Duch, "Emerging Democratic Values," p. 86; William M. Reisinger, Arthur H. Miller, Vicki L. Hesli, and Kristen Hill Maher, "Political Values in Russia, Ukraine and Lithuania: Sources and Implications for Democracy," *British Journal of Political Science* 24 (1994): 216–218; Jeffrey W. Hahn, "Continuity and Change in Russian Political Culture," in Frederic J. Fleron, Jr., and Erik P. Hoffmann, eds. , *Post-Communist Studies and Political Science: Methodology and Empirical Theory in Sovietology* (Boulder: Westview Press, 1993), pp. 319–322.

47. Bahry, "Society Transformed?" Bahry reanalyzes data from three surveys taken at different times: the Harvard Project of refugees to Europe after World War II, which reflects attitudes shaped in the 1920s, 1930s, and early 1940s; the SIP data from the emigre survey in the United States in the late 1970s; and a Times-Mirror survey conducted in 1991. This method allows her to compare public opinion on comparable issues for the *same* generations across different surveys taken at different times and to track change and continuity in opinion *across* generations. She finds that both the earlier and later studies found an essential consistency in the values of the prewar generations, even though members of those generations had grown much older by the 1970s and 1980s.

48. Bahry, p. 544.
49. The *Washington Post* journalists Peter Baker and Susan Glasser present a vivid portrait of these groups in their book, *Kremlin Rising: Vladimir Putin's Russia and the End of Revolution* (New York: Scribner, 2005), Chapter 3, "Time of the Patriots."
50. Claire Bigg, "Here Comes the Sun for Putin's Patriotic youth," *RFE/RL Russian Political Weekly*, July 26, 2005.
51. From the text of the letter faxed to foreign educational institutions by Vassili Yakemenko, head of the Russian Agency for Youth Affairs, on March 22, 2010. Many of the foreign students who responded to the invitation were unable to attend because they were unable to obtain visas in time. See Yulia Taranova, "Russian Bureaucracy Stymies Pro-Kremlin Youth Retreat," *New York Times*, July 5, 2010.
52. Elena Lisovskaya and Vyacheslav Karpov, "New Ideologies in Postcommunist Russian Textbooks," *Comparative Education Review* 43:4 (1999): 522–532.
53. A recent textbook given high-profile Kremlin endorsement for use in high school history classes lays out the current ideological positions of the authorities. It praises Gorbachev's leadership for introducing democratic freedoms and market reforms, but criticizes him for allowing the Soviet state to collapse. Likewise, it praises Yeltsin for seeking to make the break from communism irreversible, but criticizes him for allowing the integrity of the state to weaken. The 2000s is called the era of "sovereign democracy," and praised for rebuilding state authority and standing up for Russia abroad while also consolidating the market economy and Russia's integration into the international economy. The general theme of the book is that in view of Russia's harsh climate, enormous territorial expanse, and thousand-year old traditions of state-centered development, the country "needs a consolidating force" that can only come in the form of a centralized state.

   See A. V. Filippov, *Noveishaia istoriia Rossii, 1945–2006 gg.: Kniga dlia uchitelia* (Moscow: Prosveshchenie, 2007).
54. RFE/RL Newsline, October 31, 2007.
55. Polit.ru, September 10, 2008.
56. Ul'iana Makhkamova, "Shkol'naia shizofreniia," *Nezavisimaia gazeta*, September 8, 2008.
57. Richard Rose, *Understanding Post-Communist Transformation: A Bottom-Up Approach* (Routledge, 2009), pp. 187. The breakdown of responses was as follows: Twenty percent said "definitely with the CIS," 46 percent said "more the CIS than Western Europe," 6 percent said "definitely with Western Europe," and 28 percent said "more with Western Europe than the CIS." The survey was taken in 2008 by the Levada Center.
58. Levada Center, February 15, 2007. http://www.levada.ru/press/2007021501.html.
59. "Shkol'niki Rossii predpochli izuchat' svetskuiu etiku," *Vedomosti*, February 24, 2010; Polit.ru, March 26, 2010.
60. Sarah Oates, "Television, Voters, and The Development of the 'Broadcast Party'," in Vicki L. Hesli and William M. Reisinger, eds., *The 1999–2000 Elections in Russia: Their Impact and Legacy* (Cambridge: Cambridge University Press, 2003), pp. 29–50; Oates, "Framing Fear: Findings from a Study of Election News and Terrorist Threat in Russia," *Europe–Asia Studies* 58:2 (2006): 281–290; Oates, "Media, Civil Society, and The Failure of the Fourth Estate in Russia," in Alfred B. Evans, Jr., Laura A. Henry, and Lisa McIntosh Sundstrom, eds., *Russian Civil Society: A Critical Assessment* (Armonk, NY: M. E. Sharpe, 2006), pp. 57–72.

For an examination of how television viewers interpret the news stories they watch, see Ellen Mickiewicz, *Television, Power, and the Public in Russia* (Cambridge: Cambridge University Press, 2008).

61. A number of journalists have been killed. For example, the journalist Anna Politkovskaya, who wrote for one of the last-remaining independent-minded national newspapers, was murdered at her apartment building in Moscow on October 7, 2006. She had received numerous death threats as a result of her reports of massive human rights abuses committed by federal and regional forces in Chechnia. She was the 42nd journalist murdered in Russia since the collapse of the Soviet Union. Pavel Gusev, who is editor of the daily newspaper *Moskovskii Komsomolets* and heads the media committee of the Public Chamber, declared in 2007 that Russia was the second most dangerous country in the world for journalists, after Iraq.

RFE/RL Newsline, October 10, 2006; Ibid., April 2, 2007.

Some suspected Chechen president Ramzan Kadyrov of being behind Politkovskaia's murder, since she had written a number of exposes of his rule and was working on an article about torture in his prisons at the time she was killed. However, as with most of the other murders of journalists and human rights activists, the crime has still not been solved. Three suspects were tried for her murder but acquitted. The procuracy has ordered a new investigation.

62. Andrew E. Kramer, "50% Good News is the Bad News in Russian Radio," online edition of *The New York Times*, April 22, 2007. http://www.nytimes.com/2007/04/22/world/europe/22russia.html?_r=1&oref=slogin&pagewanted=print.

63. RFE/RL Newsline, February 12, 2008.

64. Polit.ru, October 10, 2008.

65. Kelly McMann has documented how authorities in some regions suppress independent newspapers and broadcast outlets, preventing opposition groups from enjoying any publicity and keeping unwelcome investigative reports from appearing. Kelly M. McMann, *Economic Autonomy and Democracy: Hybrid Regimes in Russia and Kyrgyzstan* (Cambridge: Cambridge University Press, 2006).

66. Internet service providers would be held legally responsible for the content on any sites to which they provide access. Providers would have to block access to any site deemed extremist. Natalia Kostenko, Anastasiia Golitsyna, and Anton Osipov, "Za vse otvetia provaidery," *Vedomosti.ru*, October 1, 2008.

On Russian policy toward the Internet, see Marcus Alexander, "The Internet and Democratization: The Development of Russian Internet Policy," *Demokratizatsiiya* 12 (2004): 607–627, and Anton Troianovski (2008). Playing by new rules: Soft power and the fight for Russian cyberspace. Cambridge, MA, Harvard University, Senior thesis, and Anton Troianovski and Peter Finn, "Kremlin Seeks to Extent Its Reach in Cyberspace," *Washington Post*, October 28, 2007. http://www.washingtonpost.com/wp-dyn/content/article/2007/10/27/AR2007102701384_pf.html.

67. Polit.ru, April 20, 2010.

68. Bruce Elting, Karina Alexanyan, John Kelly, et al. *Public Discourse in the Russian Blogosphere: Mapping RuNet Politics and Mobilization* (Cambridge, MA, Berkman Center for Internet and Society at Harvard University, Report number 2010-11, October 19, 2010).

69. A recent survey found that only 14 percent of Internet users follow the news online, while three quarters are members of social networking sites. Moscow Times, "Poll Finds No New Internet Users This Year," September 18, 2009.

70. A valuable study of ethnic-nationalist mobilization in the Russian Federation is Dmitry P. Gorenburg, *Minority Ethnic Mobilization in the Russian Federation* (Cambridge: Cambridge University Press, 2003).

71. Shamanism refers to a set of religious practices centered on the role of shamans, holy individuals who are intermediaries between this world and the unseen forces and spirits of the supernatural. See "Introduction to Russia and Eurasia," *Encyclopedia of World Cultures, volume VI*, Russia and Eurasia/China (Boston, MA: G. K. Hall & Co., 1994), p. xxxi.

72. Peter Reddaway and Robert W. Orttung, eds., *The Dynamics of Russian Politics: Putin's Reform of Federal-Regional Relations* (Lanham, MD: Rowman & Littlefield, 2004).

Interest Groups and Political Parties

INTEREST ARTICULATION: STATISM VS. PLURALISM

Regime change in Russia has had a powerful impact both on people's interests and on the way interests are organized—that is, both the demand side and the supply side of interest groups. Decentralization, market reforms, privatization, ideological liberalization, and the opening of the country to the outside world have reshaped people's needs and desires. At the same time, political liberalization has also allowed people to mobilize in defense of common interests. The wider diversity of interests in society and the greater freedom for association have resulted in a far more differentiated spectrum of interest associations than existed under the old regime. But although there is much more organized *interest* articulation than there was in the past, the stricter state controls over interest articulation in the 2000s have limited the diversity of *political* expression.

Chapter 4 argued that the provision of honest and effective government is a public good; people face a collective action dilemma in trying to obtain good government. Public goods are goods that anyone may enjoy whether they have expended any effort to obtain them or not, and the supply of these goods is not diminished as people use them. To explain where public goods such as honest and effective governance come from, we must look at both the supply side and the demand side. The problem of explaining the supply of good government arises because, as we know, public goods always tend to be undersupplied.[1] This occurs because few people are willing to take upon themselves the cost of organizing collective action for the common good of large groups of people if their own share of the benefit is worth less than the cost of the effort they make to achieve it. Those who do organize groups for collective benefit are often seeking some other private benefits for themselves by doing so. Some may have aspirations to become political leaders, for instance. By going to the trouble of mobilizing a group around a cause, they gain name recognition and followers.[2]

It is easier to organize people for a collective endeavor if some organizational resources are already in place. If people belong to an organization, or share ties through previous acquaintance, it is easier to reach them and draw them into a collective endeavor. If organizational entrepreneurs have to start from scratch, and go around to people one by one to persuade them to sign a petition or contribute dues or turn out for a demonstration, large-scale collective action is much harder to produce. Consequently, when a regime changes, we would expect that interests that can be mobilized through existing organizational channels will have an easier time being heard than interests that are not already organized.

The same logic applies to the political calculations of leaders. Leaders who can take control of existing organizations, and make them vehicles for representing new groups of constituents, have an advantage winning influence over activists who have to start a movement or party from scratch. Therefore, even in a time of deep change in society, the way political and organizational resources were structured in the past will affect the way interests are articulated in the new regime. The legacy of the past therefore affects the *supply* of interest groups.

On the *demand* side, that is, what people *want* from government, social interests are strongly affected by a major change such as the shift from state socialism to market capitalism. In Russia, the demise of the old state-socialist economic system, where the state was the universal employer, has affected everyone. In the first years of Russia's transition, a small minority of people became wealthy, while most people grew poorer and more insecure. Inequality rose sharply, both across social strata and across regions. The collapse of communist ideology has also spurred a number of groups to form around extremist ideologies, including xenophobic forms of Russian nationalism. Most groups, however, have formed around shared interests, such as those related to their livelihoods, their avocations, their common needs, or shared experiences.

Interest articulation is thus affected both by the degree to which people are able to organize for collective action and by the shift in their own definitions of what they want and need from government. People's interests and identities create a potential for mobilization in the political arena, but whether that potential is realized depends a good deal on the distribution of organizational resources and on the strategies of leaders who hope to build popular followings. In this chapter, we will examine how the regime change has affected people's material and social interests. We will also discuss the change in the organizational channels through which people convey their demands to the policymakers.

Socialism and Bureaucratic Politics

The forms of interest articulation have changed enormously since the communist era. The Soviet regime did not tolerate the open pursuit of any interests except those authorized by the state. Soviet authorities encouraged the formation of a number of public organizations, such as labor unions organized by branch of the economy, professional societies for creative artists, and associations for particular groups of the population, such as youth, women, and veterans. But the regime controlled these organizations tightly and treated them as means of guiding the participation of the population in public life. Stalin defined public organizations as "transmission belts" through which the state directed society.[3] The party carefully controlled the recruitment of leaders to these associations through the nomenklatura system.

At the same time, behind-the-scenes bureaucratic maneuvering for power and advantage was intense. Government agencies, regional governments, and leadership factions vied quietly but vigorously for influence over policy and appointments. They were not allowed to appeal openly to the public for support, so the public had no means of holding leaders accountable, but they used methods familiar to bureaucratic infighters throughout the world: building tacit coalitions, manipulating the flow of information, and favoring clients with patronage benefits. Sometimes the expression of demands and ideas took the form of clandestinely circulated contraband literature that the regime treated as subversive.[4]

There was constant bureaucratic lobbying by state officials to increase their own organizational status and power. These included the centralized branch agencies that managed both the economy and society and the leaders of the republics and regions of the union. Between the bureaucracy and the policymakers at the top there was a relationship of mutual dependence. The party leadership needed the branch and regional structures to achieve their policy goals. In turn, the heads of ministries, state committees, republics, and regions needed the support of top party leaders for their institutional and career interests. As the center grew weaker, and depended more on the support of the state officialdom, the idea of any serious reform of the system became more and more threatening.[5]

As the articulation of interests was regulated by the Communist Party, and there could be no open, active competition among political parties or interest groups for support, the Communist Party was the major arena for weighing alternatives and deciding policy. In the Stalin era, party policies such as the collectivization of private farms were carried out using enormous coercion: Collectivization resulted in the loss of millions of lives through the killing, deportation, and starvation of peasants.[6] But in the post-Stalin era, as government became more bureaucratized, corrupt, and incoherent, entrenched interests grew adept at ensuring that the system served them. Any policy initiative that threatened to upset the existing distribution of power was watered down before it was adopted, and often was further blunted, distorted, or forgotten as it was implemented. Paradoxically, policymakers at the top of this seemingly centralized political system lacked the authority to break through the mass of bureaucratic inertia. In many areas, they even lacked the information needed to appraise the real state of affairs.

The statist model of interest articulation was upset by *glasnost'*. *Glasnost'* stimulated an explosion of political expression which in turn prompted groups to make political demands and participate in elections. It is hard today to appreciate how profound the impact of *glasnost'* on the Soviet society was: Suddenly it opened the floodgates to a gathering stream of startling facts, ideas, disclosures, reappraisals, scandals, and sensations. But if Gorbachev expected that *glasnost'* would result in expression generally favoring his own strategy of *perestroika*, or restructuring, of Soviet socialism, he must have been surprised at the range and intensity of new demands, grievances, ideas, and pressures that erupted. In sufficiently loosening the party's controls over communication to encourage people to speak and write freely and openly, Gorbachev also relinquished the controls that would have enabled him to limit political expression when it went too far.

Ideology and organization in the Soviet regime were so tightly intertwined that by releasing controls over the ideological limits of speech, Gorbachev was giving up the party's traditional power to control public organizations. As people voiced their deep-felt demands and grievances, others recognized that they shared the same beliefs and values, and made common cause with them, sometimes forming new, unofficial organizations. Thus, as we have seen, a direct result of *glasnost'* was a wave of participation in "informal"—that is, unlicensed and uncontrolled—public associations. Daring publications in the media made people recognize that they shared common interests with others and prompted them to come together to form independent associations. When the authorities tried to limit or prohibit such groups, they generated still more frustration and protest. Associations of all sorts formed: groups dedicated to remembering the victims of Stalin's terror; ultranationalists who wanted to restore tsarism; nationalist movements in many republics. The devastating explosion of the nuclear reactor at Chernobyl' in 1986 had a tremendous impact in stimulating the formation of environmental protest, which also fed nationalist movements in Belarus and Ukraine.[7]

The mobilization of large-scale political activity led to the creation of new organizational outlets for nationalist movements, independent labor unions, and electoral coalitions. Some of these movements evolved into channels of interest articulation and aggregation in the post-Soviet era.[8]

Democrats, "Reds," and "Browns"

In Russia, as new organizations espousing political goals proliferated in the late 1980s, three distinct ideological tendencies arose. The first centered on principles of individualism, liberal democracy, market economy, the rule of law, and a Western orientation for Russia. Champions of these values were generally called "democrats." The second was a conservative, sometimes even Stalinist, version of Marxism-Leninism, whose advocates made up for their limited base of popular support with flights of extravagant rhetoric. They yearned for strong leadership, centralized state power, an assertive foreign policy, a collectivist, centrally planned economy, and preservation of an imperial Soviet Union—for them, Stalin was a heroic figure in Russian history.

The third stream of ideology drew on conservative Russian and Slavophile nationalism. Like the ultra-Marxists, the nationalists wanted Russia to have a hierarchical and imperial state and rejected Western political and economic influences. They believed, however, that not Marxism but older Russian cultural values such as Orthodox religion should be the source for rebuilding society's exhausted moral fabric. At a deeper philosophic level, the conservative nationalists also rejected the rationalism and materialism associated with Marxism. But in more practical day-to-day politics, the conservative nationalists and the ultra-Marxists often found common cause in their hatred for the West's impact on Russia (and in other forms of reactionary nativism, such as antisemitism). Thus, the "red" Marxist-Leninists often allied with the "brown" nationalists in opposition to the democratizing trends in Russia.[9] The "red–brown" strain of thought and feeling has continued to be powerfully felt in Russian politics to the present day. Later, we shall say more about communist and nationalist groups in today's Russia.

Toward Pluralism

The collapse of the Soviet regime brought a final end to the regime's ideological controls over political expression, which had already been weakened by Gorbachev's reforms. The transition created an opportunity for the rise of a variety of new groups that voiced a wide range of demands. But besides these fundamental political changes, the post-1991 period brought about another change of equal importance. The elimination of the state's monopoly on productive property resulted in the formation of new class interests, among them those of new entrepreneurs, commercial bankers, private farmers, and others interested in protecting rights of property and commerce. Another important category of interests was that of the managers of state-owned enterprises, who were facing a radically changed environment as state orders dried up and as Yeltsin's privatization program took effect. Organized labor too found itself in a new position dealing with managers of privatized enterprises rather than, as in the past, with administrators of state property. Unions themselves were divided among competing labor federations. Also divided were the farmers: While private farmers were represented by an association pressing for legal guarantees and state support for private farming, the collective farmers formed a powerful association and political party. Meanwhile, new associations representing banks, consumers, deceived investors, city governments, disabled persons, soldiers' mothers, defense industries, abused women, and a host of other interests began to form. No longer did the state demand that organized groups serve a single, state-defined political agenda, as was the case under the old regime. Now, groups could form freely to represent a diversity of interests, compete for access to influence and resources, and define their own agenda. Today, it is estimated that there are about a quarter of a million nongovernmental organizations (NGOs) in existence.[10]

Political scientists have observed that interest groups generally pursue either "inside" or "outside" strategies for influencing policy. That is, either they tend to concentrate their resources on cultivating close, friendly relations with key policymakers or they seek to build large public followings and membership bases that can apply pressure on policymakers through elections, demonstrations, letter-writing campaigns, and media attention.[11] The effectiveness of insider strategies depends on establishing relations of trust, which generally requires that the group's representatives and the policymakers keep each others' confidences. That can make it difficult to judge how powerful an "insider" group is. In the case of Russian groups, we see various combinations of strategies. Some older organizations that survived into the new era cling to their organizational assets and legacies and take advantage of their "insider" access to the state. Some that have sprung up from scratch also work closely with legislative and executive authorities, but others play "outsider" roles, trying to influence government by mobilizing public attention and support. Still others try to use both.

The rapid changes in the structure of social relations have meant that both old and new organizations have had a difficult time keeping a firm base of support. Some organizations that appeared influential at first have turned out to be little more than an empty shell. Other interest groups have proven to be very strong politically even though they are not formally organized. Some formerly cohesive groups have split. The diversification of interests has generated a wide range of opportunities for organizers and activists.

The Soviet pattern of interest articulation was *statist*—that is, the Soviet state sponsored and controlled interest groups. In the 1990s, the prevailing pattern of interest articulation shifted to *pluralism,* where multiple groups competed for members and influence. In the 2000s, the regime attempted to introduce elements of *authoritarian corporatism* into the state's relations with interest groups. In authoritarian corporatism, the state seeks to centralize the representation of recognized sectors and groups. It consults with and even funds some organizations, while ignoring or repressing others. Under Putin and Medvedev, the regime has sought to set the terms of the relationship between interest groups and policymakers. For example, partly to discourage NGOs from seeking help abroad and partly to ensure that they do not challenge the regime's hold on power, the state funds many NGOs. In 2010, President Medvedev ordered the state to spend 1 billion rubles—about $33 million US—on a competitive grants program for NGOs.[12]

Another way in which the regime seeks to channel and manage civil society is the institution of the Public Chamber, which is an organized forum through which certain societal groups are represented and consulted on public affairs. The regime chooses which associations are invited to participate in the Public Chamber and even controls the selection of those representatives. Openly oppositional groups are subject to harassment and suppression. Interest groups thus need to choose whether to accept the boundaries of the role the regime has defined in order to exercise some influence or to risk the consequences of open defiance of the regime. Most regional governments also have similar Public Chambers through which the regional administration consults with local interest groups.

It will be helpful to illustrate the patterns of interest articulation in contemporary Russian by examining four organizations in closer detail: the Russian Union of Industrialists and Entrepreneurs, the League of Committees of Soldiers' Mothers, the Federation of Independent Trade Unions of Russia (FITUR), and the Russian Orthodox Church. These comprise both "old" and "new" types of interests and organization and will illustrate a range of strategies for collective action.

The Russian Union of Industrialists and Entrepreneurs   The case of the Russian Union of Industrialists and Entrepreneurs, which represents big business, is the most powerful interest group in Russia. Its case illustrates three points: like some other inherited Soviet-era organizations, it has proven resilient in the face of the considerable changes that have taken place in society; second, although the interests of big business are aligned with the market economy, businesses still lobby for assistance from the state; and finally, although big business in Russia today is far stronger than any other organized interest, the state still has the upper hand in dealing with it.

Privatization sharply changed the environment for industry. Most formerly state-owned industrial firms are now wholly or partly privately owned. Their directors have come to respond to the incentives of a market economy, rather than those of a state socialist economy. Under the old regime, managers were told to fulfill the plan regardless of cost or quality and profit was not a relevant consideration.[13] Now, managers are motivated to maximize profits and to increase the productive value of their firms. They also need to work together to lobby government for favorable policies on taxation, pensions, regulation, foreign trade, and numerous other issues. The principal channel for interest articulation by big business is the *Russian Union of Industrialists and Entrepreneurs (RUIE)*.

Its members include both the old state industrial firms (now mostly private or quasi-private) and the financial–industrial conglomerates headed by so-called "oligarchs."[14] For its first 15 years, its president was Arkadii Vol'skii, who had been a senior CPSU official in charge of the Central Committee department overseeing industrial machine building. During the Gorbachev period, Vol'skii headed an association of the heads of state enterprises called the "Scientific–Industrial Union."[15] The new organization sought to preserve economic ties among enterprises to offset the breakdown of the old system of central planning. In 1991, the group reorganized as the RUIE. Although the RUIE professed to have no explicit political goals, it did seek to defend the interests of state industry—including their interest in obtaining credits and production orders—as well as to prevent the interruption of supply and trade ties in the face of economic upheavals.

In the 1990s, the RUIE twice tried to enter electoral politics in alliance with the main trade union association, forming a joint party and running candidates for the State Duma. The results were very poor both times. But as an insider advocate for big business, the RUIE has been highly effective. It has been an influential behind-the-scenes source of policy advice for government and parliament. Government takes it seriously. The 320,000 businesses belonging to it account for some 60 percent of Russian GDP. It has more than 100 regional and sectoral branch organizations.[16]

Consistent with its strategy of managing the interest articulation process, the Putin regime took steps to unite all big businesses under the RUIE.[17] In 2000, Putin let it be known that he wanted the oligarchs to join the RUIE rather to continue engaging in their free-wheeling independent interest articulation.[18] (As the then president Vol'skii diplomatically put it, "the interests of the oligarchs are too diverse to create their own public association, and the RUIE can help them conduct civilized lobbying."[19]) The RUIE expanded its in-house capacity for working with the government and the parliament in drafting legislation. It maintains a number of specialized internal working groups that develop policy positions on a wide range of issues such as land reform, tax law, pension policy, bankruptcy legislation, reform of the natural gas, energy and railroad monopolies, securities regulation, and the terms of Russia's entry to the WTO. By marshalling expertise, pooling the clout of its members, and maintaining friendly relations with the government, parliament, and presidential administration, the RUIE has become a powerful force in shaping policy on a wide range of issues. To be sure, individual firms still lobby government for firm-specific benefits. But the RUIE is a recognized participant in high-level government and parliamentary policy making.

RUIE also takes public positions on a variety of policy issues, pressing the government to move in particular directions. For instance, in September 2009 it wrote an open letter to President Medvedev complaining that the authorities were doing too little to back up their call for more innovation with action. Business, declared the letter, was still waiting for clear signals from the government about the specifics of what it would do to promote high-tech industry, such as making strategic investments in infrastructure, reforming the educational system, reducing corruption, and lowering taxes.[20] RUIE also won the right to sit in on meetings of the government.[21]

At the same time, the regime keeps the RUIE's influence well within limits. For example, the Kremlin has helped to create two other business associations, OPORA, with a mandate to represent the interests of small and medium-size business firms, and "Business Russia," which is active in party politics. When Putin or Medvedev meets with business leaders, they often invite representatives of all these associations to the meeting, signaling that for all its prominence, RUIE is not the sole voice of business and that the regime will set the terms for business's participation in policy making.

The limits of the RUIE's capacity to speak for business became dramatically evident when Putin launched his campaign against the *Yukos* oil firm (see Close-Up 6.1: The Yukos Affair). When the arrests of top leaders of Yukos began in July 2003, RUIE confined itself to mild expressions of concern. Its members, evidently fearful of crossing Putin, chose not to defend Yukos's head, Mikhail Khodorkovsky, or to protest the use of police methods to destroy one of Russia's largest oil companies. Instead, they promised to meet their tax obligations and to do more to help the country fight poverty. Putin pointedly avoided meeting with RUIE and other business association leaders from November 2003 to July 2004—and then agreed to meet with them only on the condition that the subject of Yukos not be discussed. Perhaps if big business had taken a firm stand, they could have affected the outcome of the case. But the desire by each individual firm to maintain friendly relations with the government and fear of government reprisals undercut business's capacity for collective action. RUIE thus chooses its battles carefully and works to pursue its interests within the limits set by the regime.

CLOSE-UP 6.1

The Yukos Affair

One of the most sensational episodes of the Putin era was the dismantling of the powerful private oil company Yukos and the jailing of its CEO, Mikhail Khodorkovsky. Khodorkovsky's career began in the late 1980s, when he was a young Komsomol activist working in the Moscow city government and used his Komsomol resources and connections to start a bank called Menatep. Financing from the Menatep bank enabled Khodorkovsky and his associates to acquire—at a bargain basement price—80 percent of the shares of the Yukos oil company when the government privatized it under the "loans for shares" plan in 1995. At first, like some of the other newly wealthy business tycoons, Khodorkovsky sought to squeeze maximum profit from the firm by stripping its assets. Soon, however, Khodorkovsky's business strategy changed, and he began to invest in the productive capacity of the firm. He made Yukos the most dynamic of Russia's oil companies. Khodorkovsky discovered that by adopting Western business practices, the company could increase its value. He reformed corporate governance practices and got Yukos's shares listed on foreign stock exchanges. By improving the efficiency and transparency of the firm, Khodorkovsky made the company more attractive to investors. As share prices rose, so did Khodorkovsky's own net worth. At its peak in 2002, the company's assets were estimated to be worth about $20 billion, of which Khodorkovsky owned nearly $8 billion. He was Russia's wealthiest citizen.

Meantime, like the American robber barons of an earlier era who sought to improve their public image through conspicuous philanthropy, Khodorkovsky created a foundation called Open Russia and launched several charitable initiatives in Russia, such as funding schools, hospitals, science, cultural exchange programs, and other causes. The company funded housing for its workers and youth programs for their families in regions where it operated. Khodorkovsky recruited some distinguished international figures to his foundation's board. He was also active in Russian politics, helping to fund the parties Yabloko and the Union of Rightist Forces, and lobbying successfully against increases in taxes on oil exports. Critics accused him of wanting to control parliament. There was talk that he intended to seek the presidency.

Khodorkovsky flaunted his independence. At a Kremlin meeting in February 2003, Khodorkovsky sparred with President Putin over a deal by which a state-owned oil company had acquired a private firm, complaining directly to Putin that the deal was corrupt. Without consulting with the Kremlin, he began talks with foreign oil companies on selling a significant share of Yukos stock. In April 2003, Yukos and another oil company, Sibneft', announced an agreement to merge, which would have created Russia's largest oil company and the fourth largest oil company in the world. In June 2003, he signed an agreement with China under which Yukos would build a major oil pipeline from Siberia to China that would supply a quarter of China's oil imports. The prospect of a privately owned oil pipeline directly threatened the state's pipeline monopoly, which ensured the state's control over both producers and consumers.

At some point in spring 2003, the Putin administration concluded that Khodorkovsky and Yukos had grown too powerful. In a series of actions beginning in July 2003, the state initiated a campaign to break up and take over the company. Several top figures in Yukos and companies associated with it were arrested and charged with fraud, embezzlement, tax evasion, and even murder. One case involved a privatization deal going back to 1993. The police searched the offices of the company and a number of its affiliates, seizing files and computer hard drives. They even raided the office of an orphanage sponsored by Open Russia.

In October 2003, masked commandos seized Khodorkovsky from his private plane at an airport in Siberia. He was charged with fraud and tax evasion. The state presented claim after claim against the company, ultimately demanding $15 billion in unpaid taxes from the company. The state deployed the tax police, the secret police, the procuracy, the courts, and the media in its campaign. When one Moscow judge issued a ruling favoring Yukos, she was removed from the case. The government moved to take over the company's assets. In August 2004, the government froze Yukos' bank accounts. In December 2004, it seized Yukos' main production subsidiary, Yuganskneftegaz, and auctioned it off to a cut-out firm, which three days later sold it to Russia's only state-owned oil company, Rosneft. (Rosneft's board chairman, Igor Sechin, is deputy prime minister and a long time associate of Putin from St. Petersburg; he is considered to be the head of the "silovik" faction in the leadership.) In May 2005, Khodorkovsky was sentenced to nine years' imprisonment and sent to a prison camp in Siberia. He remains in jail.

In 2008, the regime brought new charges against him, claiming that he embezzled some 350 million tons of oil by buying it at cost from Yukos-owned production units, selling it abroad at market prices, and laundering the proceeds. A number of observers—including the head of the RUIE—expressed skepticism about the charges, noting that they appeared to amount to a second trial for the same crimes Khodorkovsky was convicted of in the first case. At his trial, Khodorkovsky called the new charges absurd and noted that the company had paid the state 40 billion rubles in taxes on the oil he was charged with stealing.[22] Most observers concluded that the new charges were brought in order to tack a lengthy new sentence on Khodorkovsky and prevent him from being released in 2014 upon the expiration of his original sentence.

Many reasons for the government's campaign against Yukos and Khodorkovsky have been suggested. Some argue that Khodorkovsky, through his open involvement in party politics, violated Putin's rule that big business stay out of high politics. Another explanation is that Yukos was the target of a struggle among bureaucratic factions over the distribution of control over lucrative resources. Certainly, Khodorkovsky's independence defied Putin's policy of placing all major oil and gas companies under state control so as to use energy policy to advance the state's global interests. Khodorkovsky evidently calculated that Yukos was too big to crush, but the regime was willing to prove him wrong.

The validity of the government's case is unclear. The government may well have had legal grounds for charging Yukos with tax evasion and tax fraud—but since

(continued)

Russian law makes little distinction between legal tax avoidance and illegal tax evasion, it is hard for outsiders to judge. Certainly, the fact that Yukos was singled out for this treatment while other firms were not suggests that there were strong political motives at work: The Yukos affair sent a clear signal that big business's rights were contingent on the favor of the political authorities.

Whatever the motives behind the Putin administration's actions, the Yukos affair shows that the regime is willing to manipulate the legal system for political purposes, that many of the most important political contests in Russia are fought out within the state bureaucracy rather than in the open arena of public politics, and that the fight to redistribute control of Russia's most lucrative natural resource assets continues to be a driving force in Russian politics.

On the Yukos affair, see William Tompson, "Putting Yukos in Perspective," *Post-Soviet Affairs* 21:2 (2005): 159–181; Richard Sakwa, *The Quality of Freedom: Khodorkovsky, Putin, and the Yukos Affair* (New York: Oxford University Press, 2009).

The League of Committees of Soldiers' Mothers   The Soviet regime sponsored several official women's organizations, but these mainly served propaganda purposes. During the *glasnost'* period, a number of unofficial women's organizations sprang up to voice the interests of groups who were otherwise unrepresented. One such group was the Committee of Soldiers' Mothers. It formed in the spring of 1989, when some 300 women in Moscow marched to protest the end of student deferments from military conscription. In response to their actions, Gorbachev agreed to restore the deferments. In 1990 and 1991, Gorbachev also acceded to other demands made by the Soldiers' Mothers, including creating a body to investigate noncombat-related deaths of servicemen, improving social benefits for the families of deceased servicemen, and granting a provisional amnesty to soldiers who deserted the army as a result of intolerable abuse.[23] The organization has continued to operate since then and to maintain its focus on issues concerning military service. One of its enduring and most widely shared causes is its demand that the army end the common practice of subjecting new conscripts to brutal hazing, which results in numerous deaths, including by suicide, and maiming of soldiers each year.[24] The group also monitors abuses associated with the spring and fall call-ups of young men to the army and counsels families on how young men can avoid being drafted. The organization itself is relatively decentralized, maintaining a small central organization and operating through local committees in hundreds of towns and a network of thousands of volunteers.

The onset of large-scale hostilities in Chechnia in 1994–1996 and 1999–2000 stimulated a new burst of activity by the Soldiers' Mothers. The organization helped families locate soldiers who were missing in action or captured by the Chechen rebel forces, sent missions to Chechnia to negotiate for the release of prisoners and to provide proper burial for the dead, and collected fuller information about the actual scale of the war and of its casualties than the Russian military. With time, the organization became one of the most sizable and respected civic groups in Russia.[25] One of the movement's greatest assets has been its moral authority as the voice of mothers defending the interests of their children; this stance has made it hard for their opponents to paint them as unpatriotic or power hungry. The organization has also avoided taking an explicitly antimilitary stance and has welcomed opportunities to cooperate with the military in such causes as ending hazing in the ranks. For example, the newspaper *Novaia gazeta* ran an experiment in cooperation with the Soldiers' Mothers and a few military commissariats (conscription centers): they handed out cell phones to new recruits, so that if they were subjected to serious hazing, they could phone the procuracy or family members. Asked to comment on this initiative, President Medvedev replied: "Good idea. The crimes committed in the army are dangerous above all for their latency, because only a very insignificant percentage of them get to the military procuracy or the military investigator, not to mention to court."[26] One imagines that military commanders are less enthusiastic than President Medvedev about the experiment.

The League cooperates with the General Procurator's office in gathering evidence for the criminal prosecution of those who have violated the law by abusing soldiers. It also continues to devote most of its efforts to helping soldiers and their families deal with their particular problems. Thus, it performs multiple functions, combining political activity with services to clients. Unlike many Russian associational groups, the League has chosen to remain independent of government, not seeking any special privilege or recognition. As Elena Vilenskaia, one of the founders of the Committee of Soldiers' Mothers in St. Petersburg, put it, "we realized we had to form an organization of a completely different type. Not a committee which is manipulated by someone, but something fundamentally new, constructive. From the beginning, we separated ourselves from all central structures."[27]

The League of Committees of Soldiers' Mothers has won international recognition for its work and has presented reports to international organizations such as the UN Commission on Human Rights, the European Commission, and Amnesty International.[28] The League's high international profile and willingness to challenge the authorities over the sensitive issues of the Chechen War and the hazing of conscripts has often brought it into conflict with the authorities.[29] So far, however, its prestige at home and abroad has helped protect it from being shut down by the regime.

The Federation of Independent Trade Unions of Russia   The cases of the RUIE and the Committees of Soldiers' Mothers illustrate the point that the old regime was rich in state-sponsored mass organizations but poor in social capital that could provide institutional resources to new interests seeking to organize and voice their demands. Yet in some cases, the official mass organizations served to foster skills and social ties that became important resources for interest organizations in the post-Soviet environment. The RUIE suggests that an organization built upon a Soviet-era association could adapt itself successfully to the new postcommunist environment and become an influential business association. The League of Committees of Soldiers' Mothers, in contrast, formed as an informal organization in the *glasnost'* period and has consciously chosen to keep its distance from the smothering embrace of the state. The RUIE made use of inherited networks of contacts and organizational resources from the old regime, whereas the Soldiers' Mothers group built itself up from scratch, taking advantage of the Internet to link branch organizations across the country as well as winning international recognition. Its prestige at home and abroad, and its willingness to cooperate with the authorities when necessary and to avoid a directly political role for the most part, have helped preserve it.

The *Federation of Independent Trade Unions of Russia* is the successor of the official trade union federation under the Soviet regime.[30] It has adapted and survived, but is ineffective as a voice for organized labor despite inheriting substantial organizational resources from the old Soviet trade union movement. In the Soviet era, virtually every employed person belonged to a trade union. Branch trade unions represented all employed persons in a given industry, from shopworker to top management. In turn, all branch and regional trade union organizations were part of a single labor federation. With the breakdown of the old regime, some of the member unions became independent, while other unions sprang up as independent bodies representing the interests of particular groups of workers. Nonetheless, the shell of the old official trade union organization survived and is called the FITUR. It remains by far the largest trade union federation in Russia; as of 2010, it claims to represent 95 percent of all unionized workers in 41 all-Russian branch trade unions, operating through 79 territorial branches.[31] But these figures are dubious. A survey of one region in 2008 found that only about 15 percent of employed people considered themselves members of a trade union and only 15 percent could say what it is that trade unions do for them (although more than half wished to belong to a union that would defend their interests).[32] By comparison with big business, the labor movement is fragmented, weak, and unable to mobilize workers effectively for collective action.

The FITUR inherited valuable real estate assets from its Soviet-era predecessor organization, including thousands of office buildings, hotels, rest homes, hospitals, sports facilities, and children's camps. These generate a substantial stream of income for the FITUR leaders ($300 million per year, according to one 2001 estimate)[33] and spare the organization the necessity of depending on workers' dues to maintain its central staff.[34] It also inherited the right to collect workers' contributions for the state social insurance fund. Although the FITUR formally lost the right to collect and distribute social insurance funds, it still has substantial de facto control over these streams of income and their use. These assets and rights give leaders of the official unions considerable advantages in competing for members (for instance, they can deny members of rival unions from occupying apartments owned by the FITUR). They also incline the FITUR's officials to be more concerned about protecting their own organizational interests than in advancing those of the workers.[35]

The FITUR lacks effective control over its regional and branch members. Much of its effort is expended on fighting other independent unions to win a monopoly on representing workers in collective bargaining with employers rather than in joining with other unions to defend the interests of workers generally.[36] The central leadership of the FITUR spends much of its time cultivating close, clientelistic relations with powerful political leaders. The FITUR takes pains to clear any protest actions with the Kremlin. For example, it sought official blessings to hold an all-Russian political rally in October 2008, assuring the authorities that the marchers would employ only "peaceful slogans."[37] The organization is so fearful of upsetting its friendly relations with the authorities that in the midst of the severe economic crisis of late 2008, as unemployment was spreading throughout industry, it refused to release figures on the number of layoffs. This was because, as one of its officials in Moscow explained, doing so might have the effect of lowering the stock share prices of the companies![38]

The ineffectiveness of the FITUR was most clearly shown by its tepid response to the severe deterioration in labor and social conditions that occurred through the 1990s. Despite high unemployment, severe wage arrears, and a sharp drop in living standards, there was much less protest than might have been expected. Certainly, there was some labor mobilization in the 1990s, mainly over wage arrears. Surveys found that in much of the 1990s, in any given year, three quarters of all workers received their wages late at least once.[39] But recent research has found that much of the labor protest in the 1990s was in fact organized by regional governments as a tactic for putting pressure on the central government to pay back wages and pensions; trade unions were unable or unwilling to organize strikes themselves, but did so when governors backed them.[40]

In the 2000s, owing to the economic recovery, wages and pensions were generally paid on time, and labor unrest sharply subsided. But, once again, when the recession hit in 2008 and unemployment rose to over 10 percent, there was very little labor protest. There were a small number of strikes, particularly at foreign-owned plants (where the authorities are more willing to allow workers to strike), but the numbers were very small: in all of 2008, there were only four officially registered strikes and only one in 2009.[41]

Why have trade unions been unable or unwilling to mount large-scale strikes and protests despite the hardships of the transition in the 1990s and the recession in the late 2000s? One reason is workers' dependence on their workplaces for a variety of social benefits administered through the enterprise, such as pension contributions, cheap housing, and access to medical clinics and day-care facilities.[42] A second reason is the organizational structure of the FITUR, which replicates that of the Soviet trade unions. The fact that all members of each enterprise (blue collar, clerical, technical, and managerial) belong to the same union militates against mobilization around class interests. A third reason is that despite the use of collective bargaining between workers and managers in many enterprises, most enterprises still use a variety of bonuses and job coefficients to supplement the pay of individual workers. Moreover, they pay a substantial portion of wages under the table so as to avoid paying payroll taxes. As a result, workers have less incentive to organize around common interests than they would if earnings were more equal and more transparent.

A final reason is the close, clientelistic relationship between the leadership of the FITUR and government authorities. Any time that FITUR threatens any serious labor protest, the government threatens to take away its access to the distribution of social funds. Like the RUIE, therefore, the FITUR for the most part prefers to cultivate a docile relationship with the political authorities rather than to exert its independence. Yet it is fearful of losing its ability to speak for the workers. When wildcat strikes occur, they demonstrate that workers have been unable to channel their grievances through the official unions. Frustrated with the sorry state of the FITUR, which cannot credibly represent the collective interests of workers, and concerned that the recession could provoke uncontrolled worker unrest, the Kremlin has attempted to build up alternative trade unions that would command greater legitimacy among workers and put competitive pressure on the FITUR. So far, however, the leadership of FITUR has managed adeptly to thwart pressures for reform—it is far more effective at looking out for the interests of its own staff than those of Russia's workers.

The Russian Orthodox Church   The great majority of the Russian people—as many as 89 percent, depending on how religious affiliation is measured—identify themselves with the Russian Orthodox Church.[43] The Russian Orthodox Church dates its origins to Prince Vladimir's baptism in 988 in the Kievan city-state, and considers itself to be the historic partner of the Russian state and people, providing spiritual guidance to society and sanctification of state authority in return for the state's protection. Its view of itself as a state church is at odds with the constitutional precept of the separation of church and state.[44]

Historically, the church was closely allied to the state authorities. For most of the two centuries before the Bolshevik Revolution, according to historian Firuz Kazemzadeh, "the Church acted as an arm of the State, teaching obedience to the government, glorifying absolutism, and serving as a spiritual police."[45] After the communists took power, the Russian Orthodox Church was not banned, but it was subject to persecution, at times violent, and to intense surveillance by the authorities. Young people were strongly discouraged from attending services, while party members and political officials understood that their careers would be jeopardized if they openly practiced religion. Appointments of senior clergy had to be cleared by the state and some clergy were KGB agents. The church's public pronouncements had to be supportive of the state. For example, during the Cold War, church officials actively participated in the Soviet regime's propaganda campaign for "peace and justice" in the world, which was always directed against the "imperialist" world's policies and never the communist bloc's. The church did not die out, as Soviet officials had once predicted it would, but its public role was severely restricted.

The collapse of communism allowed the church to regain much of its status and freedom.[46] Under legislation passed in 1990, the church acquired the right of legal personhood, entitling it to own property and enter into contractual agreements. Many churches and monasteries that had been seized by the state were restored to the church, often in considerable disrepair. Religious education became legal. The church has also benefited from the eagerness of the political elite to associate itself with the church. Beginning with Gorbachev's celebration of the millennium of Russian Christianity in 1988 and continuing with President Yeltsin's attendance at major church events and Moscow Mayor Luzhkov's forceful drive to rebuild the Cathedral of Christ the Savior, torn down under Stalin, numerous Russian political leaders have found it expedient to embrace the church as a symbol of Russian national unity, continuity, and statehood. Although the 1993 constitution proclaimed the separation of church and state, state leaders have looked to the Orthodox Church to bless their actions. The Patriarch, for example, attended the inaugurations of Russian Presidents Yeltsin, Putin, and Medvedev. When Boris Yeltsin died in 2007, he was given (at President Putin's insistence) a state religious funeral at the Cathedral of Christ the Savior in Moscow.[47]

The end of the Soviet regime brought with it a religious awakening in Russia and other former Soviet republics. Many, including young people, sought to rediscover their religious heritage or to find a new religious identity. Thousands of foreign missionaries arrived to proselytize. Denominations and sects that had operated underground began to practice openly. New Protestant and Catholic churches were established. Muslim and Jewish organizations also gained strength. Various fringe sects won adherents. The Orthodox Church responded to the new activity by calling on the state to protect it against foreign competition. The church drew a sharp distinction between those religions that had a long history on Russian soil, and hence posed less of a threat, and those which were new and alien to it. Regarding proselytism from abroad as a hostile invasion,[48] the Church pressured the president and parliament for protectionist legislation that would ban foreign missionary activity and would, in effect, require a state license for the exercise of the new religious freedom guaranteed under the Russian constitution.

The idea of such a law was very popular among lawmakers, particularly nationalists and communists, who wanted to align themselves publicly with the moral authority of the church. In 1997, the Duma passed and President Yeltsin signed a law that gave the church much of what it wanted. The law was euphemistically called "On Freedom of Conscience and Religious Associations." Declaring that there were four religious communities that were historically indigenous to Russia—Orthodox Christianity, Islam, Judaism, and Buddhism—the law required that any other religious organization that wanted to operate on Russian soil would have to reregister with the state by the end of 1998. If it wanted to use the word "All-Russian" *(Rossiiskii)* in its name, an organization would have to demonstrate that it had operated in Russia for at least 50 years and had local branches in at least half the regions of the country. Alternatively, it could register if it could prove that it had a central organization and at least three regional branches and had existed in Russia for at least 15 years. Moreover, the law listed a number of grounds on which registration could be denied. Foreign missionaries would only be allowed to operate in Russia if they were invited by registered religious organizations.[49]

Many Russian and international religious groups were alarmed by this law. As experts noted, it was directed not against Islam, Judaism, or Buddhism, but against rival Christian groups that the Orthodox Church considered to be "destructive totalitarian sects," as the Patriarch termed them.[50] Several groups challenged the constitutionality of the law. In November 1999, the Constitutional Court upheld the main tenets of the law but softened others. It ruled that the state could restrict the activity of foreign missionaries and could ban those groups that violated human rights and Russian law. But it also declared that the clause that religious organizations had to prove they had existed for 15 years did not apply to groups registered before the law was passed or to congregations that are part of centralized organizations.[51] A ruling several months later by the court went further and invalidated the other retroactive provisions.[52] Meantime, the deadline for registering religious organizations was extended, and several groups that were initially denied were later registered.

The Orthodox Church holds that "the Russian people culturally, spiritually, and historically are the flock of the Russian Orthodox Church."[53] In contrast to the Western Christian doctrine of separation between the authority of the state and the authority of religion, Russian Orthodoxy regards church and state as interlocked elements of an organic national community.[54] It considers religious identification to be an attribute of nationality, not simply a matter of individual taste, and it regards the Russian Orthodox Church as the patrimony of the Russians—whether they are believers or not. Therefore, it is hostile to any efforts at conversion by outsiders, arguing that Western missionaries are trying to buy Russians' souls with promises of material prosperity. The Orthodox Church is amenable to coexisting with other religious communities in Russia, such as Muslims, Jews, and Buddhists, so long as the boundaries among the ethnic groups belonging to each religious community are respected. But it is deeply antagonistic to other Christian groups that believe that Russia should be religiously pluralistic. Because state leaders, both liberal and communist, have been solicitous of the church for their own political interests, they have been unwilling to cross the church on matters of religious politics. The church's animosity toward the Catholic Church, for example, has made it impossible for the pope to visit Russia. The church has also sought to exert influence on matters of public education and culture. For instance, in January 2007, the head of church, Patriarch Aleksii II, denounced the teaching of evolution in the schools.[55] The church also considers unacceptable any concept of universal human rights that places "human rights as the highest and universal foundation of public life, to which religious views and practice must be subordinate."[56]

Although the state formally adheres to the constitutional principle of separation between church and state, in practice it has encouraged the participation of the four major recognized religious communities in public life. This has given a number of opportunities to the Russian Orthodox Church in particular to exert its influence. For example, the Ministry of Education named a high-ranking bishop of the church to the state council on educational standards. A television channel has devoted a program, called "The Church and the World," to Orthodox issues, such as how a believer should live in the contemporary world.[57] In the 1990s, the church was granted a license to import cigarettes for resale in Russia without paying import tariffs, which it used to develop a large and profitable business.[58] The church has also succeeded in lobbying the state to appoint Orthodox priests as chaplains in the armed forces.[59] It has been unable, however, to persuade the authorities to make religious instruction a mandatory subject in the schools. As already stated in the previous chapter, the state has instead opted to give parents a choice among different approaches to ethical instruction in the schools—an Orthodoxy-based curriculum, curricula based on other faiths, or a secular-humanist approach.

Thus, the Russian Orthodox Church has formed a relationship of reciprocal dependence with state authorities, as in the prerevolutionary era: It looks to the state for protection, privileges, and influence in society, and in turn it grants the state authorities moral sanction for their actions. Any change in this symbiotic relationship will probably come from within the church, as believers demand that the church reduce its reliance on the state for its power and status and instead draw its strength from the commitment of the faithful.

New Sectors of Interest

We have seen that in a time when people's interests themselves are changing rapidly as a result of social change, both old and new organizations find it hard to stay united. As is true everywhere, smaller groups have an easier time acting collectively than do large, dispersed groups. We have also noted a pattern of behavior in which groups that gained new freedom in the post-Soviet era have used their influence to block competing organizations from recruiting supporters—as with the FITUR's effort to use the new Labor Code to win exclusive collective bargaining rights on behalf of organized labor, and the Russian Orthodox Church's efforts to deny equality to competing religious denominations.

Overall, the trend has been an evolution in structure of interest articulation from statism to pluralism, and more recently to an authoritarian version of corporatism. The legacy of the Soviet model survives in the case of organizations such as the trade unions and RUIE. Elements of authoritarianism are evident in the regime's efforts to limit the political rights of interest groups, and elements of corporatism are evident in the effort to draw selected interest groups into formal consultative relationships with the regime.

Still, the system of interest articulation is far more pluralistic than it was in the Soviet period. Tens of thousands of new associations speak for interests that had never been organized in the past, such as the Committees of Soldiers' Mothers and tens of thousands of other organized associations. Among these are organizations that promote the interests of particular categories of officials, business, or social groups, such as associations for governors;

associations of mayors of small towns and of mayors of closed cities; associations of small businesses and of entrepreneurs; associations for particular industries, such as the beer brewing industry; and associations for particular categories of the population, such as the Association of Indigenous Peoples of the North and the Far East.

Movements of automobile owners have been one of the most active categories of social interests. In 2002, a group called the Public Organization for the Defense of the Rights of Owners of Cars with Right-Hand Steering Wheels registered in Vladivostok. Press reports indicated that the aim of the group was to lobby against new customs duties on imported cars (many Japanese cars imported from the Far East have right-hand steering wheels).[60] An association called the Federation of Automobile Owners of Russia organized rallies to protest a government bill to double the property tax on cars. Within days, the United Russia party announced that it would kill the legislation.[61] The motorists have been particularly aroused over the abuses of driving privileges by officials. For example, in 2005, a car carrying the governor of Altai Krai struck the car of an ordinary citizen, Oleg Schcherbitskii, as Shcherbitsky was making a left turn. The governor was killed. Schcherbitskii was charged with failing to yield to the governor's car, was convicted, and was sentenced to four years in a labor colony. Motorists all across the country protested by flying white ribbons from their cars. The public outcry persuaded United Russia to switch its stance and call for Schcherbitskii's release. An appeals court then overturned the verdict.[62] Since then, motorists' protests have become common and often effective. A current campaign is the "blue buckets" movement in Moscow to protest the overuse of flashing blue lights on the cars of government officials who are able to bypass normal traffic rules, often with fatal results. Drivers drive around with blue plastic buckets attached to the top of their cars to mock the blue lights. The Duma, not amused, has passed legislation attempting to restrict the blue buckets movement and other protest activity by organized motorists.[63] Remarkably, President Medvedev then vetoed the bill.

Thousands of groups espousing charitable, social services, environmental, consumers' rights, and human rights causes have also formed. One of the most prominent is Memorial, which arose in the Gorbachev period to honor the memory of the victims of Stalin's repressions and which has continued to work to protect human rights and democratic freedoms.[64] Russian civic groups operate under very difficult circumstances, including unpredictable and sometimes hostile treatment by the authorities; scarcity of office space and other material resources; obstacles to communication with prospective members and with other groups; and habits of secretiveness and hoarding of information. Faced with economic and political pressure, many attempt to win budget support from government. Some are simply fronts for commercial activity, and many are only sporadically active. Although only a very small number of citizens are members of such organizations, many more benefit from their activity. Taken together, they represent a substantial sector of independent civic activity.

In some regions, NGOs have cooperated with the local authorities on specific issues. For example, some NGOs are working with law enforcement agencies to improve policing and detention practices and to give training to police on handling domestic violence incidents.[65] One Siberian NGO offered free breast cancer screening exams, and a thousand women responded. Recognizing the pent-up demand for better women's health services, the local government offered funds to the NGO so that it could conduct similar screening sessions throughout the region. A center for Siberian NGOs (the Siberian Civic Initiatives Support Center) has been working with several local governments to develop better mechanisms for building citizen input into policy making. Several citizen-based advocacy groups have mounted campaigns for environmental protection (in one recent case, they joined in a successful movement to persuade the authorities to reroute a planned oil pipeline to reduce the chance that it could contaminate the pure water of Lake Baikal).[66]

The regime's policy toward NGOs has sought to steer the NGO sector into cooperative relations with the state. It has not imposed comprehensive political control over NGOs, as in the Soviet era, but neither has it allowed them full autonomy. Putin and Medvedev have repeatedly argued that Russia needs a vigorous civil society, but they have also sought ways to structure and limit the political influence of Russian NGOs.[67] In 2006, following claims that Western intelligence services were funding some Russian NGOs, Putin sponsored new legislation tightening state control over NGOs. The new legislation imposed stringent new registration requirements and expanded financial controls over their activity. All existing NGOs had to reregister. Compliance with the new rules was burdensome for many groups (for instance, they had to report the current home addresses and passport numbers of all the founding members of the organization), and a number of groups were denied reregistration on the grounds that their forms were improperly filled out. Several thousand groups have been shut down in this way. In effect, the law gave the authorities a convenient pretext to refuse registration to groups that the regime found objectionable on political grounds.

At the same time, the regime has also sought to create formal mechanisms for consultation and collaboration with NGOs. In November 2001, the authorities convened a large assembly called the "Civic Forum" in the Kremlin's Palace of Congresses (where in the past, the Communist Party used to hold its congresses every five years). Some 5,000 delegates representing civic groups from all over Russia assembled. President Putin and most of the senior officials of the presidential administration and government attended the meeting. Addressing the assembly, Putin had warm words for the principle of civil society, observing that "civil society cannot be formed at the initiative of government officials" and disavowing any desire to subordinate civil society to the state. Rather, he noted that civil society "grows up on its own, feeding on the spirit of freedom" and cited the Internet as an example of the way state and society can work together for mutual benefit.[68] The meeting broke into a number of thematic working sessions, which drew up resolutions that were signed by members of the civic associations and the government. Ultimately, however, little came of these documents, although one or two found their way into subsequent government policy planning on issues such as the problem of homeless children.

Some government agencies at both the federal and the regional levels have set up advisory bodies where NGOs can provide officials with information and recommendations. For example, the Ministry of Health and Social Development established a public advisory council comprising citizen advocacy groups, including organizations representing people suffering from hemophilia, cancer, diabetes, multiple sclerosis, and other conditions. The council's charge was to inform the ministry about problems in distributing medication to patients in need.[69] Similarly, the Ministry of Justice consults with NGOs working with law enforcement agencies and the prison system to identify problems before they become cases sent to the European Court of Human Rights.[70] Relations between NGOs and the authorities are not always harmonious, but constructive cooperation between state and civil society is much more likely to be found in spheres having to do with social policy and law enforcement than in more directly political areas such as election monitoring and human rights advocacy.

Another means by which the state tries to manage its relations with civil society is through the Public Chamber. As Chapter 3 noted, the Public Chamber was formed at Putin's urging after the Beslan tragedy. It was intended to give various social associations a channel to bring their ideas and opinions to the attention of the authorities in order to make policy more effective and responsive and to monitor the quality of public life. Similar consultative bodies already existed in a number of regions and several Western countries. The legislation creating the Public Chamber passed in 2005 and the body was formed soon thereafter. The chamber has 126 members, drawn from a wide array of organizations (including the media; business; sports; environmental protection groups; the Orthodox Church; medical, legal, and academic professions; and youth groups). President Putin named the first 42 members, who in turn chose another 42. These 84 then selected the final 42. No openly oppositional figures are represented in the chamber (nor did they wish to join), but the chamber did recruit a number of prominent intellectuals and social figures, such as the world chess champion Anatolii Karpov.[71]

Although the Public Chamber has been careful to avoid taking directly political stands on controversial issues, it has weighed in on some topical questions. For instance, it called for softening some of the more repressive provisions of the 2006 law on NGOs. Perhaps of greater significance is the fact that regional governors have also been encouraged to create (or reorganize) public chambers in their own regions. Such chambers give governors opportunities to meet regularly with leaders of local civic groups, hearing their views and helping them in turn to shape public opinion.[72] Participation in such chambers gives some local NGOs greater legitimacy in voicing the interests of the groups they represent. In regions where such chambers did not already exist, the creation of a Public Chamber at the federal level encouraged the governors to establish similar chambers in each region—and to invite local

NGOs to join them. Thus, a paradoxical consequence of the pattern of authoritarian corporatism is that while it has limited freedom for some interest groups, it has simultaneously expanded it for others—especially those that are willing to work within the constraints set by the regime to advance the interests of their constituencies.

Generally, the regime pursues a three-pronged strategy: some groups—those that are explicitly opposition oriented—are repressed; others are offered channels for cooperation with the regime on the authorities' terms; and still others are purely synthetic creatures formed by the regime to siphon off support from more autonomous organizations. Still, there are a good many groups that are neither repressed, coopted, nor fictitious. The Internet allows movements to spring up overnight to protest particular actions by the authorities. But institutionalizing collective action is far more difficult and requires groups to define their relations with the regime.

INTEREST AGGREGATION AND THE PARTY SYSTEM: RETURN TO A ONE-PARTY REGIME?

In democratic political systems, political parties are indispensable mechanisms for converting citizens' demands and groups' interests into policy options that give citizens choice and control over government. In the Soviet era, the single party—the CPSU—sought to guide all public organizations and serve as the sole means for aggregating the multiple interests of a complex society. Since the end of the communist era, a number of parties have arisen, but a stable, competitive party system has not formed. The dominance of United Russia in the 2000s suggests that Russia is returning to a new form of single-party rule.

Interest aggregation refers to the combining of the demands of various groups of the population into programmatic options for government. Typically, this is a by-product of the activity of political parties as they compete for voter support in elections and organize to assume responsibility for governing. Parties propose policy programs that they hope will attract wide support, generalizing the interests of the many in order to win a share of governing power. Although other political institutions also aggregate interests, among them the mass media, parliaments, and large interest groups, it is parties that are the quintessential agency performing this vital task of the political process. Indeed, most political scientists share the view that "modern democracy is unthinkable save in terms of parties."[73] This is because a competitive party system offers voters both choice and accountability: Party electoral competition gives voters a choice over competing policy directions for government and a chance to hold public officials responsible for their performance. Without parties to organize the alternatives for policy, and compete for power, the citizens lack the ability to participate in policy making.[74] Thus, whether the democratic institutions in Russia are working or not depends on how well parties are serving to aggregate interests, define choices for voters, and hold politicians accountable.

Most of the Russian parties that sprang up in the 1990s had shallow roots; often they formed just before an election, and then faded away soon afterward. Neither voters nor politicians developed lasting ties to them. In the 2000s, the regime has attempted to bring about greater stability to the party system but to place it under tight state control. In particular, it has worked to give the pro-Kremlin party, United Russia, a dominant position among the parties and to place the rival parties into a clearly marginal role.[75] The regime has taken a number of steps to accomplish these goals. Legislation passed in 2001 and 2004 raised the requirements for registration of parties: A party must have 50,000 members and branches in at least half the regions of the country to be legally registered. Moreover, only registered parties (and not other kinds of public organizations) are allowed to run candidates in elections. The new rules resulted in a massive winnowing out of the field. There were over 40 registered parties in 2003. By 2010, only seven parties were still registered with the Ministry of Justice.[76] All the rest had either lost their registration or merged with others to remain viable.

In addition, legislation passed in 2005 eliminated single-member district seats from the Duma, so that all 450 seats in the 2007 election were filled by party lists. Parties had to collect large numbers of signatures or put down sizable deposits to qualify to run and had to win at least 7 percent of the vote to win seats. All these provisions made it still harder for small parties to compete. The tough registration requirements also give federal and local authorities more legal grounds for denying parties access to the ballot. Parties supportive of the authorities are routinely registered in regional and local elections; parties that take an opposition stance find signatures on their petitions disqualified or their candidates removed from the ballot for various alleged administrative violations.

Table 6.1 lists the most prominent political parties as of late 2007 together with their levels of popular support.[77] As it shows, United Russia has come to occupy a dominant position in the party spectrum. Other parties have been effectively sidelined.

TABLE 6.1

Party Support, January 2010

Party	Percent
United Russia	65
Communist Party of the Russian Federation	17
Liberal Democratic Party of Russia	10
A Just Russia	6
Yabloko	1
Right Cause	<1
Patriots of Russia	<1

Source: Levada Center, Accessed July 14, 2010.
Note: Distribution of responses to question: "If elections to the State Duma were being held now, for which party would you vote?" Percentage of those with a stated preference.

In the 1990s, Russian parties tended to adopt one of two political strategies. Some espoused a particular ideological outlook, while others avoided taking a clear policy stance and instead identified themselves with broad, vague appeals to support the status quo. Of those with a definable ideological stance, three main strains were apparent: democratic, communist, and nationalist. Democratic parties favored a capitalist economy, liberal democracy, and a Western orientation. The communists supported a state-dominated economic and political system, and the nationalists had a pro-imperial or pro-ethnic nationalist, anti-Western orientation. The nonideological parties offered a bland mixture of appeals to noncontroversial values, such as "centrism," "unity," "pragmatism," and "a strong state." Often such parties were simply political machines for officeholders and were commonly termed "parties of power." United Russia is far and away the most successful of the "parties of power." Its rise to a dominant position in the 2000s has transformed the party system, but echoes of the battles of the 1990s are still heard in elections today.

Let us examine these categories more closely.

Party Families

Democratic Parties   Democratic parties embodied the hope that the collapse of communism would lead to an open, pluralistic, political order respecting political and civil rights and a market-based economy. Some democrats prefer a more laissez-faire approach to the economy, and others a form of social democracy. But they would all agree that Russia must guarantee political and economic freedoms for its citizens, protect private property rights, and strengthen the rule of law, and they fight against socialist and collectivist tendencies in the political and economic spheres.

Russia's democrats first mobilized in the *glasnost'* era. After suffering setbacks in the 1993 and 1995 elections, some leaders of the democratic forces pooled their resources and formed a new electoral alliance called the Union of Right Forces (SPS, for its Russian initials) to compete in 1999. They put a trio of younger leaders at the top of their party list, and their campaign emphasized that Prime Minister Putin had endorsed (if rather vaguely) their economic program. This time their strategy paid off, and they entered parliament. In 2003 and 2007, however, facing harassment from the authorities, along with falling voter support, SPS again fell below the 5 percent threshold in the Duma party list vote. In fall 2008, they agreed to dissolve as a party and re-form, with two other organizations, as a new, business-oriented party called Right Cause, with a friendly relationship with the regime, and led by a troika of three coequal leaders. Several long-time leaders of SPS resigned in protest, charging that the new structure was an instrument of the Kremlin.[78] By all indications, the formation of the new party was indeed engineered by the authorities and served the purpose of splitting the hard-line opposition elements away from the rest of the democratic forces, and then moving the latter into a cooperative relationship with the regime. In any event, the party was largely paralyzed by conflicts among its three leaders.[79]

Yabloko considers itself the "democratic opposition" to the government. For many years, it was headed by the prominent political figure Grigorii Yavlinsky. It espouses a general theme of a socially oriented economy and a pro-Western external policy, as well as championing causes such as environmental protection, anticorruption, and effective local self-government. Yavlinsky himself ran for the presidency in 1996 and again in 2000, receiving around 7 percent of the vote in 1996 and 5.8 percent in 2000, but did not run in 2004 or 2008. Yabloko has consistently refused to form an electoral alliance with other democratic parties, contributing to the persistent fragmentation of the democratic camp. Nationally, Yabloko's support has fallen from the 10 percent level that it enjoyed in the 1990s to about 1 percent, although it still has pockets of support in Moscow and St. Petersburg. It was represented in the first, second, and third Dumas, but has not cleared the electoral threshold in the fourth and fifth Dumas. It has some representation in regional and local assemblies.

Communist Parties   The Communist Party of the Russian Federation (CPRF) is the major successor party to the old CPSU. Other splinter groups exist that are more militantly Stalinist; the CPRF has cautiously embraced certain elements of the market and has declared that it no longer believes in violence and revolution as means to achieve its policy goals. It vehemently opposed the market reforms and privatization programs of the Yeltsin era.[80] CPRF continues to oppose the market-oriented policies of the Putin regime. The CPRF also takes a nationalist stance, for instance attacking Western influence in Russia. Its leader, Gennadii Ziuganov, has sought to align the party with the religious and spiritual traditions of Russian culture, glossing over Marx's and Lenin's militant enmity toward religion. Ziuganov frequently invokes the traditional mutual support between the Russian state and the Russian Orthodox Church.

The CPRF has a substantial organizational base, a well-defined electoral following, a large but declining membership, a large network of local party newspapers, and, probably most importantly, the tradition of Communist Party discipline, which it inherited from the Communist Party of the Soviet Union. Divisions within the party are usually kept from exploding, although periodically the party expels dissidents. But the CPRF has clear weaknesses as well. Ziuganov lacks broad personal appeal, but no other communist leader enjoys wide support in the party. CPRF voters tend to be older than average, and the party appeals to them by its association with the old regime. Moreover, it is ideologically straitjacketed: If it moves too much to the center of the political spectrum, it will lose its distinctiveness as a clear alternative to the government, but if it moves further to the left, it will marginalize itself. The result is that the CPRF's share of the electorate is declining, but the party has been unable to mobilize new groups of voters. While the ideology, reputation, and organization of the communists give them a certain baseline amount of electoral support, that support is declining, and they have been unable to attract new groups of followers.

Nationalist Parties   The most visible nationalist party, the Liberal Democratic Party of Russia (LDPR)—Zhirinovsky's party—differs from the communists in certain important respects. Zhirinovsky's party stresses the national theme, even more than the communists, appealing to feelings of injured ethnic and state pride. Zhirinovsky calls for aggressive foreign policies and harsh treatment of non-Russian ethnic minorities. However, his economic policy is much fuzzier. While demanding that the government relieve the distress of Russians who have suffered under market reforms, he also distances himself from the socialist economic system of the past and poses as a "third force," which is neither tied to the old communist regime nor to the new order. Finally, he also sends a clear message of support for harsh authoritarian rule to deal effectively with Russia's enemies without and within.

Zhirinovsky cultivates a vivid, theatrical, even clownish, public persona, which works effectively on television. He appeals to many voters who are disaffected with both the government and the communists. However, bombastic as Zhirinovsky's rhetoric is, the party's actual voting record in the Duma is extremely supportive of the authorities. Zhirinovsky's party is also famous for putting figures identified with organized crime onto its candidate lists.[81] Rumors have circulated for years about the price for buying a good place on the list. Some consider the LDPR to be a business enterprise more than a political party.

Zhirinovsky's LDPR has been the most successful of the parties competing for the nationalist vote. A great many other parties have attempted to build successful followings around themes such as the need to restore the Soviet Union, or to make Russia a great world power again, or to cleanse Russia of the ethnic "outsiders" who contaminate it, or to bring back the tsar. But these parties have either failed in their bid for parliamentary votes and then splintered and faded or have concentrated their efforts on forming a small but dedicated corps of militant followers.

There are a number of small militant nationalist groups that have adopted proto-fascist ideologies and organizational models. An example is the National Bolshevik Party. The NBP has repeatedly been refused registration on the grounds that it is extremist. It mixes extreme leftist and extreme nationalist themes: It is hostile to capitalism, to the West, to immigrants, and to the authorities. It does not have a serious political following, but it has been effective at attracting attention with publicity stunts. Once a group of its activists took over a government reception office near the Kremlin and unfurled a banner outside the window that read, "Putin Quit Your Job!" Another time a group occupied offices in the Ministry of Health after arriving in fake police uniforms and demanding the evacuation of the building. They then threw a portrait of Putin out of the window. They have squirted mayonnaise onto the head of the Central Election Commission and committed other acts of what they call "food terrorism."[82] Meantime, its leader, a writer named Eduard Limonov, who was sentenced to a four-year term in jail for illegal weapons possession, protests that his party is a victim of political oppression.

The many small nationalist groups feature a variety of ideological tendencies: Some want to see Russia form a great Eurasian union, while others focus on ridding Russia of ethnically alien elements. The inability to define a common national program has been one of the factors inhibiting unity among the nationalist forces. Another has been their tendency to devote their energies to street protests rather than party-building.

Parties of Power Although many parties have called themselves centrist, that usually means that they lack any distinct policy positions that they could be held accountable for. In some cases, parties that are closely allied to the authorities call themselves centrist to reinforce their commitment to stability and continuity. Certainly, the most successful "party of power" to have arisen—United Russia—considers itself to be centrist. For example, in its publicity, it describes itself as the "party of Russian political culture," "the party of sovereign democracy," "the party of stability, of self-reliant people."[83] At the same time, it does have a programmatic tendency. Sometimes it calls itself "right-centrist," because it supports market-oriented and pro-business policies, such as cutting taxes and reducing regulation. Often it calls its philosophy "social conservatism." Voters see the party as positioned on the right side of the spectrum—three quarters of citizens believe that United Russia wants to "continue and deepen market reforms" and to treat the West as an "ally or friend."[84] Its identification with Vladimir Putin is total; Putin is the chairman of the party (although not a member of it!) and, according to the chairman of the party's Supreme Council, the Duma speaker Boris Gryzlov, he is the country's "national leader" "regardless of what post he occupies."[85] Before the 2007 Duma election, one party supporter, a well-known circus performer named Askold Zapashnyi, was quoted as saying, "we must beg Vladimir Vladimirovich to remain for another term. God does not bestow such a leader upon the country every year. We don't want our children to be abandoned."[86]

For the United Russia party, this strategy of embracing Putin is risky. It can succeed only so long as Putin is both powerful and popular. If Putin comes back as president, the party will probably continue to be regarded as the party of Putin. If not, the party will need to find a new patron in the Kremlin.

United Russia uses a variety of levers to maintain its dominant position in the political system. At election time, it pressures federal and local election commissions to disqualify popular opposition parties and candidates. It dominates the airwaves. Recently, for example, one of its Duma deputies was made the host of a talk show about legal issues, a move that observers interpreted as a way of positioning him to defend the party's positions in televised debates in the 2011 election campaign.[87] Its access to financing from both state and private sources enables it to far outspend its rivals in election campaigns. And, in some cases, it encourages the falsification of election results to ensure the outcomes it desires.[88] Some of these efforts would appear to be unnecessary, because the party enjoys a considerable base of political support.[89] But, like dominant parties in other authoritarian regimes, it goes to great lengths to ensure its control over elections as a way of discouraging its opponents from uniting against it.[90]

The forerunner of United Russia as a party of power was "Our Home Is Russia." It originated in the run-up to the 1995 parliamentary elections, when President Yeltsin's political advisors decided to use the Kremlin's political resources to create a pro-government, centrist but moderately reformist, political movement. Yeltsin asked the then prime minister Chernomyrdin to head it. Benefiting from government official support and promoting a reassuring image of stability and pragmatism, Our Home won 10.3 percent of the list vote in the December election. However, Our Home never succeeded in defining a clear programmatic position, and was mostly a coalition of officeholders, particularly big-city mayors, regional governors, and presidents of ethnic republics. For this reason, it soon became known as "the party of power." And once Chernomyrdin was dismissed from the government in 1998, Our Home imploded. In 1999, it only won 1.2 percent of the list vote. It dissolved soon thereafter.

The 1999 election was peculiar in that it offered voters at least three parties that had some claim to being a party of power. Besides Our Home Is Russia, two other blocs that had strong links to the state authorities also competed. The Fatherland–All Russia alliance united several powerful regional leaders and its list was headed by former Prime Minister Evgenii Primakov. But the real phenomenon of 1999 was the third "party of power," Unity. Unity formed only three months before the election, by all accounts with the active assistance of Boris Berezovsky and President Yeltsin's entourage in the Kremlin. Its trump card was Vladimir Putin. Appointed prime minister on August 9, 1999, Putin actively aided in the formation of the new movement, commenting at one point that "as a citizen," he intended to vote for Unity. Thus, state officials who wondered which was the "true" party of power (fearing to back the wrong party!) could safely conclude that Unity was the right choice, particularly as Putin's popularity soared. As the once-dominant Fatherland–All Russia bloc's ratings fell, Unity's support rose: Unity went from 4 percent on November 2 to 9 percent on November 22 to 18 percent on November 29, and it received 23.3 percent of the vote on election day.[91] The reason for its success was that governors and other elites quickly switched their allegiance to it once they saw that it was going to be the *real* party of power.

In parliament, Unity became the vehicle through which President Putin could enact his legislative program. Voting with remarkable discipline, Unity's members formed alliances with other parliamentary factions and passed nearly every bill proposed by Putin and the government.[92] Unity liked to describe itself as a "ruling party," but in fact it did not control either the government or the presidency: It was largely the parliamentary appendage of a very strong president. Putin spoke vaguely about the desirability of building a viable party system and even of moving to the point where parties would name the candidates for president. But, like President Yeltsin before him, he himself found it expedient to remain above the battlefield of party politics. Still, the

Kremlin lent its considerable resources to ensure the Unity would dominate the next parliament. In December 2001, "Fatherland" (Moscow Mayor Yuri Luzhkov's party) merged with Unity to form "United Russia." The Kremlin signaled to federal and regional officeholders that it expected them to support United Russia in the Duma election of 2003. The result was a landslide electoral victory and an overwhelming majority in the Duma. United Russia succeeded in capitalizing both on President Putin's popularity and on the steady improvement in the economy.

In 2006, the Kremlin formed another party of power to siphon off opposition to United Russia from the left side of the spectrum. Called "A Just Russia" *(Spravedlivaia Rossiia)*, it is headed by Sergei Mironov, the chair of the Federation Council. The party espouses a left-centrist, broadly social-democratic, orientation, stressing the need for improved pay for workers, assistance to the poor, and higher pensions for the elderly. It periodically offers mild criticism of United Russia for tieing itself too closely to the government and big business and promises to fight "wild capitalism," to nationalize natural resources, and to provide free, state-funded housing, education, and medical care to all citizens. The Kremlin appears to want A Just Russia to survive but to remain weak, giving it just enough encouragement to enable it to recruit some leaders and some voters, but not enough to allow it to displace United Russia from a dominant position. In the 2007 Duma elections, it won 7.7 percent of the vote (to United Russia's 64.3 percent), and in regional elections in 2008, it generally won 7–8 percent of the vote (to UR's 50–80 percent share). The party did not run its own candidate for president in the 2008 election, instead endorsing Dmitrii Medvedev.

A Just Russia is not, of course, an opposition party in any meaningful sense of the word. Actual open competition between United Russia and A Just Russia would result in the risk of a divided elite, which in turn could spur an uncontrollable cascade of open popular mobilization.[93] Most likely, the Kremlin seeks to allow A Just Russia to win just enough votes to siphon off support from the communists and nationalists, but not enough to pose a serious threat to United Russia's dominance. The Kremlin has repeatedly created similar parties to draw off support from independent parties, give politicians additional channels for winning office, and manage party competition. The formation of a new pro-business party to replace SPS is the latest example of this tactic.

Many authoritarian regimes use dominant parties as a means to coordinate the political ambitions of politicians, structure electoral competition, ensure reliable voting majorities in legislatures, and build popular loyalty to the regime. Such regimes tend to be more durable if they have such parties than if they do not.[94] But maintaining the party over time and across the country requires the investment of regime resources. The regime must make it worthwhile for other powerful interests in the society, such as business and regional elites, to work on its behalf. Maintenance of a true ruling party, as the history of the Soviet regime illustrates, is not only incompatible with democratic party competition but also a check on personal dictatorship.

Parties and Elections

Since the first competitive elections held in the early 1990s, the greatest impetus to the development of political parties has been the Duma elections. Each round of elections (1993, 1995, 1999, 2003, 2007) has stimulated a burst of organizational activity by parties.[95] Presidential elections, on the other hand, held in 1991, 1996, 2000, 2004, and 2008 have not had a similar effect. Because Russia's presidential system encourages the president to avoid making commitments to parties, presidential elections have tended to concentrate attention on the candidates' personalities rather than their policy programs and therefore have even undermined party development. The same has been true of gubernatorial elections. Other factors as well inhibited the development of a competitive party system in the 1990s, including the trend for big business to sponsor candidates directly, the rise of governors' political machines, and the tendency for the Kremlin to intervene in the electoral system, both by sponsoring parties of power and by selective backing of individual gubernatorial and mayoral candidates. Political scientist Henry Hale terms these "party substitutes."[96] The weakness of independent parties in the 1990s allowed Putin's regime to concentrate its resources on a single, dominant "party of power" in the 2000s.

Historically, the development of parties in Russia in the past two decades has been stimulated by parliamentary elections much more than by presidential elections. This began under Gorbachev, in 1989, with the elections of deputies to the new USSR Congress of People's Deputies. This election campaign stimulated the mobilization of democratic activists intent on electing reformers to the Congress. The activists of 1989 then became the core of a democratic movement in the 1990 elections to the Russian Congress of People's Deputies. Partisan factions in both legislative assemblies became the nuclei of political parties. The 1993 election to the new State Duma was the impetus to yet another wave of party formation, as 13 parties registered and competed for seats. Two years later, 43 parties competed in the December 1995 Duma election—far more parties than could possibly be accommodated, given that the same five percent threshold rule was kept. In the end, only four parties crossed the five percent threshold: the communists, Zhirinovsky's LDPR, the Our Home Is Russia bloc formed around Prime Minister Chernomyrdin, and the Yabloko party. Of these, the communists were the most successful, winding up with nearly one-third of the seats in the Duma. Altogether, half of the votes were cast for parties that failed to win any seats on the party list ballot.

The 1999 election was dominated by the question of who would succeed Yeltsin as president. Many federal and regional officeholders wanted to rally around a new "party of power" in order to protect their positions. The Unity party, formed in August by a group of backroom Kremlin strategists to give Putin a base of electoral support, came from nowhere to win a remarkable 23 percent of the party list vote in December. Unity swallowed some of its former rivals to become United Russia, and the Kremlin decided to give it the full benefit of its administrative help in the 2003 election. United Russia won 38 percent of the party list vote and wound up with two-thirds of the seats in the Duma. The communists lost almost half their vote share, and the democrats did even worse; for the first time, none of the democratic parties won seats on the party list vote. The result underscored Putin's determination to eliminate any significant alternatives to his policies and power. In 2007, the rival parties were pushed still further to the sidelines as United Russia was credited with winning almost two-thirds of the vote. The regime went to massive lengths to guarantee the desired electoral outcome, denying rival parties access to the ballot, airtime on television, and opportunities to campaign; in a number of regions, outright fraud was used in tallying the votes.[97]

Table 6.2 indicates the results of the party list voting in the 1999, 2003, and 2007 Duma elections, and how they were converted into parliamentary parties' seats in the Duma.

Unlike parliamentary elections, presidential elections have had very little positive effect on party development. The three individuals who have run and won in Russia's presidential elections—Yeltsin, Putin, and Medvedev—all conspicuously avoided running as partisans. (Technically, sitting presidents may not be party members—but this would hardly be a bar to a president who wanted to change the law.[98]) Rather, all three evidently calculated that they would have broader appeal if they chose *not* to run as party candidates and emphasized instead their personal qualities and their devotion to broad national goals. To be sure, some of the major challengers have represented

TABLE 6.2

Votes and Seats

	3rd Duma (2000–2003)		4th Duma (2003–2007)		5th Duma (2007–2011)	
	Party list vote (%)	Seats in Duma (%)	Party list vote (%)	Seats in Duma (%)	Party list vote (%)	Seats in Duma (%)
Unity/United Russia[a]	23.32	18.4	37.4	68	64.3	70
OVR	13.33	10.2				
CPRF	24.29	20.2	12.65	11.56	11.57	13
LDPR	5.98	3.9	11.49	8	8.14	9
SPS	8.52	7.3	3.97	0	0.96	0
Yabloko	5.93	4.8	4.32	0	1.59	0
Motherland/ A Just Russia[b]			9.04	8.67	7.74	8

Abbreviations:
OVR = Fatherland–All Russia
CPRF = Communist Party of the Russian Federation
LDPR = Liberal Democratic Party of Russia
SPS = Union of Rightist Forces
[a]Unity merged with OVR in 2001 to form United Russia.
[b]A Just Russia formed in 2006 from the merger of Motherland, the Pensioners Party, and the Party of Life.

parties or political movements, among them the leaders of the communist party, the LDPR, and Yabloko.

In his two presidential election campaigns, 1991 and 1996, Boris Yeltsin, however, did present himself as the clear alternative to a restoration of communism. The 1996 election saw a remarkable turnaround in his electoral fortunes. At the beginning of 1996, his approval was in single digits.[99] But Yeltsin's displays of vigor during the campaign, his lavish promises to voters, and his domination of media publicity, all contributed to a remarkable surge in popularity and a second-round victory over Gennadii Ziuganov, his communist rival. The campaign took its toll on Yeltsin. Soon afterward, he had a major heart surgery and for much of his second term he was in poor health.

Putin's two elections, in contrast, focused on his reputation for competence and decisiveness. In 2000, he had the advantage of being acting president and ran the equivalent of a "rose garden" campaign, going about the normal daily business of a president rather than venturing out and asking for people's votes. He counted on the support of officeholders at all levels, a media campaign that presented a "presidential" image to the voters, and the voters' fear that change would only make life worse. His rivals, moreover, were weak. Several prominent politicians prudently chose not to enter the race against him. In the event, Putin won an outright majority in the first round. He won reelection as president in 2004 in a landslide, with over 71 percent of the vote. The Kremlin's use of administrative carrots and sticks (known in Russian as the "administrative resource"), its egregious manipulation of media coverage of the election, and Putin's genuine popularity all combined to make the outcome a foregone conclusion. Moreover, Putin's decisive victory underscored the point that United Russia needed Putin far more than Putin needed the party.

Medvedev's 2008 election answered two questions: whether Putin would leave the presidency, and in what capacity he would remain in power. Putin's support for Medvedev, together with the massive administrative interference in the elections by the Kremlin, ensured that the election proceeded according to the plan. Medvedev was officially reported to have received 70 percent—slightly less than Putin had officially received in 2004, but better by more than a 2:1 margin than his three rivals combined.

Table 6.3 lists the results of the presidential elections in 2000, 2004, and 2008, together with the party affiliations, if any, of the candidates.

Until the mid-2000s, there was a great deal of turnover in the parties. Politicians were constantly starting new parties, only to abandon them after the election. Voters had relatively shallow attachments to parties and often associated them with particular politicians' personalities rather than with specific ideological stances. Each new election presented voters with a substantially new set of party choices, making it hard for voters to develop any lasting attachments to parties or to make sensible judgments about parties' past or future performance. As Richard Rose puts it, Russia had "a floating party system."[100] The electoral cycle of 2007–2008 suggests that this pattern may now be at an end. The party system has apparently developed an anchor in the form of a lasting, stable, dominant party of power—United Russia.

TABLE 6.3

Russian Presidential Elections in the 2000s (Percentage of Valid Vote)

	2000 (%)	2004 (%)	2008 (%)
Vladimir Putin	52.94	71.31	–
Gennadii Ziuganov (CPRF)	29.21	–	17.72
Vladimir Zhirinovsky (LDPR)	2.7	–	9.35
Grigorii Yavlinskii (Yabloko)	5.8	–	–
Nikolai Kharitonov (CPRF)	–	13.74	–
Dmitrii Medvedev	–	–	70.28
Andrei Bogdanov (DPR)	–	–	1.3
Other	6.53	10.71	–
Against all candidates[a]	1.88	3.45	–

Putin and Medvedev won in the first round by wide margins in each race.
Abbreviations:
CPRF: Communist Party of the Russian Federation
LDPR: Liberal Democratic Party of Russia
DPR: Democratic Party of Russia
[a]The "against all candidates" option was not available on the 2008 ballot.

Party Strategies and the Social Bases of Party Support

The establishment of the dominant party regime has changed the way parties represent different social groups. In the 1990s, there were some systematic links between particular social groups and particular parties. For instance, younger and better-educated voters tended to support the democratic parties, while older and less-educated voters supported communist and nationalist parties. But as the United Russia party has gained dominance, it has appealed to all parts of the society. As a result, social structure has become less and less significant as an influence on voting patterns, while voters' attitudes toward the authorities in general and Putin in particular have become the most important predictor of voting preferences.

Table 6.4 reports the result of a survey in December 2007, just after the Duma election. It seeks to elicit the reasons that voters voted for or against United Russia. The results suggest that voters of all camps tend to see United Russia as the embodiment of President Putin's political legacy. The challenge for United Russia in the future will be to establish a basis of support that goes beyond simply its identification with Putin. The party will need to cultivate more lasting attachments based on its ability to deliver policy benefits to the voters. Putin and other Kremlin officials have warned the party that it cannot hope to feed off the Kremlin's life support system forever—though they are unwilling to cut it loose. For other parties, the 2007–2008 elections confirmed the new reality that United Russia is likely to enjoy a dominant position for years to come. Other parties have been relegated to playing a small, marginal role in national politics and concentrating their efforts on winning seats in regional parliaments. Most politicians have recognized that career success today requires hitching their wagon to the principal party of power—United Russia.

TABLE 6.4

Grounds for Support of United Russia

If you voted for United Russia, why?

Wanted to support V. Putin	46
I like this party, I trust it	32
I don't especially like this party, but the others are even worse	3
I wanted to vote the same way as everyone else	2
I was forced to vote for it but I didn't especially want to	<1
Other	<1
Hard to answer	15

If you voted against United Russia, why?

It's not a bad party, but I like the one I voted for better	16
I don't like the monopolism of this party, its special position	11
I don't like the idea of this party, I don't agree with its policy course	9
I figured that United Russia would get a lot of votes and could manage without my vote	8
I don't like the actions of the authorities in my region, I don't trust them	4
I wanted to express mistrust in V. Putin	3
I don't like the party leaders of United Russia	2
Poor, uninteresting advertising; boring election campaign	<1
Other	3
Hard to answer	43

Some say that these elections were a referendum about confidence in Vladimir Putin. Others say that these were ordinary parliamentary elections. Which of these viewpoints is closer to your own opinion?

	All respondents	United Russia	CPRF	LDPR	A Just Russia
More with the first	65	74	54	40	66
More with the second	19	14	28	41	20
Hard to answer	16	12	18	19	14

Source: All-Russian Center for the Study of Public Opinion (VTsIOM),
http://wciom.ru/index.php?id=268&uid=9406, accessed July 11, 2008;
Press release no. 840, December 19, 2007; Political attitudes and the vote for
United Russia (Survey conducted December 8–9, 2007. N=1600).
Note: Support for United Russia strongly reflects attitudes toward Vladimir Putin.

The Future of the Party System

Several factors help account for the fact that Russia failed to develop a competitive party system. Among these are the powerful presidency, the weakness of civil society, the fading of the ideological cleavages produced by the regime change, and the success of the authorities in building a single, dominant party of power—United Russia. Strong presidentialism undermines the ability of parties to promise that electoral success will translate into policy influence, since the president can choose a government largely of his own liking. Under these circumstances, politicians prefer to join the Kremlin-backed bandwagon. As a result, neither the dominant party nor its marginal rivals are capable of performing the functions of aggregating the interests of citizens and formulating practical policy options. Elections have been turned into shows of support for the current regime.

It is possible that United Russia will outlast the Putin–Medvedev era. Much will depend on whether future leaders will continue to rule using authoritarian methods. If so, they are likely to find it convenient to use a dominant party to mobilize voters in elections, build majorities in legislatures, and manage the careers of ambitious politicians. The Kremlin's political strategist, Vladislav Surkov, has indicated that he would like to see United Russia dominate the political system for 10 or 15 years or more, ensuring that the long-term goals of the Putin–Medvedev leadership are achieved.[101] To make United Russia into a successful, long-lasting party of power that ensures continuity in policies and power across elections, the Kremlin will have to give up some of the informal, personalized political practices that it currently uses to rule and give United Russia the autonomy to succeed—or to fail.

NOTES

1. Mancur Olson, *The Logic of Collective Action: Public Goods and the Theory of Groups* (Cambridge, MA: Harvard University Press, 1965).
2. Kay Lehman Schlozman, Sidney Verba, and Henry Brady, "Participation is Not a Paradox: The View from American Activists," *British Journal of Political Science* 25 (1995): 1–36.
3. According to Gregory J. Kasza, such "administered mass organizations" as Stalin-era trade unions and youth groups have been a characteristic feature of a number of the mobilizing regimes of the twentieth century. Gregory J. Kasza, *The Conscription Society: Administered Mass Organizations* (New Haven, CT: Yale University Press, 1995).
4. Frederick C. Barghoorn, "Faction, Sectoral and Subversive Opposition in Soviet Politics," in Robert A. Dahl, ed., *Regimes and Oppositions* (New Haven, CT: Yale University Press, 1973), pp. 27–88.
5. Philip G. Roeder, *Red Sunset: The Failure of Soviet Politics* (Princeton: Princeton University Press, 1993).
6. Robert Conquest, *The Great Terror: A Reassessment* (New York: Oxford University Press, 1990). The terrible famine of 1932, which struck the Ukraine and certain other regions with particular force, was itself the product of deliberate policy as Stalin and his associates expressly prohibited sending relief to the affected areas, apparently in order to break any resistance to the collectivization campaign.
   See also Robert Conquest, *The Harvest of Sorrow: Soviet Collectivization and the Terror-Famine* (New York: Oxford University Press, 1986).
7. Jane I. Dawson, *Eco-Nationalism: Anti-Nuclear Activism and National Identity in Russia, Lithuania, and Ukraine* (Durham, NC: Duke University Press, 1996).
8. On the emergence of informal social groups in the glasnost' period, see Judith B. Sedaitis and Jim Butterfield, eds., *Perestroika from Below: Social Movements in the Soviet Union* (Boulder, CO: Westview, 1991) and Michael Urban, *The Rebirth*

of Politics in Russia (Cambridge: Cambridge University Press, 1997). A valuable overview of the emergence of nationalist movements in the Gorbachev period is Chapter 4, "Nationalism and Nation-States: Gorbachev's Dilemmas," in Ronald Grigor Suny, ed., *The Revenge of the Past: Nationalism, Revolution, and the Collapse of the Soviet Union* (Stanford: Stanford University Press, 1993), pp. 127–160.

9. The labels "red" and "brown" are widely used to refer to these ideological tendencies in Russian discussions. "Red," of course, is the symbolic color of the Bolsheviks, of communism and revolution; it was the dominant color of the Soviet flag. "Brown" represents extremist nationalism, after the "brown shirts" who were early Nazi followers of Adolf Hitler in Germany in the 1920s. Thus, they are regarded as quasi-fascist ultranationalists.

10. Ul'iana Makhkamova, "Obshchestvennye organizatsii ne bedstvuiut," *Nezavisimaia gazeta,* June 18, 2008.

11. Jack L. Walker, Jr., *Mobilizing Interest Groups in America: Patrons, Professions, and Social Movements* (Ann Arbor, MI: University of Michigan Press, 1991), p. 9.

12. Polit.ru, May 13, 2010.

13. In a system where all prices were set by the state, there was no meaningful measure of profit in any case. Indeed, relative prices were profoundly distorted by the cumulative effect of decades of central planning. The absence of accurate measures of economic costs is one of the major reasons that Russia's economy continues to be so slow to restructure.

14. Chapter 7 will discuss the oligarchs in more detail.

15. Information on Civic Union may be found in Stephen White, Graeme Gill, and Darrell Slider, *The Politics of Transition: Shaping a Post-Soviet Future* (Cambridge: Cambridge University Press, 1993), pp. 166–169. A more detailed study is Peter Rutland, *Business Elites and Russian Economic Policy* (London: Royal Institute of International Affairs, 1992). See also Michael McFaul, "Russian Centrism and Revolutionary Transitions," *Post-Soviet Affairs* 9:3 (July/September 1993): 196–222; Wendy Slater, "The Diminishing Center of Russian Parliamentary Politics," *RFE/RL Research Report* 3:17 (April 29, 1994), discusses the fate of Civic Union through the 1993 elections.

16. Information drawn from the RUIE's Web site, http://www.xn—o1aabe.xn—p1ai/Default.aspx?CatalogId=1054, accessed July 14, 2010.

17. One observer termed the Putin regime's strategy "managed pluralism." See Harley Balzer, "Managed Pluralism: Vladimir Putin's Emerging Regime," *Post-Soviet Affairs* 19:3 (2003): 189–227.

18. Peter Rutland, "Business and Civil Society in Russia," in Alfred B. Evans, Jr., Laura A. Henry, and Lisa McIntosh Sundstrom, eds., *Russian Civil Society: A Critical Assessment* (Armonk, NY: M. E. Sharpe, 2006), p. 85.

19. *Segodnia,* October 7, 2000.

20. Mikhail Sergeev, "Biznes priznaetsia v nedoverii k prezidentu," *Nezavismiaia gazeta,* September 24, 2009.

21. Polit.ru, January 11, 2010.

22. Mansur Mirovalev, "Khodorkovsky Pleads Not Guilty in Court," *Moscow Times,* April 22, 2009.

23. Lisa McIntosh Sundstrom, "Soldiers' Rights Groups in Russia: Civil Society Through Russian and Western Eyes," in Alfred B. Evans, Jr., Laura A. Henry, and Lisa McIntosh Sundstrom, eds., *Russian Civil Society: A Critical Assessment* (Armonk, NY: M. E. Sharpe, 2006), p. 180.

24. Figures on the number of soldiers who die each year as a direct or indirect result of hazing (*dedovshchina*) are hard to come by. According to the Ministry of Defense, only 16 soldiers died as a result of improper treatment in 2005. However, another 276 committed suicide, and 1064 died as a result of "crimes and incidents." Polit.ru, January 27, 2006. The Prosecutor General reported in August 2006 that, so far that year, 17 servicemen had died as a result of hazing and over 100 had been injured, and that there had been some 3,500 reported cases of hazing. *RFE/RL Newsline*, August 4, 2006. In 2008, a leader of the Soldiers' Mothers Committee was quoted by Reuters as saying that up to 3,500 Russian soldiers die each year from "various accidents and suicides." *RFE/RL Newsline*, February 14, 2008. An official report by the Public Chamber in 2009 states that there had been 604 noncombat deaths in the military in 2008, of which half were by suicide. Polit.ru, January 30, 2009.

Occasionally, a particularly shocking case comes to light, resulting in a public outcry and provoking the military to arrest and try those guilty. But despite the public and official condemnation of the practice, it clearly continues.

25. http://www.soldiersmothers.spb.org/, On the Soldiers' Mothers, see Lisa McIntosh Sundstrom, *Funding Civil Society: Foreign Assistance and NGO Development in Russia* (Palo Alto, CA: Stanford University Press, 2006); Valerie Sperling, *Organizing Women in Contemporary Russia: Engendering Transition* (Cambridge: Cambridge University Press, 1999), pp. 206–207; *Christian Science Monitor*, February 24, 2000.

26. *Novaia gazeta*, interview with President Medvedev, April 15, 2009. http://www.novayagazeta.ru/data/2009/039/01.html.

27. Quoted in Annemarie Gielen, "Soldiers' Mothers Challenge Soviet Legacy," on Web site of Initiative for Social Action and Renewal in Eurasia, www.isar .org/isar/archive/GT/GT8Gielen.html. July 5, 2002.

28. Sundstrom, "Soldiers' Rights Groups," p. 182.

29. James Richter, "Evaluating Western Assistance to Russian Women's Organizations," in Sarah E. Mendelson and John K. Glenn, eds., *The Power and Limits of NGOs: A Critical Look at Building Democracy in Eastern Europe and Eurasia* (New York: Columbia University Press, 2002), p. 80.

30. On the transformation of the trade unions as a result of the regime transition, see Paul Kubicek, *Organized Labor in Postcommunist States: From Solidarity to Infirmity* (Pittsburgh: University of Pittsburgh Press, 2004); Sue Davis, *Trade Unions in Russia and Ukraine, 1985–1995* (New York: Palgrave, 2001); and Linda J. Cook, *Labor and Liberalization: Trade Unions in the New Russia* (New York: The Twentieth Century Fund Press, 1997).

31. Figures taken from its Web site, at http://www.fnpr.org.ru/n/252/4890.html, accessed November 29, 2010.

32. Ol'ga Morozova, "Profsoiuzy ne pomogaiut," *Vedomosti.ru*, July 8, 2008.

33. Davis, *Trade Unions in Russia and Ukraine, 1985–1995*, p. 202.

34. Konstantin Savel'ev, "Netrudovye rezervy Mikhail Shmakova," *Nezavisimaia gazeta*, March 12, 2009. There is no clear accounting of the extent of the FNPR's property holdings or the amount of annual revenue they bring in.

35. Ibid., p. 203.

36. The FITUR reached a Faustian bargain with the government over the terms of a new Labor Relations Code, which was adopted in 2001. Under the new legislation, employers no longer have to obtain the consent of the unions to lay off workers. But collective bargaining will be between the largest union at each enterprise and the management unless the workers have agreed on which union

will represent them. Thus, the new labor code favors the FITUR at the expense of the smaller independent unions.

37. Polit.ru, September 30, 2008.
38. Viktoriia Kruchinina, "Zasekrechennaia bezrabotitsia," *Nezavisimaia gazeta*, December 4, 2008.
39. Richard Rose, *New Russia Barometer VI: After the Presidential Election* (Glasgow: Centre for the Study of Public Policy, University of Strathclyde, Studies in Public Policy No. 272), p. 6; Richard Rose, *Getting Things Done with Social Capital: New Russia Barometer VII* (Glasgow: Centre for the Study of Public Policy, University of Strathclyde, 1998), p. 15. In 1996, the question was, At any point during the past 12 months, have you received your wages or pension late? In 1996, 78 percent responded yes, 21 percent no. In 1998, the question was, At any point during the past 12 months, have you received your wages late? 75 percent responded yes, 25 percent no.
40. Graeme B. Robertson, "Strikes and Labor Organizations in Hybrid Regimes," *American Political Science Review* 101:4 (2007): 781–798.
41. Unofficial estimates indicated that there were about 60 actual strikes in 2008 and about 100 in 2009. Sergei Kulikov and Mikhail Sergeev, "Rossii grozit protestnoe obostrenie," *Nezavisimaia gazeta*, February 18, 2010.
42. Linda J. Cook, *Labor and Liberalization: Trade Unions in the New Russia* (New York: The Twentieth Century Fund Press, 1997), pp. 76–77.
43. Another 9–10 percent identify with other faiths: 8–9 percent are Muslim, 0.5–0.6 percent are Buddhist, and 0.2–0.3 percent are Jewish. *RFE/RL Newsline*, October 3, 2000, citing estimates published in *Nezavisimaia gazeta—religii*. Estimates vary widely, depending on the way religious affiliation is understood—as religious heritage or active practice. Some experts believe the number of Muslims in Russia to be as high as 14 or 15 percent. Another survey in December 2008 found that 73 percent considered themselves Orthodox, 6 percent Muslim, 11 percent nonbelievers, and 3 percent believers but with no specific religious affiliation. Polit.ru, December 10, 2008. About 30 percent of the population regularly attend religious services and participate in other church practices. Stanislav Minin, "Poluvotserkovannye kak nemnogo beremennye," *Nezavisimaia gazeta,* June 2, 2008.
44. An accessible and sympathetic introduction to Orthodox history and doctrine is Timothy Ware, *The Orthodox Church* (New York: Penguin Books, 1984).
45. Firuz Kazemzadeh, "Reflections on Church and State in Russian History," in John Witte, Jr. and Michael Bourdeaux, eds., *Proselytism and Orthodoxy in Russia: The New War for Souls* (Maryknoll, NY: Orbis Books, 1999), p. 237.
46. John Dunlop, "The Russian Orthodox Church as an "Empire-Saving" Institution," in Michael Bourdeaux, ed., *The Politics of Religion in Russia and the New States of Eurasia* (Armonk, NY: M. E. Sharpe, 1995), pp. 15–40; Dimitry V. Pospielovsky, "The Russian Orthodox Church in the Postcommunist CIS," in Michael Bourdeaux, ed., *The Politics of Religion in Russia and the New States of Eurasia* (Armonk, NY: M. E. Sharpe, 1995), pp. 41–74; John Garrard and Carol Garrard, *Russian Orthodoxy Resurgent: Faith and Power in the New Russia* (Princeton: Princeton University Press, 2008).
47. Timothy J. Colton, *Yeltsin: A Life* (New York: Basic Books, 2008), p. 446. Yeltsin himself was not religious, but Putin recognized the symbolic power of a religious ceremony to mark a high state occasion.
48. Metropolitan Kirill of Smolensk and Kaliningrad, "Gospel and Culture," in John Witte, Jr. and Michael Bourdeaux, eds., *Proselytism and Orthodoxy in Russia: The New War for Souls* (Maryknoll, NY: Orbis Books, 1999), p. 74.

49. *Segodnia*, June 19, 1997.
50. *RFE/RL Newsline*, September 22, 1997.
51. Ibid., November 24, 1999; *Segodnia*, November 24, 1999.
52. This came in a case involving the Jesuits, whose right to registration was upheld by the Constitutional Court in April 2000, although the Society had existed in Russia only since 1992.
53. *RFE/RL Newsline*, February 14, 2002.
54. John Witte, Jr., "Introduction—Soul Wars: The Problem and Promise of Proselytism in Russia," *Emory International Law Review* 12:1 (Winter 1998): 38.
55. *RFE/RL Newsline*, January 30, 2007. There is a diversity of opinion within the Orthodox Church over how far to concede to the modern world. In summer 2008, the Church declared Bishop Diomid of Chukotka and Anadyr a schismatic after he condemned the Church for going astray by embracing democracy, facilitating globalization, and agreeing to dialogue with other faiths. He was removed from his post as bishop after he pronounced anathema on the current leaders of the Church and was required to move into a monastery as an ordinary monk. *Nezavisimaia gazeta*, November 27, 2008; Polit.ru, September 16, 2008; *Moscow Times*, June 30, 2008.
56. Polit.ru, June 26, 2008.
57. Ibid., September 4, 2009.
58. Alexandra Odynova, "Orthodox Businessmen Get a Patron Saint," *Moscow Times*, December 11, 2009.
59. Elina Bilevskaia, "RPTs tozhe zaimetsia modernizatsiei," *Nezavisimaia gazeta*, April 24, 2010.
60. Polit.ru, November 28, 2002.
61. Ibid., November 23, 2009.
62. Ellen Barry, "Road Rage at the Kremlin," *New York Times*, November 28, 2009. http://www.nytimes.com/2009/11/29/weekinreview/29barry.html?scp=3& sq=russia&st=cse.
63. Alexander Bratersky, "Blue Bucket Protests Draw Duma's Attention," *Moscow Times*, May 4, 2010; Polit.ru, July 9, 2010. Among other things, the legislation would require drivers to give three days notice before holding any public action.
64. Nanci Adler, *Victims of Soviet Terror: The Story of the Memorial Movement* (Westport, CT: Praeger, 1993).
65. Brian D. Taylor, "Law Enforcement and Civil Society in Russia," *Europe–Asia Studies* 58:2 (2006): 193–213.
66. I am indebted for information about the Siberian Civic Initiatives Support Center to Sarah Lindemann-Komarova. Its Web site is www.cip.nsk.su.
67. Balzer, "Managed Pluralism."
68. Polit.ru, November 21, 2001; *RFE/RL Newsline*, November 26, 2001.
69. Vladimir Frolov, "NGOs Starting to Make an Impact on the State," *Moscow Times*, June 2, 2008.
70. Viktoriia Kruchinina, "V Rossii rastet 'tiruremnoe naselnie," *Nezavisimaia gazeta*, September 25, 2008.
71. On the Public Chamber at the federal level, see James Richter, "Putin and the Public Chamber," *Post-Soviet Affairs* 25:1 (2009): 39–65.
72. Novgorod's governor, for example, has had such a consultative body in place for many years. See Natalia Dinello, "What's So Great About Novgorod-the-Great: Trisectoral Cooperation and Symbolic Management," *NCEEER Working Paper* (Washington, DC: NCEEER, 2001).

73. Quoted in Richard Rose, Neil Munro, and Stephen White, *The 1999 Duma Vote: A Floating Party System* (Glasgow: Centre for the Study of Public Policy, University of Strathclyde, 2000), p. 3.

74. E. E. Schattschneider, *The Semi-Sovereign People* (New York: Holt, Rinehart and Winston, 1960), pp. 140–141; Robert A. Dahl, *Polyarchy: Participation and Opposition* (New Haven, CT: Yale University Press, 1971).

75. Ora John Reuter and Thomas F. Remington, "Dominant Party Regimes and the Commitment Problem: The Case of United Russia," *Comparative Political Studies* 42:4 (2009): 501–526; Vladimir Gel'man, "From 'Feckless Pluralism' to 'Dominant Power Politics'? The Transformation of Russia's Party System," *Democratization* 13:4 (2006): 545–561.

76. These were United Russia; the Communist Party of the Russian Federation; the Liberal Democratic Party of Russia; Patriots of Russia; Yabloko; A Just Russia; and Right Cause. Taken from the Web site of the Ministry of Justice: http://www.minjust.ru/ru/activity/nko/partii/, accessed July 14, 2010.

77. The figures are taken from the Levada Center (formerly VTsIOM) and reflect percentages supporting the given party of those intending to vote.

78. Sergei Borisov, "Novyi shans dlia pravykh," *Nezavisimaia gazeta*, October 1, 2008; Polit.ru, September 29, 2008; October 2, 2008.

79. In spring 2010, two of the three coleaders agreed that the party should be headed by a single leader, but needed the presidential administration to decide who that should be.
    Mariia-Luiza Tirmaste, "Nam nuzhen glavnokomanduiushchii i oboz s proviantom," *Kommersant*, April 20, 2010.

80. On the CPRF, see Joan Barth Urban and Valerii D. Solovei, *Russia's Communists at the Crossroads* (Boulder: Westview Press, 1997) and Richard Sakwa, "Left or Right? The CPRF and the Problem of Democratic Consolidation in Russia," *Journal of Communist Studies and Transition Politics*, 14:1 & 2 (March/June 1998): 128–158.

81. For example, a founding member of the notorious Tambov organized crime gang was elected to the Duma in 1995 on the LDPR list. See Vadim Volkov, *Violent Entrepreneurs: The Use of Force in the Making of Russian Capitalism* (Ithaca, NY: Cornell University Press, 2002), pp. 112–113.

82. Peter Finn, "Kremlin Not Amused by Life of This Party," *Washington Post*, August 16, 2005.

83. Slogans taken from the party's Web site, http://www.edinros.ru/news.html, accessed February 13, 2007.

84. Timothy J. Colton and Henry Hale, "The Putin Vote: Presidential Electorates in a Hybrid Regime," *Slavic Review* 68:3 (2009): 473–503; Timothy J. Colton and Henry Hale, "Russians and the Putin–Medvedev Tandemocracy: A Survey-Based Portrait of the 2007–08 Election Season," *Problems of Post-Communism* 57(2) (2010): 3–20.

85. *RFE/RL Newsline*, October 17, 2007.

86. Ibid.

87. Elina Bilevskaia, "Obrechennye na debaty," *Nezavisimaia gazeta*, July 14, 2010.

88. Mikhail Myagkov, Peter C. Ordeshook, and Dimitri Shakin, *The Forensics of Election Fraud: Russia and Ukraine* (Cambridge: Cambridge University Press, 2009).

89. Colton and Hale, "The Putin Vote," "Russians and the Putin–Medvedev Tandemocracy."

90. Beatriz Magaloni, *Voting for Autocracy: Hegemonic Party Survival and Its Demise in Mexico* (Cambridge: Cambridge University Press, 2006).

91. Olga Shvetsova, "Resolving the Problem of Pre-Election Coordination: The Parliamentary Election as an Elite Presidential 'Primary," in Vicki Hesli and William Reisinger, eds., *Elections, Parties and the Future of Russia: The 1999–2000 Elections* (Cambridge: Cambridge University Press, 2002).

92. Thomas F. Remington, "Presidential Support in the Russian State Duma," *Legislative Studies Quarterly* 31:1 (2006): 5–32.

93. Such a scenario occurred in the cases of the "colored revolutions" in Serbia, Georgia, and Ukraine in 2000, 2003, and 2004, respectively. See Michael McFaul, "Conclusion: The Orange Revolution in a Comparative Perspective," in Anders Aslund and Michael McFaul, eds., *Revolution in Orange: The Origins of Ukraine's Democratic Breakthrough* (Washington, DC: Carnegie Endowment for International Peace, 2006), pp. 165–195. On the Orange Revolution and its predecessors, see Close-up 9.1, in Chapter 9.

94. Jason Brownlee, *Authoritarianism in an Age of Democratization* (Cambridge: Cambridge University Press, 2007); Jennifer Gandhi and Adam Przeworski, "Authoritarian Institutions and the Survival of Autocrats," *Comparative Political Studies* 40:11 (2007): 1279–1301; Jennifer Gandhi, *Political Institutions Under Dictatorship* (Cambridge: Cambridge University Press, 2008); Beatriz Magaloni, *Voting for Autocracy: Hegemonic Party Survival and Its Demise in Mexico* (Cambridge: Cambridge University Press, 2006).

95. On the political campaigns surrounding the 1989 and 1990 elections include Brendan Kiernan, *The End of Soviet Politics: Elections, Legislatures, and the Demise of the Communist Party* (Boulder: Westview Press, 1993); and Michael McFaul and Sergei Markov, *The Troubled Birth of Russian Democracy: Parties, Personalities, and Programs* (Stanford: Hoover Institution Press, 1993). For accounts of the elections of 1993, 1995, and 1999, see Stephen White, Richard Rose, and Ian McAllister, *How Russia Votes* (Chatham, NJ: Chatham House Publishers, Inc., 1997) and Richard Rose and Neil Munro, *Elections Without Order: Russia's Challenge to Vladimir Putin* (Cambridge: Cambridge University Press, 2002). On the 2003 election and its impact on party development, see Henry Hale, *Why Not Parties in Russia? Democracy, Federalism, and the State* (Cambridge: Cambridge University Press, 2006).

96. Hale, *Why Not Parties in Russia?*

97. Mikhail Myagkov, Peter C. Ordeshook, and Dimitri Shakin, *The Forensics of Election Fraud: Russia and Ukraine* (Cambridge: Cambridge University Press, 2009).

98. Hale, *Why Not Parties in Russia?* p. 206.

99. Stephen White, Richard Rose, and Ian McAllister, *How Russia Votes* (Chatham, NJ: Chatham House, 1997), p. 254.

100. Rose and Munro, *Elections Without Order*, pp. 118–119.

101. Surkov made these comments at a United Russia party school session on February 7, 2006. They are taken from the United Russia Web site: http://www.edinros.ru/news.html?id=111148, accessed March 13, 2006. He noted that Japan's Liberal Democratic Party and Sweden's Social Democrats had each held power for 40 years or more and that there was nothing strange or undemocratic about such party dominance.

Between State and Market

THE DUAL TRANSITION

Russia's transition from communism brought about an overhaul of both its political and economic systems. This is because the two were tightly intertwined. The communist political system rested on state ownership of all productive wealth, thus eliminating class divisions based on property ownership and allowing the Communist Party to manage the economy on behalf of the state. Observing the sharp difference between Russia's and China's economic performance in the 1990s and 2000s, many observers argue that Russia's strategy of loosening political controls and engaging in radical economic reform opened the door to a surge of corruption, oligarchic predation, and extremes of wealth and poverty before the economy began recovering. Many, therefore, both in China and elsewhere, consider China to offer a far more successful model of national development. In China, the communist party has maintained tight political controls and moved more slowly to dismantle state economic controls and has been far more successful in achieving sustained economic growth. Certainly, China's thriving economy is all the more impressive when compared to the spectacle of breakdown and decline seen in Russia over the last decade, as Figure 7.1 and Tables 7.1 and 7.2 show. Note that Figure 7.1 shows per capita income levels in Russia and China as expressed in terms of "purchasing power parity," which provides a more accurate estimate of the actual incomes based on the purchasing power of incomes in the country. The figure underscores the sharp drop in incomes in Russia before their recovery in the 2000s, in contrast to the much steadier trend in China for average incomes to rise.

Considering the dismal economic performance of the Soviet model and the dynamic rates of growth in most market-oriented economies, few doubt that a market economy leads to both higher economic growth and greater dynamism over the long term than does state socialism. But Russia's transition from a state-controlled economy to a market system resulted in economic depression,

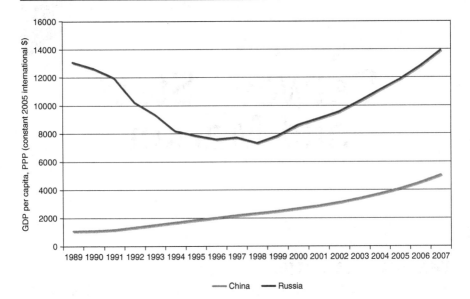

— China — Russia

FIGURE 7.1
GDP Per Capita: Russia and China, 1989–2008

the collapse of social welfare structures, and the concentration of wealth and power in the hands of a small group of tycoons. Based on Russia's experience, therefore, many argue that liberalization of the economy should wait until the institutional infrastructure of capitalism is in place and that democratization should wait until the economy has reached a sufficient level of growth so that conflicts over redistribution do not undermine political order.[1]

When compared with other postcommunist countries, Russia's growth performance is lower than that of the successful Central European countries but higher than most of the post-Soviet countries. Figure 7.2 provides the figures on economic growth in several postcommunist countries, taking the economy as of 1990 as a baseline for tracking annual growth or decline of GDP through 2007. Those countries that remade their economies along capitalist lines were most successful, while those that reformed only partially experienced the deepest declines before beginning to recover. The great debate, therefore, is between those who think Russia's reforms in the early 1990s were too radical, too "Bolshevik," to succeed, and those who believe that Russia's reforms did not go far enough to eliminate the distortions blocking the breakthrough to a dynamic of self-sustaining growth.[2] The fact that Putin's accession to power coincided with economic recovery in Russia makes it hard to resolve this debate conclusively—all the more since world oil prices experienced a steady rise during Putin's presidency.

Certainly, the economy Putin inherited had few of the institutions needed for a successful market economy: impartial regulatory bodies to referee market competition; law enforcement and judicial bodies to enforce contracts and property rights; financial markets to allocate capital efficiently; transparent corporate

TABLE 7.1

Russian Annual GDP Growth and Price Inflation Rates, 1991–2009

Year	1991	1992	1993	1994	1995	1996	1997	1998	1999	2000	2001	2002	2003	2004	2005	2006	2007	2008	2009
GDP	−5	−14.5	−8.7	−12.6	−4.3	−6	0.4	−11.6	3.2	7.6	5	4	7.3	7.1	6.4	7.4	8.1	5.6	−7.9
Inflation	138	2323	844	202	131	21.8	11	84.4	36.5	20.2	18.6	15.1	12	11.7	10.9	9	11.9	13.3	8.8

Source: Press reports of Russian State Statistical Service (www.gks.ru).
Note: GDP is measured in constant market prices.
Inflation is measured as the percentage change in the consumer price index from December of one year to December of the next.

TABLE 7.2

Comparison of Russian and Chinese Development

	GDP per capita[a]	Inequality (%)[b]	Life expectancy (%)[c]	Literacy (%)[d]	Market capitalization[e]	Foreign direct investment[f]	Internet users per 100 people[g]
Russia	14,706	44	67.8	99.5	116.4	73	31.9
China	5,515	47.8	73.1	93.7	189.8	148	22.5

Source: World Bank, World Development Indicators.
[a] GDP per capita in 2008, PPP (constant 2005 international $).
[b] Income share of top quintile of income earners (2005).
[c] Life expectancy at birth (2008), total (years).
[d] Literacy rate, adult total (percent of people ages 15 and above) (2008).
[e] Market capitalization of listed companies (billions of current $US) (2008).
[f] Foreign direct investment, net inflows, 2008 (BoP, billions of current US$).
[g] 2008.

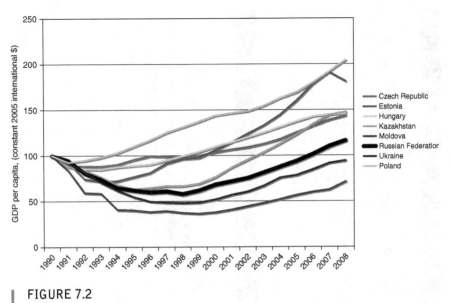

FIGURE 7.2

Comparative Postcommunist Economic Performance, 1990–2008 (1990 = 100)

governance and protection for shareholder rights; wide access to information about economic activity; insurance markets to spread the risk of business activity. Nor were the representative political institutions, such as parties and parliament, able to channel popular demands for fair play in the economy into public policy. Many Russians resented the fact that the privatization of state assets in the 1990s allowed a handful of unscrupulous oligarchs to loot the state's wealth. Under these circumstances, Putin's strategy of renationalizing the industries most critical to his domestic and foreign policy goals, while encouraging market capitalism in the rest of the economy, has enjoyed a broad base of public support.

Stabilization

To understand the mixture of state control and market capitalism that characterizes Russia's economy today, we have to go back to the beginning of the 1990s and examine the radical reforms enacted under Yeltsin. Russia pursued two major sets of reforms in the 1990s, macroeconomic *stabilization* and *privatization*. In Russia, the stabilization program was nicknamed "shock therapy," which underscores its drastic and painful nature, and the fact that government policy makers had few good choices. Stabilization imposes an austerity regime on an economy after a period of severe budget deficits and raging inflation (whether open or repressed) in order to restore a balance between what society spends and what it earns. It is always a response to a fiscal crisis, comparable to an emergency-room operation on a patient bleeding to death. In the case of economies, the trauma is uncontrollable inflation— skyrocketing prices, plummeting currency, and a huge shortfall of revenues to meet government obligations.[3]

The point of stabilization is to stabilize the money and prices, which requires eliminating chronic sources of inflation. This means making drastic cuts in state spending, raising taxes, ending price controls, and eliminating restrictions on foreign trade so that foreign products can compete with domestic ones. Structural reform of this kind always lowers the standard of living for some or most groups of the population, at least in the short run. Therefore, until living standards begin to rise again, such reform creates powerful political opponents. These include the groups that formerly had enjoyed the benefits of state-controlled wages and prices, high state spending to subsidize priority sectors of the economy, protection from competing foreign industries, and welfare entitlement programs. In many countries undergoing stabilization programs, these groups are well organized, voicing their opposition to reform through strong trade unions, associations of directors of state-owned firms, and political parties whose primary constituencies are those most vulnerable to reform.

Those who are made worse off by stabilization are not the only enemies of reform, however. Joel Hellman has argued persuasively that in a number of the postcommunist countries, it was precisely the "early winners" from reform who stepped in to block subsequent measures to open the economy to free competition. These included managers who acquired ownership rights to monopoly enterprises and then worked to shut out potential competitors from their markets. Others were state officials who benefited from collecting "fees" to issue licenses to importers and exporters or permits for doing business. Still others were bankers who took out cheap state-subsidized loans from the Central Bank and then lent out money to entrepreneurs at exorbitant rates. Many enterprise directors set up profitable sideline businesses, while using the state enterprise as a cheap source of production equipment, raw materials, and labor; the state enterprise then recorded losses, while the private sideline business made the director and his friends a tidy profit. All these newly advantaged groups cultivated ties with policy makers who protected them from both a rollback of the reforms and their advancement to the next stage. They thus sought to lock in their rents—that is, profits made above what they would have received if the market were fully competitive. Hellman argues that these rent-seeking groups were a powerful brake on reform in postcommunist countries such as Russia.[4] The result was that after the initial reforms, the economy did not become more open to competition: Those who took advantage of the initial steps prevented the deepening of reform.

The Russian stabilization program took shape in the fall of 1991. The August 1991 coup had fueled support for radical reform. The response to the coup was a surge of support for Yeltsin and his radical reform program both in the Russian Congress of People's Deputies and in society more generally. Addressing the Congress on October 28, 1991, Yeltsin demanded special powers to enact radical reform by decree and, on November 1, received them by a decisive margin. He named himself prime minister and head of government and formed a cabinet of young, radically minded intellectuals drawn from academic institutes. Egor Gaidar, then 35 years old, became deputy prime minister and overall architect of the reform program. Yeltsin proceeded to issue a set of decrees liberalizing foreign trade and the circulation of hard currency.[5] On January 2, 1992, under Yeltsin's political protection, the new government undertook a major initiative to push Russia toward a market system by abolishing most controls on wholesale and retail prices and by cutting government spending sharply.

Almost immediately, opposition to the new program began to form. Within two weeks of the introduction of the program, Ruslan Khasbulatov, chairman of the Russian Supreme Soviet, spoke out strongly against the program and called on the government to resign. Since Yeltsin formally was head of government, this was a direct attack on Yeltsin. Yeltsin's vice president, Alexander Rutskoi, sided with Khasbulatov and the opposition in parliament. Economists and politicians chose sides. Dispassionate analysis of, and even basic information about, the effects of the stabilization program became virtually impossible to get. The shock therapy program was an easy target for criticism, even though there was no consensus among critics about what should be done instead. Opponents demanded that the pace of reform be slowed so that Russians would have more time to adjust to the new conditions; they complained that the Gaidar team might be capable theorists but had no idea how to run a government. They demanded creation of a safety net to cushion the blow of the transition for the indigent, the elderly, and the displaced. It became commonplace to say that the program was all shock and no therapy.

Evaluating Stabilization

Why did Yeltsin and his government adopt so radical a program of reform? The fact is that they had very little choice. They were faced with several undesirable alternatives, and they chose the least bad among them.[6] The breakdown of state planning and administrative controls over the economy had proceeded very far. Ministries and regional governments were no longer responding to the old hierarchical command system, but a system of market-based price signals was not in place that could guide producers and consumers. In their power struggle, leaders such as Gorbachev, Yeltsin, and Khasbulatov had freely issued decrees giving away valuable assets or rights that left the state with ever fewer means to control the economy.[7] Hyperinflation was about to erupt, and the policy makers needed to bring demand and supply in the economy back into some rough equilibrium.[8] Like policy makers in other countries facing a financial collapse, they adopted a draconian combination of tax hikes, spending cuts, and monetary stringency.[9] The program led immediately to a severe and protracted economic recession.

One line of criticism directed against the Yeltsin–Gaidar government, its Western advisers, and the international financial organizations that were supplying loans was that they were seeking to "de-industrialize" Russia—that is, trying to destroy the great industrial plant that had been built up at such cost over many years. Some of the critics went further and said that the West was deliberately trying to sabotage Russia by forcing it to follow the shock therapy prescription. Communists and nationalists got a rise out of audiences by depicting Gaidar and the other radical members of the 1992 government as the traitorous hirelings of a malevolent, imperialist West.

A more widespread viewpoint, however, is that the principles underlying the reform program were fundamentally flawed.[10] These ideas are sometimes referred to as the "Washington consensus" because they represented the conventional advice promoted by the United States and many economists in the 1980s and 1990s. The Washington consensus emphasized macroeconomic stabilization, privatization, deregulation, and trade liberalization as ways of squeezing out inflationary pressures and injecting painful but necessary doses of competitive pressure into the economy. The idea was to reduce the amount of state intervention into the economy as much as possible and as quickly as possible. You can't jump across an abyss in gradual steps, they pointed out; if you prolong the pain of reform, the opposition will only grow stronger.

Gaidar and his team embraced this philosophy, for both economic and political reasons. Economically, they believed that Russia would never progress if it remained wedded to a Stalin-era industrial system where the heavy and defense industries received the lion's share of investment, while consumer goods and services sectors were perennially starved of resources. Politically, they wanted to act as quickly and decisively as possible in order to make movement toward the market economy irreversible. The team of reformers who enacted stabilization in Russia in 1992 acted on the assumption that they had only a very short window of opportunity in which to act, or otherwise the forces opposed to market capitalism—communists and their supporters, powerful state officials and enterprise managers, workers and peasants dependent on state-owned factories and farms—would rise up and restore the old system. Therefore, the reformers had to be pragmatic. They calculated that they would have to make concessions to potential allies, such as industrial managers and regional governors, by giving them a stake in the success of reform, and they used the privatization program to do so.[11] The problem was that because insiders ("early winners") ended up with so many advantages, they acted to block further reform and thus protracted the pain of transition.

Both critics and defenders of the program assume that the government's policies actually had the effects they intended. In fact, the program was never fully carried out. Moreover, many officials simply circumvented the policies. Directors of important industries wheedled credits out of the Central Bank (which was not under the government's control) and persuaded ministries to place orders for products simply to keep production going.[12] Rather than respond to the new financial austerity, many directors simply continued to turn out and ship their products without being paid, allowing interenterprise arrears to mount. Or, since money was tight, enterprises formed elaborate barter chains with other enterprises. The Gaidar government lacked full control over the state bureaucracy, so it could not completely shape the structure of incentives to which enterprise managers responded. The credibility of its policies was never secure. Since the effectiveness of a stabilization program depends on producers' calculation of the government's commitment to staying the course, the government's imperfect control over the money supply distorted the effects of the policy. Moreover, the government did not carry out price liberalization fully, but maintained controls on energy and electric power rates. This may have protected consumers and producers, but it let severe price distortions accumulate throughout the economy.

The Gaidar team inherited an economy on the verge of breakdown. Through 1991, as traditional lines of control via the Communist Party and state bureaucracy weakened, regional and local governments began erecting barriers to interregional trade. Some set tariffs; others erected roadblocks preventing the "export" of goods from their territories. Moscow and other big cities introduced identity cards to prevent out-of-towners from coming in and purchasing goods from the relatively better stocked stores in cities. The network of internal wholesale and retail trade was breaking down. Administrative measures probably would have failed to restore them, short of martial law. But the drastic price liberalization of January 2, 1992, which allowed producers and retailers to set any price that the market could bear for most goods and services, immediately eliminated the internal trade wars and restored the circulation of goods, albeit at high and often ruinous prices.

Privatization

Stabilization was followed shortly afterward by another, equally important program—the privatization of state assets. In contrast to the shock therapy program, privatization at first enjoyed considerable public support, which helped offset the unpopularity of stabilization. Privatization is the transfer of ownership of state enterprises to private owners. Economic theory holds that under the right conditions, private ownership of productive assets is more efficient for society as a whole than is monopoly or state ownership, because in a competitive environment, owners are motivated by an incentive to maximize their property's ability to produce a return. Whereas a monopolist does not care if the firm he or she owns is inefficient, the owner of the firm in a market system wants to increase the productivity and therefore the market value of the firm. For this reason, most economists consider it essential to transfer ownership of state assets from the state to private owners as part of the transition from socialism to a market economy in order to stimulate growth and productivity in the economy as a whole. In short, a system of clearly established property rights benefits not only the individual owners but also the whole society.

The theory is generally valid. But, as is often true of valid theories, much can interfere with its application to the real world.

We must distinguish the privatization of state-owned firms in Russia from the creation of new, private start-up businesses. Although private entrepreneurs have created a large number of new, independent businesses, these are usually small in scale. Moreover, there has not been a net increase in the number of such businesses over time. In contrast, the fate of the formerly state-owned enterprises has enormous political importance. This is because the great majority of the population are tied to those enterprises for their livelihoods and for the range of social benefits that are supplied through jobs at state enterprises.

Moreover, *how* enterprises are privatized is deeply political. One method is to simply give away state assets to the public as a democratic gesture that quickly turns the entire population into property holders and gives them a stake in the reform process. An alternative is to require auctions in which groups and individuals submit competitive bids to purchase assets, thereby creating real value that can be used as investment capital, but allowing rich or corrupt elements of the population to capture control of state enterprises. Russia combined these two methods, first distributing free vouchers to all citizens, who were then able to use the vouchers to bid for shares of privatized firms at special auctions, and then holding auctions of shares for cash.

Giving people the right to start private businesses was much less controversial than was the design of the privatization program. As early as 1986, Soviet law was changed so as to permit individuals and family members to start their own businesses, as well as to allow groups of people to start private commercial businesses organized as cooperatives.[13] Small-scale firms have sprouted up, although as a sector, small business is much smaller than in Western economies and has not grown in the last decade (the number of small businesses has not risen much above 1 million). In the United States, firms employing fewer than 500 people employ just over half of all workers. In Russia, small businesses—defined as those employing 100 or fewer workers—account for only about 16 percent of all employment.

Firms that are fully or partly state owned are often large, while start-up private firms tend to be small (about two-thirds of private firms are small in scale). The privatization of larger state firms affects the livelihoods of large numbers of employees. Because many towns were built around giant enterprises, privatization of a state firm can affect a whole region. And of course, privatization of important industrial or natural resource assets has substantial implications for the distribution of wealth.

For these reasons, privatization programs are profoundly political acts. Someone must decide how to set value on state enterprises in the absence of capital markets; whether to privatize enterprises for cash or for government-provided coupons; how much to favor the workers and managers of the enterprise in gaining control over their own workplace; whether to allow foreigners to buy privatized enterprises; and which levels of government can privatize which assets. Disputes over these issues have often stalled privatization programs in countries undergoing the transition from communism. The decisions that Russia made in the 1990s about privatization are still the subject of passionate debate and bitter recrimination.

Voucher Privatization   In the first wave of privatization in 1991 and 1992, buyers used cash rather than state-issued vouchers to buy state firms. But cash privatization had the effect of making the rich richer and giving ownership of enterprises to the officials who had run them before. Ordinary citizens often were excluded from benefiting from the most profitable opportunities as insiders acquired the stock of the most promising firms. And the poor, of course, had no chance at all to buy shares. In the interests of dispersing ownership rights as widely as possible, parliament's law envisioned that all citizens would be given special bank accounts to buy shares of privatized enterprises.

In April 1992, as opposition to the stabilization program was gaining force, Yeltsin issued a decree launching a program of voucher privatization beginning in the fourth quarter of 1992. Under the program, every citizen of Russia would be issued a voucher with a face value of 10,000 rubles (the equivalent of about $30). People would be free to buy and sell vouchers, but they could only be used to acquire shares of stock in privatized enterprises through auctions, where voucher owners could bid vouchers for shares of enterprises. People were also allowed to use their vouchers to acquire shares of mutual funds investing in privatized enterprises or they could sell them to other people. The program was intended to ensure that everyone became a property owner instantly. Politically, the aim was to build support for the economic reforms by making citizens into stock owners and thus giving them a stake in the outcome of the market transition. The designers of the program hoped that even though the voucher privatization program did not itself represent new investment capital, it would eventually spur increases in productivity by creating meaningful property rights.[14]

Beginning in October 1992, 148 million privatization vouchers were distributed to citizens. The program established three ways in which state enterprises could be privatized by means of voucher auctions. These methods differed according to how much stock could be acquired by employees of privatized enterprises and on what terms. Each method balanced the demands of managers and workers of state enterprises for control over their own enterprises against the demand of outsiders for the right to bid freely for shares, and each combined the objective of letting citizens acquire stock for free with that of creating a real capital market where stock had tradable value. The State Privatization Committee oversaw the privatization process. This powerful agency and its chairman, Anatolii Chubais, became targets of attack from all sides—from those accusing the committee of selling off assets too cheaply and not protecting enterprises to those distressed at the way in which state managers usually wound up with the controlling share of stock. With Yeltsin's protection, however, Chubais carried out the program over the objections of all critics.

Chubais's team was reluctant simply to give away Russia's vast capital stock to the powerful state enterprise directors. Instead, it wanted to diffuse ownership rights as broadly as possible. The political realities, however, dictated that the government allow enterprise directors certain advantages. In the short run, the consent of the directors to the program was essential to maintaining economic and social stability in the country. The managers also represented one of the most powerful collective interests in the country. The government, therefore, allowed a good deal of "insider privatization," in which senior enterprise officials acquired the largest proportion of shares in privatized firms. In most enterprises, both ownership and control wound up in the hands of the managers.[15]

Around 18,000 medium- and large-scale firms were privatized by 1996. Privatization for most of them did not immediately bring about major changes in the way they were run. One reason is that privatization did not result in an infusion of new investment capital to modernize their plant and equipment and another is that managers strenuously resisted allowing their firms to be taken over by outside investors. Asked in one major survey of enterprise directors whether they would be willing to sell a majority of the shares of their enterprise to an outside investor who would bring the capital needed to invest in modernizing the firm, two-thirds said they would not be willing. In other words, they preferred to remain majority owners of an unprofitable enterprise than the minority owners of a much more profitable one.[16] Very few firms experienced much management turnover and even fewer engaged in extensive restructuring of their operations to make them more productive or efficient.

All vouchers were to have been used by December 31, 1993. President Yeltsin extended the expiration date until June 30, 1994. By that time, 140 million vouchers had been exchanged for stock out of 148 million originally distributed, according to Anatolii Chubais.[17] Some 40 million citizens had become property owners. About 70 percent of large- and medium-sized firms and 80 percent of all small businesses had been privatized. The voucher privatization phase had ended. The next phase was to bring about the privatization of most of the remaining state enterprises, but by means of auctions of shares for cash. This also included the infamous "loans for shares" scheme that we will discuss later. By 1996, about 90 percent of industrial output was being produced by privatized firms and about two-thirds of all large- and medium-sized enterprises had been privatized.[18] As of 2006, nearly 80 percent of all Russian firms, accounting for just over half the work force and about 70 percent of GDP, were in the private sector.[19]

Once the voucher privatization campaign was completed, the government turned to other methods to sell off shares in state enterprises. One method used in 1995–1996 came to be called "loans for shares." Although ownership rights and wealth had been concentrated before this, the program enabled a handful of ambitious entrepreneurs to acquire title to some of Russia's most desirable assets at low prices. The episode resulted in the emergence of the so-called "oligarchs," a handful of wealthy magnates who took advantage of the government's weakness in the mid-1990s to acquire ownership and control over some of Russia's most lucrative natural resource, industrial, and media assets. (See Close-Up 7.1: Russia's Oligarchs.)

How "loans for shares" worked can be illustrated by the case of Norilsk Nickel, a giant metallurgical firm in Russia's North that is the world's largest producer of nickel. An inefficient, debt-ridden behemoth of a company, Norilsk Nickel was also potentially one of Russia's most valuable assets. In 1995, with elections approaching and the government desperate for cash, a prominent entrepreneur named Vladimir Potanin proposed a deal to the government. His bank would bid on the right to manage a block of 51 percent of the shares of Norilsk Nickel in return for granting a loan to the government. If after a year's time the government failed to repay the loan, the bank would have the right to purchase the shares outright. He proposed conducting similar auctions for several other companies of strategic importance as well. Yeltsin and the government approved the plan despite the fact that it was clearly designed to turn over ownership of some of Russia's crown jewels to a small coterie of tycoons. Potanin's bank organized the auctions and the banks he controlled were the sole bidders for Norilsk Nickel. Not surprisingly, his

CLOSE-UP 7.1

Russia's Oligarchs

The term "oligarchs" refers to a small group of wealthy and powerful individuals who succeeded in taking advantage of the opening of the Russian economy to acquire control of Russia's most lucrative industrial and natural resource assets.[20] Political contacts helped them win crucial licenses and monopolies early in the postcommunist period; by building up great economic empires, they also grew powerful in the political realm.

The rise of the oligarchs was helped by Yeltsin's privatization policies, but in fact they got their start well before the Soviet regime fell. As the system of centralized administrative control over economic resources collapsed in the late 1980s, well-placed officials in the party, the KGB, and the Komsomol (Soviet Youth League) began cashing in on their power and privileges. Some quietly liquidated the assets of their organizations and squirreled the proceeds away in overseas accounts and investments.[21] Others created banks and businesses in Russia, taking advantage of their insider positions to win exclusive government contracts and licenses and to acquire financial credits and supplies at artificially low, state-subsidized prices in order to transact business at high, market-value prices. Great fortunes were made overnight. Access to capital and contacts from the old regime helped these new *biznesmeny* considerably. Some called this wave of quasi-market activity "nomenklatura capitalism." By the time the Soviet regime fell and the Yeltsin government began to try to establish a working market economy, some of the nomenklatura capitalists had already entrenched themselves as powerful players.

The concentration of financial and industrial power extended to the mass media. One of the most prominent financial barons, Boris Berezovsky, who controlled major stakes in several banks and companies (including Aeroflot), acquired an 8 percent stake in the main state television company, ORT, and one of Berezovsky's banks was part of a banking consortium that owned another 38 percent of ORT. Berezovsky himself became deputy director of the company and exerted extensive influence over its programming. Berezovsky and the other ultrawealthy and well-connected tycoons who controlled these empires of finance, industry, energy, telecommunications, and the media became known as the "oligarchs." Through the "loans for shares" program, Yeltsin and his entourage gave them a royal opportunity to scoop up some of Russia's most desirable assets in return for help in his reelection effort. In the spring of 1996, with Yeltsin's popularity at a low ebb, the oligarchs agreed to help secure Yeltsin's reelection. How much money they poured into Yeltsin's reelection campaign is still a matter of dispute—some say the quantity was relatively insignificant—but there is no question that the media properties they controlled promoted the cause of Yeltsin's reelection. The media painted a picture of a fateful choice for Russia, between Yeltsin and a return to totalitarianism, directly serving Yeltsin's campaign strategy and unquestionably helping him win.

Some saw the oligarchs as a cabal controlling Yeltsin's administration and, through it, Russia. Boris Berezovsky was being more boastful than candid when he declared in October 1996 that there was now a group of seven individuals who controlled banks and businesses that together controlled half of the economy and wielded substantial political power. Berezovsky was overstating their cohesiveness as a group because once Yeltsin was reelected, the oligarchs fell out and began feuding with one another. The 1998 financial crash hurt all of them and nearly wiped several out. Their influence depended on the unique environment of Yeltsin's presidency, when a weakened Yeltsin, faced with substantial political opposition and uncontrollable government deficits, gave them enormous assets at bargain basement prices.

Putin's presidency sharply altered this situation. In July 2000, Putin met with several of the most influential oligarchs. There he laid down a new set of terms for the relationship between the state and big business. Putin promised that the oligarchs' property would be secure, however unsavory the manner in which it had been acquired, so long as they kept their noses out of high politics and as long as they were investing in Russia rather than sending their money abroad.[22] Since then, most of the oligarchs have been content to abide by the new rules of the game. They have competed to build political machines at the level of regional government, but generally refrain from seeking broader political influence. However, a few of the original oligarchs tempted fate, openly opposing Putin. They paid a high price for their defiance. Through a series of criminal and civil prosecutions in 2000–2001, Putin forced Boris Berezovsky and another prominent oligarch, Vladimir Gusinsky, to relinquish their substantial media holdings. Both men are now under indictment and living abroad. These actions, together with the campaign to destroy Khodorkovsky and Yukos, sent a clear signal: So long as heads of big businesses do not challenge the president, they are welcome to amass wealth. But as soon as they cross Putin, they will be crushed.

Putin's campaign to break the power of the old oligarchs, however, did not end the concentration of money and power. Under Putin, a new set of oligarchs has gained prominence. They have benefited from their personal associations with Putin and their membership in social and professional networks based in the security police (the so-called "silovik" wing of the regime). They have grown wealthy from control over nationalized assets, including those seized from the Yeltsin-era oligarchs. Because they represent a different alliance of commercial wealth and political power than the oligarchs represented in the 1990s, political scientist Daniel Treisman has dubbed this group "Putin's silovarchs."[23]

bid won. A year later, when the government failed to repay the loan, Potanin proceeded to acquire majority ownership in Norilsk Nickel. This was an astonishing bargain: For $170 million, Potanin bought a company whose output now accounts for close to 2 percent of Russia's GDP.[24] At the time, however, the company was being run inefficiently and well below capacity. However unsavory the loans for shares scheme was, it did have the result that Norilsk Nickel and the other firms that were acquired by oligarchs improved their efficiency substantially.

The case of Norilsk Nickel was only one example of the infamous "loans for shares" scheme. Controlling interests in several of Russia's largest oil companies were auctioned off to other oligarchs, also at dirt-cheap prices. The entire "loans for shares" program stands as one of the most flagrant examples of the cozy, collusive relationship between Russia's oligarchs and the Yeltsin regime. Along with the other forms of privatization, "loans for shares" resulted in extremely high levels of ownership concentration in Russia. As of 2003, the top 10 families in Russia owned approximately 60 percent of the value of the stock market. This is high by European standards, but it is characteristic of other middle-income developing countries, and it is lower than in the United States and Europe a century ago. Moreover, close analysis suggests that firms owned by oligarchs in Russia have been more productive than state-owned firms.[25]

Consequences of Privatization   Initially, privatization contributed little to the urgent task of modernizing and retooling the economy. Vouchers, the instrument used in the first phase for mass privatization, were not inflationary because they could not be used as legal tender for other transactions.[26] But neither were they forms of productive capital, as stocks and bonds are in countries with established financial markets. So, the vouchers did not expand the pool of resources enterprises could use to increase productivity and efficiency. They were intended as an impetus to a process that would end in the consolidation of a market economy. The policy makers believed that mass privatization would establish an interest on the part of new property owners in increasing the value of their assets, which they would achieve by investing in the modernization and retooling of the firms. In turn, the need for capital would induce a healthy capital market into being. However, the lack of an institutional infrastructure for market exchange and a lack of confidence in the future deterred entrepreneurs from investing capital. Capital investment rates in Russia rose substantially in the 2000s, but they were extremely low in the 1990s (and capital flight very high). When the worldwide recession struck in 2008, capital again fled the country. Generally, capital investment in Russia remains below the levels of other transitional economies.[27] An international survey of investors in 2009 found that Russia and other CIS countries were ranked at the bottom of a list of emerging markets. China, Brazil, India, Central Europe, Latin America, Africa, and the Middle East were all ranked higher.[28]

There is a famous theorem in economics that holds that *if* the costs of economic transactions are sufficiently low, then regardless of how property rights over some set of economic assets are initially allocated, bargaining among owners will eventually achieve a socially efficient distribution of ownership and control rights over those assets as owners buy and sell property and enter into mutually advantageous contractual relations.[29] That is, each asset ultimately winds up with its highest and best use. But note the *if*. The theorem stipulates that the distribution of property rights reaches the social optimum *if* the costs of bargaining and reaching agreements among owners are low and *if* the state enforces property and contract rights. In fact, in any real society, the costs of transactions—the absence of trust, incomplete information about the qualities of what is being sold, the problem of enforcing an agreement after it has been reached—can be formidable.[30] In Russia, the uncertainty surrounding the change in economic and political conditions made transaction costs extremely high. As a result, owners of many firms preferred to capitalize on their political leverage and take advantage of inefficiency rather than to maximize the value of their assets. For example, many owners initially stripped newly privatized firms of assets and sent the proceeds to offshore bank accounts. Many owners avoided restructuring their firms and depended on state life-support systems such as cheap loans and subsidies.[31] Many newly wealthy owners preferred to spend their money on lavish consumption rather than to reinvest it in their firms. Only in the late 1990s, when the political system became more predictable, did private owners begin to behave as though they care more about the long-term value of the assets they owned than about maximizing short-term returns.

Weak Capital Markets and the August 1998 Crash   Privatization was carried out in the absence of effective, impartial institutions regulating capital markets. The channels by which market economies convert private savings into investment in companies, such as financial institutions, pension and insurance funds, and stock and bond markets, were also weak in Russia. For so large a country, with so great an industrial potential, stock and bond markets are small.[32] In the 1990s, many enterprises, starved for working capital, failed to pay their wages and taxes on time and traded with one another using barter. By 1998, at least half of enterprise output was being "sold" through barter trade.[33] Barter creates a world of unreal values, a "virtual economy," where it is impossible to calculate the cost of goods and where investors cannot make intelligent judgments about where capital investment will have the greatest return. A virtual economy is profoundly inefficient.[34]

By the mid-1990s, the government's own long- and short-term goals were in conflict. In the long run, the government hoped privatization would create property rights and capital markets. But in the short term, the government needed to raise cash to compensate for shortfalls in its tax revenues. Privatization allowed the government to generate budget revenue by auctioning off state-owned shares of stock in industrial firms. Unfortunately, the government found that demand for shares was often weak and sold off the assets at embarrassingly, even scandalously, low prices. Moreover, at the same time the government was trying to auction off shares in enterprises, it was also trying to raise revenues by issuing bonds (GKOs) at extremely high rates of return.[35] The market for the lucrative GKOs crowded out the capital market for investment in industry. One government policy goal—that of financing budget expenditures by issuing bonds—was in direct competition with another—that of accelerating private ownership of state-owned enterprises.

Making matters worse was a collapse in oil prices on the world market. The price of a barrel of oil on the world market fell in half from January 1997 to December 1998, cutting deeply into Russia's export earnings. International markets were also shaken by a financial crisis that rippled across Asia, and nervous investors pulled out of many emerging markets. This double blow of external pressure and an unsustainable fiscal situation at home pushed Russia's government into a debt trap. The government needed to borrow to meet current obligations. To pay off the interest on the loans it had taken out, it needed to raise still more cash, which it did through still more borrowing, including credits from the IMF, high interest-bearing domestic bonds, and privatization. As lenders grew worried that the government could not make good on its obligations, they demanded ever-higher interest rates, deepening the trap.

Finally, in August 1998, the bubble burst. The state could not honor its obligations. The government declared a moratorium on its debts and let the ruble sink against the dollar. Overnight, the ruble lost two-thirds of its value and credit dried up.[36] Government bonds held by investors became almost worthless. Importers went out of business. The effects of the crash rippled through the economy. The sharp devaluation of the ruble made exports more competitive and gave an impetus to domestic producers but also significantly lowered people's living standards. Although recovery began surprisingly fast, the 1998 crash was the culmination of nearly a decade of economic decline.

How severe was the economic depression of the 1990s? No doubt official figures overstate its depth. Consumption fell less than production. Observers skeptical of official output statistics pointed out that in the past, managers had every reason to *overstate* their actual output, since they were under pressure to fulfill the production plan, whereas now they were more likely to *understate* their output in order to avoid taxes. Moreover, the very structure of national income shifted. Much more of Russia's economic activity is occurring in the sphere of services, which is poorly captured in output statistics. The share of services in the economy dropped much less than that of industry or agriculture. There is certainly a great deal of off-book economic activity taking place, some of it legal but untaxed and some of it illegal.

Still, Russia's economic decline in the 1990s was deeper and more protracted than was the Great Depression experienced by the United States or Western Europe following 1929. It was about half as severe as the catastrophic drop caused by the effects of World War I, the Bolshevik Revolution, and the Civil War.[37] The depression in the 1990s was the aggregate result of many individual survival strategies. Starved of cash, some enterprises formed alliances with regional governors to pay lower taxes to the regions, while pressuring the regional branches of the federal tax collectors to let them defer their tax obligations to the central government.[38] Recognizing that major oil, gas, and electric power firms were suffering from huge unpaid bills from their customers, the federal government effectively allowed them to avoid paying much of their federal taxes in return for keeping key customers, such as military bases and major industrial enterprises, supplied with energy and fuel. Each link in the chain coped with the shortage of cash and credit in the economy, but the net outcome was a deep structural crisis. The government was perennially short of money with which to meet its obligations, including pensions and pay for teachers and other state employees. People coped by working outside the official economy, earning unrecorded incomes and hoarding money. Banks and other financial institutions were failing to convert savings into investments into the economy; instead, they made money by speculating in currency markets.

The Recovery   Beginning in 1999, however, the economy began to recover. The recovery was driven by three factors. First, many domestic firms that had not been competitive when the value of the ruble was relatively high against the dollar suddenly became competitive on domestic and foreign markets. Second, President Putin's early policy moves reassured many economic actors that he was intent on restoring order in the state and establishing a business-friendly economy. Third, and perhaps most importantly, the prices of oil and gas began rising again on the world market. By January 2008, the world price of oil was about 10 times what it had been in December 1999—rising from about $10 per barrel to about $100. But, partly because of the windfall revenues from rising oil prices, Putin failed to carry out more fundamental reforms of the economy, leaving the economy acutely vulnerable to the shock of the worldwide financial crisis that exploded in fall 2008.

Still, from 1999 to 2008, the economy enjoyed 10 years of solid growth. Total output grew at an average rate of over 7 percent per year. Money began circulating again. Barter transactions largely ended; enterprises started paying taxes and wages on time; the government paid out pensions on time. Real incomes rose to well above their 1998 levels, as wages and pensions increased. Unemployment fell from over 13 percent in 1998 to less than 7 percent as of the beginning of 2008.[39] The number of people living in poverty fell by over one-third, from over 30 percent at the end of the 1990s to under 20 percent in 2008. Higher tax collections allowed the government to realize significant budget surpluses, which it has used to pay off the foreign debt and to create a reserve fund (called the stabilization fund) that was kept as insurance against a new recession (the government used it actively when the crisis struck in 2008) and to reduce inflationary pressures. As Figure 7.1 shows, by the end of 2007, according to official figures, Russia's GDP per capita, expressed in purchasing power, was 10 percent above what it had been in 1990.

However, because so much of Russia's growth has been driven by the rising prices of oil and gas on the world market, Russia is subject to the same "paradox of plenty" that afflicts other oil-rich economies. Sometimes, in fact, a dependence on natural resources for export-based revenues is called the "resource curse."[40] A former economic advisor of Putin has warned of the "Venezuelanization" of Russia, meaning that Russia may be falling into the trap of allowing high resource-based revenues to drive populist fiscal policies, increased state control over the economy, and authoritarian political tendencies—to the detriment of both long-term economic performance and democracy. William Tompson, an economist with the Organization for Economic Cooperation and Development (OECD), argues that while Russia is far from being a classic petro-state, the windfall from high energy prices has allowed Putin to roll back the democratic trends of the 1990s and to avoid enacting structural reforms of the economy.[41]

The sharp drop in world oil prices brought a devastating shortfall in budget revenues; the budget deficit for 2009 was over 7 percent. The government drew down its reserve funds to support the economy and to prevent a collapse in the value of the ruble. The severity of the financial crisis underscored the dangers of depending on natural resources as the basis for the economy. Although Putin and Medvedev frequently point out that Russia cannot depend solely on high world energy prices for its economic well-being, they rely on access to resource-based revenues as an alternative to relinquishing control over human and natural resources. Energy-based revenues are a convenient way for them to maintain political support through generous distributive programs. But when international oil prices fall heavily, the resulting financial crisis reveals the underlying weaknesses in the economy.

Boom and Bust Cycles

Both Vladimir Putin and Dmitrii Medvedev have declared that they intend to place the economy firmly on the path of self-sustaining growth by creating a climate conducive to investment and innovation. In Putin's first term, some reformers who were part of the Gaidar team of the early 1990s—including Gaidar himself—were involved in drafting legislation on tax reform, administrative reform, privatization, and other policies. Putin's initial legislative agenda sought to lower marginal tax rates, protect property rights, reduce burdensome government regulation of business, liberalize the labor market, shift the pension system more toward pension insurance and private savings, eliminate the tariff and bureaucratic obstacles that prevent Russia's entry into the World Trade Organization (WTO), and create a market for buying and selling land. Legislation on most of these reforms was enacted. Putin's team also successfully fended off demands to raid the stabilization fund for additional spending, which might have wrecked macroeconomic stability. Focused spending on infrastructure improvement, education, healthcare, and agriculture helped reverse decades of stagnation and neglect in the social sphere.

But by 2003, the president's commitment to economic reform faltered. Some of the most ambitious plans were quietly shelved, such as the aim of breaking up the large natural monopolies and overhauling the state bureaucracy. Instead of trying to restructure the giant natural gas monopoly Gazprom into several competing companies, Putin decided to use it as a means to expand state control over the entire oil and gas industry. The government's attention to the reform of the housing and utilities sectors and the electric power monopoly abated. Plans to restructure the dangerously shaky banking industry were forgotten. Instead, the government began taking back control of major oil, gas, electric power, automotive, machine-building, aviation, nuclear power, and other enterprises; the most visible of these was the drive to break up Yukos and absorb its most lucrative assets into the state-owned oil company Rosneft.[42] Previously, private enterprises in several strategic sectors, such as oil, shipbuilding, aviation, truckbuilding, and telecommunications, were brought partly or wholly back under state ownership.[43] The percentage of stock owned by the state in Russia's 20 largest companies was 11 percent at the end of 2003, but rose to almost 40 percent by early 2007.[44] In most cases, Putin placed individuals from the security services into prominent positions overseeing these firms, rather than people skilled in economic management.[45] Often, the state resorted to blackmail and forced bankruptcy to take over target firms, then redistributed them to key bureaucratic allies in the security services—a process that came to be known as "velvet reprivatization."[46]

The government also began squeezing foreign investors out of their majority stakes in major oil and gas ventures, forcing them to accept minority shares as a condition of doing business.[47] In short, Putin's growth agenda was overtaken by a new emphasis on placing big business under tight state control and renationalizing some firms of strategic importance.

At the same time, the leadership forfeited the opportunity to undertake more fundamental reforms that might have put Russia on the path toward sustained economic growth and reduced its vulnerability to swings in the world financial and economic system. The government did not place the housing and utilities sector on a market footing, sensitive to the explosive quality of popular expectations that rates for heating, electric power, and other services should remain low. The outburst of social protest in January 2005 when the government attempted to replace a number of in-kind social benefits with cash payments—a reform badly bungled in design and implementation—frightened the leaders and led them to shelve any further plans to put basic services on a fully market footing. As of 2010, after 18 years of negotiations, Russia still had not joined the WTO.[48] As a result, a number of Russian economic sectors, such as banking, insurance, and telecommunications, were not exposed to international competition. This left them dependent on and vulnerable to the shifting pressures of political interests in the Kremlin.

The 2008 financial crisis, which developed into a full-blown recession, exposed these structural weaknesses. Like the 1998 crash, the new crisis originated abroad but was exacerbated by structural weakness in the economy. Globally, the financial crisis of fall 2008 brought a sudden freezing of bank credit worldwide, a sharp decline in the values of stocks and other financial assets, a decline in consumer confidence, and the beginning of a serious slowdown or recession in most major economies. Russia was hit hard, beginning with a sell-off on the stock market after Russia invaded Georgia in August 2008 and accelerating as the worldwide financial panic spread. By the end of October 2008, the total value of Russian stock shares was three-quarters lower than the value in the beginning of the year, the largest drop in value of any stock market in the world.[49] Private pension funds suffered large-scale withdrawals; almost $500 million were withdrawn in the first 10 months of the year, almost $100 million in October alone. Investors' flight from the markets was triggered by the fact that the economy depended so heavily on oil and gas revenues at a time when the world market price of oil fell from its high of around $140 per barrel in the spring to below $50 by December. The effects of the collapsing stock market and plummeting energy prices then rippled out into the rest of the economy, including manufacturing and commerce.

The resulting recession hurt Russia's economy more than any other G-20 economy: output in 2009 fell 7.9 percent. Unemployment rose to over 10 percent of the economically active population, but many workers who were nominally employed were forced to take unpaid leaves or work short hours, or were simply not paid the wages they were owed. One survey in May 2009 found that 38 percent of the workforce faced wage arrears.[50] Real incomes fell sharply, particularly in the sectors that had prospered during the good years—finance, retail commerce, construction and energy.[51] Meantime, inflation remained high, cutting further into people's purchasing power (see Table 7.1).

Cities that depended on a single major industry—what Russians call "monocities"—were also hit hard. For example, the town of Togliatti, in Samara Oblast, is home to the giant automaker AvtoVAZ, the manufacturer of Lada cars. Until the recession, the firm employed about 100,000 people, or about one out of every seven adults in the town. Nearly every other business in the city depends on the health of AvtoVAZ. Most of the town's budget revenues are generated by the firm.[52] The crash cut sales of the company's cars by over 40 percent in 2009, requiring AvtoVAZ to turn to the federal government for a bailout. The government helped craft a restructuring plan for the company, gave it funding for debt relief and new investment, persuaded the French automaker Renault to increase its stake in the company, and eased around 27,000 workers off the payroll (some were given early retirement, and others were offered new jobs in other enterprises). Altogether the government pumped more than 75 billion rubles (about US$2.5 billion) into propping up the company. Although AvtoVAZ is probably the most visible case of a distressed company in a company town, the government estimates that there are another 300–400 such cities elsewhere in Russia, and that as many as a quarter of the urban population live in them. At least one hundred of them are at or near the point of crisis.[53] It is hard to imagine how the government can keep them all on life support.

Fortunately, thanks to the government's prudence in building up a cushion of foreign exchange and reserve funds, it had more options with which to cope with the 2008 crisis than it did in the 1990s. The government had accumulated about $180 billion in the stabilization funds created from surplus oil and gas revenues, plus about $350 billion in currency reserves. This allowed the government to pump money into job creation, higher public sector salaries, improved unemployment benefits, and increases in pensions. Altogether, Putin told a group of miners in March 2009, the government's various efforts to prop up the economy were costing the equivalent of 12 percent of GDP.[54] By 2010, as world energy prices rose again, Russia's economy slowly recovered.

The crisis of 2008–2009 was global, but its effect on Russia exposed the economy's weaknesses. Heavily dependent on revenues from exports of oil and gas and other raw materials, Russia has not yet built an economic system capable of generating self-sustaining economic growth. It inherited an economy from the Soviet regime that was entirely owned and governed by the state and that still reflects the bias of the Soviet planners to concentrate their investment in heavy and extractive industry organized in large-scale enterprises. In good times, the temptation for Russian rulers to build their political coalitions around the distribution of economic rents is very strong, and in hard times, the government needs to use the revenues from its natural resource wealth to maintain social stability.

Social Conditions

The economic changes in the country have had an enormous impact on living standards. For most of the 1990s, unemployment, inflation, and nonpayment of wages and pensions led to distress and insecurity for a majority of households before living standards recovered in the 2000s. As of 1998, according to Richard Rose's New Russia Barometer survey, only 29 percent of respondents said that they had adjusted to living in the new economic system. By 2008, this had risen to 66 percent.[55] People grew more optimistic about the economy. However, the devastating economic crisis beginning in 2008 weakened the sense of confidence most people were feeling about the future. A June 2010 survey found that almost three quarters of the population saw the current economic situation as a crisis and 11 percent saw it as "catastrophic."[56]

The recovery in the 2000s overcame most of the severe social dislocations of the 1990s, when a rising unemployment and the persistent lag of wages behind prices led to a sharp rise in poverty. At least 30 percent, and as many as 40 percent, of the population, depending on the measures used, were classified as living in poverty at the end of the 1990s. Since most single-parent households are headed by women, rising unemployment pushed more women and children than men into poverty.[57] Also vulnerable to the economic disruptions of the 1990s were groups whose incomes were paid directly out of the state budget, such as those living on pensions and disability payments, as well as teachers, scientists, and healthcare workers. Although they received periodic increases in their earnings levels, these were insufficient to keep up with rising prices. People often went for months without receiving their wages or pensions. By 2008, however, rising incomes, falling unemployment, and steady increases in pensions and other social payments had reduced poverty to less than 20 percent of the population.

However, income inequality rose sharply in the 1990s and then more gradually during the recovery of the 2000s. Rising inequality has been caused by many factors. In the 1990s, it was the result of the lag of wage increases behind price inflation, the sharp rise in unemployment, the deterioration of the pension and other social assistance systems, and the concentration of vast wealth in the hands of a small number of people. In the 2000s, despite declining poverty, inequality continued to rise as a result of sharp disparities in wage levels (two workers in the same occupation and in the same region might have widely different wages depending on the firm where they work[58]), the extremely high earnings of managers in industries such as energy and finance, and the Putin regime's shift to a flat (13 percent) income tax and abolition of estate taxes. As a result of both government policy and current economic trends, therefore, economic prosperity is benefiting the upper ends of the income distribution much more than the lower end. This helps explain the sharp rise in the number of Russian billionaires. According to *Forbes*, the number of billionaires in Russia shot up from 60 to 110 between 2007 and 2008.[59] At one point, as many as a dozen of them had seats in the Federation Council.[60] But the financial crisis hit the rich hard: on average, they lost around half their wealth in the 2008 crash.[61]

One commonly used measure of inequality is the Gini index, which is an aggregate measure of the total deviation from perfect equality in the distribution of wealth or income. A society where one person receives all the income would have a Gini index of 1; the value for a society in which everyone received the same income would be 0. In a highly egalitarian country such as Finland, Sweden, or Norway, the Gini index for income distribution stands at about 25. Countries with moderately high levels of income inequality, such as Great Britain, France, and Italy, fall in the range between 27 and 37. High-inequality countries such as the United States have a Gini index of around 45. In Russia, the Gini index nearly doubled during the early 1990s, rising from 26 in 1987–1990 to 48 in 1993–1994. Inequality in Russia was higher than in any other postcommunist country except Kyrgyzstan.[62] As the economy began to recover and poverty fell, the Gini index declined slightly, to just under 40, before creeping back up in the late-2000s to over 42 (still somewhat below the level of income inequality in the United States). As in the United States, the top 20 percent of income earners receive about half of all income. In 2009, the richest tenth of the population in Russia received over 16 times as much income as did the poorest tenth, up from 14 times in 2002. The actual level of income inequality is probably considerably greater than the official figure because of the large scale of unreported, "off-book" income due to tax evasion.

The continuing rise in inequality and absence of a growing middle class is a matter of some concern to Russian leaders. In his address to the State Council on February 8, 2008, President Putin declared that the current level of income inequality was "absolutely unacceptable" and should be reduced to more moderate levels; he called for measures that would bring about an expansion of the middle class. Its share of the population, he declared, should reach 60 or even 70 percent by 2020.[63]

Another disturbing dimension of the social effects of transition has been the erosion of public health. Although public health had deteriorated in the late communist period, the decline worsened after the regime changed. Mortality rates rose sharply, especially among males. Life expectancy for males in Russia is at a level comparable to poor and developing countries. The economic recovery and greater sense of stability in society helped bring about an improvement in life expectancy, so that by 2010, male life expectancy at birth was about 63 and that for females about 75.[64] The extraordinarily high disparity between male and female mortality is generally attributed to the higher rates of abuse of alcohol and tobacco among men. Other demographic indicators are equally grim. The then prime minister Fradkov told a cabinet meeting in July 2006 that only 30 percent of newborns "can be described as healthy," and that "there are more than 500,000 disabled children in need of various forms of treatment, and also some 730,000 orphans or abandoned children."[65] Russia's mortality rates from cardiovascular disease and tuberculosis are about three times higher than in Europe or the United States.

Russia's leaders consider the demographic crisis to pose a grave threat to the country's national security because of both the army's inability to recruit enough healthy young men and the growing shortage of labor in some regions.[66] Until very recently, Russia's population shrank by up to three quarters of a million people each year due to the excess of deaths over births. Demographers estimate that Russia's population could fall by over one-third by 2050. The finance minister, Alexei Kudrin, said at a meeting of government ministers in August 2008 that "we are entering a demographic abyss. We will build factories but the number of people employed in them will fall."[67]

Russia's growing reliance on immigrant labor is causing other problems, similar to those experienced in Europe and the United States. Experts believe that there are 7–8 million immigrants in Russia, most from other countries of the CIS.[68] The government has introduced a quota system, by which, each year, businesses submit their requests for new immigrant labor for the following year. The rising number of immigrant workers in the economy, particularly evident in large cities, has led to serious social tensions. Many are victims of unscrupulous employers and physical violence by xenophobic thugs. Anti-immigration groups periodically stage protests demanding that the immigrants be sent back to their home countries. The immigration issue has provoked urgent debates over appropriate policy responses. It is unquestionable, however, that Russia's need for immigrant labor will rise as its economy grows and the country carries out its large-scale plans to expand oil and gas production and build major infrastructure projects, while the supply of available domestic labor diminishes.[69] The government has run a program to attract Russians living in other CIS countries to return to Russia, but so far, very few have responded.

The Putin regime took some early steps toward placing the economy on a path where it could sustain growth through continuing productivity improvement, but these measures fell short of their goal as the leaders chose instead to take advantage of the windfall gains from high world energy and commodity prices to cement their political support among the elite and general public. If the regime is to meet its long-term goals of economic reform, it will have to overhaul the relationship between state and market. The Soviet state used central planning to direct enterprises on what to produce and how to use resources. Much of the economy was geared to heavy industry and defense production, and government ministries directly administered each branch of the economy. In postcommunist Russia, there must be an entirely different relationship between the state and the economy if the economy is to follow a path of self-sustaining growth. It must set clear rules for economic activity, regulate markets, enforce the law, supply public goods and services, and promote competition. The legacy of tsarist and Soviet economic models, the size of the country, and the harshness of its climate mean that Russia's economy will continue to feature a large role for the state in regulating economic activity and redistributing resources.

President Medvedev is undoubtedly right when he declared that the economy suffers from the effects of centuries of deeply entrenched corruption, dependence on raw materials exports, and a habit of depending on the government to solve problems.[70] He has also declared that "no matter how many state-owned companies we have, modernization will happen, above all, through private businesses, and only if there is competition" and that "The state should not tear the apples from the tree of economics. What the government should do is help to grow our apple orchard, develop our economic environment."[71] But the strong signals coming from the president that Russia must fundamentally shift the structure of its economy and the attitudes of its population have had little impact so far. The only major concrete result of Medvedev's modernization drive is a large-scale state-funded program to build a Russian equivalent to Silicon Valley—where innovative start-up companies can try out new technologies—in a town outside Moscow. It is doubtful that this project will have the transforming effect on the structure of the economy that would be needed to realize President Medvedev's vision.

NOTES

1. For a vehement expression of this point of view, see the recent writings of the former chief economist of the World Bank, Joseph E. Stiglitz. Stiglitz attacks the "Washington Consensus" and the radical liberalization policies it pursued in the 1980s and 1990s. He is especially critical of IMF policy in Russia. See Joseph E. Stiglitz, *Globalization and Its Discontents* (New York: W. W. Norton & Co., 2002); Joseph E. Stiglitz, *Making Globalization Work* (New York: W. W. Norton & Co., 2006).
2. Among those critical of the radical reforms of the early 1990s are Stephen F. Cohen, *Failed Crusade: America and the Tragedy of Post-Communist Russia* (New York: W. W. Norton, 2001); Peter Reddaway and Dmitri Glinski, *Tragedy of Russia's Reforms: Market Bolshevism Against Democracy* (Washington, DC: U. S. Institute of Peace, 2001); Jerry F. Hough, *The Logic of Economic Reform in Russia* (Washington, DC: Brookings Institution Press, 2001). Among those arguing that the reforms did not go far enough in removing obstacles to an open, competitive market system are Anders Aslund, *Building Capitalism: The Transformation of the Former Soviet Bloc* (Cambridge: Cambridge University Press, 2002); Anders Aslund, *Russia's Capitalist Revolution: Why Market Reform Succeeded and Democracy Failed* (Washington, DC: Peterson Institute for International Economics, 2007); and Andrei Shleifer and Daniel Treisman, *Without a Map: Political Tactices and Economic Reform in Russia* (Cambridge, MA: MIT Press, 2000). Shleifer and Treisman argue that the compromises made by the reformers were conscious concessions to important stakeholders in order to weaken resistance to the larger goals of the reforms.
3. If the inflation is hidden or repressed, it means that price controls prevent the market from reflecting inflationary pressures with continuously increasing prices. In those cases, the hidden inflation takes the form of widening shortages and black markets. Whether the inflation is open or repressed, it has the same destructive effect on productive activity: no one wants to invest in any activity where the benefits will only be felt in the future. Productive investment, as a result, plummets.
4. Joel S. Hellman, "Winners Take All: The Politics of Partial Reform in Post-communist Transitions," *World Politics* 50:1 (1998): 203–234.
5. "Hard currency" is the term used for the U.S. dollar, German mark, Japanese yen, and other national currencies that are freely traded on world markets and used as currency reserves by governments. Soft currencies are those where governments set a value and then protect that value against foreign currency markets. Thus, they do not have an established international market value.

6. Shleifer and Treisman, *Without a Map*; William Tompson, "Was Gaidar Really Necessary? Russian 'Shock Therapy' Reconsidered," *Problems of Post-Communism* 49:4 (July/August 2002): 12–21.

7. For example, Russia's largest oil company Lukoil was created by a directive issued by the Russian Council of Ministers in November 1991, shortly before the final dissolution of the Soviet Union. Needless to say, creation of this company enabled a small group of owner-managers to become hugely wealthy overnight. See Peter Maass, "The Triumph of the Quiet Tycoon," *New York Times Magazine*, August 1, 2004.

8. Economists generally say that once prices start rising by 50 percent a month and more, the economy is in a state of hyperinflation.

9. For a discussion of stabilization in Poland, see Jeffrey Sachs, *Poland's Jump to the Market Economy* (Cambridge, MA: MIT Press, 1993).

10. Cf. Joseph Stiglitz, *Globalization and Its Discontents* (New York: Norton, 2002), esp. ch. 5, "Who Lost Russia?" and Stiglitz, *Making Globalization Work*.

11. A good account of the political choices faced by the reformers is Shleifer and Treisman, *Without a Map*. For memoirs by two of the key policy makers from the period, see Anatolii B. Chubais, ed., *Privatizatsiia po-rossiiski* (Moscow: Vagrius, 1999); Yegor Gaidar, *Days of Defeat and Victory* (Seattle: University of Washington Press, 1999).

12. Joseph R. Blasi, Maya Kroumova, and Douglas Kruse, *Kremlin Capitalism: Privatizing the Russian Economy* (Ithaca, NY: Cornell University Press, 1997), p. 171; Andrei Shleifer and Daniel Treisman, *Without a Map: Political Tactics and Economic Reform in Russia* (Cambridge, MA: MIT Press, 2000), p. 42. A good account of the Central Bank's high-handedness in this period is Juliet Johnson, *A Fistful of Rubles: The Rise and Fall of the Russian Banking System* (Ithaca, NY: Cornell University Press, 2000), ch. 3, "The Central Bank of Russia," pp. 64–97.

13. In a cooperative, all the employees are coowners of the business and share in its profits.

14. The goals of the privatization program are laid out in a volume of essays by its chief Russian designers and their Western advisers. See, in particular, Anatoly B. Chubais and Maria Vishnevskaya, "Main Issues of Privatisation in Russia," and Maxim Boycko and Andrei Shleifer, "The Voucher Programme for Russia," both in Anders Åslund and Richard Layard, eds., *Changing the Economic System in Russia* (New York: St. Martin's Press, 1993), pp. 89–99 and 100–111. Another book by three individuals closely involved in the privatization program gives both lucid theoretical rationalization and frank insider insight into the program. See Maxim Boycko, Andrei Shleifer, and Robert Vishny, *Privatizing Russia* (Cambridge, MA: MIT Press, 1995).

15. Pekka Sutela, "Insider Privatization in Russia: Speculations on Systemic Changes," *Europe–Asia Studies* 46:3 (1994): 420–421.

16. Blasi et al., *Kremlin Capitalism*, pp. 179–80. The authors conducted a major national annual survey of the managers of privatized enterprises in Russia.

17. Radio Free Europe/Radio Liberty Daily Report, July 1, 1994.

18. Blasi et al., *Kremlin Capitalism*, p. 50.

19. *Rossiiskii statisticheskii ezhegodnik 2005* (Moscow: Goskomstat Rossii, 2006), pp. 148, 349; Rudiger Ahrend and William Tompson, "Fifteen Years of Economic Reform in Russia: What Has Been achieved? What Remains to be Done?" *OECD Working Paper No. 430*, ECO/WKP(2005)17 (Paris: OECD, 13 May 2005), p. 23.

20. Similar oligarchs have also arisen in Ukraine and several other postcommunist countries, where the state opened the economy just enough to allow entrepreneurs to profit from partial reform but not enough to force them to compete with other entrepreneurs on a level playing field.
21. Steven L. Solnick, *Stealing the State: Control and Collapse in Soviet Institutions* (Cambridge, MA: Harvard University Press, 1998).
22. Peter Rutland, "Putin and the Oligarchs," in Dale R. Herspring, ed., *Putin's Russia: Past Imperfect, Future Uncertain* (Lanham, MD: Rowman & Littlefield, 2003), p. 141.
23. Daniel Treisman, "Putin's Silovarchs," *Orbis* (2007): 141–153.
24. http://www.nornik.ru/page.jsp?pageId=about.
25. Daniel Treisman has argued that the loans for shares scheme, while unsavory, was actually a catalyst for the recovery in the 2000s. He shows that the firms run by the oligarchs performed better in the 2000s than firms that remained under state ownership. Daniel Treisman, "'Loans for Shares' Revisited," *Post-Soviet Affairs* 26:3 (2010): 207–227. For a reconsideration of the role played by the oligarchs more generally, see Sergei Guriev and Andrei Rachinsky, "The Role of Oligarchs in Russian Capitalism," *Journal of Economic Perspectives* 19:1 (2005): 131–150.
26. They were backed by the federal government's share of the proceeds of the sale of stock from state enterprises. Each enterprise had to offer at least 35 percent of its stock for vouchers. This corresponded to the share of ownership that the federal government claimed for itself. The federal government's share in the sale of privatizing enterprises was thus distributed to the citizens in the form of vouchers.
27. The OECD estimates that Russia's rate of gross fixed capital investment as a share of GDP is about 18 percent, compared to around 40 percent for China. Organization of Economic Cooperation and Development, *OECD Economic Surveys: Russian Federation* (Paris: OECD, November 2006), pp. 26–27.
28. Igor' Naumov, "Rossiia i SNG opustilis' na dno ivestitsionnogo mira," *Nezavisimaia gazeta*, May 15, 2009.
29. This is known as Coase's Theorem, after the economist Ronald H. Coase. It is very often misrepresented: Coase was calling attention to the sensitivity of markets to the costliness of transactions. Where contracts and property rights are not consistently enforced and information is scarce, the theorem predicts that the initial distribution of property rights will be an obstacle to efficiency-improving economic exchange.
30. This perspective underlies the field of institutional economics. Cf. Douglass C. North, *Institutions, Institutional Change and Economic Performance* (Cambridge: Cambridge University Press, 1990).
31. Blasi et al., *Kremlin Capitalism*; Michael McFaul, "State Power, Institutional Change, and the Politics of Privatization in Russia," *World Politics* 47 (1995): 210–243.
32. They continue to be small by world standards. For example, the total capitalization of Russia's 300 largest companies reached around $250 billion in fall 2004, which is less than the capitalization of General Electric. *Kommersant-Dengi*, September 14, 2004.
33. European Bank for Reconstruction and Development (EBRD), *Transition Report 1998: Financial Sector in Transition* (EBRD: London, 1998), p. 186.
34. On the virtual economy, see Clifford G. Gaddy and Barry W. Ickes, "Russia's Virtual Economy," *Foreign Affairs* 77 (September–October 1998): 53–67; and David Woodruff, *Money Unmade: Barter and the Fate of Russian Capitalism* (Ithaca and London: Cornell University Press, 1999).
35. In spring 1996, when the presidential election campaign was at its height, Russian state treasury obligations were selling at ruinously high interest rates—over 200 percent effective annual yields on six-month bonds. Little wonder that investors

were uninterested in the stock market. Because of the instability of the political climate and the fear of default, the great bulk of this paper was short term.

36. Thane Gustafson, *Capitalism Russian-Style* (Cambridge, England: Cambridge University Press, 1999), pp. 2–3, 94–95.

37. The Russian Civil War (1918–1921) was fought between the Bolshevik ("Red") forces and the anticommunists ("Whites") following the Communist Revolution. The Whites comprised a diverse set of enemies of the new regime—among them both monarchists and socialists—whose inability to unite against the Bolsheviks ensured their ultimate defeat at the hands of the Red Army.

38. Shleifer and Treisman, *Without a Map*, pp. 113–136.

39. *Rossiiski statisticheskii ezhegodnik 2008* (Moscow: Goskomstat, 2008).

40. It is now well established that countries that rely on natural resources for a high proportion of national income tend not to invest in other sources of productivity (such as human capital) and fail to develop effective institutions of accountability and governance. For this reason, they tend to have weaker long-term economic performance and to undergo transitions away from democracy. See Terry Lynn Karl, *The Paradox of Plenty: Oil Booms and Petro-States* (Berkeley: University of California Press, 1997); Michael L. Ross, "The Political Economy of the Resource Curse," *World Politics* 51:2 (1999): 297–322; Michael L. Ross, "Does Oil Hinder Democracy?" *World Politics* 53:3 (2001): 325–361. For a discussion of Putin's Russia as a "petro-state," see Marshall I. Goldman, *Petrostate: Putin, Power, and the New Russia* (New York: Oxford University Press, 2008).

41. William Tompson, "A Frozen Venezuela? The 'Resource Curse' and Russian Politics," in Michael Ellman, ed., *Russia's Oil and Natural Gas: Bonanza or Curse?* (London: Anthem Books, 2006), pp. 189–212; also see William Tompson, "The Political Implications of Russia's Resource-Based Economy," *Post-Soviet Affairs* 21:4 (2005): 335–359 and M. Steven Fish, *Democracy Derailed in Russia: The Failure of Open Politics* (Cambridge: Cambridge University Press, 2005), pp. 114–138.

42. OECD Russia Survey 2006, p. 38.

43. Goldman, *Petrostate*, pp. 133–135.

44. William Tompson, "Back to the Future? Thoughts on the Political Economy of Expanding State Ownership in Russia," *Les Cahiers Russie: The Russia Papers* 6 (2008): 1–2.

45. Goldman, *Petrostate*, p. 193.

46. Some of these practices were outlined in a scandalous interview that appeared in a prominent business newspaper. The interviewee, who had handled many of these transactions, indicated that the head of the group carrying them out was Igor' Sechin, a deputy prime minister considered to be the leader of an informal bureaucratic clan uniting a number of figures tied to the security police. See Maksim Kvashe, "Partiiu dlia nas olitsetvoriaet silovoi blok, kotoryi vozglavliaet Igor' Ivanovich Sechin," *Kommersant*, November 30, 2007, p. 20.

47. Goldman, *Petrostate*, pp. 128–133.

48. Conditions of WTO membership include the consent of all existing members as well as the elimination of tariff and other trade barriers. Putin and Medvedev regard WTO membership as useful as a way of putting competitive pressure on Russian industry. However, they have been under pressure from Russian producers to make as few concessions to the WTO as possible. Because of this, and because of objections from other members of the organization, Russia's accession negotiations have dragged on for more than 15 years.

49. Sergei Kulikov, "Rossiia stala autsaiderom," *Nezavisimaia gazeta*, October 28, 2008.

50. "Na zaderzhku zarplaty zhaluetsia tret' rossiian," *Vedomosti*, July 20, 2009.

51. Polit.ru, March 6, 2009.
52. "Mer Tol'iatti: sotsial'naia obstanovka v gorode odnoznachno napriazhennaia," *Vedomosti*, September 8, 2009.
53. Polit.ru, July 8, 2009; September 29, 2009; December 15, 2009; Sergei Kulikov, "Gradoobrazuiushchii vzryv," *Nezavisimaia gazeta*, December 15, 2009.
54. Ibid., March 12, 2009.
55. Richard Rose, *Understanding Post-Communist Transformation: A Bottoms-Up Approach* (New York: Routledge, 2009), *pp. 173–179.*
56. Anastasiia Bashkatova, "Ekonomicheskie ministry pochemu-to ne vyzyvaiut doveriia," *Nezavisimaia gazeta,* June 10, 2010.
57. Gail Kligman, "The Social Legacy of Communism: Women, Children, and the Feminization of Poverty," in James R. Millar and Sharon L. Wolchik, eds., *The Social Legacy of Communism* (Washington, DC: Woodrow Wilson Center Press and Cambridge University Press, 1994), p. 261; Mary Buckley, "The Politics of Social Issues," in Stephen White, Alex Pravda, and Zvi Gitelman, eds., *Developments in Russian and Post-Soviet Politics*, 3rd ed. (London: Macmillan, 1994), pp. 192–194.
58. Simon Clarke, "Market and Institutional Determinants of Wage Differentiation in Russia," *Industrial and Labor Relations* 55:4 (2002): 628–648.
59. Nikolaus von Twickel, "Rich Get Richer as Poor Get Poorer," *The Moscow Times*, August 8, 2008.
60. Heidi Brown, "Russia: The World's Richest Government," *Forbes.com*, April 1, 2008, http://www.forbes.com/2008/03/28/russia-billionaires-duma-biz-cz_hb_0401 russiapols_print.html, accessed April 2, 2008. However, the financial crisis of 2008 had hit a number of the tycoons hard. One expert estimated that the total worth of the top 25 on the Russian Forbes list fell by $240 in just 5 months. Philip P. Pan, "Russian Elite Look to Kremlin for Aid as Wealth Evaporates," *Washington Post*, October 17, 2008.
61. Philip P. Pan, "Russian Elite Looks to Kremlin for Aid as Wealth Evaporates," *Washington Post*, October 17, 2008.
62. The World Bank, *Transition: The First Ten Years—Analysis and Lessons for Eastern Europe and the Former Soviet Union* (Washington, DC: World Bank, 2002), p. 9.
63. Quoted from Vladimir Putin's address to an expanded session of the State Council, February 8, 2008, "On the Strategy of Development of Russia to 2020," From http://president.kremlin.ru/text/appears/2008/02/159528.shtml.
64. Sergei Kulikov, "Pravitel'stvo ustroilo demograficheskii vzryv," *Nezavisimaia gazeta*, February 18, 2010.
65. *RFE/RL Newsline*, 20 July 2006.
66. Russian military commanders reported that one-third of the men they had called up in the fall of 2004 were unfit to serve as a result of health problems. Polit.ru, December 9, 2004.
67. Sergei Kulikov, "Nuzhnye liudi v nuzhnom meste," *Nezavisimaia gazeta*, September 10, 2008.
68. Alex Anishyuk, "Immigrants Make Up 10% of Work Force," *The Moscow Times*, March 31, 2010, citing a report commissioned by the United Nations.
69. The government estimates that the working-age population will fall from about 90 million in 2008 to 77.8 million in 2020. Kulikov, "Nuzhnye liudi v nuzhnom meste."
70. Dmitrii Medvedev, "Go Russia!," September 10, 2009, http://eng.kremlin.ru/text/speeches/2009/09/10/1534_type104017_221527.shtml.
71. "Medvedev Targets Investment Boost, Tax Cuts," *The Moscow Times*, June 18, 2010.

Politics and the Law

DEMOCRATIZATION AND THE RULE OF LAW

In Russia, the law has often been an instrument of power rather than an impartial constraint on the state. Consequently, one of the most important goals of democratic reformers since the end of the Soviet era has been to establish the rule of law, that is, to make the enforcement of law independent of the will of the authorities. In this effort, there have been mixed results. The legal system continues to be subject to corruption and political abuse. The regime has tried to weaken the ability of wealthy private interests, such as oligarchs and organized crime, to manipulate the legal system but have made it more susceptible to influence from the political authorities. Presidents Putin and Medvedev often emphasize the importance of the rule of law, yet the regime frequently bends judicial institutions to its will when major political interests are at stake.

The constitutional scholar Stephen Holmes has distinguished between the "rule of law" and "rule by law." In rule-by-law, a powerful elite concentrating political power uses law to protect its prerogatives. In rule-of-law, power is sufficiently dispersed among groups and organizations in society to prevent any one group from monopolizing access to the law. Many citizens and groups can call upon the law to defend their rights and interests. The range and variety of their resources help to keep the judiciary independent of political influence.[1] Merely reforming legal codes and institutions by itself is not sufficient to make the legal system impartial. As Holmes argues, "Russia's legal reforms will succeed only to the extent that the country as a whole develops in a liberal, pluralistic, and democratic direction."[2]

In the Soviet regime, the authorities regarded the law as an extension of state power, to be used for the state's purposes.[3] However, the mass terror under Stalin led Stalin's successors (who themselves had felt the terrible insecurity and fear that terror instills) to limit the arbitrary power of the secret police. After Stalin's death in 1953, legal reformers fitfully attempted to reform the codes of law and procedure so as to build more guarantees of rights into the legal system. One of the most important institutional changes made in the late 1950s was to place the secret police under stricter legal control. Extrajudicial trials, judgments, and sentences, which were a common practice at the time of Stalin's terror, were prohibited, and criminal defendants were granted important rights. New codes of criminal law and criminal procedure were adopted, and official policy promoted a concept of "socialist legality." Like many slogans of the post-Stalin period, this was a formula meant to gloss over incompatible goals. The idea was that the legal system, while still subordinate to the party, should be less subject to political abuse.

In fact, in the post-Stalin era, the party and police continued to use legal procedures as a way of legitimating actions taken in the service of the regime's power and security. The criminal codes themselves contained articles providing legal penalties for "anti-Soviet agitation and propaganda" and for "circulation of fabrications known to be false which defame the Soviet state or social system."[4] In the post-Stalin period, these were frequently used against individuals who wrote or circulated works (whether fiction or nonfiction) that the regime judged to be anti-Soviet. Alternatively, the authorities sometimes resorted to the practice of declaring a dissident mentally incompetent and forcibly incarcerating him in a mental hospital, where he could be further punished by being administered mind-altering drugs.[5] The continuation of these practices as means of political repression into the late 1980s attests to the inability of the law to protect the rights of individuals whom the party or KGB for any reason considered a threat.

When Mikhail Gorbachev came to power in 1985, one of his major goals was to strengthen the legitimacy and authority of legal institutions. He declared the establishment of a "law-governed state" (*pravovoe gosudarstvo*) to be one of the cardinal objectives of his reform program.[6] By a "law-governed state," Gorbachev meant that both rulers and ruled would obey the law. Its opposite would be a condition where the rulers exercised power arbitrarily; the rulers could freely violate the state's own constitutional and statutory rules, as had often happened under the Soviet regime when Communist Party, KGB, and other officials often ignored constitutional and legal norms in exercising their power, but they expected their subjects to obey the law. Since 1991, the ideal of the law-governed state has continued to attract lip service from Russian leaders even when they took actions violating the constitution. Vladimir Putin, for instance, declared that Russia must be governed by a "dictatorship of law," which certainly has ambiguous implications (does it mean that the law must be supreme over the state or a dictatorship by means of law?).

Likewise, Dmitrii Medvedev, himself formerly a law professor, uses the language of rights, freedom, and law in emphasizing the importance of constitutional democracy. In his presidential address to parliament in November 2008, he declared, "the Constitution has set out the path for the renewal of Russia as a free nation, as a society for which the highest value is the rights and dignity of every person."[7] Statements of this sort by the country's leaders are not necessarily cynical or hollow. Like their Soviet predecessors, Russian rulers today want the law to serve as a source of social order and a constraint on the arbitrary behavior by state officials. Bureaucrats' ability to bend the law to their own purposes is a far more immediate threat to the leaders' ability to achieve their goals than is the remote prospect of organized popular resistance.

The clash between these competing impulses—the leaders' desire to manipulate the law for political purposes versus their interest in promoting it to reinforce state stability and predictability—helps account for the zigzag nature of legal reform over the past two decades. A number of reforms have strengthened legal institutions by making them less subject to political abuse. The judicial system has grown somewhat more independent and effective. Several legal principles essential to a democratic and pluralistic society have been established. One of the most significant changes is the creation of a Constitutional Court empowered to adjudicate disputes arising between the branches of government and between the federal level of government and the constituent territories. A body of law recognizing private property rights has been adopted.

At the same time, the legal system is still not fully independent of the authorities. At the federal level, the sweeping informal power of the president limits the courts' ability to apply the law impartially. For instance, the Constitutional Court has been unwilling to cross the president on matters concerning presidential prerogatives; under Yeltsin, the court was willing to defy the president occasionally, but in the 2000s, the court has never tried to check the president. Many lower court rulings go unenforced because of the ability of powerful interests to flout judicial decisions, and some decisions clearly reflect high-level political intervention. At the regional and local levels, courts remain susceptible to political influence. On a range of contentious issues—electoral disputes, federalism issues, property rights conflicts, national security cases— the courts routinely bow to the will of those in power. Although this can mean that the courts can sometimes uphold federal law against wayward local officials when the federal authorities want to curb regional autonomy, it also means that the courts almost never issue a ruling that defies the president. At the regional level, governors tend to have similar influence over the courts, routinely intervening in cases where their political interests are affected.

A second problem is corruption. Russian surveys have found that the courts and police are among the most highly corrupted of Russian institutions. To some extent, this stems from the rapidity of the change in the political and economic system. The meltdown of the Soviet system created opportunities for criminals to amass wealth and use it to corrupt law enforcement officials. Legitimate business owners often find themselves forced to turn to illegal protection rackets because the police and courts fail to protect their basic interests.[8] Many citizens report that they cannot afford to turn to the law for the redressal of their grievances, because they cannot afford to pay the bribes that they believe are expected. Trust in the courts and procuracy is low, as Table 5.1 showed.[9] President Medvedev himself acknowledged the gravity of the problem in a meeting with a group of senior judicial officials in May 2008, noting that "[unjust] decisions, as we all know, do happen and come as a result of different kinds of pressure, like telephone calls and—there's no point in denying—offers of money."[10] Medvedev has explicitly denounced the prevalent "legal nihilism" in the country, the tendency to view the law as a nuisance to be got around rather than a binding constraint on behavior.

Legal reformers emphasize two basic principles: individual rights should take precedence over the power of the state, and judicial power should be separated from legislative and executive power. Observance of these two principles would represent a large step toward greater respect for law and away from the many abuses of law that the Soviet state committed in the past. For instance, the Bolsheviks held that as "revolutionary justice" was higher than any written law, the rights and obligations of rulers and citizens must be subordinate to the political interests of the regime. But this instrumental view of the law was not held by the Bolsheviks only. Many in and outside of President Yeltsin's administration expressed a similar view that the goal of eliminating the foundations of communist rule took precedence over observance of the letter of the law: the populace must obey the law—but the authorities (*"vlast'"*) could choose when to observe it and when not to, according to their judgments of expediency.

The problem is that although the leaders want state officials and citizens to treat the law as binding, they routinely intervene in the workings of the law when important political interests are at stake. Compared with the Soviet era, however, there is far less overt repression of real or imagined political opponents, because there is much wider freedom of expression and association. Today, there are no provisions in the criminal code outlawing "anti-state agitation and propaganda." But in individual cases the authorities do use various articles of the criminal code for political repression. In several cases, the authorities have used criminal prosecutions on charges of tax law violations, embezzlement, and other crimes, as well as civil suits for recovery of debts, in campaigns against individual businesspeople. A good example is the use of selective prosecution to dismantle the Yukos oil firm so that it could be taken over by the state. (See Close-Up 6.1, the Yukos Affair, in Chapter 6.) In other cases, the authorities use the provisions in the code outlawing "extremist" activity or "inciting religious or ethnic hatred" as ways of prosecuting individuals whose protests are too overt for the authorities' liking.[11] Probably the commonest form of political repression, however, does not use the law at all: sometimes individuals are simply beaten up by the police or by anonymous thugs if their political activity offends the authorities.[12]

Judicial reform affects many interests, including the bureaucratic self-interest of the agencies directly responsible for law enforcement. For centuries, the most important agency for law enforcement in Russia has been the *procuracy*. It is charged with supervising the judicial system, investigating crimes, preparing and prosecuting cases, and ensuring that the rights of *both* state *and* individuals are upheld. Historically, it has been the most prestigious and powerful component of the legal system. Accordingly, judicial reformers have long tried to shift the balance of power away from the procuracy and toward the judiciary in protecting individual legal rights. But the procuracy has managed to block many of the reforms that have been proposed.

Judicial Reform

Full establishment of the rule of law would mean that no arm of the state would be able to influence or violate the law for political ends. In turn, this would require that the judiciary be independent of the executive. As in the Soviet era, however, judges continue to be subject to political pressures, some direct, some indirect. As President Medvedev's comments above suggested, one notorious form of political influence is called "telephone justice." This refers to the practice whereby an official or some other powerful individual privately communicates instructions to a judge on a particular case.[13] "Telephone justice" in the Soviet era could take the form of instructions from the Communist Party to judges to be especially harsh in passing sentences on a particular class of criminals if the party was attempting to conduct a propaganda campaign against a social problem, such as alcoholism, hooliganism, or economic crimes. Or, an official might tell a judge to go easy on a particularly well-connected defendant. Today similar confidential instructions to judges are likely to come from the presidential administration or the office of a regional governor. And besides these political threats, the independence of the judiciary is also compromised by the prevalence of corruption.

Since 1989, reforms of Russia's legal system have sought to improve the effectiveness and independence of judicial institutions and to strengthen individual legal rights vis-à-vis the state. These institutional and statutory changes have often met resistance from powerful agencies of the state. Moreover, once adopted, formal rules intended to strengthen the independence of the judiciary are often subverted in practice by the authorities. Still, the range of cases in which judges and prosecutors are able to enforce the law impartially has expanded substantially. Moreover, there is now an enormous realm of civil transactions involving private property that are—for the most part—outside the direct political purview of the authorities. But by the same token, the large stakes often involved in such cases induce many parties to legal disputes to resort to bribes and threats to achieve their goals.

Let us now consider three domains of the legal system in particular: the procuracy and other agencies of law enforcement, the judiciary and in particular the Constitutional Court, and the codes of law and legal procedure.

Law Enforcement

Russia's legal system traditionally vested a great deal of power in the procuracy: It was considered to be the most prestigious branch of the law. The procuracy is somewhat comparable to the system of federal prosecutors in the United States, but has wider powers and duties. The procuracy is given sweeping responsibilities for fighting crime, corruption, and abuses of power in the bureaucracy and for both instigating investigations of criminal wrong-doing by private citizens and responding to complaints about official malfeasance. The procuracy has the primary responsibility for bringing criminal cases to court. It supervises the investigation of a case, prepares the case for prosecution, and argues the case in court. In addition, the procuracy has traditionally been seen by officials as the principal check on illegal activity and abuses of power. One of the procuracy's assigned tasks is to supervise all state officials and public organizations to ensure that they observe the law.

The procuracy investigates matters of wrongdoing throughout the state. For instance, after President Medvedev declared that improving the quality of elementary education was a top priority, the procuracy throughout the country responded by investigating instances of administrative and criminal wrongdoing on the part of school teachers and administrators. In one region, the procuracy found the directors of two schools guilty of violating the administrative code when they discovered broken toilets, windows without glass panes, and leaking roofs at their schools. In a district in Pskov oblast, a procurator fined the heads of four rural schools 500 rubles each for serving the children uninspected vegetables grown in school gardens and for using chipped and cracked plates. In Buryatiia, the procurator discovered that computers delivered to schools were not being used. In one school in Ivanovo, the Internet was connected only in the director's office. A procurator in a city in Amur oblast brought charges against a school administrator for padding his payroll.[14] Accounts such as these illustrate the point that the procuracy is held responsible for enforcing laws and rules in every sphere of the state and at every level of power. As the then Procurator General Vladimir Ustinov put it in a speech in May 2004, since civil society in Russia is so underdeveloped, the procuracy has assumed the functions of civil society in curbing abuses by the state bureaucracy.[15]

Formally, the regional branches of the procuracy are subordinate to the Procurator General in Moscow. In the 1990s, however, many local procurators formed alliances with governors, without whose support they were unable to maintain their offices and pay their staff. This led to a serious weakening of the center's law enforcement capacity. Therefore, as soon as he entered office, President Putin worked to recentralize the procuracy so that it could enforce federal law throughout the country. When Putin created the seven new federal "super-districts" in May 2000, the procuracy announced that it was creating new district level branches of the procuracy in each federal district. These were charged with riding herd on the procuracy offices in each of the subjects of the federation and thus helping to recentralize control within the procuracy. The new district offices were instructed to comb through regional statutes to find instances of laws contradicting federal law and to correct those problems. They found hundreds of such cases in each federal district and pressed regional legislative and executive bodies to rewrite the offending legislation. Putin hailed this effort for "its important role in implementing the important task of creating a unified legal space in the country."[16]

The procuracy has substantial political influence, which it exercises to protect its institutional prerogatives. Complaining that its resources leave it grossly underequipped to meet even the most elementary demands placed upon it, such as investigating the most serious violent crimes and bringing the offenders to justice, the procuracy's representatives plead for more resources rather than for fewer responsibilities. The procuracy has lobbied in defense of its institutional prerogatives when it believed that a proposed reform would weaken its power. For example, it staunchly opposed giving arrested persons the right to consult with an attorney at any time during the pretrial investigation; it opposed the adoption of the jury trial system; it fought reforms giving the courts the right to review procurators' decisions on the pretrial detention of criminal suspects; and it battled (unsuccessfully) to retain the responsibility to supervise criminal investigations when Putin created a new, autonomous hierarchy to supervise criminal investigations. The procuracy has won some of its fights, and in others, it has succeeded in watering down reforms intended to strengthen other legal institutions. Both Russian statist traditions (including the experience of legal institutions in the Soviet and prerevolutionary eras) and Russia's use of a continental system of legal procedure[17] reinforce the procuracy's central role in the judicial system. However, the reformed Criminal Procedure Code that came into effect on July 1, 2002, significantly reduced the legal powers of the procuracy by providing that warrants for arrests, wiretaps, searches, seizures, and a number of other pretrial procedures could no longer be issued by the procuracy, but only by the courts.[18]

Because of the centrality of the procuracy in the Russian legal system, the position of Procurator General—who directs the procuracy throughout the country—is of considerable political sensitivity. The president nominates a candidate for Procurator General to the Federation Council, which has the power to approve or reject the nomination. Likewise, the president must obtain Federation Council approval to remove the Procurator General. Only rarely in post-communist Russia has the Procurator General taken a position directly opposing the president, but in one important case, the procuracy did demonstrate its political independence. In February 1994, the State Duma approved an amnesty for several categories of persons, including those who were in jail awaiting trial for their participation in the attempted coups d'état of August 1991 and October 1993. The 1993 constitution gave the Duma the power of amnesty, although no law had yet been adopted specifying how this power was to be exercised. However, President Yeltsin expressed outrage at the decision and his advisors presented a variety of legal opinions purporting to demonstrate that the Duma's action was unlawful. Nonetheless, the Procurator General at the time, although believing that the Duma had exceeded its constitutional powers, complied with the Duma's decision, and ordered the release of the prisoners. When President Yeltsin pressured him to halt the release, the procurator refused to comply and resigned instead. The release was duly carried out. Then, for several months afterward, the Federation Council refused to confirm Yeltsin's nominee for a new Procurator General.[19]

Under Yeltsin, the procuracy exercised greater independence of the executive branch; since Putin came to power, the procuracy has been a loyal instrument of the Kremlin's political will. Some of its efforts have been devoted to enforcing federal law throughout the country and checking abuses by regional officials. But some have clearly served to stifle political opposition. In high-profile cases, the procuracy's actions are closely coordinated with the Kremlin. Former Procurator General Ustinov said that he met at least once a week with President Putin in order to "report" to the president, although he insists that the procuracy is entirely independent of the authorities in its enforcement of the law.[20] This is a doubtful claim, however. The record suggests that the procuracy is often used as an instrument against figures whom the Kremlin wants to remove from the political arena.

In June 2006, Putin removed Ustinov as Procurator General and replaced him with Yuri Chaika, who had been Justice Minister. Curiously, Putin then named Ustinov Minister of Justice. This move—a promotion for Chaika but a demotion for Ustinov—seems to have been part of a larger bureaucratic battle among Kremlin factions relating to control over the law enforcement agencies, because in 2007, over Chaika's resistance, a new body called the Investigative Committee was created within the structure of the procuracy. It was assigned the responsibility of managing the investigation of major crimes but was effectively outside the supervision of the procurator. The impression that this was part of a larger turf war was reinforced when the head of the Investigative Committee proceeded to arrest the deputy minister of finance and the head of the federal antinarcotics agency, only to be forced to fire his own top investigator over accusations of corruption several months later. This war among the country's top law enforcement agencies was undoubtedly related to the succession from Putin to Medvedev. It demonstrates that control over law enforcement is subject to politicization as bureaucratic factions seek control of the instruments of coercion in order to settle scores with rival factions. The gravity of such in-fighting also creates an urgent desire on the part of many in the political elite that there be a single all-powerful leader at the top who can prevent such struggles from weakening the country's security.

A number of agencies besides the procuracy have responsibilities for law enforcement. Some of them are administered by the Ministry for Internal Affairs (MVD), and others are specialized successor bodies of the old Soviet-era KGB (Committee for State Security).

The MVD manages both regular uniformed police (known as the *militsiia*) and militarized security forces that carry out riot control and other functions. The ministry also maintains specialized police forces, such as the traffic police. As a uniformed service wielding coercive power, the MVD is one of the "force structures" (*silovye struktury*). It is also widely criticized for corruption, brutality, and ineffectiveness. In November 2009, a police major in Novorossiisk posted videos to his personal Web site appealing to President Medvedev to address the deep problems in the MVD, such as corruption, poor working conditions, and criminal investigations of innocent people. The videos caused a national scandal when they were reposted on YouTube, where they received more than a million hits in a week.[21] Other widely publicized episodes of police abuses at the same time forced the problems of the MVD to the top of the political agenda. In response, President Medvedev issued a decree making several far-reaching changes in the MVD's structure and personnel. He fired two deputy ministers and replaced them with individuals from the presidential administration, as well as making several other top-level appointments. He issued a decree reducing the number of employees in the central office of the ministry by half, from 20,000 to 10,000, and ordered a sweeping reorganization, a further 20 percent cut in the number of employees by 2012, and a pay increase for the remaining employees. He submitted a package of legislation to the Duma tightening sanctions for misconduct by police officials.[22] These were dramatic gestures (he fired more MVD officials at one stroke than President Putin had done in eight years).[23] But success in his effort to transform the culture of the MVD will require long-term sustained pressure from the top.

In the Soviet era, the KGB, or Committee for State Security, exercised very wide powers. These included responsibility for both domestic and foreign intelligence. The KGB also conducted extensive surveillance over society to prevent political dissent or opposition, and in its exercise of power, it often operated outside the law. In October 1991, following the August 1991 coup (when the KGB chairman was one of the principal organizers of the seizure of power), Yeltsin dissolved the Russian republican branch of the KGB and divided it into several new agencies: the Ministry of Security, which was to guard the state's security in domestic matters; the Foreign Intelligence Service, which took over the KGB's overseas espionage and intelligence functions[24]; the Federal Agency for Governmental Communications and Information (FAPSI), which maintained security in the country's telecommunications system, the Federal Border Guard Service (FSP), and the Federal Tax Police (FSNP). The reorganization altered the structure and mission of the successor bodies, but they were never subjected to a thorough purge of personnel. Although many of the archives containing documents on the past activities of the secret police[25] have been opened to inspection, thus exposing many aspects of the Soviet regime's use of terror, no member or collaborator of the security service has ever been prosecuted for these actions. None of the KGB's informers have been exposed to public judgment. Indeed, the security police claim that they were themselves a victim of Stalin's arbitrary rule and terror.

Throughout the 1990s, the successor bodies were further reorganized. In 1993, the Ministry of Security was reorganized as the Federal Counter-Intelligence Service, and in 1995, President Yeltsin reorganized it yet again into the Federal Security Service (FSB), assigning it comprehensive duties and powers. From a senior Russian government official's description to the press of the new body's mandate, we can get an idea of how wide ranging the FSB's powers are. The new FSB, he stated, would "be able to infiltrate foreign organizations and criminal groups, institute inquiries, carry out preliminary investigations, maintain its own prisons, demand information from private companies, and set up special units and front enterprises." Its duties would include foreign intelligence activities to boost Russia's "economic, scientific, technical, and defense potential" and "to ensure the security of all government bodies."[26] The authorities have continued to expand the FSB's range of duties. In 2009,

President Medvedev declared that in addition to its responsibilities for counter-intelligence and fighting terrorism, nationalism, and extremism, the FSB was also supervising the effectiveness of the use of government money to bail out banks and businesses in the current economic crisis.[27] The FSB has also found ready support for the expansion of its powers to oversee political life. In July 2010, the Duma passed legislation sponsored by the FSB giving it the right to issue preventive warnings to individuals that their behavior was nearing the limit of permissible behavior and that they risked violating the law against extremism. The law passed with almost no debate despite the objections of human rights activists and the country's human rights commissioner.[28]

The security agencies have been skillful at adapting to the new post-Soviet political environment and have found new security tasks that enable them to retain power and resources. An example is the FAPSI, which is responsible for ensuring the security of state telecommunications. FAPSI is believed to provide telecommunications services to a number of governmental, financial, and commercial organizations, giving it privileged intelligence-gathering opportunities. A further step in the strengthening of the state security police under President Putin was the decision in March 2003, enacted in a series of presidential decrees, to merge FAPSI and the Federal Guard Service into the FSB. Since both of these services had operated as divisions of the KGB in the Soviet era, observers commented that the FSB was returning to the old model of "superagency."

Although they have been eager to aggrandize power, the security agencies have a reputation for competence and honesty. Many former security officers have been recruited to work for private organizations. And a number of leading politicians have background in the security organs, including, most famously, Vladimir Putin. Putin has drawn upon the security agencies for many of his senior personnel appointments. Certainly, a number of figures who were associates of Putin while he worked in the KGB have wound up with senior positions in the executive branch and as heads of major government-run business corporations—often simultaneously.[29]

Their broad responsibilities and the secrecy surrounding their operations make the FSB and other security agencies extremely difficult to monitor. Effectively, the only institution to which they are accountable is the president. Putin and Medvedev, meantime, have continued to expand the mandate and budget of the security agencies. Like their predecessors, they have chosen to give the security services broad autonomy in return for their political support.

The Judiciary

In contrast to the clout that the procuracy has traditionally wielded in Russia, the bench has been relatively weak and passive. Traditionally, judges have been the least-experienced and lowest-paid members of the legal profession and the most vulnerable to external political and administrative pressure.[30] This situation is changing; the professionalism and prestige of the bench have been rising.[31] But in order for judges to exercise their powers impartially and without fear of retribution, the political environment in which they operate must value the principle of judicial independence. However, the regime changes in Russia have had contradictory effects on the development of an effective, autonomous, judicial branch. In the 1990s, the rise of powerful business interests, coupled with the reach of organized crime, subverted judicial autonomy. In a few instances, judges were murdered when they attempted to thwart organized crime. In the 2000s, judges have been reluctant to cross the executive branch.

In addition, many judges have left the bench to take higher paying jobs in other branches of the legal profession. As the volume of court cases that come before the courts increase, judges find themselves hard-pressed to keep up. There are around 30,000 judges in courts of general jurisdiction. They hear almost six million cases each year.[32] The workload of the courts continues to rise as market relations spread and more and more disputes spill over into the courts. Despite the introduction of a new institution of "bailiff-enforcers" in 1997 to assist in ensuring parties to legal judgments comply with court decisions, courts still often find it difficult to implement their decisions in the face of determined resistance.[33] Judges continue to complain that there are too few bailiffs to enforce judgments and provide security in courtrooms.

In the Soviet system, judges were formally elected by the local soviet of the jurisdiction in which they served; in actuality, they were part of the Communist Party–controlled nomenklatura system and thus were appointed to their positions by the party staff. Reforms beginning in the late 1980s attempted to increase judges' independence by lengthening their term of office and placing their election into the hands of the soviet at the next-higher level to that of the jurisdiction in which they served. But this still allowed powerful regional executives to sway judicial decision making. Therefore, in the early 1990s, reformers pushed a law through the parliament giving the power of appointment of all federal judges to the president, although the president must choose from among candidates screened and proposed by judicial qualifications commissions. The president was also obliged to take into account the suggestions of the legislatures of the regions where federal judges would serve. Judges now have lifetime terms, but under legislation passed in 2001, they must retire at age 65 (at 70 for the highest courts).

The judicial reform law passed at the end of 1996 took a significant step in the direction of establishing a single legal order throughout the Russian Federation.[34] Over the objection of some of the heads of the national republics and other regions, both chambers of parliament and the president agreed that all courts of general jurisdiction would be federal courts and would be guided by federal law, the federal constitution, and the instructions of the federal Supreme Court. The law establishes an institution of local justices of the peace (*mirovye sud'i*), which had existed in Russia in the prerevolutionary era, who consider minor cases. These courts have spread rapidly and now hear a large proportion of all civil and criminal cases. It is important to note that in contrast to the United States' multitiered federal system of courts, Russia's law establishes a common federal judiciary throughout the country.[35]

With Putin's active support, trial by jury has been introduced into court-rooms throughout the country for serious criminal cases. The jury system remains controversial. Supporters believe that it helps make citizens consider themselves to be part of the legal system, and, by extension, the political system, rather than passive and helpless objects of its will. Jury service, at least in theory, allows people to experience directly the responsibilities associated with democratic self-government. Reformers assert that jury trials also make the legal system more honest and effective, since it is more difficult for police, investigators, prosecutors, and judges to get away with abuses and misconduct. Finally, they argue that the jury trial redresses the bias of criminal procedure by countering the strong advantages traditionally possessed by the procuracy and establishing a more level playing field between accuser and accused. Trial by jury certainly is not a *necessary* condition for democracy: other judicial fact-finding procedures are also perfectly consistent with democratic principles. But in Russia, where there are long traditions of local self-government and strong if latent norms of egalitarianism and communalism, the jury trial may indeed have indirect effects that reinforce democratic values. Moreover, it is an institution with substantial roots in Russian society. It was introduced and widely used in Russia as part of the great reforms of the 1860s, and juries became an important instrument of civic participation.[36] Following the October Revolution in 1917, however, the Bolsheviks eliminated the jury trial.

As in the Anglo-American world, juries are somewhat more sympathetic to defendants than judges would be; acquittal rates are significantly higher than in regular courts.[37] Some of the acquittals have prompted second thoughts about the jury system. For example, in 2006, a jury in St. Petersburg acquitted a group of youths who had been accused of killing a Vietnamese student out of ethnic hatred. Eight of the 17 accused were let off entirely, and the rest were convicted of other charges. In another 2006 trial involving a gang of Russian youths armed with chains and knives who had beaten a 9-year-old Tajik girl to death, a jury concluded that the charges of murder had not been proven and that therefore the accused were not guilty of her murder. The youths were found guilty of hooliganism instead, and given light sentences. In a third case, involving the hate killing of a student from the Congo, four accused youths were acquitted. These cases attest either to the sloppy work of the investigators and prosecutors or to the sympathies of jury members with the young men accused of the charges.[38] One indication that the jury system is having an effect on the administration of justice is the fact that in fall 2008, the government pushed through a law barring the use of jury trial in cases involving charges of terrorism, espionage, and "inciting mass unrest."[39]

The courts of general jurisdiction form a pyramid of local and regional courts. At its pinnacle is the Russian Supreme Court, which hears cases referred from lower courts and also issues instructions to lower courts on judicial matters. Its reasoning in rendering decisions is published and may be taken as guidance by lower courts in reaching decisions (bringing the Russian system closer to the recognition of legal precedents as binding). The Supreme

Court does not have the power to challenge the constitutionality of laws and other normative acts adopted by legislative and executive bodies. That power is assigned by the constitution to the Constitutional Court. Under the constitution, judges of the Supreme Court are nominated by the president and confirmed by the Council of the Federation. Likewise, the chairman of the Supreme Court is appointed by the president and confirmed by the upper house.

There is another system of courts designed to adjudicate cases arising from civil disputes between firms, including bankruptcy proceedings, and between firms and the government. These are called "arbitration" or "commercial" courts *(arbitrazhnye sudy).*[40] There is one arbitration court in each subject of the federation, and there are another 10 interregional courts to hear appeals. At the apex of this system stands the Supreme Arbitration Court. Like the Supreme Court, the Supreme Arbitration Court is both the highest appellate court for its system of courts and the source of instruction and direction to lower commercial courts. Also, as with the Supreme Court, the chairman of the Supreme Arbitration Court is nominated by the president and confirmed by the Council of the Federation. As the volume of commercial transactions in Russia has grown, so has the workload of the arbitration courts. Currently, they hear about one million cases per year.[41] A growing number of these cases arise from tax disputes (including a rapidly growing number of cases, often successful, when private firms take the government's tax authorities to court). The new commercial courts have issued a number of crucial rulings that have helped establish the legal foundation for a market economy. The courts have often had a hard time enforcing their rulings, but the new institution of judicial bailiffs has helped somewhat. Moreover, enterprises sometimes find it useful to obtain a ruling in a dispute against another enterprise, even if they are unsure whether it will be enforced, in order to have a precedent that they can use in future litigation.[42] Two-thirds of businesspeople report that they would prefer to go to court to settle their disputes than to turn to executive bodies, the media, criminal structures, or other channels. The vast majority—83 percent—believe that they stand a good chance of defending their rights in court if the other party is another enterprise. But if the other party is a regional or local government, 70 percent think their chances of winning are low.[43]

In 2001, the Putin administration sponsored legislation to reform the judicial system. One of the aims of the reforms was to increase the accountability of judges for their actions, but increasing accountability conflicted with the goal of increasing independence. After extensive deliberation by legal experts, judges, presidential staff people, and parliamentarians, the reforms were enacted. They consisted of a substantial increase in judges' salaries and improvement in their working conditions; organizational changes in the way judges were appointed and removed; and the changes to the criminal procedure code that were noted earlier that expanded the rights of judges to supervise pretrial criminal procedures.[44] Putin also reformed the system of judicial qualifications commissions, which regulate the selection and disciplining of judges, by bringing a larger number of laypeople onto them.[45] Reports indicate that Putin used this reform to place a number of representatives of the executive branch—including former security police officials—onto the regional commissions.[46] Putin's reforms were ostensibly designed to increase the status and political independence of the judiciary and to expand the judicial protection of civil liberties. Undoubtedly, the president wanted to increase the autonomy of the judiciary vis-á-vis regional and business interests, consistent with his aim of centralizing power. President Medvedev has also called for increasing judicial independence and fighting corruption in the judiciary and for adopting a new code of ethics for judges. One small indication that the president's attention to the problem of judicial ethics was bearing fruit occurred when the deputy chairman of the Supreme Court resigned in February 2009 after his son was arrested on charges of accepting a bribe.[47] Such a gesture is extremely rare in Russia.

The Constitutional Court

The creation of the Constitutional Court is one of the more important achievements of the democratization movement of the late 1980s and early 1990s. Because the Soviet regime had no legal institution to ensure that legislative and administrative acts of the state conformed with the Soviet constitution, legal reformers in the Gorbachev period called for creating a constitutional court, equivalent to such bodies as the Constitutional Council in the French Fifth Republic or the Constitutional Court in Germany, which would rule on the constitutionality of laws and would adjudicate disputes between the union and the republics. As a cautious initial experiment with such a body, a constitutional amendment creating a "committee on constitutional supervision" (*komitet konstitutsionnogo nadzora*) was passed in December 1988. This body came into being on January 1, 1990. The committee's first official decision, in September 1990, found that Gorbachev had acted unconstitutionally when he had decreed earlier in the year that as president he had the power to forbid or allow demonstrations within Moscow. Gorbachev did not challenge the committee's ruling. But the committee found itself powerless to overcome the paralyzing effects of the "war of laws" between union, republican, and local government authorities. Moreover, since it was not a court, the committee could not adjudicate cases. Nevertheless, the committee's creation set an important precedent.

The committee dissolved along with the rest of the union government in December 1991. Russia, however, had established a constitutional court by a constitutional amendment in July 1991. The 15 members of the Constitutional Court were elected by the Congress of People's Deputies for life terms. The Congress elected a relatively young legal scholar, Valerii Zor´kin, as chairman.

The Russian Constitutional Court made several significant decisions in its first year. Among them was a finding in December 1991 that President Yeltsin's decision to merge two state ministries into a single body was unconstitutional; the president complied with the decision, establishing the precedent of effective judicial review. Another important decision concerned

Yeltsin's decrees in the fall of 1991 outlawing the Communist Party and nationalizing its property. Reviewing the constitutionality of his actions, the court held in November 1992 that Yeltsin acted within his rights when he banned the Communist Party's executive organs but that he had no right to prohibit members of the party from forming primary organizations (PPOs or cells). Moreover, the court said that the state had the right to confiscate the party's property, but that in cases where the title of an asset was unclear or disputed, only the Supreme Arbitration Court could rule on the state's rights. This decision was widely regarded as juridically sound and politically shrewd, in that it allowed both the communists and the president's side to claim victory. The court also, perhaps wisely, avoided taking sides on the president's assertion that the CPSU was itself unconstitutional. The court thus positioned itself as a politically neutral institution. This was no mean achievement in the tense, polarized environment of the time.

The court then tried to intervene in the severe confrontation that arose between President Yeltsin and the Congress of People's Deputies in December 1992 over the rightful powers of the president and the legislature. Initially, Chairman Zor´kin proposed that a national referendum be held to decide on the basic constitutional principles to govern Russia, and both sides initially agreed. Soon, however, Zor´kin began siding with parliament against the president, revealing a zeal more political than judicial. In October 1993, following Yeltsin's decrees dissolving parliament and calling for new elections and a constitutional referendum, Yeltsin also suspended the operation of the Constitutional Court. The following summer, with the new constitution adopted, the new parliament passed a law on the Constitutional Court, according to which there were to be 19 members and the members themselves would elect their own chairman. Thirteen of the original members of the court remained members (including Zor´kin, whom Yeltsin removed as chairman of the court but who continued to be a full member of it and was elected chairman of the court again in 2003). The president then nominated six new justices to fill the vacancies on the court and presented them to the Council of the Federation for confirmation. The Council refused to confirm three, and the stage was set for a new round of political bargaining between the president and parliament until eventually the full complement of 19 judges was confirmed.

As soon as it started work again in 1995, the court began establishing its right to interpret the constitution. It ruled on several ambiguous questions relating to parliamentary procedure. It overturned some laws passed by ethnic republics within Russia and struck down a provision of the Criminal Code that limited individual rights. Generally, in cases involving disputes between individuals and state authorities, the court has favored individual rights. For example, in 2009 the court ruled that a person may not be declared mentally incompetent in his absence, or forcibly confined to a psychiatric facility without a court hearing.[48] In another ruling, the court found in favor of a soldier who was forced to stay in the military six months beyond his termination date while the military conducted a criminal investigation against him.[49] The court regularly issues decisions upholding individual rights against the state.

The court has also made a number of significant rulings in the area of federal relations where it has been asked to delimit the powers of the regions vis-á-vis the federal government. Generally, it has defended the unity of the federation in the face of the regions' demands for autonomy. Throughout the 1990s, the court rendered a series of decisions upholding federal law against the efforts by regional executives and legislatures to assert their autonomy. In the 1990s, however, the court recognized that the federal government had only limited capacity to enforce its decisions in the regions.

The election of President Putin changed the political balance sharply. Putin made it clear that he intended to reclaim for the federal government some of the power and prerogatives that had been claimed, de facto, by regional governments. The court issued an important ruling in 2000 that was consistent with Putin's push for uniformity and centralization. In a case dealing with the constitutionality of several provisions of the constitution of the Gorno-Altai ethnic republic, the court was asked to rule whether the republic had the right to declare itself "sovereign" and to claim the natural resources located on the republic's territory as its own "property." The court ruled that not only did the provisions on sovereignty and the ownership of natural resources violate the federal constitution (on the grounds that only the Russian Federation is sovereign) but declared explicitly that the analogous provisions in all the other republic constitutions that contained such points were also unconstitutional. To drive the point home, the court met with the heads of the constitutional courts of all six republics whose constitutions possessed such provisions. It explained that these provisions were all automatically rendered invalid and should be removed. Clearly, the court was taking advantage of Putin's vigorous drive to centralize power to assert its own legal doctrine of the primacy of federal law and constitution over regional claims to sovereignty.

Because the court has been politically prudent, reluctant to issue a decision that will be flagrantly ignored, it has tiptoed cautiously around the huge domain of presidential authority. In the Yeltsin period, however, the court did limit the president's power. One instance was its ruling in the "trophy art" case, when it decided that President Yeltsin was required to sign a law after both chambers of parliament overrode his veto.[50] Another was its decision that the use of the proportional representation system in the electoral law to elect half of the deputies of the Duma was entirely compatible with the constitution (observers generally thought that the case, which was brought by one of the regional legislatures, had the tacit support or even sponsorship of the Kremlin). And the court ruled that President Yeltsin was not entitled to run for a third term.[51] In other and more significant cases, however, the court has tended to side with the president. One of the court's first and most important decisions concerned a challenge brought by a group of communist parliamentarians to the president's edicts launching the war in Chechnia. The court ruled that the president had the authority to wage the war through the use of his constitutional power to issue edicts with the force of law.

The Constitutional Court proceeds by deciding whether to accept a case or inquiry. (It receives some 15,000 petitions each year.) Usually if it does so, it has determined that a challenge to an existing law, decree, or official action has legal merit. It then holds hearings where parties and experts representing both sides of the issue make statements to the court. Each side listens to the arguments presented by its opponents and seeks to counter them with superior arguments. The court then takes the information presented under advisement and renders its judgment. Dissenting opinions are published separately, but in recent years, there have been very few of these; the court far prefers to speak with a single voice.

The court tends to act slowly. Most cases require 2–4 weeks to decide, with most of that time being spent on the painstaking task of drafting their decision. The court issues only about 20 full rulings per year. The court issues, however, several hundred "findings" (determinations or *opredeleniia*) per year. These fall short of being full rulings on a case but find that the issues it raises were decided in a previous case. It therefore has begun to introduce a form of law by precedent. This form of decision making eases the strain on the court's growing workload.

The court has been in a difficult position in the Putin period. It has sought to steer a course between being regarded as a tool of the president and crossing the president on a significant issue only to have its ruling flagrantly ignored. Court Chairman Zor´kin has frankly acknowledged the authoritarian elements in the current regime, but argues that all civilized states combine strains of authoritarianism and democracy and that "for Russia the main thing is to find a way between the Scylla of bureaucratic caprice (*chinovnich'ego proizvola*) and the Charybdis of anarchic powerlessness."[52] Zor'kin's comments suggest a keen appreciation of the limits of the court's independence and its need to rely on the executive for enforcement of its rulings.

Putin meantime made clear his power over the court by pushing a law through parliament that moved the seat of the court to St. Petersburg as of May 2008 over the objections of the judges. This change of venue is widely regarded by observers as an effort to reduce the court's political prestige by distancing it from the network of central state bodies headquartered in Moscow.

Yet, despite the severe political constraints within which it is forced to operate, the Constitutional Court has established a place for itself in the political system. It has often upheld the civil and constitutional rights of individuals in cases involving the actions of state officials, and it has clarified that in the system of courts it has the exclusive right of constitutional review. It is possible that over time, through the slow accumulation of decisions involving the interpretation of the constitution, the court will gain in political legitimacy and become a constraint on unchecked executive power.[53]

Reforms in the Law Codes

In addition to the changes in judicial institutions, Russia has made far-reaching modifications to the codes of criminal, civil, and administrative law and procedure over the last two decades. The changes have expanded formal protections for individual legal and civil rights, and established rules consistent with a capitalist economy. More generally, they create legal conditions for civil society through laws recognizing the rights of social and public organizations such as religious communities, political parties, charitable associations, labor unions, and business firms. To a surprising degree, this legislation has been passed following a laborious process of bargaining and consensus building among interested groups, including judges, legal experts, and politicians, rather than by decree or dictate.

One of the milestones of statutory reform is the Civil Code, which regulates civil relations among individuals, organizations, and the state and provides legal guarantees for property rights.[54] Another important achievement was the new Criminal Code, finally signed into law by President Yeltsin in June 1996 following a year and a half of negotiations and deliberations among specialists, concerned state bodies, the presidential administration, and members of parliament. The new code brought the criminal law into closer conformity with the demands of the post-Soviet environment. It reduced the number of crimes subject to capital punishment, differentiated closely among crimes according to their seriousness, emphasized the need to protect individual legal rights as opposed to the state's interests, decriminalized some activities that had been illegal in the Soviet era, and at the same time introduced definitions of new types of crimes that had been previously unheard of, such as money laundering and unfair competition. The set of laws reforming the judiciary adopted in December 2001 was a significant step toward improving the working conditions of courts and expanding the legal powers possessed by courts.[55] In 2002, a new Code of Criminal Procedure was passed that increased individual legal rights.[56] For these statutory changes to bring about major progress toward real judicial independence, however, the necessary political conditions must also be met and political interference in the operation of the justice system be ended.

Growing Salience of International Law

A final dimension of movement toward greater judicial independence has been the increasing importance of international law. Nowhere is this more evident than in the sphere of human rights. In 1996, Russia formally joined the Council of Europe (an organization of 47 countries in Europe that publicly pledge to adhere to the principles of democracy and human rights), and in 1998, it ratified the European Convention of Human Rights. Under the rules of the Council of Europe, citizens in any of the member countries are entitled to send a complaint to the European Court of Human Rights (ECHR) in Strasbourg about abuses of their rights by their own countries' law enforcement, judicial, or criminal corrections institutions. Over the last decade, the number of petitions to the ECHR from Russia has exploded, from around 2,500 in 2001 to over 10,000 a year today. Of the roughly 100,000 cases pending before the court, nearly one-third come from Russia and the backlog is growing rapidly.[57] Generally, these claims concern cases where a court's decision on the payment of a pension claim or another social benefit has not been implemented, conditions of incarceration in prison, and violations of the legal rights of suspects by the police. A number of cases arise from Chechnia as a result of the disappearance of family members or crimes committed by the federal army.

The court itself has become increasingly concerned about the growing burden of such cases coming from a single country and has urged Russia to ratify an agreement that would speed up court procedure. Until recently, Russia balked, fearing that the court's rulings would nearly all find in favor of the plaintiffs and against the state (already some 95 percent of the 800 Russia-related cases that the court has decided have been resolved against the Russian authorities).[58] In January 2010, however, under pressure from President Medvedev, the parliament ratified the agreement. The Constitutional Court, moreover, ruled that courts of general jurisdiction in Russia must agree to review cases and the state must pay damages and restore the individuals' rights in civil or criminal cases where the ECHR has ruled in favor of the individual.[59] A major test of the Russian state's willingness to comply with the European Court of Human Rights will come in a trial involving the Yukos company. In 2004, Yukos's lawyers petitioned the ECHR to take up the case, arguing that the Russian government's actions against the company were "unlawful, disproportionate, arbitrary and discriminatory, and amounted to disguised expropriation."[60] The trial began in 2010. Depending on the court's ruling, the Russian government may face a serious challenge to its avowed commitment to comply with the ECHR's legal norms.

OBSTACLES TO THE RULE OF LAW

The structural and statutory changes that have been made in Russia's legal system, and the far higher level of political pluralism, have expanded civil rights substantially compared to those in the Soviet era. Individuals and organizations have greater opportunity to defend their rights through the legal system than they did in the Soviet era. Still, the reforms have not ended the arbitrary use of state power by the authorities, and the manipulation of the legal system for political purposes by those in power has continued. The threats of terrorism and extremism have also given the authorities the opportunity to enact restrictions on the civil rights of individuals and groups. The repeated claim that shadowy "foreign interests" are trying to break up Russia's integrity as a state has been used to justify enacting a series of legislative and administrative measures that limit the freedom of individuals, political groups, and the mass media.

Other obstacles to the rule of law are long standing and persistent. Bureaucratic autonomy and nontransparency continue to be a barrier to the rule of law, by allowing state officials to defy the will of both executive and legislative policy makers and apply law arbitrarily. Together with the widespread corruption in the legal system, the pattern of the abuse of law by the authorities undermines respect for the law. Let us consider these issues in greater detail.

Bureaucratic Rule Making

The profound inertia of a heavily bureaucratized state remains a challenge for central policy makers no less than for democratic accountability. In Russia today, as in Russia in centuries past, the power of the state's rulers is frequently thwarted by the tendency of administrative agencies to issue rules—decrees, regulations, instructions, orders, directives, circular letters, and many other kinds of official and binding rules, many of them secret—applying not only to subordinates in the same agency but, often, also to other governmental agencies and to Russian citizens generally. In the Soviet period, the practice of bureaucratic rule making through what are called "sublegal normative acts" was extremely widespread. Some indication of the magnitude of this practice is suggested by the fact that over the first 70 years of Soviet power, the USSR legislature adopted fewer than 800 laws and decrees, whereas over the same period, the union-level government issued hundreds of thousands of decrees and other normative acts. Tens of thousands of more binding rules issued by particular government ministries and state committees also remained on the books. The profusion of rules and regulations, complementing, interpreting, and often contradicting one another, creates ample opportunities for evasion, as well as incentives for powerful individuals to cut through the jungle of red tape. Although the rules and regulations that the departments issue are supposed to be consistent with both the language and spirit of the law, in practice they frequently gut it, so that reforms adopted by the legislature may be eviscerated by the time they reach the level where they are supposed to be acted upon.

The 1993 constitution did not give parliament an explicit right to oversee (*kontrolirovat´*) the executive branch, a power considered essential in a separation of powers system.[61] The constitutional changes sponsored by President Medvedev in November 2008 did, however, include a provision explicitly enabling parliament to oversee government.[62] Parliament has several other oversight powers as well, among them the budget process, investigations, hearings, and the Auditing Chamber.[63] These would allow parliament to ensure bureaucratic compliance with legislative requirements if parliament were inclined to use them. But parliament in the 2000s has been so thoroughly dominated by the executive branch that it has exercised almost no actual oversight over government.

Moreover, legislative acts are frequently vague and general. A persistent problem with legislation passed by the Federal Assembly and signed into law is that as laws pass through the legislative mill, their more controversial points are removed or replaced with bland statements that give bureaucrats wide latitude to issue rules "interpreting" the law. The ambiguity of formal rules invites a reliance on "informal institutions" by state officials and ordinary citizens alike.[64] Officials have wide latitude to use state institutions for their own personal benefit and to minimize openness and transparency in their work.

Personalization of power, secretiveness, and excessive discretion in the hands of administrative officials are obstacles not only to the primacy of law but also to the ability of a central leader to ensure the implementation of his policies. For this reason, Putin and Medvedev have repeatedly denounced the bureaucracy's propensity to sidetrack federal laws and decrees with rules and regulations that distort or block the federal laws. Putin demanded a major reform of the entire system of state service in order to raise the quality and professionalism of civil servants. In 2002, he issued two decrees laying out general principles to guide the state bureaucracy, but these were extremely broad. Legislation was passed in 2003 and 2004 codifying the organizational principles of the state service that regulated recruitment, pay, evaluation, and promotion.[65] In 2003, Putin issued another decree demanding a comprehensive reform of the structure and operation of the state bureaucracy.[66] This resulted in a reorganization of the federal executive in March 2004 that was widely regarded as a failure. In late 2005, the government issued a new document intended to improve the efficiency, responsiveness, and transparency of state administration.

President Medvedev has kept up the rhetorical pressure on the bureaucracy, denouncing bureaucratic interference in society in ringing language[67]:

> Meantime the state bureaucracy, as it did 20 years ago, is guided by the same mistrust toward free individuals, toward free activity. This logic pushes it to dangerous conclusions and dangerous actions. The bureaucracy periodically terrorizes business [literally, "gives it nightmares"] so that it won't do something wrong. It takes control of the mass media so that they don't say something wrong. It interferes in elections so that the wrong person doesn't get elected. It pressures the courts so that they don't condemn the wrong person for something. And so on. As a result, the state apparat is the biggest employer, the most active publisher, the best producer, its own judge, its own party and, in the end, its own populace. This system is absolutely ineffective and creates only one thing—corruption. It engenders mass legal nihilism, it contradicts the Constitution, it impedes the development of institutions of an innovative economy and democracy.
>
> A strong state and an all-powerful bureaucracy are not the same thing. The first is needed for civil society as an instrument of development and support of order, for the protection and strengthening of democratic institutions. The second is fatally dangerous for it. So our society must be calm, insistent, and not put off till tomorrow the development of the institutions of democracy.

Medvedev's vehement language denouncing arbitrary behavior by the state bureaucracy is some indication that the leadership is frustrated by its inability to bring the state bureaucracy fully under its control. So far, the administrative reform measures attempted under Putin and Medvedev have failed to achieve their goals, and the severe constraints they have imposed on free competition among parties and interests in the political arena make it unlikely that either parliament or the courts will be able to check the "all-powerful bureaucracy."

Terrorism and National Security

Terrorism and the measures taken to combat it pose twin threats to the rule of law in Russia as in other contemporary states. The large-scale violent attacks against civilians carried out by radical Islamic groups in the United States, Europe, Africa, and Asia have prompted even democratic states to adopt policies giving the authorities far-reaching powers to restrict civil liberties in the interest of fighting terrorists.[68] These powers are readily subject to abuse by rulers wishing to suppress their political opposition. In several Central Asian states, for instance, the authorities have suppressed a number of religious and political groups by charging their leaders with complicity in terrorist acts (acts that in some cases may have been staged by the authorities themselves as a pretext to eliminate their rivals). In Russia, the terrorist threat has been used by authorities to expand the government's powers to restrict civil and political liberties.

As Close-Up 3.1 (Chapter 3) indicated, Russians in recent years have been the victims of a series of shocking terrorist incidents. Some of these have involved attacks against military, police, and civilian targets, and others have taken the form of seizing large numbers of civilians as hostages. The series of terrorist attacks in 2004 had a particularly high political impact, because they revealed how serious were the problems of corruption, indiscipline, and incompetence among the agencies charged with protecting the country's security.

Putin responded to the terrorist attacks with a series of laws intended both to centralize political power and to expand the powers of the security police. As we saw in Chapter 3, Putin took advantage of the Beslan crisis to push through legislation abolishing the direct election of regional governors, create the Public Chamber, and eliminate all single-member district elections to the Duma. More directly related to the antiterrorist campaign was legislation passed in 2006 that assigned the FSB primary responsibility for fighting terrorism in the country and, giving it increased powers to command the armed forces in case of an act of terrorism, to wiretap individuals suspected of terrorist activity, and even to shoot down hijacked airplanes. The law outlaws organizations "whose purposes and actions include the propaganda, justification, and support of terrorism."[69] A second law passed in 2006, following the capture and killing of several Russian diplomats in Iraq, authorizes the president to use both armed forces and special forces against terrorists outside the borders of Russia.[70] Several observers have commented that this law, in effect, legalizes assassinations overseas of individuals designated as terrorists.[71]

The threat of terrorism and its concomitant, extremism, has also been broadly cited as justification for other laws and policies allowing the authorities to restrict political rights. For example, one of Putin's justifications for the law tightening rules on the operation of nongovernmental organizations (NGOs) was that it would "secure our political system from interference from outside, as well as our society and citizens from the spread of terrorist ideology."[72] A law passed in 2007 amended the Criminal Code to provide a three-year prison sentence for anyone convicted of politically or ideologically motivated vandalism.[73] Procuracy officials have proposed legislation to restrict the ability of extremist organizations to use the Internet.[74] Extremism and terrorism can be used very readily as pretexts for political repression. For example, in 2008, a person who criticized the police on his blog on the Internet was arrested for extremist activity.[75] Later that year, the procuracy accused the 2×2 television cartoon network of promoting extremism for broadcasting an offensive episode of South Park ("Mr. Hankey's Christmas Classics") just as the network's broadcast license was up for renewal. The chairman of the Duma's committee on youth affairs added menacingly that "the cartoons that 2×2 broadcasts are undermining the moral foundations of society and exerting a negative influence on the rising generation, propagating cruelty, violence, and sexual promiscuity."[76]

Russia is no different from any other modern society in having to balance principles of individual rights against the real threat to society posed by terrorist and extremist organizations. Certainly, crimes motivated by ethnic and religious prejudice have grown and the threat of terrorism is real. But in Russia, compared with democratic states, the constraints on arbitrary and politically motivated use of legal instruments stemming from the open competition of parties, media, elections, and interest groups are weak. As a result, the powers that the Russian regime has aggrandized in response to the terrorist attacks of the past few years are likely to be abused, as the authorities punish unflattering media coverage of their activity and suppress opposition groups on the suspicion that they are extremist or are abetting terrorism. In view of the history of the exploitation of law for political repression in the Soviet era and again today, the recent antiterrorist and antiextremist legislation has ominous implications for the rule of law.

Organized Crime and Corruption

Organized Crime   A threat of another kind to the principle of the rule of law is the widespread corruption of state officials and the power of organized crime. These are closely related: The worsening of corruption after the end of the communist regime owes a great deal to the rapid growth in the power of organized crime in the 1990s. Certainly, the police often appear to be incapable of solving major crimes committed by organized crime groups. Hundreds of prominent individuals—politicians, businesspeople, bankers, journalists, and others—have been assassinated in contract murders, but few cases have resulted in an arrest, let alone a conviction. A number of Duma deputies have been murdered. Journalists and human rights workers have been targeted. In July 2009, Natalya Estemirova, a human rights activist in Chechnia working with Memorial, was abducted outside her home and murdered; as of a year later, there had still been no arrests in the case. In October 2006, Anna Politkovskaya, a journalist who had written scathing exposes of the tactics used by federal forces in Chechnia and by the Moscow-backed government in Chechnia, was murdered. The following month, a former KGB officer, Alexander Litvinenko, was killed by radiation poisoning in London (the individual whom British police believe committed the murder was elected to the Duma on the LDPR party list, giving him legal immunity). Two prominent banking officials were also murdered in the fall of 2006. All were believed to have been victims of contract killings. Criminal gangs extensively use contract killings to settle accounts.

They are also closely tied to structures of the state. The Minister of Internal Affairs, Rashid Nurgaliev, commented in 2007 that one-tenth of Russia's regions were "under the control of organized crime groups, who often face little or no official resistance."[77] One Russian expert on the subject estimated that Russia had as many as 10,000 organized crime groups, employing some 300,000 people."[78]

Analysts agree that two conditions foster the entrenchment of organized crime: first, the state bureaucracy is highly susceptible to corruption and has allowed organized crime to penetrate it deeply, and second, regular businesses frequently find it impossible to operate except by turning to organized crime for "security services," which include paying protection rackets, forcing partners to make good on agreements, and obtaining scarce supplies. The persistence of crime and corruption is the product of a vicious circle formed by the interlocking relationship among three sets of factors: government, legitimate business, and criminal organizations. Many businesses, both small-scale entrepreneurs and the owners of large companies, purchase protection from protection rackets (of course, racketeers often commit acts of violence against businesses to force them to purchase their protection services). Government, particularly the police, is weak and is weakened further by corruption. Organized crime groups penetrate both business and government, providing business with services such as protection as well as short-term loans and the enforcement of business contracts, and paying off law enforcement officials to let them operate with impunity.[79] Experts estimate that at least half of the income of organized crime groups goes to paying bribes to state officials.[80]

Each side in this triangle depends on the others. Businesses frequently find that they must pay bribes to corrupt government officials simply to be able to operate or to be allowed to get around the law. Moreover, unable to count on the courts to protect their property rights and enforce their business agreements, they often turn to organized crime rackets for protection. Taking advantage of the state's inability to enforce the law (and, through penetration of the state, keeping it weak), organized crime preys on business and corrupts government. And government officials often find it easier, safer, and more lucrative to accept bribes than to fight crime and corruption or to provide legitimate public goods such as fair enforcement of the laws. The fact that Russia is a federal state probably exacerbates the problem, since the existence of governments at different levels multiplies the number of officials who demand bribes as condition for doing business.[81]

Corruption   Corruption is fed both by the interests of businesses in evading legal rules and by organized crime rackets that want to keep government subservient. Although corruption is notoriously difficult to measure with any precision, all observers agree that it has increased substantially since the end of the Soviet period and still further under Presidents Putin and Medvedev—probably because of the large increase in public and private incomes due to rising international oil prices. It is widespread both in everyday life and in dealings with the state. President Medvedev has called corruption "a systemic challenge, a threat to national security, the sort of problem that engenders mistrust on the part of citizens in the very possibility for the state to bring order and guarantee security" and made the fight against corruption one of his top priorities as president.[82] In 2008, he sponsored legislation that, for the first time, explicitly defined corruption on the part of state officials, set stiff standards for hiring and evaluating officials, and sought to enlist popular involvement in the fight to eradicate it. However, as President Medvedev himself acknowledged two years later, the legislation has had little impact on the problem.[83]

Medvedev is correct to regard corruption as pervasive and profoundly destructive. Studies by Russian think tanks show that its scale is staggering. A survey of small business by the National Institute for the Systematic Study of the Problems of Entrepreneurship found that about half of all small businesses pay bribes to officials and about one-fifth pay protection money to criminal rackets. Seventy percent paid some portion of wages to workers in unreported, off-tax forms, and over half made off-book payments to suppliers. Over time, the number of businesses giving bribes to officials had increased (probably because fewer are paying racketeers protection money).[84] Another independent study, conducted by the National Association of Electronic Traders and an interregional NGO called "Against Corruption," found that about one-fourth of the money allocated by the state for procurement orders—equivalent to some $40 billion—was skimmed off by government and businesses through corruption.[85] A study by the Institute of Social Forecasting and the Institute for Comparative Social Research found many regular forms of corrupt transactions between government and business concerning the parliament, the media, the state procurement system, the judicial system, the tax agencies, and so on. For instance, purchasing a seat in parliament cost between $2 and $5 million. To obtain federal budget funds might cost 30–40 percent of the cost of the project. Winning a lawsuit in court cost 10 percent of the sum contested. To write off a tax debt cost up to half the sum of the unpaid taxes. Kickbacks to win a state procurement contract typically cost 20 percent of the sum of the contract.[86] As more money has flowed into Russia, thanks to higher oil and gas prices, the scale of corruption has grown. The head of the Institute for National Strategy estimates that the volume of money involved in corrupt transactions doubled between 2006 and 2008. If in 2006, the total amount of corrupt payments was $240 billion (a sum about the size of the federal budget), by 2008, it had doubled and reached at least $480, or one and one-half times the size of the budget.[87] The eye-popping revelations about the scale of corruption in Russia published in the press in recent months no doubt reflect the high-level attention that President Medvedev has paid to the problem. But it also shows how serious a drag the problem of corruption is on the economy and society and how gravely it threatens state capacity.

Corruption in Russia has deep roots and many Russians assume that it is an ineradicable feature of Russian society. Comparative studies of corruption demonstrate, however, that the culture of corruption can be changed by changing the expectations of the public and the government. For example, some countries have created powerful independent agencies to fight corruption. When the top political authorities back them up, people begin resisting corruption and refusing to engage in it, and government officials begin providing services without expecting to receive bribes.[88] The key is for the political leadership to make a serious commitment to fighting corruption and to reinforce this commitment with institutional reform and sustained attention. In Russia, the authorities' commitment to eradicating corruption is undermined, however, by the fact that prosecutions usually focus on officials who have already fallen out of favor with the authorities. The question is not whether the leadership recognizes the problem, but whether they have the political will to address it.

CONCLUSION

Despite some steps toward realizing the ideal of the rule of law since the end of the communist regime, Russia remains closer to a system of rule-by-law than to the rule-of-law. The precedence of law over political and administrative power in the state would reduce the ability of officials in the bureaucracy, the security police, and the president to exercise power arbitrarily. Respect for the law on the part of officials and citizens would help establish habits of civic initiative and responsibility, which are essential to democracy. These are among the reasons that legal reformers in Russia have propagated the ideal of the "law-governed state." As with many other institutional reforms, however, success in the realm of law will ultimately require a commitment on the part of the highest officials in the country. It would require them to take a long-term view of the importance of the rule of law for economic progress and to refrain from abusing legal institutions for their short-term political gains. It will also require the development of political pluralism where resources for political influence are widely distributed, allowing groups to monitor the behavior of state officials and preventing any one group from monopolizing access to the law.

The radical implications of a shift to a law-governed state have generated opposition from a number of entrenched interests both inside and outside the state. In some cases, the opposition comes from bureaucratic unwillingness to relinquish administrative power. In other cases, it stems from the lucrative opportunities that lax and corrupt practices create for self-enrichment by officials. Many who wield power and many in the population continue to hold the traditional skeptical attitude toward the law—the view that law is no more than an instrument of those in political power. However, there is ample evidence that a substantial base of support exists for the concept of law as a set of impartial rules to which both state officials and ordinary citizens would be subordinate.

But there are still many obstacles to the realization of the rule of law. The inefficiency and corruption of law enforcement bodies, the penetration of the state by organized crime, and the old habit on the part of Russian rulers and Russian citizens of treating the law instrumentally continue to impede progress toward the primacy of law. In recent years, the state has taken a number of steps that compromise the independence of the judiciary. Although Putin and Medvedev have sponsored reforms that strengthen efficiency and accountability in the legal system, it appears that they are more intent on making law independent of regional and business interests that might interfere with their own power than they are with advancing the rule of law. The regime's use of the procuracy, tax organs, and courts to prosecute selected targets on political grounds, and the wave of new legislation strengthening the powers of the security police in the face of terrorism and extremism, indicate that the Kremlin will not soon relinquish its political influence over the legal system.

NOTES

1. Stephen Holmes, "Introduction," *East European Constitutional Review* 11:1/2 (Winter/Spring 2002): 91.
2. Ibid., p. 92.
3. A seminal study of the influences on the development of law in the Soviet Union is Harold J. Berman, *Justice in the U.S.S.R.*, rev. ed. (Cambridge, MA: Harvard University Press, 1963).
4. Full texts of these articles of the RSFSR Criminal Code together with commentary will be found in Harold J. Berman, ed., *Soviet Criminal Law and Procedure: The RSFSR Codes*, 2nd ed. (Cambridge, MA: Harvard University Press, 1972). Analogous articles were contained in the criminal codes of other republics as well.
5. Sidney Bloch and Peter Reddaway, *Psychiatric Terror: How Soviet Psychiatry Is Used to Suppress Dissent* (New York: Basic Books, 1977).
6. On the legal reforms of the Gorbachev period, see Donald D. Barry, ed., *Toward the "Rule of Law" in Russia? Political and Legal Reform in the Transition Period* (Armonk, NY: M. E. Sharpe, 1992); and Alexandre Yakovlev with Dale Gibson, *The Bear That Wouldn't Dance: Failed Attempts to Reform the Constitution of the Former Soviet Union* (University of Manitoba, Canada: Legal Research Institute, 1992).
7. Presidential message to parliament, November 5, 2008 http://www.kremlin.ru/appears/2008/11/05/1349_type63372type63374type63381type82634_208749.shtml.
8. Federico Varese, *The Russian Mafia: Private Protection in a New Market Economy* (New York: Oxford University Press, 2001); Vadim Volkov, *Violent Entrepreneurs: The Use of Force in the Making of Russian Capitalism* (Ithaca, NY: Cornell University Press, 2002).
9. See p. 133.
10. Natalia Krainova, "Medvedev Orders Cleanup of Courts," *The Moscow Times*, May 21, 2008 http://www.moscowtimes.ru/article/600/42/367572.htm.
11. *Vedomosti.ru*, May 28, 2008.
12. For example, in April 2008, Moscow police beat up members of a group of people who were participating in a demonstration against police brutality. Earlier that month, a respected political analyst was assaulted by two unknown individuals. As he had received a series of threatening phone calls after he had filed a lawsuit accusing United Russia of committing election fraud in the Duma election the

previous December, he was convinced that the attack was an effort to force him to stop his activity. *RFE/RL Newsline*, April 8, 14, 2008.

13. Alena Ledeneva, "Telephone Justice in Russia," *Post-Soviet Affairs* 24:4 (October–December, 2008): 324–350.

14. Dmitrii Kamyshev, "Vypolnenie Poslannogo," *Kommersant Vlast* 45:798 (November 17, 2008).

15. *RFE/RL Newsline*, May 17, 2004.

16. Quoted in Brian D. Taylor, "Russia's Regions and Law Enforcement," in Peter Reddaway and Robert W. Orttung, eds., *The Dynamics of Russian Politics: Putin's Reform of Federal–Regional Relations*, Vol. II (Lanham, MD: Rowman & Littlefield, 2005), p. 74.

17. Inquisitorial procedure is contrasted with the adversarial model used in Anglo-American judicial proceedings. In the inquisitorial system, the presiding officer (judge, magistrate) actively seeks to determine the full truth of the case at hand rather than serving as an impartial referee in a contest between an accuser and a defendant. In Soviet and Russian tradition, the powerful procurator is the central figure in the proceeding; the judge may actively participate in questioning witnesses and ruling on matters of law, but the procurator is expected to serve the higher cause of justice and not simply to present the state's best case against the accused. From the standpoint of the Anglo-American tradition, this puts the procurator in a potentially contradictory position: While the procurator is required to ensure the legality of the entire proceeding (including, as appropriate, the obligation to defend the accused's rights), he or she must also seek to prosecute and win the case. Since the procurator has already overseen the pretrial investigation and concluded that there is sufficient evidence to proceed with the trial, it is extremely rare for a procurator to decide that the case lacks merit and should be dropped. From the standpoint of the Anglo-American criminal process, it is as though the procurator were wearing the hats of prosecutor, defender, judge, and jury all at the same time. In any case, in Soviet times, judges tended to be highly deferential to the procurators. As a result of the procuracy's power and prestige, very few criminal cases in the Soviet period resulted in acquittal, although in some cases, a higher court set aside a questionable conviction or remanded it for further investigation, effectively reversing a lower court's verdict.

    For a discussion of the Soviet procuracy that places it in the context of both Western continental models and earlier, Russian historical precedents, see Berman, *Justice in the USSR*, pp. 238–247.

18. Peter H. Solomon, Jr., "Putin's Judicial Reform: Making Judges Accountable as well as Independent," *East European Constitutional Review* 11:1/2 (Winter/Spring 2002): 121.

19. Donald D. Barry, "Amnesty Under the Russian Constitution: Evolution of the Provision and Its Use in February 1994," *Parker School Journal of East European Law* 1:4 (1994): 437–461.

20. From an interview with *Komsomol'skaya Pravda*, July 19, 2002, cited in *RFE/RL Newsline*, July 19, 2002.

21. Natalya Krainova, "New YouTube Videos Criticize Corruption," *The Moscow Times*, November 16, 2009.

22. The MVD's allies in the Duma worked to water down these sanctions. For example, one of them provided that if a policeman commits a crime, the fact that he is a law enforcement official would be treated as an exacerbating circumstance and result in a higher sentence if convicted. The Constitutional Court warned that such a provision might be unconstitutional, and the Duma dropped it.

Ivan Rodin, "KS prishel na pomoshch' MVD," *Nezavisimaia gazeta,* April 16, 2010.

23. Alexandra Samarina, *"Territoriia bezopasnosti Dmitriia Medvedeva," Nezavisimaia gazeta,* February 18, 2010.

24. The ten "sleeper" spies living under false identities who were arrested in the United States by the FBI in June 2010 for illegal activity and deported to Russia soon afterward worked for the Foreign Intelligence Service.

25. The KGB was the institutional successor to the powerful instruments of coercion that the Soviet regime used since the revolution to eliminate its political enemies, including the Cheka (created within 6 weeks of the October Revolution), the GPU, and the NKVD. In the post-Stalin era, according to its press representatives, the KGB had nothing in common with these predecessor organizations and was dedicated to upholding the law while carrying out its mission of defending the security of the state and its citizens. Often KGB press representatives discussed the modern efforts of the organization in combating drug trafficking and terrorism. Evidently keen to be portrayed in a positive light in the media, the KGB promoted itself in the 1980s as a heroic organization, a body performing its difficult duties with scrupulous respect for the law as well as with ingenuity and courage.

26. OMRI Daily Digest, April 7, 1995.

27. Irina Granik, "FSB vnedril v bor'bu s krizisom," *Kommersant,* January 30, 2009.

28. Polit.ru, July 9, 2010; Ivan Pavlov and Alexandra Samarina, "Gosduma podderzhit FSB v bor'be z ekstremizm," *Nezavisimaia gazeta,* June 4, 2010.

29. Perhaps the most prominent of these figures is Igor' Sechin, who was deputy chief of the presidential administration under Putin and then moved with Putin to the government in May 2008, when he became deputy prime minister in charge of strategic industries (including oil and gas). Sechin is simultaneously chairman of the board of Russia's main state oil company, Rosneft. He worked closely with Putin in the St. Petersburg city government in the 1990s before moving to Moscow with Putin in 1996. Sechin is considered to have a background in the KGB and to be the head of a bureaucratic faction associated with the security services. On the recruitment of officials from the security agencies into top positions in the presidential administration and government under Putin, see Olga Kryshtanovskaya and Stephen White, "Putin's Militocracy," *Post-Soviet Affairs* 19:4 (2003): 289–306.

30. Eugene Huskey, "The Administration of Justice: Courts, Procuracy, and Ministry of Justice," in Eugene Huskey, ed., *Executive Power and Soviet Politics: The Rise and Decline of the Soviet State* (Armonk, NY: M. E. Sharpe, 1992), pp. 224–231.

31. Kathryn Hendley, "Putin and the Law," in Dale R. Herspring, ed., *Putin's Russia,* 3rd ed. (Lanham, MD: Rowman & Littlefield, 2007), p. 108.

32. Hendley, "Putin and the Law," p. 110. Of these, 1.2 million are criminal cases. *Vedomosti,* October 20, 2006.

33. On the new system of bailiffs, see Todd S. Foglesong and Peter H. Solomon, Jr., *Courts and Transition in Russia: The Challenge of Judicial Reform* (Boulder, CO: Westview Press, 2000), pp. 165–171; also Peter L. Kahn, "The Russian Bailiffs Service and the Enforcement of Civil Judgments," *Post-Soviet Affairs* 18:2 (April–June 2002): 148–181.

34. Eugene Huskey, "Russian Judicial Reform After Communism," in Peter Solomon, ed., *Reforming Justice in Russia, 1864–1994* (Armonk, NY: M. E. Sharpe, 1997).

35. All courts of general jurisdiction must apply the federal constitution, federal criminal and civil law, and procedural codes. The only nonfederal courts operating at

the regional level are the constitutional courts of ethnic republics and the "charter courts" in regular administrative territorial units. These courts adjudicate disputes involving a republican constitution or the charter of a subject of the federation, but they too must adhere to federal statutory and constitutional law. There are also specialized military courts for cases involving the armed forces.

36. In one of the most famous trial verdicts in Russian history, Vera Zasulich, a young Russian revolutionary who had attempted to assassinate the chief of police of St. Petersburg in 1878, was acquitted by a jury following a fiery speech by her lawyer that scathingly denounced the injustices of the Russian government.

37. In jury trials, the acquittal rate was 8.5 percent in 2002 but less than 1 percent in ordinary trials.
Hendley, "Putin and the Law," p. 113. Note that a majority of 7 votes out of the 12 jurors suffices to decide on a conviction, but only 6 votes are needed to acquit. Solomon, "Limits," p. 103.

38. *Vedomosti*, October 20, 2006.

39. Polit.ru, November 13, 2008. This could readily be used to prevent defendants in cases involving political demonstrations from being tried by juries.

40. It is misleading to call these "arbitration" courts, since they use judicial procedure, not arbitration, to adjudicate disputes. They were created out of the "arbitration boards" used in Soviet times to resolve disputes among economic entities such as enterprises and ministries, but now form a separate branch of the federal judiciary.

41. *Polit.ru, May 20, 2009.*

42. See Kathryn Hendley, Barry W. Ickes, Peter Murrell, and Randi Ryterman, "Observations on the Use of Law by Russian Enterprises," *Post-Soviet Affairs* 13:1 (January–March 1997): 19–41.

43. From a survey by VTsIOM, reported in Mikhail Malykhin, "Kazhdyi desiatyi rossi-iskii biznesmen gotov pribegnut' k pomoshchi kriminal'nykh struktur," *Vedomosti*, June 30, 2010.

44. Peter H. Solomon, Jr., "Putin's Judicial Reform: Making Judges Accountable as Well as Independent," *East European Constitutional Review* 11:1/2 (Winter/Spring 2002): 117–123.

45. Hendley, "Putin and the Law," pp. 106–107.

46. *RFE/RL Newsline*, August 26, 2005.

47. *Roza Tsvetkova, "Pokazatel'nyi ukhod," Nezavisimaia gazeta, February 18, 2009.*

48. *Polit.ru, March 18, 2009.*

49. Anna Pushkarskaia, "Konstitutsionnyi sud pristupil k demobilizatsii," *Kommersant*, March 18, 2009; Polit.ru, April 20, 2009.

50. This case arose when President Yeltsin refused to sign a law that parliament had passed that he considered unconstitutional. The law nationalized cultural artifacts and artworks that the Soviet Army had seized in Nazi-occupied Europe during World War II. Parliament overrode his veto, but Yeltsin still refused to sign. Parliament sent a protest to the Constitutional Court, which found that Yeltsin had no right to withhold his signature when parliament overrode a veto; it did find some provisions of the law unconstitutional but warned that a president had no right to declare a duly passed law unconstitutional—only the court had that power.

51. *Segodnia*, February 21, 2000.

52. Anna Pushkarskaia, "S nezavisimost'iu sudov moglo byt' i khuzhe," *Nezavisimaia gazeta*, April 16, 2010; Anna Pushkarskaia, interview with Valerii Zor'kin, *Kommersant*, May 7, 2009.

53. A comprehensive study of the court emphasizing its success in institutionalizing its role despite the growing authoritarianism of the current regime is Alexei Trochev, *Judging Russia: Constitutional Court in Russian Politics, 1990–2006* (Cambridge: Cambridge University Press, 2008).

54. Parts 1 and 2, recognizing private property and regulating commercial transactions, passed in 1994 and 1995; Part 3, regulating inheritance rights, passed in 2001. An important amendment to the Civil Code passed in early 2001, when the Duma lifted a suspension on the right to buy and sell land.

55. For a review of these laws, see Solomon, "Putin's Judicial Reform," pp. 117–123.

56. Hendley, "Putin and the Law," p. 104.

57. Kommersant, March 22, 2007; Yuri Chernega and Viktor Khamraev, "Gosduma otkazyvaetsia ot davleniia na Evropeiskii sud," *Kommersant.ru*, November 11, 2008.

58. Polit.ru, January 29, 2010.

59. Ibid., February 26, 2010.

60. "Yukos, Russia Face Off at Last in Strasbourg," *The Moscow Times*, March 4, 2010.

61. John D. Huber and Charles R. Shipan, *Deliberate Discretion? The Institutional Foundations of Bureaucratic Autonomy* (Cambridge: Cambridge University Press, 2002).

62. This was signaled by a new requirement that the prime minister deliver a report once a year on the performance of the government.

63. The Auditing Chamber *(Schetnaia palata)* is an auditing agency created by the parliament, comparable to the General Accounting Office in the United States. Like the GAO, it serves the legislative branch by conducting audits of the books of executive agencies and presenting reports of its findings.

64. Vladimir Gel'man, "The Unrule of Law in the Making: The Politics of Informal Institution Building in Russia," *Europe–Asia Studies* 56:7 (November 2004): 1021–1040; Peter H. Solomon, Jr., "Law in Public Administration: How Russia Differs," *Journal of Communist Studies and Transition Politics* 24:1 (2008): 115–135.

65. *OECD Economic Survey*, pp. 128–129.

66. Polit.ru, August 13, 14, and November 21, 2002; OECD Economic Survey Russian Federation 2006, p. 125.

67. From the president's message to parliament, November 5, 2008, as published on the president's Web site: http://www.kremlin.ru/appears/2008/11/05/1349_type63372type63374type63381type82634_208749.shtml.

68. In the United States, the Patriot Act, passed a month after the September 11 attacks, significantly expands government power to conduct surveillance of U.S. citizens suspected of involvement in terrorist activity, allows indefinite detention of noncitizens, and creates a new category of crime called "domestic terrorism."

69. Polit.ru, February 27, 2006; *RFE/RL Newsline*, March 7, 2006.

70. Ibid., July 5, 2006.

71. The secret police conducted one such operation even before the law was passed. In 2004, two Russian agents were arrested, tried, and convicted in Qatar for the assassination of a former Chechen rebel leader and his son and bodyguard. The Qatar authorities released them after five months in prison. Upon their return to Russia, they were awarded with decorations.

72. Polit.ru, November 30, 2005.

73. *RFE/RL Newsline*, April 19, 2007.

74. Ibid., June 22, 2007, April 14, 2008.

75. Polit.ru, November 11, 2008.

76. Anna Malpas, "'South Park' Episode Called Extremist," *The Moscow Times*, September 9, 2008; Polit.ru, September 23, 2008.
77. Quoted in *RFE/RL Newsline*, March 15, 2007.
78. Ibid.
79. Varese, The Russian Mafia; Vadim Volkov, "Who Is Strong When the State Is Weak? Violent Entrepreneurship in Russia's Emerging Markets," *Beyond State Crisis? Postcolonial Africa and Post-Soviet Eurasia in Comparative Perspective*. Ed. Mark R. Beissinger and Crawford Young (Washington, DC: Woodrow Wilson Center, 2002), pp. 81–104.
80. Polit.ru, September 24, 2008.
81. Political scientist Daniel Treisman has conducted a comparative analysis of corruption in Russia and other countries. He found that most of the explanation for corruption in countries lay in the following four factors: relatively low per capita income, low experience with democracy, low level of foreign trade, and the country's federal structure. Once these factors were accounted for, Russia was not particularly more corrupt than other countries. See Daniel Treisman, "The Causes of Corruption: A Cross-National Study," *Journal of Public Economics* 76:3 (2000): 399–457.
82. Polit.ru, June 25, 2008.
83. Elina Bilevskaia, "Mnogokratnaia shtrafnaia korruptsiia," *Nezavisimaia gazeta*, July 15, 2010.
84. *Kommersant*, April 25, 2007.
85. *RFE/RL Newsline*, October 18, 2007.
86. Elena Ivanova, "Vziatki otkatilis," *Vedomosti.ru*, February 6, 2008.
87. Nikita A. Krichevskii, "Aktual'nye predlozheniia na vechnuiu temu: kak dolzhna stroit'sia strategiia bor'by s korruptsiei," *Nezavisimaia gazeta*, June 11, 2008.
88. Susan Rose-Ackerman, *Corruption and Government: Causes, Consequences, and Reform* (Cambridge: Cambridge University Press, 1999), pp. 159–162.

Russia and the International Community

R ussia's thousand-year history of expansion, war, and state domination of society has left behind a legacy of autocratic rule and a preoccupation with defending national borders. In the twentieth century, Russian society experienced several traumas that deeply affected its relations with the outside world. Twice the regime collapsed—in 1917 and again in 1991—and twice world wars took tens of millions of lives. During the Soviet era, civil war and Stalin's terror killed tens of millions more. Little wonder that Russians should regard the preservation of statehood in an anarchic world as the foremost priority for their country. Likewise, this history of catastrophe, much of it self-induced, helps explain why Russians place their trust in rulers who can ensure the security and stability of the state. It also explains the strongly pragmatic streak in Russian foreign policy since the end of the Soviet era: Russian leaders tend to be acutely sensitive to the international balance of power and their country's place in it. However bitterly they may regard the loss of their country's status as a superpower, Russians have little desire to provoke a conflict with the United States or other international powers.

Russians harbor a high sense of insecurity about their country. A survey in February 2009 found that 37 percent of respondents believe that Russia faces a foreign military threat at present.[1] A 2007 survey sponsored by the European Union found that almost half of Russians regard the European Union as a threat to Russia, and specifically to its financial and industrial independence. Only a third consider Europe as a neighbor and partner with which Russia should develop long-term relations.[2]

Some of this insecurity stems from the fear that outside powers will take advantage of the state's vulnerability at a time of regime change.[3] Russians historically have learned to associate periods of domestic turmoil with attempts by foreign powers to exploit Russia's weakness. Interludes of regime collapse and civil disorder, such as the Time of Troubles in the early seventeenth century or the fall of the Romanov dynasty in 1917 during World War I, which led to the February and October Revolutions, tempted external powers to intervene in Russia and seize Russian-ruled territories. Many Russians today regard the period of the late 1980s and early 1990s in a similar light, believing that Gorbachev's concessions to the West, his willingness to allow the union to dissolve, and his abandonment of Communist Party rule left Russia weakened and humiliated and subject to the dictates of the West. A major source of Russian suspicion of outside powers is the widespread view that the West is trying to squeeze Russia out of its traditional sphere of influence. This includes the belt of countries in Eastern Europe, but especially the states of the former Soviet Union. Suspicion of the United States in particular is widespread. One survey of 18- and 19-year-olds in summer 2007 found that almost 80 percent believed that the "United States is trying to impose its norms and way of life on the rest of the world," and almost 70 percent disagreed with the proposition that the United States "brings more good than harm."[4] A survey of the general population found that Russians were almost evenly divided between those who consider the American CIA a terrorist organization (30 percent) and those who think it is not (32 percent).[5]

The Putin–Medvedev foreign policy has addressed the widespread sense of insecurity and loss following the collapse of the Soviet state. The worldwide increase in the price of oil from 1999 to 2008 strengthened their hand in this effort and the collapse of oil prices in October 2008 weakened it. The regime's policy is far from seeking to isolate Russia from the international capitalist economy, as the Soviet regime did. Nor is it intending to compete with the United States as a global superpower. However, it has sought to increase its leverage in the former Soviet region. This has created a dilemma: As Russia expands its influence around its perimeter, countries on its borders have hedged their bets by improving relations with the United States and China.

Thus, a classic "security dilemma" has arisen in the relations between Russia and some of its neighbors. In a security dilemma, efforts by one country to increase its invulnerability to pressure from another take the form of actions that the other country finds threatening. The latter country therefore takes actions to increase its own security, which come at the expense of the first country. The nuclear arms race between the United States and the Soviet Union during the Cold War is a prime example of this trap: Neither side was able to achieve security in the face of the other's capacity for massive nuclear retaliation, which led both sides to redouble their efforts to make their nuclear weapons invulnerable to attack.

Russia and its southern neighbor Georgia have also been locked in a security dilemma. As Georgia, fearing Russian domination, has pushed hard to align itself with the United States and NATO and against Russia, Russia has responded with increasing pressure on Georgia. In August 2008, war broke out between the two countries. The immediate cause of the war was the dispute over the status of two ethnic enclaves on Georgian territory, Abkhazia and South Ossetia. Abkhazia lies on the Black Sea, while South Ossetia is contiguous to Russia (in fact, it borders on North Ossetia, one of Russia's ethnic republics). The leaders of both territories declared their independence from Georgia in the early 1990s. Georgia refused to acknowledge these claims to independence. War broke out between forces in both territories and Georgia in the early 1990s. Once peace was restored, Russia maintained peacekeeping forces in both regions. Over time, Russia built up its military and economic support for each, although never quite going so far as to recognize their independence. Talks between their leaders and Georgia over their political status failed: Georgia was willing to grant them wide autonomy within Georgia but their leaders held out for complete independence.

In August 2008, Georgia launched a military assault to reestablish Georgian control over South Ossetia. It bombarded South Ossetia's capital city, Tskhinvali, and other positions, evidently expecting to take control of the territory before Russia could respond. Georgia's attack resulted in casualties among South Ossetian militiamen and civilians, Georgian civilians living in the region, and some Russian peacekeepers. Russia (which was evidently expecting the attack) responded vigorously, not only defeating the Georgian forces in South Ossetia, but pushing them out of Abkhazia as well, and occupying a buffer zone around both territories. Following urgent international diplomatic intervention, Russia pulled back its forces to Abkhazia and South Ossetia. Shortly after the cease-fire, Russia recognized the independence of both territories—although of the rest of the world, only Nicaragua and the Palestinian group Hamas chose to follow suit.

International observers condemned Russia's actions as an act of aggression or, at the very least, a gross overreaction. At the same time, many also criticized Georgia's president for foolishly provoking the Russian response. Russia's victory was in many ways hollow, because although it gave Russia a military foothold in Georgia, it did not increase Russia's regional security or international prestige. The five-day war underscored Russia's dilemma as it seeks to expand its influence in the territory of the former Soviet Union and at the same time to win recognition as a stakeholder in the international community. The war reflected the reality that when Russia acts unilaterally to expand its power and security in its immediate sphere of influence, it often provokes counterreactions that only leave it more insecure.

ENERGY AS AN INSTRUMENT OF POWER

The Russian–Georgian war was an exceptional event in that it involved the direct application of military force. More typical of Russia's effort to rebuild its status as regional superpower is its use of energy resources for political influence. It has used these to consolidate its control over the economies and infrastructures of the former Soviet region—what Russians call "the near abroad." In part, Russia is making use of the close integration of the energy and transportation infrastructure left behind by the Soviet Union. As a defense minister commented in October 2003, "The CIS [Commonwealth of Independent States] is a very crucial sphere for our security. Ten million of our compatriots live there, and we are supplying energy to them at prices below international levels. We are not going to renounce the right to use military power there in situations where all other means have been exhausted." On the same day, speaking in another Russian city, Putin declared that Russia would never give up control of the pipeline system in the former Soviet states. The pipelines were built by the Soviet regime, he observed, and only Russia can keep the system operating, "even those parts of the system that are beyond Russia's borders."[6]

Certainly, Russia regards the former Soviet region as lying in its sphere of interest. In an interview with the Russian press in August 2008, following the war with Georgia, President Dmitrii Medvedev declared that there are regions "in which there are privileged interests. In these regions are located countries with which we have traditionally friendly, cordial relations, historically special relations. We will work very attentively in these regions and develop such friendly relations with these states, with our close neighbors." In answer to a question from a journalist as to whether the high-priority regions were those on Russia's borders, Medvedev explained: "those are of course bordering regions. But not only them."[7] It is not clear what nonbordering regions Medvedev had in mind, although perhaps they included Serbia. In any case, Medvedev was reconfirming a tenet of post-Soviet Russian foreign policy: that the region of the former Soviet Union constituted a sphere in which Russia believes it has special, "privileged," interests, much as with the Monroe Doctrine of 1823, when the United States declared Latin America to be a region in which it has exclusive prerogatives.

Russia has used energy as a principal instrument for building and maintaining its influence in the former Soviet sphere. This is in part a reflection of a basic geopolitical reality: Russia has to export energy to sustain its economy. Therefore, Russia's economic growth and status as a great power depend on maintaining its exports of oil and gas. This in turns means that Russia relies on ensuring a reliable way to get its oil and gas to world markets. Likewise, Europe depends on imported Russian energy, especially Russian gas. Russia's gas accounts for about a quarter of European gas consumption.

Thus, both Russia and its neighbors depend on secure transit routes for oil and gas. For instance, three-quarters of Russian gas exports to Europe go through Ukraine and most of the rest transits through Belarus. Therefore, Russia is deeply concerned about the possibility that Ukraine or Belarus could divert gas or block Russian exports (as they have done). One reason for the strategy of using energy to consolidate control over the pipeline infrastructure in the region, therefore, is to guarantee uninterrupted access to its European markets. Both Russia and Europe have proposed new alternative pipeline routes for shipping gas from Russia to the West in order to reduce the dependence on existing pipeline routes. Moreover, Russia has sought to diversify its customer base by entering major energy agreements with Japan and China for oil and liquefied natural gas.

Under Putin, the state and semi-state energy firms have become instruments of Russia's strategy to increase its political influence in the former Soviet region. The largest of these firms is the state gas monopoly Gazprom.

Gazprom is a behemoth. It has over 400,000 employees. Its market value at its peak in May 2008, before the rapid drop in energy prices later that year, was estimated at $363 billion, making it the fifth largest publicly traded company in the world at that time.[8] President Medvedev (who served as the chairman of the board of directors of Gazprom until he became president) said that Gazprom alone was responsible for providing one-fifth of federal budget revenues.[9] Although it has taken several steps toward improving the transparency of its corporate governance, it is still widely criticized by foreign observers (and by some Russian officials) for its resistance to reform and reluctance to modernize its operations.[10] Gazprom has a near-total monopoly over the extraction, processing, and distribution of natural gas in Russia and, through a series of acquisitions, is now one of the largest oil firms as well. It owns and controls the entire gas pipeline system in Russia and much of the pipeline system in neighboring countries. In recent years, Gazprom has raised prices substantially on the gas it sells to Russia's neighbors, phasing out Soviet-era price subsidies and bringing the prices much closer to world market prices. Although Russian leaders and Gazprom managers insist that they are basing these decisions on market forces, the price increases have had the consequence of allowing Gazprom to acquire greater control over the pipeline networks within the neighboring transit countries as part of the price agreements.

For example, Gazprom had been selling gas to Ukraine for about $50 per thousand cubic meters, then as negotiations for a new contract began in 2006, Gazprom raised the price to about $220 (close to the price paid by West European customers). Gazprom offered to take partial control in Ukrainian pipelines or shares in Ukrainian companies as payment, but Ukraine refused. By January 1, 2006, no new contract had been signed. Russia cut the gas supply to Ukraine, and Ukraine in turn cut the supply of Russian gas to Europe. Eventually, an agreement was reached. Russia agreed to supply gas to Ukraine at a discounted price through a shadowy supply company that was partly owned by Gazprom and partly by a firm whose principals have been investigated by the authorities in Ukraine and United States for their ties to organized crime.[11] Similarly, Gazprom raised prices to Moldova, the Baltic States, Georgia, Armenia, and Belarus. In several cases, it negotiated deals under which it acquired stakes in the pipeline companies of the partner country in return for substantial price discounts on gas. Currently, Gazprom owns a majority stake in the gas pipeline transiting Belarus that delivers gas to Europe, and it owns all the gas pipelines transiting Armenia. The prize is the Ukrainian gas pipeline network, and Gazprom is attempting to use its negotiating leverage to offer price concessions on gas for greater control over Ukraine's pipeline system.[12]

Russia has also consolidated its control over the electric power networks of neighboring countries. The Russian national electric power company, Unified Energy Systems (UES), bought Armenia's electric power generation and distribution system through an offshore subsidiary.[13] The UES company has also acquired substantial stakes in the electric power companies of other neighbors, including Georgia and Moldova, and aims to expand its holdings in

Latvia, Lithuania, Belarus, Ukraine, Tajikistan, and Kyrgyzstan, as well as several other countries such as Bulgaria, Romania, and Turkey.[14]

Russia's success in using energy to leverage economic power into political influence has encouraged many Russians to express a desire to see the former Soviet Union reconstructed under Russian domination. A former KGB chairman was quoted in late 2003 to the effect that "if we do not reassemble the Soviet Union, we have no future at all." The popular minister for emergency situations, Sergei Shoigu, campaigning for the United Russia party, said he hoped "to live to see the day when we have one big country within the borders of the [former] Soviet Union."[15] A political strategist with close Kremlin ties declared that the only way Russia could thrive in the twenty-first century was to dominate "the post-Soviet space," which was its natural "historical–geographical area." Another strategist commented that Putin needed to offer Russians an inspiring new national project, which could only be a "Great Russia": "history has left us no other choice," he argued. "Russia can only be great."[16] Putin himself said that the countries of the CIS were "now working to restore what was lost with the fall of the Soviet Union but are doing it on a new, modern basis," in a speech at Lev Gumilev University in Kazakhstan in June 2004.[17]

THE CIS AND ITS PROGENY

Although some leaders pay lip service to the idea that the CIS can serve as the organizational framework for a restored union, Russia has invested little in the effort. As we discussed in Chapter 1, the CIS was formally created simultaneously with the dissolution of the Soviet Union by agreement of the leaders of Russia, Ukraine, and Belarus in December 1991. Yeltsin and his colleagues regarded the CIS as a vehicle for maintaining the ties linking the states of the former Soviet Union until a new framework was worked out. Many in the Russian leadership assumed that the breakup of the union would be temporary and that once the former Soviet states saw that they could not survive on their own, the union would be restored in some new form. Neither Russia nor other successor states were willing to devote much effort to building a strong CIS: The other states feared Russian dominance in it, while Russia preferred to concentrate on carrying out its own far-reaching political and economic reforms. In any event, the CIS never became more than a loose framework for periodic consultations among its members.

Certainly, one major obstacle to the growth of integration and hence of coordinating power for the CIS is the enormous difference between Russia's power and size and the power and size of the other members. As Table 9.1 indicates, Russia's population is almost three times larger than that of the next most populous member, Ukraine. Russia was never willing to turn over sovereign power to any organization not under its immediate control, and the other member states of the CIS were unwilling to turn over much power to a governing body controlled by Russia. This issue simply underscores the point

TABLE 9.1

Population and Income of Former Soviet States, 2008 (Excluding the Baltic States)

	Population (millions)	GDP, PPP Per Capita (constant 2005 intl $)
Russian Federation	141.95	14,706
Western neighbors:		
Ukraine	46.25	6,721
Moldova	3.6	2,704
Belarus	9.68	11,340
Transcaucasus:		
Armenia	3.08	5,611
Azerbaijan	8.68	8,100
Georgia	4.3	4,586
Central Asia:		
Kazakhstan	15.67	10,458
Kyrgyz Republic	5.28	2,025
Tajikistan	6.84	1,761
Turkmenistan	5.04	6,119
Uzbekistan	27.31	2,455

Source: World Bank, World Development Indicators.

that the Soviet Union itself functioned as a sovereign state only by submerging Russia's own status as a political actor within the larger Soviet state and investing power instead in the Communist Party–dominated structures of the union. For this reason, Russia probably had no chance of becoming a democratic state until it jettisoned the union. But without Russia, of course, there could be no union.

Another reason that the CIS has not achieved deeper integration is that some of its members regard Russia as a potential threat and seek to protect themselves by forming security and economic partnerships with the West and with China. Former Soviet republics Estonia, Latvia, and Lithuania, which never joined the CIS, are members of NATO (legally the United States never recognized them as union republics of the USSR), and Ukraine and Georgia, which were members of CIS, have sought to join NATO.[18] Several CIS members formed a loose alliance called GUUAM as a counterweight to Russia (Georgia, Ukraine, Uzbekistan, Azerbaijan, and Moldova).

Moreover, the United States has established a presence in the former Soviet region. Following the September 11, 2001, attacks on the United States by Al Qaeda–backed terrorists, the United States sought and received basing privileges at air force facilities in two former Soviet republics in Central Asia,

Kyrgyzstan and Kazakhstan. The immediate reason for American use of these bases was to support American air strikes against the Taliban regime in Afghanistan. Russia accepted this American military presence on the condition that it be for a limited time and restricted in scope, recognizing that the removal of the Taliban regime also served Russian security interests. The United States also sent military trainers to build up the Georgian army, evidently to reassure Georgia that the United States supported it in its defiance of Russia, and the United States also provided generous military aid to Georgia.

Russia has grown increasingly resentful of this American presence in its neighborhood. President Medvedev gave voice to this hostility in his remarks to parliament in November 2008, when he accused the United States of seeking to encircle Russia with a ring of military bases, missile systems, the "unrestrained" expansion of NATO, and other "gifts." Accusing the United States of fomenting the Georgian war in order to have a pretext to introduce NATO war vessels into the Black Sea, he commented that the war in Georgia and the global financial crisis were "two very different problems" sharing "a common origin"—that is, the United States' policy of imposing its will on the rest of the world.[19] Probably, the single most threatening scenario in Russian eyes would be for Ukraine to enter NATO. Russia views this prospect in somewhat the same way the United States would react if Mexico joined a Russian-led military alliance.

Thus, because of the differing foreign policy orientations of the members of the CIS, and because of the expansion of U.S. and NATO power eastward, the CIS never became a new state structure filling the vacuum left by the collapse of the old union. Therefore, the Putin and Medvedev leadership has instead chosen to work through subsets of the CIS for specific sets of tasks. Four in particular are important: the so-called "union state" between Russia and Belarus, the Eurasian Economic Community, the Collective Security Treaty Organization, and the Shanghai Cooperation Organization (SCO).

The Russia–Belarus Union

The leaders of Russia and its smaller Western neighbor, Belarus (formerly known as Belorussia), have made sporadic attempts to form a union since the mid-1990s. Belarus is led by its dictatorial president Alyaksandr Lukashenka, who has pinned his hopes for a political future on a union of Belarus and Russia. This would elevate his own political status to that of a coequal with Russia's president and tie his country's failing economy to Russia. Six times between 1996 and 1999, Presidents Yeltsin and Lukashenka held showy ceremonies at which they signed agreements promising to unite their two countries.[20] New institutions (such as a joint parliament) were created on paper, but neither side was willing to cede any real power to the union structures.

In 2002, President Putin poured cold water on the idea of a union by pointing out the obvious—that Russian could never allow a union with Belarus to proceed at the expense of Russia's economic or political interests. Then, at the end of 2006, the relationship took a further sharp downturn when Russia more than doubled the price Belarus would have to pay for natural gas and imposed a substantial new export tax on oil shipped to Belarus. Belarus initially refused to pay the higher rates and imposed a transit fee for oil shipped across Belarus territory. Russia in turn accused Belarus of siphoning off oil from the pipelines sending oil from Russia via Belarus to Europe and cut off the supply of oil to Belarus for three days. Belarus then shut off the supply of oil through its pipelines to Europe, sending shockwaves throughout Europe. The incident dramatized both the illusory nature of the Russian–Belarus "union" and the willingness of Russia to use coercive tactics to force its neighbors to accept its terms for energy purchases. Clearly, Russia was unwilling to continue subsidizing Belarus with cheap energy for the sake of a special political relationship. Putin has made it clear that if Belarus is to merge with Russia, it will be as a constituent federal subject of Russia, rather than as a coequal state.

The Eurasian Economic Community

Under the CIS's auspices, a customs union made up of Russia, Belarus, Kazakstan, Kyrgyzstan, and Tajikistan formed. The objective was to facilitate trade among the members by eliminating customs barriers. In 2000, the members formally created the "Eurasian Economic Community (EEC)," along the lines of the European Community. Under the weighted voting scheme it uses for decision making, Russia has the preponderance of decision-making power. In addition to lowering trade barriers among the member states, the group has also discussed energy cooperation. Although EEC has not developed into a real economic community, under its auspices, Russia, Belarus, and Kazakhstan signed a treaty forming a new Customs Union in December 2009. The new union is also unlikely to affect actual trade relations among the three countries. For example, Russia has not dropped the export duties on oil it exports to Belarus. Likewise, Belarus food and other industries are heavily protected and would be devastated if tariff barriers on imported products from Russia were lifted. The status of the new customs union was further confused by the fact that Putin, as prime minister, in 2009 unexpectedly announced that Russia would join the World Trade Organization as a bloc with its two partners in the customs union, Belarus and Kazakhstan, only to abandon the plan quietly a few months later.[21]

The Collective Security Treaty Organization

If the EEC resembles—at least formally—a post-Soviet European Community, the Collective Security Treaty Organization (CSTO) resembles a post-Soviet NATO. The CSTO was formed by a treaty in April 2003 out of a predecessor agreement, the Tashkent Treaty, established originally in 1992. It is devoted to collective defense and promotes the principle of collective response to security threats. Its members, Russia, Armenia, Belarus, Kazakhstan, Kyrgyzstan, and Tajikistan, maintain elements of the old Soviet unified air defense grid.

They have also agreed to form their own rapid deployment force with Russian paratroopers as its core element. The CSTO's role has been limited. It facilitates consultations among members on responses to terrorist threats.[22] It also gives Russia a way to expand its own military bases in Central Asia and a platform for political declarations (such as warnings against NATO expansion). But it has been overshadowed as an instrument for collective action by the Shanghai Cooperation Organization.

The Shanghai Cooperation Organization

The Shanghai Cooperation Organization (SCO) comprises Russia, China, Kazakhstan, Kyrgyzstan, Uzbekistan, and Tajikistan. It is a vehicle through which Russia, Central Asian states, and China coordinate security policies dealing with the cross-border flows of drugs, weapons, and terrorists. It was formed in 2001 and has evolved rapidly. An indication of its significance is the fact that when the heads of government of its members meet, the leaders of India, Pakistan, and Iran attend as observers.[23] The SCO has planned joint military training exercises (to address a hypothetical terrorist threat) and adopted joint declarations about regional security policy. Under its auspices, a regional antiterrorist center was created in Kyrgyzstan under Russian military command. In July 2005, the SCO formally requested that the United States set a deadline for the removal of its military forces from the airbases in Kyrgyzstan and Uzbekistan, and shortly afterward, Uzbekistan formally requested the United States to withdraw from the base it was leasing there. This followed a bloody incident in May when Uzbek security forces killed several hundred protesters, provoking strong U.S. criticism of the regime's actions and a cooling of U.S.–Uzbek relations. The American withdrawal from Uzbekistan was viewed by Russian analysts as a loss for American influence in the region and a gain for Russia.[24] Russia regards the SCO as an organization with considerable potential to counterbalance American influence in Central Asia, but it cannot count on the SCO to give unqualified support to its own initiatives.[25] For example, following the war with Georgia in August 2008, Russia won only a tepid endorsement of its actions from the organization. Moreover, none of the members either of the CSTO or the SCO followed Russia in recognizing the independence of Abkhazia and South Ossetia.[26] Thus, Russia's effort to use multilateral diplomacy as a way of multiplying its international leverage has limits when its actions meet with resistance from its partners.

OBSTACLES TO REGIONAL HEGEMONY

Although Russia's economic and military influence in the former Soviet region has increased as a result of these organizational initiatives and its immense energy resources, it faces serious challenges to its effort to dominate the region. First is the fact that several of its neighbors are weak states with repressive regimes and uncertain stability. In recent years, there have been several large-scale popular protest movements against autocratic and unpopular governments in the region. Two of them (Georgia's "Rose Revolution" in fall 2003 and Ukraine's "Orange Revolution" in fall 2004) represented democratic movements aimed against efforts by old guard leaders to falsify the results of elections in order to hold on to power.[27] In another case, that of Kyrgyzstan, a popular uprising in 2005 succeeded in driving the president from office but not in establishing democratic rule. In all three countries, the popular movements formed in reaction to massive election fraud and swelled until they ultimately forced the presidents to resign. (See Close-Up 9.1: The Orange Revolution.) But whereas these revolutions were generally regarded as democratic breakthroughs by Western observers, they were deeply unsettling to the Russian authorities because they threatened the seeming stability of the region. The Orange Revolution in Ukraine was particularly embarrassing to Russia because Russia had intervened so openly in the election campaign in favor of its preferred candidate, who ultimately had to relinquish power in the face of massive popular protest and a unified Western stance against his efforts to manipulate the outcome. Russia's inability to prevent a humiliating political defeat reinforced the fears of many officials in the Kremlin that they could not be sure how deep popular discontent runs in Russia and neighboring states, and their conviction that Western agents were stirring up trouble against them. As if to reinforce these fears, a new wave of popular protests erupted in Kyrgyzstan in November 2006, indicating that the new regime's stability was also tenuous. Mass rioting in spring 2010 again led to the expulsion of Kyrgyzstan's president. In that case, Russia was thought to have helped instigate the uprising.[28]

CLOSE-UP 9.1

The Orange Revolution

Ukraine's presidential election of 2004 resulted in a fiasco for Russian policy. Of the two leading candidates—Prime Minister Viktor Yanukovych and former prime minister Viktor Yushchenko—Russia strongly favored Yanukovych with visible and heavy-handed support. Yanukovych took a line favoring closer ties between Russia and Ukraine. He promised, for example, that if elected he would make Russian (along with Ukrainian) a state language of Ukraine and would introduce dual citizenship so that Ukrainian citizens could be citizens of Russia as well. Putin made no pretense of neutrality. Yanukovych was given prominent play in the Russian media. For example, he was shown, together with Ukraine's president Leonid Kuchma, meeting with Putin to celebrate Putin's birthday in October and addressing a national congress of Ukrainians in Russia at the Kremlin. President Putin went so far as to pay a three-day visit to Ukraine on the eve of the first round of the election, where he made clear Russia's backing for Yanukovych. Russian political consultants and strategists were sent to Ukraine to ensure Yanukovych's victory.

(continued)

Yanukovych was closely tied to the political establishment in Ukraine and to some of Ukraine's leading oligarchs. Much of his support came from the Russian-speaking industrial regions of eastern Ukraine. Yushchenko, in contrast, had a reputation as a competent, honest reformer. He had served as prime minister for 1999–2001 and before that as chairman of Ukraine's Central Bank. Much of his support came from the western regions of the country, where Ukrainian national feeling and antagonism toward Russia is strong. The cultural and political divide between the nationalist West and the pro-Russian East in Ukraine was expressed with unusual intensity during the campaign. Many participants and observers claimed—with the hyperbole that elections often fan—that the contest between Yanukovych and Yushchenko represented a choice between Russia and Europe in Ukraine's basic political orientation.

The election campaign was marked by substantial acrimony and dirty tricks. In the course of the campaign, Viktor Yushchenko was poisoned. In early September, he became violently ill and had to be rushed for treatment to Vienna. He recovered sufficiently to resume campaigning later in September, but his face had been badly disfigured. Later, pathologists in Vienna reported that he had been poisoned with a high dose of dioxin, the active ingredient in the powerful defoliant Agent Orange. The fact that the night before he fell ill he had had dinner with the head of Ukraine's secret service only fueled suspicions about who had poisoned him.

The first round, held on October 31, resulted in a dead heat between the two top finishers, Yushchenko and Yanukovych. Yushchenko received 39.87 percent of the vote, while Yanukovych received 39.32 percent. The runoff took place on November 21. Putin paid another visit to Ukraine to aid Yanukovych. Exit polls on the day of the voting suggested that Yushchenko had a comfortable lead. However, the country's Central Electoral Commission declared Yanukovych the winner, by 49.46–46.61 percent. Observers from Europe and the United States reported, however, that there had been widespread falsification. The Organization for Security and Cooperation in Europe (OSCE's) election observation mission stated that the vote fell below democratic election standards. U.S. Senator Richard Lugar, observing the election as President Bush's representative, declared in Kiev that "It is now apparent that a concerted and forceful program of election-day fraud and abuse was enacted with either the leadership or cooperation of government authorities." Two days later, the European Union announced that "we don't accept these results and we think they are fraudulent." U.S. Secretary of State Colin Powell warned of "consequences" for U.S.–Ukrainian relations if the Ukrainian authorities failed to investigate "the numerous and credible reports of fraud and abuse." Observers reported that the fraud was most prevalent in the eastern regions of the country, where Yanukovych's support was strongest.

However, President Putin rejected any suggestion of fraud. He telephoned Yanukovych to congratulate him on his victory, commenting that "the battle has been hard-fought, but open and honest." Putin and other Russian policymakers

furiously criticized the West for refusing to accept the election results. Putin called the OSCE's characterization of the election as fraudulent "inadmissible." Russia's ambassador to the European Union declared that "it's impossible not to see the direct involvement of the American Congress, individual congressmen who are spending their days and nights in Kyiv—foundations, nongovernmental organizations, consultants, experts. It's clear and obvious to everyone."[1]
An editorial comment in the Russian daily *Izvestiia* claimed that the events clearly demonstrated that the West was trying to weaken Russia by stripping away territories from its sphere of influence, but pointed out that Russia had made matters worse by intervening so ineptly.[2]

As soon as the Ukrainian election commission announced its official report, Yushchenko's supporters streamed into the central squares of Kiev and other cities to protest the official results. The demonstrations were large in scale and well organized. The opposition adopted the color orange as their symbol and wore orange ribbons and scarves. Denouncing the official results as fraudulent, they demanded new and fair elections. Led by a youth movement called "Pora" ("It's Time"), they erected tents, set up field kitchens and first-aid stations, and handed out ribbons, scarves, and literature. A 19-year-old leader of Pora noted that they had been ready for action: "We heard that Yanukovich would try to organize this fraud, and we were prepared for this kind of situation," she said. "We decided we also had to do something, to raise the people's will."[3] Hundreds of thousands of people participated; the central square in Kiev was filled with protesters 24 hours a day, day after day for nearly two weeks. Yushchenko's supporters appealed to the Ukrainian Supreme Court to nullify the results of the November 21 runoff on the grounds that they had been falsified and to require holding new elections. As the days passed and the opposition movement gained in strength, pressure on the Ukrainian authorities to find a peaceful resolution mounted.

President Putin faced a serious dilemma. Russia's support for Yanukovych and its refusal to acknowledge the election fraud in the Ukraine was already discrediting Russia in the West and threatening to spoil his plans for closer ties with Europe. A summit meeting between the European Union and Russia on November 25, overshadowed by the Ukrainian crisis, failed to produce a planned agreement on a "strategic partnership." But Putin also feared the consequences of allowing Yushchenko to win, which would complicate relations between Russia and Ukraine and represent another humiliating defeat for Russia. The Russian Duma passed a resolution on December 3 accusing the European Parliament, the European Union, and the OSCE of "destructive foreign interference in the development of the situation in Ukraine." Ukrainian president Kuchma flew to

[1]*RFE/RL Newsline*, November 29, 2004.
[2]www.izvestia.ru/comment/article763957. *November 29, 2004.*
[3]Quoted in C. J. Chivers, "Youth Movement Underlies the Opposition in Ukraine." *New York Times*, November 28, 2004.

(*continued*)

Moscow to consult with Putin to find a way out of the impasse. Representatives of the Yanukovych and Yushchenko camps met to discuss possible political solutions. Yanukovych proposed a power-sharing agreement under which the powers of the president would be reduced, the powers of the prime minister strengthened, and the two would divide the offices between them. Yushchenko, sensing that his political support in Ukraine and abroad was growing, rejected the deal and held out for a new runoff election. Yanukovych then agreed to participate in a new runoff if Yushchenko would agree to constitutional changes weakening the powers of the presidency and strengthening those of the prime minister. The two camps edged toward a deal.

On December 3, the Ukrainian Supreme Court ruled that the November 21 election was invalid due to large-scale fraud and called for holding a new election. Five days later, the Ukrainian parliament passed a package of laws that included reforms of the election system intended to reduce opportunities for election abuses and a set of constitutional amendments that would reduce the powers of the president and strengthen those of the prime minister. In effect, the legislation bundled together reforms that both camps had demanded: a cleaner election process, as Yushchenko's supporters sought, in return for a less presidentially dominant system, as Yanukovych's supporters, fearing that Yushchenko would win the December 26 election, had wanted. On December 9, at a meeting of the Russia–NATO Council in Brussels, the Russian foreign minister and the other NATO foreign ministers issued a statement declaring that all sides agreed to respect the outcome of the new elections. On December 26, the new run-off election was held. Yushchenko won with 52 percent of the vote.

Although the immediate crisis was over, the episode revealed how far apart were the interests and perceptions of Russia and the West. For many Russian policy makers, Ukraine is an integral part of Russia's sphere of influence; indeed, many Russians find it hard to conceive Ukraine as a separate country. For them, therefore, Western support for Yushchenko amounted to an effort to separate Ukraine from Russia and turn it against Russia. Many Russians were convinced that it was the CIA and other Western secret services that had underwritten the "Orange Revolution." They pointed out that events in Ukraine unfolded very similarly to those a year before in Georgia. At that time, a mass movement that became known as the "Rose Revolution" protested the large-scale falsification of presidential elections, with the West's support, and forced President Shevardnadze to leave office, bringing the young leader of the opposition, Mikhail Saakashvili, to power. (Saakashvili's supporters, which included an organized youth movement called "Kmara" or "Enough," marched on parliament carrying roses, as a symbol of their nonviolent protest.) Russians also recalled the similar sequence of events in September–October 2000 in Serbia. There, President Milosevic attempted to falsify the outcome of an election he had lost, provoking mass protests, strikes, and a march on parliament; ten days after the election, he was forced from office. For some Russians, the similarity of these events was hardly coincidental; it simply confirmed that they were all part of a concerted Western strategy to exploit the denunciation of election fraud as a means to deny Russia its traditional allies and expand Western power in Russia's natural sphere of influence.

From the standpoint of the West, such charges reflected a fundamental lack of acceptance of the force of popular demands for democratic elections. To be sure, efforts by Western foundations, NGOs, and government democracy-building programs contributed to these popular uprisings.[4] In each case, the popular movements supported the opposition because the opposition had won elections but were being denied the right to claim victory. Western assistance has gone to efforts to promote civil society, free elections, and competitive parties and therefore benefited opposition movements in the instances where the authorities attempted to steal elections. International monitoring of elections is intended to ensure that the election results are credible and the winners hold power by right, rather than by force. To regard Western insistence on fair elections in zero-sum terms, as an attempt to invade Russia's natural sphere of influence, is to ignore the substantial basis of support that existed for democratic principles. As Michael McFaul put it, "democracy is not an American plot."[5] Although President Putin ultimately found it prudent to accept the outcome of the decision in Ukraine to hold new elections, the failure of his own clumsy efforts to intervene in the election proved to be a humiliating setback and one likely to reinforce Russian grievances about the country's ambiguous place in the international system.

The Orange Revolution also illustrates the point that peaceful protest movements are better at overthrowing a repressive regime than at ensuring the stability of a new democratic regime. Within a year after the Orange Revolution, Ukrainians expressed widespread dissatisfaction with its results. Continued squabbling among the parties forming the "orange coalition" after 2004 led to a series of government failures. The two allies of the Orange Revolution, Viktor Yushchenko and Yulia Tymoshenko, fell out and competed in the 2010 presidential election against their old opponent Viktor Yanukovych. Yanukovych won with a clear majority, a result reflecting popular disillusionment with the outcome of the Orange Revolution and the economic distress caused by the 2008 recession. The aftermath of the Orange Revolution indicates that a popular revolution may be able to force a regime to call a new election but be unable to guarantee that the new regime will be any more competent or honest than its predecessor.

---

[4]Michael McFaul has evaluated the relative importance of internal and external influences in bringing about the Orange Revolution in Michael McFaul, "Importing Revolution: Internal and External Factors in Russia's 2004 Democratic Breakthrough," in Valerie Bunce, Michael McFaul, and Kathryn Stoner-Weiss, eds., *Democracy and Authoritarianism in the Postcommunist World* (Cambridge: Cambridge University Press, 2009), pp. 189–225.

[5]Michael McFaul, "'Meddling in Ukraine': Democracy Is Not an American Plot," *The Washington Post*, December 21, 2004.

There have also been outbursts of popular unrest elsewhere in Central Asia. In eastern Uzbekistan, a protest against the government in the town of Andijan in May 2005 was suppressed by violence when Uzbek security forces opened fire on several thousand demonstrators, reportedly killing hundreds of them. The government claimed that the organizers were linked to a radical Islamist movement. When the eccentric dictator of Turkmenistan died in December 2006, some feared that the succession could be contested, leading to a colored revolution in that country. However, the election was managed peacefully. Nevertheless, the fear that popular unrest could spill out into a large-scale organized protest movement and force the leaders from power strongly influences the calculations of Russian and other regional leaders and is used to justify repression against potential opposition groups.

Related to the concern over the stability of the states on its periphery is the continued threat of Islamic fundamentalist movements in Central Asia and the Transcaucasus, linked to the Taliban and other international Islamist groups. It is hard to gauge the influence of radical Islamist groups in Central Asia and the Caucasus because the authorities tend to label any manifestation of Islamic piety as politically inspired. Nevertheless, there are radical Islamic terrorist organizations operating in Central Asia, notably the "Islamic Movement of Uzbekistan (IMU)," which has been linked to several terrorist acts in Central Asia. The IMU's access to the region is eased by the fact that its militants are able to slip back and forth between Tajikistan and Afghanistan. The Tajik border with Afghanistan is very weakly controlled (the Uzbek–Afghan border is better guarded). The resurgence of the Taliban and the opium trade in Afghanistan has given the IMU an opportunity to exploit the drug trade for its own benefit. Experts estimate that the IMU controls most of the drugs trafficked across Afghanistan's borders into Tajikistan and Kyrgyzstan.[29]

Russian leaders have also consistently accused Chechen rebels of being supported by international Islamist terror groups. A prominent Chechen rebel leader killed in 2005, named Khattab, was a Jordanian who helped to infuse the Chechen independence movement with Islamic political ideology. The serious concern over the spread of international Islamist ideology helped motivate Putin's decision to offer assistance to the United States following the September 2001 attacks in New York and Washington and to cooperate with the American campaign to eradicate the Taliban regime in Afghanistan.

Finally, Russia's leverage in the region from its oil and gas wealth is precarious. For one thing, Russia needs to mix Central Asian natural gas with Russian gas in order to meet its commitments to the European market. Gazprom's ability to expand production of gas in Russia in the short term is limited; production at its major fields is declining and substantial investment will be needed to increase production significantly in the coming years.[30] Therefore, in order to meet its growing export commitments, Gazprom needs to acquire cheap gas from Turkmenistan. The reason Russia could offer Ukraine gas at a discounted price was that Russia counts on a long-term agreement with Turkmenistan for a below-market price. Russia's dependence on Central Asia for gas supply therefore requires a close political relationship between Russia and the Central Asian states together with political stability in the region. Russia's leverage over Turkmenistan, Kazakstan, and other Caspian Sea gas-producing states was substantial until the late 1990s, because all their gas had to be exported through Russian-controlled pipelines. Now, however, thanks to a new pipeline, Turkmenistan can bypass Russia and export gas directly to Iran. Moreover, in December 2009, Turkmenistan began shipping gas through a new pipeline to China. At the ceremonial opening of the pipeline, Turkmenistan's president called attention to the political importance of the pipeline when he declared that "this project has not only commercial or economic value. It is also political. China, through its wise and farsighted policy, has become one of the key guarantors of global security."[31]

Russia's control over the oil export pipelines from Central Asia faces a similar challenge. Until recently, all Central Asian and Caucasus oil was exported through Russian pipelines. Since 2005, however, when a major new pipeline from Azerbaijan through Georgia to a Turkish port on the Mediterranean Sea was laid (the "Baku-Tbilisi-Ceyhan pipeline"), Russia's monopoly on the transit of Caspian Sea oil to export markets was broken. The pipeline project, which took 10 years, was strongly backed by the United States over Russian objections; the American Secretary of Energy spoke at the opening ceremony of the pipeline. The fact that oil and gas transportation routes for energy supplies from Central Asia and the Caucasus no longer all feed through Russia diminishes Russian influence in the post-Soviet region.

RUSSIA AND THE INTERNATIONAL COMMUNITY

Russia's interest in expanding influence in its "near abroad" is not the same as creating an empire or restoring the Soviet Union. It is important to bear in mind that Russia today is far more open than it was under Soviet rule, and its leaders recognize that it cannot retreat into isolation and autarky. Putin and Medvedev have repeatedly stated that Russia's economic interests require closer trade and investment ties with the outside world and that its security requires avoiding confrontations with any powerful potential enemies. The post–Cold War environment has been more favorable to Russia's strategic interests than most observers expected, however. While having to accept the United States' preeminent military power and the limits this imposes on Russia's own security strategy (for instance, requiring it to accept NATO's expansion and the end of the ABM treaty regime), it has also given Russia new opportunities to develop its own international role by playing on the world's concerns about international terrorism. The new vulnerabilities and divisions created in the post–Cold War world and Russia's immense energy resources have given Russia new opportunities to develop influence. As it deepens its trade and investment ties with the outside world, however, its vulnerability to disruptions in the supply routes of its oil and gas exports and to the fluctuations in world commodity prices also increases.

President Medvedev is trying to harness Russian foreign policy to his long-term goal of modernizing the country's economy. Meeting with the Russian ambassador corps in July 2010, he declared that the chief tasks of Russian foreign policy are modernization and democratization of Russia. Specifically, he told them that the three top policy goals were modernization of the economy and production, strengthening institutions of democracy and civil society, and fighting organized crime. He also said that the chief partners of Russia are the United States and the European Union, and that he wanted to deepen cooperation with the Asia-Pacific region as well. Relations with the CIS countries were far down on the list of priorities that he named.[32] Medvedev has taken several steps consistent with this shift in foreign policy orientation, such as making concessions in order to reach agreement on the new strategic arms reduction treaty with the United States[33] and agreeing to impose sanctions on Iran for failing to comply with UN restrictions on its nuclear program.

The president's ability to bring about a major reorientation of Russian foreign policy is very limited, however. Given the tandem leadership, officials cannot be certain that he has a secure hold on state power or that he will remain in office beyond 2012. Moreover, it will take decades for Russia to shift its economy away from a dependence on raw materials exports, and meantime it needs the revenues from its resource wealth to finance its social programs and to overcome the destructive legacies of the Soviet era. Deeper economic integration with the outside world will serve the goal of modernization only if Russia improves its institutional capacity to encourage entrepreneurship at home.

Russia's vast size, weak state capacity, and cultural legacy of autocracy impose limits on its ability to adapt rapidly to the changing demands of the international environment. Stresses from wars and internal turmoil have encouraged Russians to prize stability and security over openness to change. The conservatism of its institutions reflects these values. However, in a competitive global environment, Russia's state structures inhibit the country's ability to take advantage of deeper economic integration with more advanced economies. Presidents Putin and Medvedev have recognized the need to overcome the temptation to collect short-term rents from Russia's natural resources and instead to carry out deep reforms of its political and economic structures that make it worthwhile for individuals to invest in endeavors, such as education and innovation, whose return will only be realized over the long term. But they have been unwilling or unable to expend the political capital necessary to make such reforms.

Russia's rulers seek to reconcile the imperative of strengthening the state with the need for economic growth and integration into the world economy. The deep impact of the global 2008–2009 recession on Russia showed that the progress the state has made in overcoming the legacies of Soviet rule is tenuous. The viability of Russia's postcommunist state depends on how responsive and adaptive its institutions are to the demands of Russia's citizens in a globalized and interdependent world.

NOTES

1. From a VTsIOM survey cited in Polit.ru, February 24, 2009.
2. From the Web site of the Levada Center: Levada-Center, February 15, 2007. Release: reception of European values by Russians http://www.levada.ru/press/2007021501.html.
3. A valuable overview of the deep continuities in the evolution of Russia's relations with the outside world through the twentieth century is Robert Legvold, "The Three Russias: Decline, Revolution, and Reconstruction," in Robert A. Pastor, ed., *A Century's Journey: How the Great Powers Shape the World* (New York: Basic Books, 1999), pp. 139–190.
4. Sarah Mendelson and Theodore Gerber, "Glavnyi vrag rossiiskoi molodezhi," *InoPressa*, August 23, 2007, http://www.inopressa.ru/print/wp/2007/08/03/13:08:26/vrag.
5. *RFE/RL Newsline*, October 16, 2007.
6. Ibid., October 10, 2003.
7. From the transcript of Medvedev's interview on August 31, 2008, as published on the presidential Web site: http://kremlin.ru/text/appears/2008/08/205991.shtml.
8. http://lenta.ru/news/2008/05/27/npf/. From May through October, Gazprom's share price fell 71 percent.
9. http://lenta.ru/news/2008/05/27/npf/.
10. Jonathan Stern, "The Future of Russian Gas and Gazprom," *Oxford Energy Forum*, November 2005, p. 14.
11. Tom Warner, "RosUkrEnergo Hits at Critics by Naming Owners," *Financial Times*, April 27, 2006.
12. When a new, pro-Russian president was elected in Ukraine in 2010, he indicated that he might be willing to sell control over the operation of its gas pipelines to a consortium that includes Gazprom in return for lower prices. Andrew E. Kramer, "Seeking Lower Fuel Costs, Ukraine May Sell Pipelines, *New York Times*, March 24, 2010.
13. *RFE/RL Newsline*, September 27, 2006.
14. *RFE/RL Business Watch*, September 23, 2003.
15. *RFE/RL Newsline*, December 1, 2003.
16. Ibid., January 5, 2004.
17. Lev Gumilev, who was the son of the famous Russian poet Anna Akhmatova, was a historian and philosopher who popularized the idea of "Eurasianism." Eurasianism is an intellectual movement emphasizing Russia's ethnic and cultural links with the peoples of Central Asia and Mongolia, as opposed to Russia's European heritage and identity.
18. Georgia formally withdrew from the CIS in 2008 following its war with Russia. NATO has offered the prospect of eventual membership to both countries.
19. President's message to parliament, November 5, 2008, http://www.kremlin.ru/appears/2008/11/05/1349_type63372type63374type63381type82634_208749.shtml.
20. Agreements or treaties of union were signed by the two presidents on April 2, 1996; April 2, 1997; May 23, 1997; December 28, 1998; and December 8, 1999.
21. Ira Iosebashvili, "Putin Ditches Unilateral WTO Bid," *The Moscow Times*, June 10, 2009; Irina Filatova, "Confusion as Customs Union Kicks Off," *The Moscow Times*, July 1, 2010; Sergei Kulikov, "Ritual'no-tamozhennyi soiuz," *Nezavisimaia gazeta*, December 1, 2009; Alex Anishyuk, "Plan to Join WTO with Customs Union Abandoned," *The Moscow Times*, April 15, 2010.

22. See Fiona Hill, "The Eurasian Security Environment," *Testimony before the US House of Representatives Armed Services Committee Threat Panel*, September, 22, 2005, p. 7; Alexander Gabuev, "Sammit v Kremle vyshel blokom," *Kommersant*, February 5, 2009.

23. Fred Weir, "Russia, China Looking to Form 'NATO of the East'?" *Christian Science Monitor*, October 26, 2005, http://www.csmonitor.com/2005/1026/p04s01-woeu.html; Nabi Abdullaev, "SCO Endorses Iranian President's Re-Election," *The Moscow Times*, June 17, 2009.

24. The United States did renegotiate its treaty with Kyrgyzstan and continues to lease an airbase there.

25. Hill, "Eurasian Security Environment," p. 7.

26. Nabi Abdullaev, "Medvedev Disappointed in Dushanbe," *The Moscow Times*, August 29, 2008; Vladimir Solov'ev, "Organizatsiia antinatovskogo dogovora," *Kommersant.ru*, September 6, 2008.

27. On the commonalities among these democratic revolutions, see Michael McFaul, "Conclusion: The Orange Revolution in Comparative Perspective," in Anders Aslund and Michael McFaul, eds., *Revolution in Orange: The Origins of Ukraine's Democratic Breakthrough* (Washington, DC: Carnegie Endowment for International Peace, 2006), pp. 165–195.

28. Andrew E. Kramer, Before Kyrgyz Uprising, Dose of Russian Soft Power," *New York Times*, April 18, 2010. Among other things, the ousted president had offended Russia by accepting a large promise of aid from Russia in return for closing the American air base there, then turning around and accepting a larger sum from the United States to reopen the base.

29. Fiona Hill, "Eurasian Security Environment," p. 5.

30. Claire Bigg, "Putin Receives Turkmen President for Gas Talks," *RFE/RL Russian Political Weekly*, 6:2, January 26, 2006. Although experts believe that Western technology and capital will be needed to develop the new fields where future gas production will be concentrated, Gazprom has recently forced international energy companies to reduce their stakes in joint ventures from majority to minority positions.

31. Alex Anishyuk, "Turkmens Start Gas Supplies to China," *Moscow Times*, December 15, 2009.

32. Vladimir Solov'ev, "Ne ot MIDa sego," *Kommersant*, July 13, 2010.

33. Russia dropped its insistence that the United States end its plans to deploy missile defense installations in Eastern Europe as a condition for signing the treaty.

INDEX